Unity for Absolute Beginners

Sue Blackman

Apress·

ISBN-13 (pbk): 978-1-4302-6779-9

ISBN-13 (electronic): 978-1-4302-6778-2

Distributed to the book trade worldwide by Springer Science+Business Media New York, 233 Spring Street, 6th Floor, New York, NY 10013. Phone 1-800-SPRINGER, fax (201) 348-4505, e-mail orders-ny@springer-sbm.com, or visit www.springeronline.com. Apress Media, LLC is a California LLC and the sole member (owner) is Springer Science + Business Media Finance Inc (SSBM Finance Inc). SSBM Finance Inc is a Delaware corporation.

For information on translations, please e-mail rights@apress.com, or visit www.apress.com.

Apress and friends of ED books may be purchased in bulk for academic, corporate, or promotional use. eBook versions and licenses are also available for most titles. For more information, reference our Special Bulk Sales–eBook Licensing web page at www.apress.com/bulk-sales.

Any source code or other supplementary materials referenced by the author in this text is available to readers at www.apress.com. For detailed information about how to locate your book's source code, go to www.apress.com/source-code/.

For my Mom, who is now finishing her first book.

Contents at a Glance

Contents

About the Author

Sue Blackman is a 3D artist and interactive applications author and instructor based in southern California. She has taught 3ds Max and game classes for artists for well over ten years in top-rated community colleges and private schools, such as the Art Institute of California, and has been lead 3D artist on games for Activision through one of their subsidiaries. She has worked in the industry for several years to help train Fortune 1000 companies, such as Boeing, Raytheon, and Northrop Grumman, to create serious games and training applications with game-based formats. She has been involved with the commercial development of real-time 3D engines for well over ten years. She is an avid tutorial writer and has created both tutorials, as a contributing author, and artwork for various 3ds Max books over the years, as well as training manuals for 3D authoring applications for serious games. She has also written for ACM Siggraph on serious games, one of her favorite topics. You can visit her web site at www.3dadventurous.com.

About the Contributor

Jenny Wang graduated with a BA in Math and minor in Computer Science from University of Southern California. After working for many years in the corporate world, she became interested in video games. She decided to combine her love of art with technology, which led to web development and 3D art creation with 3DS Max and Photoshop. Learning and working with C# and the Unity game engine, she had a blast working on this book and working with Sue Blackman. You can visit her web site at www.jennywangdesign.com.

About the Technical Reviewer

Marc Schärer Schärer is an interactive media software engineer creating cutting-edge interactive media experiences for training, education, and entertainment with his company Gayasoft (http://www.gayasoft.net) located in Switzerland, using Unity since its early days in 2007.

Marc Schärer has a strong background in the 3D graphics, network technology, software engineering and the interactive media fields. After starting programming at the age of 11, he later studied Computer Science and Computational Science and Engineering at Swiss Federal Institute of Technology Zurich before working with various teams in North America, Oceania, and Japan to create compelling interactive experiences.

With the rise in popularity of serious games, interactive education, and immersive experiences, Gayasoft focuses on researching options and technologies for the next generation of interactive and immersive experiences. We apply state-of-the-art AR and VR technologies (Vuforia, Metaio, Oculus Rift) and intuitive, innovative input technologies (Razer Hydra, STEM, Thalmic Myo, Leap Motion, Emotive Insight).

Acknowledgments

Thanks go out to Jenny Wang for her invaluable help with the research, concept testing, and 2D art assets required for this book.

Thanks also to Barry Paul and John Irvin for introducing me to the fine art of potato-gun marksmanship (I still can't believe they actually beaned a bunny with that overripe orange) and to Erik Toraasen, whose many ideas for garden-gnome gameplay threatened to push the book way over schedule. From my 3ds Max class, I'd like to thank Brad Roach for "donating" the scarecrow used for some of the Mecanim experiments, and Jenny for taking the time to investigate Mixamo for character rigging. (You can read her report in Appendix A.)

The concept for the Gnomatic Garden Defender grew out of a frustration over keeping the destructive hoards of real bunnies out of my own garden and my fascination with the long-standing British love affair with garden gnomes. Upon returning from the UK after spending two years pursuing an alternate education, I was introduced to the newly published book, *Gnomes*, with its fanciful illustrations of forest gnomes by Rein Poortvliet. A #1 seller on the New York Times list, it became the de facto reference for the modern garden gnome.

Combining a common plaster garden gnome with a home-made potato gun seemed a perfect theme for the book's project, so after creating a working prototype for the gnome, weapon, and game-play I headed out to the web to immerse myself deeper into the culture. To my great delight, I discovered I wasn't alone in my desire to arm the little folk. Shawn Thorsson's collection of "combat gnomes" so tickled my sense of the outrageous that I painted my own gnome's potato gun to loosely resemble Shawn's rocket launcher, paying homage to his marvelous creativity and craftsmanship. Be sure to check out the "finest militarized lawn ornaments in the world" at http://thorssoli.etsy.com and his blog at http://protagonist4hire.blogspot.com/.

Introduction

The Unity community is very large and very helpful. There are videos, code, and 3D assets available on any number of topics, and the Unity help documents have recently undergone a major update. But if you are new to any or all of the components of game development (scripting, 2D or 3D art asset creation and manipulation, or game design in general), you have probably discovered how overwhelming it is to make sense of it all.

One of the biggest challenges is to learn how to bring it all together. Unlike short topic videos, this book takes you through the process of creating a game that seems very simple at first glance, yet becomes more sophisticated as you work your way through the design and creation process.

One of the great advantages books have over videos is the luxury to spend time on explanations. In game development, there are always several different ways to solve design and technical problems, but there is rarely a "best" solution. And unlike a large studio, where budget and time constraints dictate a highly detailed game document, you will discover that the game design and creation process must be flexible in order to be able to finish a game or even a working prototype.

About the Unity Game Engine

Unity provides an excellent entry point into game development, balancing features and functionality with price point. The free version of Unity allows people to experiment, learn, develop, and sell games before committing any of their hard-earned cash. Unity's very affordable, feature-packed Pro version is royalty free, allowing people to make and sell games with the very low overhead essential to the casual games market.

With its huge user community, Unity removes the elitist separation between programmers, artists, and game designers that is typical of high-priced game engines. It makes it possible for anyone to take the first step to bringing their ideas to life. In this book, you will get to wear many hats as you create your first Unity game, discovering where your interests lie as well as gaining an understanding of what is required should you reach the point where collaboration becomes appealing.

Will I Have to Learn to Script?

You don't have to be a programmer to make your own game with Unity, but you will need to be able to understand enough of what the scripts do to know what can be tweaked to your advantage or decide if a particular script will suit your needs.

Most game play needs to be scripted in Unity, but there are hundreds of scripts already available that can be readily reused. Unity ships with several of the most useful. More can be found by searching the forum, Wiki, or UnityAnswers. Many forum members will even write bits of script for less adept users. In the Collaboration section of the forum, you can even find scripters looking to trade for art assets. By the end of this book, you should know enough to be able to take advantage of the wealth of material available from the Unity community.

Games, by their very definition, are about interaction; even with games that are largely controlled by physics, logic-driven cause and effect is what differentiates games from linear, plot-driven passive media. Even the most "artist friendly" game engines need scripting to move beyond simple environmental walkthroughs. If you have no previous scripting experience, you will find that this book's aim is to familiarize you with scripting a few lines at a time, while providing visual feedback as often as possible. If you find you enjoy the scripting part of the project, feel free to delve deeper into programming with a more conventional approach.

What About Math?

One of the most common things heard in the game industry by artists and programmers alike is, "If I'd known math was going to be so useful, I would have paid more attention in class." Although it helps to have a good background in math, there are plenty of resources for both code and mathematical functions to help you solve a particular problem. And, as always, there are plenty of people on the Unity Forum and Answers who may be willing to help as long as you can show that you have spent a reasonable amount of time trying to solve it yourself.

Assumptions and Prerequisites

This book assumes that you are new to scripting, 3D and game design, and/or the Unity engine.

What This Book Doesn't Cover

This book is not about conventional game design; it is more of a precursor, getting you into the habit of analyzing needs and weighing choices. Not only is creating a massive design document intimidating when you are the one who will have to implement everything, but it is likely to be unrealistic until you are more familiar with the engine and your own capabilities. More typically, you will find yourself building your game up a little bit at a time, prototyping ideas and functionality as you go along.

This is not a book on how to become a programmer. It uses programming best practices when possible, but the scripting in this book is designed to ease a non-programmer into the process by providing instant visual feedback as often as possible. While there are usually several ways to attain the same goal, the scripting choices made in this book are generally the easiest to read and understand from an artist's or designer's point of view. In this book, scripting is presented in the way a native speaker learns his own language. He is surrounded by it, immersed in it, and allowed to tinker with it to slowly gain a basic working knowledge of it. Don't worry about remembering it all. Some things you will use throughout the project, and others you will be encouraged to take note of for future reference.

Conventions Used in This Book

1. Instructions look like this.What Is the General Structure of this Book?

Tip Follow this format.

```
Code looks like this
```

Platform

This book was written using Unity 4.5 in a Windows 8 environment. Differences for shortcut keys and operating system file storage with Unity on a Mac are noted throughout the book.

Chapter 1

The Unity Editor

The most exciting part of learning a new application is getting it installed and firing it up for the first time. Following that, the most frustrating part can be the process of becoming familiar with its editing environment. Unity is no exception, especially if you are already familiar with DCC (digital content creation) applications. In this chapter, you will be introduced to the Unity editor and many of its key concepts. As this will serve as a light overview for the rest of the book, don't stress over trying to remember it all.

Installing Unity

The first order of business is to download and install Unity if you have not already done so.

Unity has two license types: free and Pro. When you download and install Unity for the first time, you will have the option of using a free 30-day trial of the Pro version. It can be selected as a third option right in the license dialog upon installing Unity or upon returning the currently active license (an option that allows you to move Pro licenses to different machines). With a few exceptions, most of the Pro features are aimed at the optimization of your projects and are beyond the scope of this book. If you are considering the purchase of Unity Pro, you should be aware that, with the exception of Windows Mobile, it will require a separate license for each of the mobile target platforms you wish to author for.

Unity User Account

Currently, after you download and install Unity, if you don't already have one, you will be required to create a Unity user account during the installation. Your user account will provide access to the downloads, Unity Forum, Unity Answers, and the Unity Asset Store. The forum provides a place for discussion of all things Unity. Answers is where you can go to get quick solutions to your queries, and the Unity Asset Store is where you can find assets of all kinds (3D models, animated characters, textures, scripts, complete game environments, etc.) to help you with your project. Once Unity is installed, you will find a direct link to each of these resources through the editor.

1

To get started, go to www.unity3d.com/unity/download.

With the account created, you can download Unity for Windows or Mac. The download site will automatically offer the version that matches the platform you are currently on.

Installing

This book was written using Unity 4.5. Because Unity regularly makes changes that can affect your projects, you may wish to use the 4.5 version even if the current version is newer. If you prefer, you *can* install multiple versions of Unity on the same machine, providing you name the folders accordingly (e.g., Unity 4.5, Unity 4.6). You may only run one instance of Unity at a time, regardless of the version. If you choose to have multiple versions, you will be required to start Unity from the desired version rather than from the desktop icon or the project itself, as the previously run version will open by default.

If that sounds like too much trouble, you can always check the book's thread on the Unity Teaching forum, http://forum.unity3d.com/forums/23-Teaching, where both errata and version-change solutions will be posted and updated as necessary. A search for the book's title will help you find its thread.

1.   Install Unity, following the prompts, including the sample project.

On a Windows machine, it will be installed in the Program Files x86 folder. Upon the release of Unity 5.0, when it will be fully 64 bit, it should install itself in the regular Program Files folder. The sample project will be installed in Documents ➤ Public Documents ➤ Unity Projects. On a Mac, you will find it in /Users/Shared/Unity.

At this point, you should now see the Unity icon on your desktop (Figure 1-1).

Figure 1-1. The Unity application icon on the desktop

2.   Click the icon to open Unity.

If you downloaded the sample project, Unity will open with it already loaded (Figure 1-2).

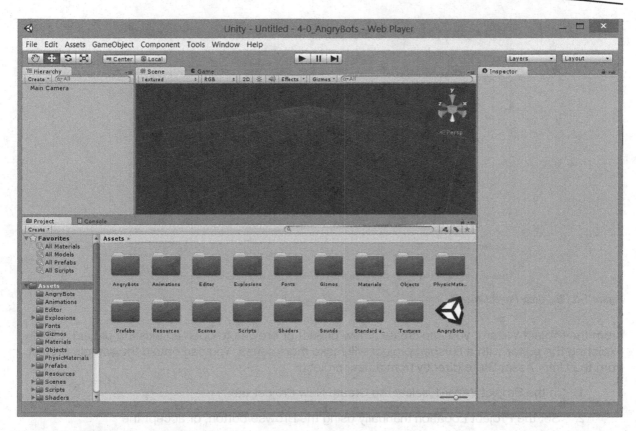

Figure 1-2. The Unity sample project loaded

If the Scene window is blank, you can double-click the Unity icon in the Assets folder to load the AngryBots scene. The demo scene Unity ships with changes occasionally, so yours may be different.

> **Tip** When opening Unity from the desktop icon, it will open the previously opened project, provided it can be found.

If you did not choose to install the sample project, you will see the Project Wizard (Figure 1-3).

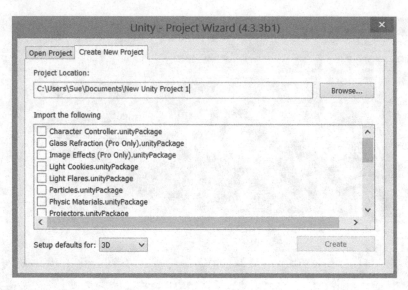

Figure 1-3. The Unity Project Wizard

From the Project Wizard, you can create a new project or browse to open an existing project. Initially, exploring the editor with a finished project will make more sense. You can obtain the sample project from the Unity Asset Store directly from a new project.

1. In the Project Wizard, select the Create New Project tab.

2. Set the Project Location manually using the Browse button, or accept the default name and location.

> **Tip**   When you create a new project, you will be creating a folder to house the project. The folder *is* the project. You can only create a new project in an empty folder.

3. With the project name and location specified, click the Create button.

The new project and, as yet nameless, *scene* opens in the Unity editor.

Originally, if you pressed the Alt key down immediately after clicking the Unity icon on the desktop, it would force the program to start with the Project Wizard. Because that required excellent timing and/or a good dose of luck, Unity finally added the option to the Preferences section. While it may seem like a nice time-saver to automatically open your last file, it has its drawbacks. If the project has become corrupted, Unity will not be able to open it (giving you access to the file menu where you can open a different file). If you are using multiple versions of Unity, it will recompile data if the last project was opened in a different version. Depending on the version, the changes made could be permanent. To avoid complications, the best practice is to set the preference to always start with the Project Wizard.

4. From the Edit menu, select Preferences.

5. Under General, turn on Always Show Project Wizard (Figure 1-4).

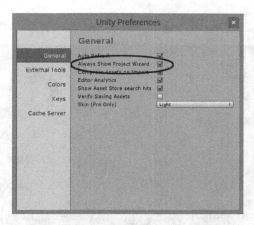

Figure 1-4. Preferences set to Always Show Project Wizard

General Layout

With the project loaded, you should see Unity sporting its default layout. If you are using the free version, the UI should appear in light gray (Figure 1-5). If you have purchased, or are evaluating, Unity Pro, the background will reflect the dark theme (Figure 1-6). For this book, the screenshots will utilize the light theme for better contrast. If you have Pro and prefer the lighter version, you can change the Skin in the General section of the Preferences.

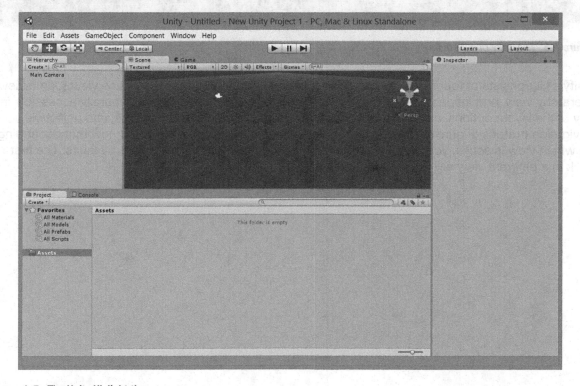

Figure 1-5. The Unity UI, light theme

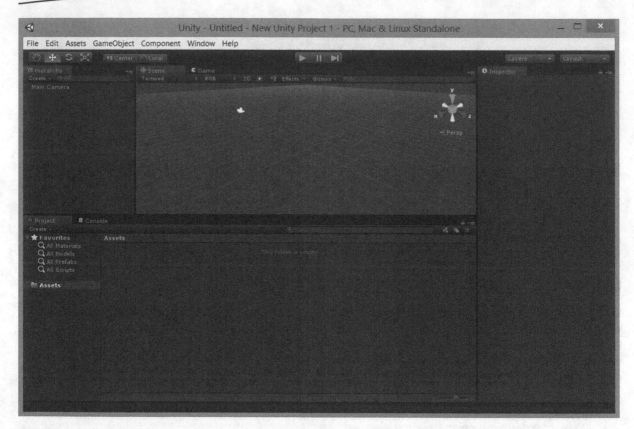

Figure 1-6. The Unity UI dark theme

Unity's UI consists of four main "views" and several important features. The Scene view, Game view, Hierarchy view, and Inspector view (typically referred to as the *Inspector*) are generally accessible in any of the layout options, as are the playback controls, coordinate system options, and object/viewport navigation buttons (Figure 1-7). If the term "views" seems a bit odd, it helps to know that depending on which view is *active*, your input (or the events it triggers) will generate different results. The first click in a different view will set the focus to it.

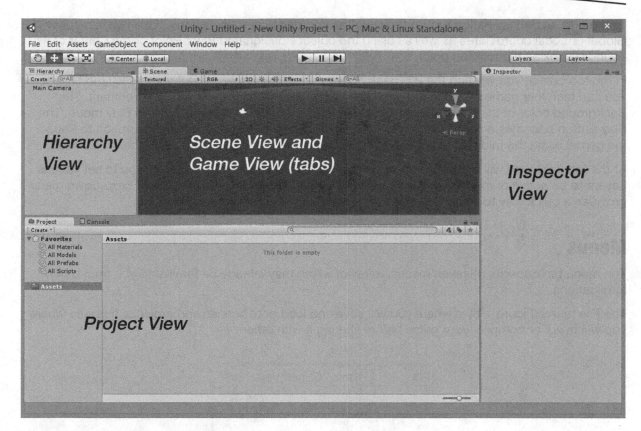

Figure 1-7. The Unity GUI and its main features

With the default layout, the main feature is the Scene view. This is where you will be able to arrange your 3D assets for each scene or level in your project.

In the tab next to the Scene view, you will find the Game view. In the default layout, when you click the Play button, the Game tab is automatically opened. The game view is where you will interact with your scene at runtime to test your game play.

To the left of the Scene/Game viewports, you will find the Hierarchy view. This is where you will find the objects that are currently in the loaded scene or level.

Below the Scene/Game view is the Project view. This contains the resources or assets available to the current project. This folder corresponds directly to the project's Assets folder on your operating system. Deleting files from the Project view will send them to the trash on your computer. If you author from an external hard drive, you should be able to locate the deleted files in the drive's own trash folder. The main point here is that there is no "undo" for these deleted files.

To the far right, you will find the Inspector. This is where you will have access to the parameters, options, and other particulars of selected assets, from the Hierarchy or Project views, as well as general project-related settings.

At the top left, you will find the navigation controls that will allow you to move and arrange objects in your scene and re-orient the Scene view itself for easier access to the various objects.

To the right of the navigation tool controls are the coordinate system options. Here you can specify Global or Local coordinates as well as using the object's designated Pivot Point or the Center of its bounding box as the rotation point.

In the top center, you will find the Playback buttons. The Play arrow will put you in Play mode, where you can test your game's functionality and presentation in a Windows or Mac environment. The Background color of the UI will also change, alerting you to the fact that you are in Play mode. The Play button becomes a Stop button once you are in Play mode. You also have the option to Pause the game, using the middle button, or to step through one frame at a time, using the right button.

At the top right, you will see two drop-down menus. The Layers button will allow you to set various Layers to be active or inactive during Play mode, or define new layers. The Layout drop-down menu provides a quick way to switch between several popular layout configurations.

Menus

The menu bar consists of seven menus, a few of which may already be familiar to you from other applications.

The File menu (Figure 1-8) is where you will save and load both scenes and projects. It is also where you will build, or compile, your game before sharing it with others.

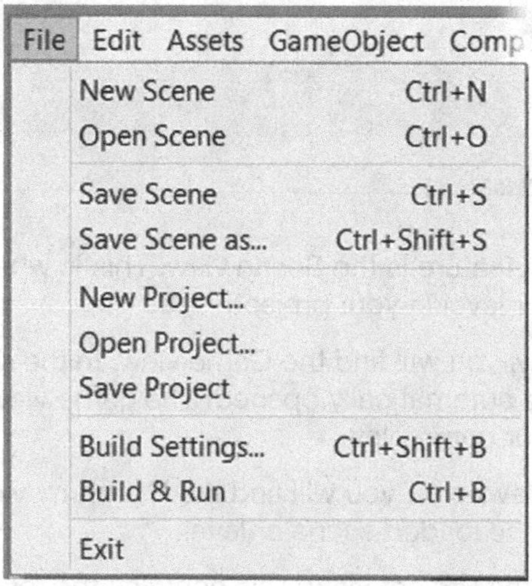

File	Edit Assets GameObject Comp	
	New Scene	Ctrl+N
	Open Scene	Ctrl+O
	Save Scene	Ctrl+S
	Save Scene as...	Ctrl+Shift+S
	New Project...	
	Open Project...	
	Save Project	
	Build Settings...	Ctrl+Shift+B
	Build & Run	Ctrl+B
	Exit	

Figure 1-8. The File menu

In the Edit menu (Figure 1-9), you will find the usual editing options: Undo, Redo, Cut, Copy, Paste, Duplicate, and Delete. The next couple of sections deal with functionality generally accessed through keyboard shortcuts or UI buttons, but that are useful for identifying the shortcuts. The Play options are fairly self-explanatory. You will investigate Find later in the chapter. The Edit menu is also where you can find access to Project and Render settings. These are settings that are not associated with any particular scene object. Preferences is where you can go to customize the Unity editor for matters other than layout. At the bottom, you can gain access to the snap options to help with the arrangement of your scene assets.

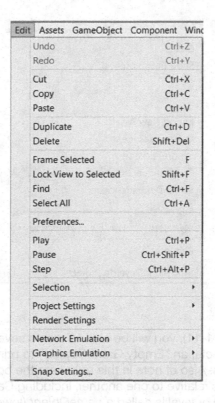

Figure 1-9. The Edit menu

In the Assets menu (Figure 1-10), you will see the various options for creating, importing, and exporting assets. This extremely useful menu can also be accessed in a couple of different places in the editor, as you will see throughout the book. Topping the list is the Create submenu. This is where you will create most of your Unity-specific assets, such as scripts, materials, and a variety of other useful things. Along with the menus for importing assets such as textures and 3D models, you will find a mainstay of Unity game development: the means of importing and exporting Unity "packages." Packages are the vehicle for transferring all things Unity with their relationships and functionality intact.

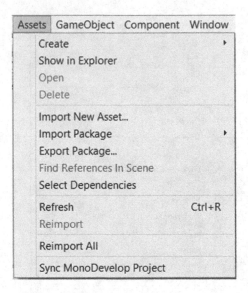

Figure 1-10. The Assets menu

In the GameObject menu (Figure 1-11), you will be able to create several types of pre-set objects, from the most basic of Unity objects, an "Empty GameObject," to primitives, lights, cameras, and a nice variety of 2D and 3D objects. Also of note in this menu are the bottom three commands. They are the means for positioning objects relative to one another, including Cameras and their views. In Unity, anything that is put in your scene or level is called a *gameObject* (lower case g). More than just Unity's name for an object, *gameObject* specifically refers to an object that inherits from the GameObject class (upper case G), that is the code that defines the top level object and its basic behavior.

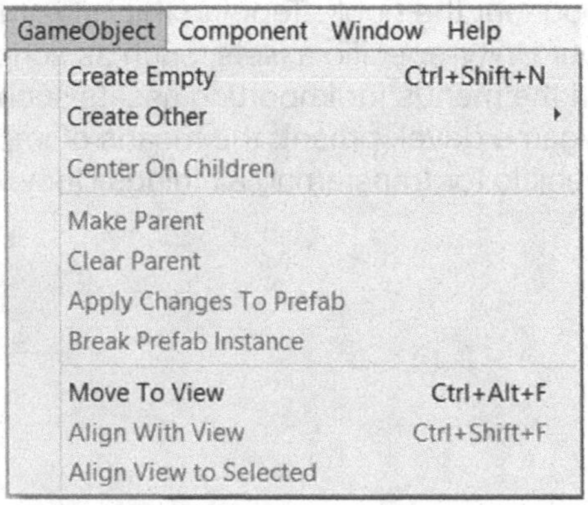

Figure 1-11. The GameObject menu

The Component menu (Figure 1-12), is where you can add components to define or refine your gameObject's functionality. Any of the "Create Other" objects from the GameObject menu *could* be built from scratch by adding the appropriate components to an empty gameObject.

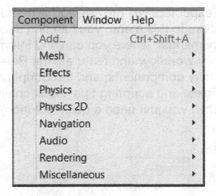

Figure 1-12. *The Component menu*

The Window menu (Figure 1-13) is where you can go to open or change focus to Unity's standard and specialty views or editors. The shortcut keys are listed if they exist. Note the Asset Store item. This will take you directly through Unity's Asset Store, where you can import assets directly into your game.

Window	Help	
Next Window	Ctrl+Tab	
Previous Window	Ctrl+Shift+Tab	
Layouts	▶	
Scene	Ctrl+1	
Game	Ctrl+2	
Inspector	Ctrl+3	
Hierarchy	Ctrl+4	
Project	Ctrl+5	
Animation	Ctrl+6	
Profiler	Ctrl+7	
Asset Store	Ctrl+9	
Version Control	Ctrl+0	
Animator		
Sprite Packer		
Lightmapping		
Occlusion Culling		
Navigation		
Console	Ctrl+Shift+C	

Figure 1-13. *The Window menu*

The Help menu (Figure 1-14), as expected, will provide you with the version number and license information of your Unity installation. In this menu, you can find access to the three main pieces of Unity documentation: the Unity manual, where you can find information on the workings and concepts behind much of the Unity workflow and features; the Reference Manual, where you can get specific information on Unity components; and the Scripting Manual, where you can find Unity-specific API classes, examples, and scripting tips. Additionally, the menu supplies links to the Unity Forum and Answers (when you just need a quick solution) and a means of reporting a bug should the need arise.

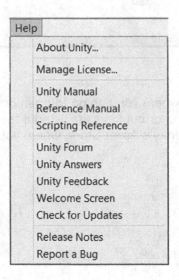

Figure 1-14. The Help menu

Getting Started

Each of Unity's "views" comes with its own options and settings. Most are along the top of the viewport or panel, but there are a few that are located at the bottom. Once again, this is just a quick overview to familiarize you with some of their key features.

If you didn't choose to download and install the sample scene, AngryBots, with your Unity install, you will need to fetch it from the Unity Asset Store if you wish to follow along with the next section's exercises. It is a free download and can be found in the Complete Projects category, Unity Technologies section.

1. From the Windows menu, select Asset Store.

2. Select the Complete Projects category.

3. Select the Tutorials subsection.

4. Select Angry Bots.

5. Click the Download button's drop-down arrow (on its right side).

6. Select Download Only.

7. Close the Asset Store window when the project has finished downloading.

8. In the Unity editor, from the files menu, select Open Project.

The Project Wizard opens (Figure 1-15).

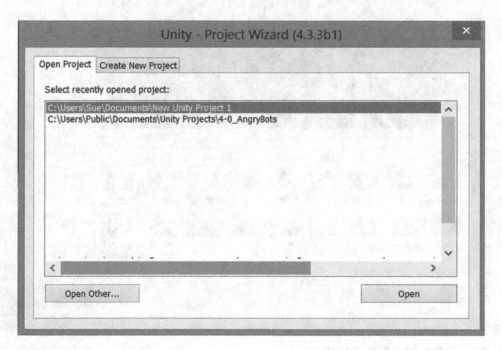

Figure 1-15. The Project Wizard

9. Select Open Other…

10. Navigate to where the project was installed, and select the parent folder, 4-0_AngryBots.

When Unity opens a project that you were previously working on, it will open to the scene you were editing or viewing. If this is the first time the project has been opened, it will open to a new, unnamed scene. Since all new scenes are created with a default camera, it won't be entirely empty, but it also won't do you much good as you check out the various views.

One of the first things you will learn to do in Unity is to keep your projects organized. While it's not mandatory to do so, you will find that most developers create a folder called *Scenes* to store the game's scenes or levels in. You will find that AngryBots does indeed have a Scenes folder, but the main scene was left on its own in the root folder. Unity helps you to locate various types of resources through the use of various icons. The icon used for scenes is, appropriately, the Unity production.

1. In the Project view, select the Assets folder in the left column and locate the AngryBots scene in the right column (Figure 1-16).

Figure 1-16. The AngryBots scene in the Project view

2. Double-click on the AngryBots scene name and/or icon to load the scene.

The contents of the scene are shown in the Hierarchy view. The Scene view reflects the last observation point from the last scene seen in the Unity editor, regardless what project it was in.

Navigating the Scene View

The first thing you will probably want to do is explore the loaded scene in the Scene view. Because viewport navigation varies quite a bit in 3D applications, this is a good place to start your Unity experience. Let's start by focusing in on an object in the Hierarchy view.

1. In the Hierarchy view, double-click on the Main Camera to focus the Scene view to it.

Tip   At the time of this writing, the double-click method to focus or find an object in the Scene view may no longer work on all platforms. An alternate means of zooming in on the selected object is to move the cursor into the viewport and press the F key. Both methods will "Frame" the selected object in the viewport.

Your exact view may vary, but from any particular location, it will be looking toward the Main Camera object (Figure 1-17). You will learn how to adjust the icon size and type in the Scene a little bit later.

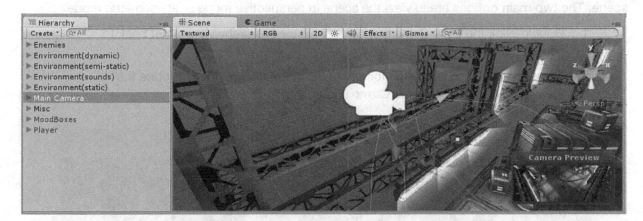

Figure 1-17. The Main Camera "found" in the Scene view

When a camera object is selected, you will also get an inset showing what it sees.

2. To orbit around the Scene view's current focus, Main Camera, hold the Alt key down on the keyboard, press the left mouse button, and move the mouse around.

The scene view is orbited around the current center.

3. Release the Alt key, press the middle mouse button or roller, and move the mouse.

The view is panned (moved up/down/left/right).

4. Holding the Alt key down once again, press the right mouse button and move the mouse.

This time, you are zooming the scene in and out. You can also zoom by rolling the middle mouse roller.

5. Release the Alt key, and continue to hold the right mouse button down as you move the mouse.

With no Alt key, the view is rotated from the viewpoint's origin.

You can also perform fly-through navigation through the scene.

6. Hold the W key down on the keyboard and then press the right mouse button. Move the mouse to perform direction changes.

The speed increases the longer the mouse button is held down, so you may want to try a few starts and stops. Try experiments with the A, S, and D keys along with the right mouse button.

Understanding the Scene Gizmo

In the Scene view, you have several options for working in the viewport as you create and refine your scene. The two main options are to view the scene in perspective mode or an isometric mode.

1. Double-click the Main Camera once again in the Hierarchy view to get back to some scene objects.

2. Using the right mouse button (or any of the alternative methods), rotate the view and observe the Scene Gizmo (Figure 1-18).

Figure 1-18. The Scene Gizmo in the upper right corner of the Scene view

The Scene Gizmo indicates the cardinal direction of the global or world directions. Currently you are seeing the view in a perspective view, Persp, but you can use the Scene Gizmo to change to an iso view, Iso. An 'iso' or isometric view is a view often used in drafting to create a 3D view without the vanishing point perspective of the human eye. Unlike perspective, where objects farther back in the scene *appear* smaller, in Iso, their size relative to each other is always correct. When coupled with the cardinal directions (front, back top, bottom, left and right), Iso will show a flat orthographic view that can make positioning objects much more accurate. When rotated off of the side or top/bottom views, the view becomes isometric. You can toggle the lable to return to a perspective view.

3. Select the Y or top view arrow on the gizmo.

The scene is seen from the top (Figure 1-19), but it's still the perspective view, as indicated by the wedge-shaped icon next to the Top label, just below the gizmo.

Figure 1-19. The perspective Top view

    4.   Click on the Top label.

Now the view is a flat orthographic view, as indicated by the three parallel bars of the new label icon (Figure 1-20).

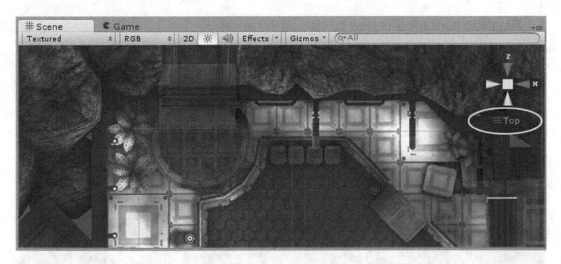

Figure 1-20. The ortho Top view

    5.   Try clicking the other Scene Gizmo arrows to see the other views.

These views will allow you to position objects with respect to each other with far more accuracy than a perspective view.

    6.   Use the right mouse button or its equivalent to rotate away from the current view.

This time the view becomes an isometric view (Figure 1-21). If you have an engineering background, you will recognize this as a typical means of depicting objects in 3D without having to calculate true (human-type) perspective. It is also used in many world-building games, such as Blizzard's Warcraft 3 or StarCraft.

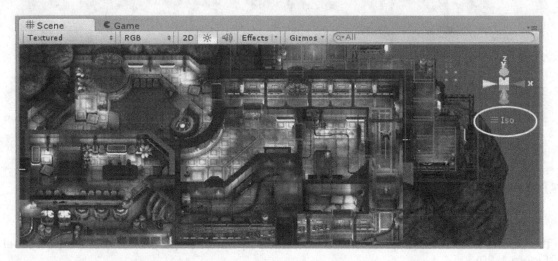

Figure 1-21. The Iso, or isometric view

7.   Return to a perspective view by clicking the iso label.

The viewport and label are returned to a perspective view (Figure 1-22).

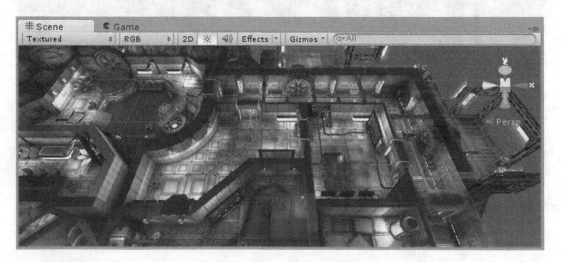

Figure 1-22. The Scene

Exploring the Views

Now that you are becoming more adept at manipulating the viewport, you can check out several of the tools and features available to you with each of the main views.

Hierarchy View

The Hierarchy view is essentially a list tree of the objects currently in the loaded or active scene. The key word here is "currently" because during run-time, objects can be "instantiated" (created on the fly) or destroyed (deleted from the scene). This is an important concept in Unity, and it is one of the reasons that most changes made during run-time are not permanent. On exiting Play mode, the Hierarchy view will be returned to its former state.

During your experimenting with the viewport, you may have accidentally clicked on an object in the Scene view. When selected that way, the hierarchy in the Hierarchy view will be expanded to show the picked object. As you may have noticed, some of the objects are children of children of the top-level objects in the scene. With this in mind, you can imagine how difficult it can be to locate particular objects in either the Scene or Hierarchy view. As the book's project comes together, you will be importing and using several prefabs (Unity's term for reference objects) and will want a quick means of locating them in the current scene.

Fortunately, Unity has a nice search function for that very purpose. At the top of the Hierarchy view, to the right of the Create drop-down arrow, you will see a small magnifying glass icon and its drop-down arrow. The drop-down menu will let you filter for All, Name, or Type. Let's start with Type (Figure 1-23).

Figure 1-23. The Search feature's filters

1. Press the drop-down arrow next to the search icon, and select Type.

2. In the text file to the right, type **camera**.

Before you can finish typing, Unity lists the cameras in the scene. In this case, there is only one, Main Camera. If you select it in the Hierarchy view, it is also selected in the Scene view, along with its view in the Camera Preview window. Note how everything else in the scene has been grayed out.

3. Return to a normal Scene view by clicking the x to the right of the word you typed in.

The Scene view is returned to normal, but the selected object remains highlighted in the Hierarchy view.

4. Next, change the filter back to All and type **confused**.

5. Select the only object that comes up, ConfusedEnemyMech.

6. Double-click to see the view focus in on it.

7. Click the x to return the view to normal.

8. This time, type in something more generic, **pipe**.

Because there are several objects in the scene with the word *pipe* in their name, the list of possible objects is quite long. In the Scene view, they are all "un-grayed," helping you to find the one you want fairly quickly (Figure 1-24).

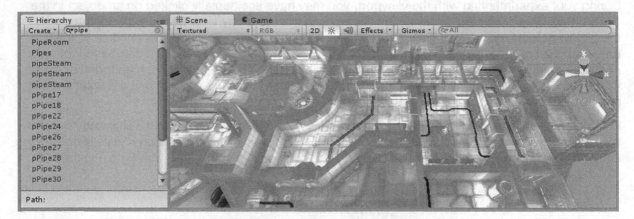

Figure 1-24. The options for a scene object with "pipe" in its name

9. Click the x to return the Scene view to normal.

Scene View

The Angry Bots scene provides you with plenty of variety to explore the Scene view's tools and features. Because there are lots of options, you will just take a look at some of the more commonly used features.

1. Deselect any objects you've got selected by clicking in a blank area of either the Hierarchy or Scene view.

2. Zoom back far enough to see about half of the scene.

3. On the far left, just under the Scene tab, click on Textured to see the other viewport display options (Figure 1-25).

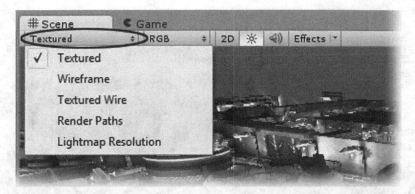

Figure 1-25. The viewport display options

Of the five, the first three should be easy to understand, especially if you have had any background in 3D modeling or have ever watched a "making of" video of any of the pioneers of the CG movie industry's 3D animated films.

4.   Try selecting Wireframe and then Textured Wire.

You may have noticed that meshes automatically show as textured wire when selected. The difference here is that the wire is black, not light blue, allowing you to continue to locate the selected item in the Scene view. In Wireframe, you can see how 3D objects came to be called "meshes," as they resemble wire meshes.

The next option to the right shows RGB (Figure 1-26). This set of display options has to do mostly with texture maps. RGB, the default, shows the red, green, blue part of an RGBA texture.

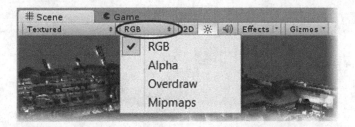

Figure 1-26. The scene view options

5.   Select the Alpha option.

If you are familiar with the alpha channel of a 32-bit texture or image, you may be thinking that Alpha is about transparency, with 0 as fully transparent and 255 as fully opaque. In Unity, however, the alpha channel can do duty as anything from a glossiness channel to self-illumination to height maps. Each of Unity's shaders is designed to make use of alpha channels of its textures to maximize effect and minimize texture usage. With the Alpha option selected for the viewport texture display, you will be able to see the alpha channel but not what it has been used for (Figure 1-27).

Figure 1-27. Textures displaying alpha channels

6. Select the Overdraw option.

Overdraw, the third option, shows how many objects must be drawn on top of each other from the current vantage point. The denser or brighter the display (Figure 1-28), the more objects there are that must at least be sorted, if not actually drawn. In mobile games, regardless of device and operating system, this type of sorting is very costly and should be kept to a minimum.

Figure 1-28. Possible overdraw problem areas showing as bright areas in the Scene view

7. Select the Mipmaps option.

The final option shows the MIP map distance, with no color being the full original-sized texture. As the tint goes from blue to clear to gold through to red, the smaller, blurrier maps are substituted, preventing the sparkly artifacting effect seen as the camera pulls back away from the object. Blue uses a blurred version of the map when the camera is close enough to see pixilation in the texture. You will learn more about MIP mapping when you work with imported images later on.

1. Zoom in close enough to the compound floor by using the mouse roller or by holding the Alt key, pressing the right mouse button, and moving the mouse to see the floor tinted blue at close range.

2. Zoom out slowly, and watch as the tint goes to no tint then to red (Figure 1-29).

Figure 1-29. Color tinting indicating which version of MIP map is shown according to the distance

An absence of tint is the native image. Blue is a blurry version of it you can use so that you won't see each and every pixel up close. Red is a blurred version of it you can use so that you won't see the sparkly artifacting common to low-resolution videos. To see the MIP maps generated from the imported textures, you can select a texture and view it in the Inspector.

3. In the Project view, select the Textures folder from the Assets folder.

4. Locate and select the AngryBots texture in the second column.

5. At the bottom of the Inspector, in the Preview window, move the slider from the far right, slowly over to the far left.

The images are shown in increasingly blurry versions. They appear pixilated as Unity zooms in closer and closer and the versions are smaller and smaller.

6. Set the Scene view drop-down menu back to its default RGB.

The next option for the Scene view is the 2D toggle. If you are creating a 2D game, it makes sense to develop in the kind of view that matches the final output. A little experimentation shows that the 2D option is a preset to the Back view, with the iso option turned on (Figure 1-30). The view points in the positive Z direction. The Scene gizmo is hidden to prevent accidental viewport manipulation. Only Pan and Zoom are available.

Figure 1-30. The 2D toggle compared with the Back/iso view

The next toggle in the Scene view turns scene lighting off and on. When the scene lights are off, the scene is lit from the user's viewpoint, straight into the scene, insuring the visible objects will be well lit. In the Angry Bots scene, the lighting has already been "baked" into most of the textures—that is, the textures themselves have been altered to appear as they are with the lighting on them. To see the lights being toggled off and on in this scene, you will need to locate one of the objects that receives dynamic lighting.

1.   In the Hierarchy view, search for mine_bot.

2.   Select one of the listed mine_bots, and double-click it to zoom in on it in the Scene view.

3.   Toggle the Scene Light button off and on to see the effect on the bot (Figure 1-31).

Figure 1-31. The Scene Lights toggle: lights on (left) and lights off (right)

Now that you've seen that the bots and not the building receive lighting, you can test the Render Paths option in the first display drop-down menu.

4. Change the first Display option from Textured to Render Paths.

5. Zoom out until you can identify the various red tinted objects.

A closer inspection will show that they are all of the objects that are also receiving dynamic light during run-time.

The next button to the right is the Play Sound Effects toggle (Figure 1-32). It toggles audio on or off.

Figure 1-32. The Sound Effects toggle

1. Toggle the Audio button on.

2. Search for and select polySurface5073 in the Hierarchy view.

3. Double-click on it to focus the Scene view to it.

The sound you hear is a 3D sound, and it can be heard only when you are close enough to the object. It is also set to be a looping sound.

The Effects drop-down menu to its right allows you to select which effects will be shown in the Scene view (Figure 1-33). The Angry Bots scene uses a Skybox for the environment and some animated materials on some of the outside decks. You can toggle them all off or on by clicking the Effects button, or you can selectively choose which you want to see from the drop-down menu.

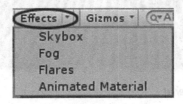

Figure 1-33. The Effects drop-down menu

4. With polySurface5073 selected, orbit the view until you have a good view of the sky and deck, and can hear the rain sound effect (Figure 1-34).

Figure 1-34. A good view of the sky and outside deck

5. Toggle the Sky box on and off.

The hazy sky disappears and reappears. The skybox is a cubic map (a six-image collection) that is added to the scene through the use of shaders. It has no actual "box" geometry, so you never have to worry about the player getting too close to it.

6. Next, toggle on Animated Materials.

7. Look closely at the deck in the Scene view, and then check out its material in the Inspector (Figure 1-35).

Figure 1-35. A close look at an animated material

This distortion/reflection effect is achieved through the floor material's shader. Many of the sample projects contain code and shaders that you can commandeer for your own projects, so they are well worth investigating, even if their functionality is past your current level of knowledge.

8. Turn off the Animated Material effect in the drop-down menu.

The next button is the Gizmos button/drop-down menu (Figure 1-36). This is where you can control which specialty icons will show in the Scene view and how they will be presented. Several types of gameObjects have standard gizmos already assigned and active in the scene. The most obvious are lights and audio, and—if you remember the new, almost empty scene when you opened the project—the camera. The gizmos help you to locate objects in the Scene view that have no mesh associated with them. The light icons, by the way, show the tint set for the specific lights they represent.

Figure 1-36. Gizmos drop-down menu

1. Navigate the Scene view until you can see a nice selection of gizmos (Figure 1-37).

Figure 1-37. A good view of some specialty icons in the scene

This view displays several spotlight icons showing the placement of lights in the wall's can light fixtures, a point light, the lightbulb icon, and a couple of audio icons associated with each of the two mine bots guarding the area.

2. Open the Gizmos list, and try adjusting the 3D Gizmos slider.

As the gizmos get larger, they start to fade out before they cover too much of the scene. As a default, they are set as 3D gizmos. They are obviously 2D icons, but they are adjusted in size depending on how close you are to them, giving you a better feel for where the actual gameObject is in 3D space. They are also occluded by mesh objects, as can be seen with the golden can lights on some of the walls. If you find the dynamic sizing distracting while working mostly in an overhead view, you may prefer to switch them to 2D.

3.   Uncheck 3D Gizmos.

All of the gizmos within view are shown at a standard size. While this is obviously not practical for a first-person vantage point, it is useful for overhead editing. 2D icons are not affected by distance.

4.   Switch the view to a top/iso view so you are looking down on the compound.

As you may remember, most of the lighting was baked into the textures, so most of the light gizmos you see are no longer in use. Fortunately, you can opt to turn icons off and on by type.

5.   Open the Gizmos list again, and click the Light icon from the icon column.

All of the light gizmos are turned off in the Scene view.

6.   Now turn off the Audio Source icons.

An overhead search of the compound should now find the lone camera icon, but you will also see several blue box outlines. Because the gizmos are associated with the components that dictate the object's features and functionality, you can also assign icons to custom scripts, because scripts are also components. In Angry Bots, several of the scripts have gizmos assigned to them.

7.   Open the Gizmos list again, and try unchecking the Rainbox gizmo check box on the far right of the script name in the Scripts section.

The blue rectangle gizmos disappear from the scene.

In Unity, you have the option of assigning custom icons as well as generic gizmos to specialty scripts. While it is beyond the scope of this book to cover that functionality, it should at least take the mystery out of some of the gizmos you come across in other people's scenes.

The last item on the Scene view bar is the now familiar search feature. While it may seem redundant to have the search featureon both views, Unity allows you to fully customize which views are turned on and where they are placed, so you could possibly find it very convenient if you are using two monitors and have the Hierarchy view far removed from the Scene view.

Game View

Having dealt with the most complicated view, you can now take a look at the Game view.

1.   Click the Game tab to the right of the Scene tab.

For the most part, the Game view is about the runtime functionality of your scene, and its tools and options reflect that as well (Figure 1-38).

Figure 1-38. *The Game view options*

On the far left, the aspect drop-down menu allows you to specify an aspect ratio so you can make sure you will be seeing what your player will see (Figure 1-39). You can also add custom, fixed sizes by clicking the Add button (the plus sign) at the bottom (Figure 1-40).

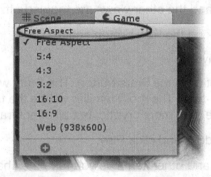

Figure 1-39. *The Free Aspect drop-down menu*

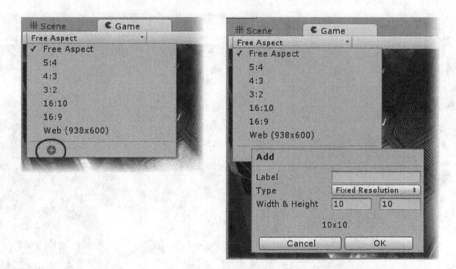

Figure 1-40. *On the left, the Add icon, and on the right, the custom option popup for a fixed-size view*

2. Click the Free Aspect drop-down menu.

3. Click the Add icon at the bottom of the Free Aspect list.

The next option is "Maximize on Play" (Figure 1-41). When toggled on, this will hide all other views and maximize the Game view on Play. If you have stipulated a fixed window size, Unity will do its best to match it.

Figure 1-41. "Maximize on Play" toggle

1. Toggle the "Maximize on Play" option on.

2. Click Play.

The Game window is maximized, and the other views are toggled off.

3. Stop Play mode by clicking the Play button again.

The views return to their original layout.

Next to the "Maximize on Play" option is the Stats button. The Stats window will show you the statistics for your game during run-time. The most familiar will be the frame rate at the upper right. The various items in the list may be a bit more cryptic, but all affect frame rate in one way or the other.

1. Toggle on the Stats window, and click Play.

2. Observe the frame rate and other items as you take the character through the compound (Figure 1-42).

Figure 1-42. The Stats window during run-time

3. Stop Play mode, and turn off the Stats window.

The last item on the Game view bar is the Gizmos toggle. Like the Effects drop-down menu, this one works as a toggle when clicked or can be set to selectively see the gizmos you prefer.

Project View

Next up is the Project view. You have already used it a few times, but it has some nice functionality that you will want to be aware of. Before going any further, it is worth a reminder that the Assets folder on your computer is the Assets folder you see in the Project view. The most important thing to remember is that you can add to the folder through the Explorer (in Windows) or the Finder (on Mac), but you should not remove or rearrange resources except from within Unity unless you also include the object's .meta file.

Besides the Create drop-down menu, which is another location from which you can access some of the Assets menu's functionality, one of the main features of the two-column Project view is the Favorites options found above the Assets folder section (Figure 1-43). It allows you to see all assets of the listed types.

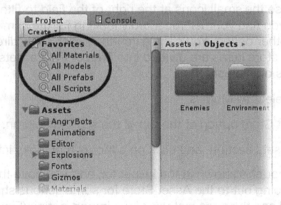

Figure 1-43. The Favorites options

1. Select each of the filters, and watch the results.

The materials are displayed on spheres as with most 3D applications. The models and prefabs are shown with thumbnail images, and the scripts are shown as a simple list with their script type icon. If you are an artist and have created most of your own models and textures, you will probably find it quicker to locate them by name. Conversely, if you are working with assets created by someone else, you may not know the names but will know the one you are looking for when you see it. To keep a good workflow for either scenario, Unity has provided a slider at the bottom of the view that will size the thumbnails up or down. More importantly, on the left end of the slider, it reverts to names with type icons.

2. Select the All Models filter.

3. In the lower right of the view, adjust the slider from left to right to see the changes in thumbnail size and presentation (Figure 1-44).

Figure 1-44. *Adjusting the thumbnail display for the models*

4.   Try selecting the folders from the Assets folder to see their presentation.

You've probably noticed the familiar Search field at the top of the Project view. With folders selected, you can type in a name or use the small icons at the right of the field to filter by type or label. You can also save the search if you find yourself repeatedly looking for the same item. When using the filters, however, you get another option. You can search the Asset Store directly if you find you need a particular asset. The store items are divided into Free or Paid assets, so you can search the thumbnail previews for items of interest.

5.   From Favorites, select All Models.

6.   Click on the Asset Store option at the top of the second column.

7.   Open the Free Assets section, and click on a model that looks interesting.

The information about the model is shown in the Inspector, and you have the option of importing it directly to your scene or going out to the Asset Store for some serious shopping (Figure 1-45, left). For the Paid Assets, you will see the price instead of the import option (Figure 1-45, right).

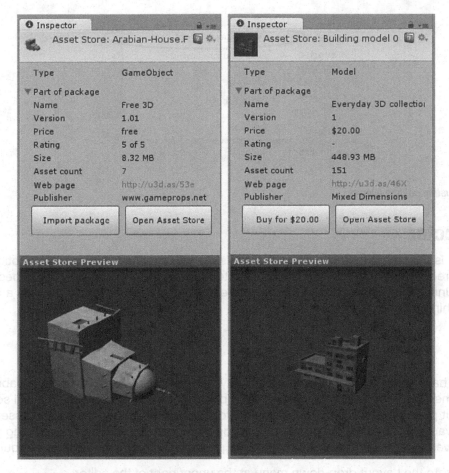

Figure 1-45. Accessing the Asset Store assets directly from the Project view: a Free asset (left), and a Paid asset (right)

8. For fun, type in **rabbit** (or some other object of interest) in the search field.

The item or related items, if any can be found, appear in the project view.

The last bit of Project view functionality will allow you to switch from the default Two Columns Layout to the original One Column Layout (Figure 1-46). These options can be located by right-clicking over the Project tab. The One Column Layout can be more useful, depending on the overall layout of the UI or where in the development process your game happens to be. You will get a chance to give it a try later in the book.

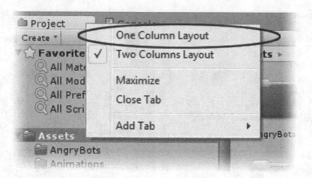

Figure 1-46. Adjusting column layouts

The Inspector

The Inspector is the last of the main views or panels. As you may have noticed, its functionality and options are directly related to the item that is selected elsewhere in the editor. As you become more familiar with Unity, you will spend a lot of time in the Inspector. It is where you will gain access to almost everything related to your game in Unity.

Layout

Now that you have spent a bit of time with the Unity views and panels, it's time to see about re-arranging them as your needs change. As you open various sample scenes, you will see many different layout preferences. The current default layout shows the loaded scene and assets folder off to nice advantage, so these are good choices for a first look. As you start developing your own games, however, you may find it useful to try other preset layouts or even customize your own.

1.   Locate the Layout drop-down menu at the upper right of the editor.

2.   Open it, and check out some of the preset layout options (Figure 1-47).

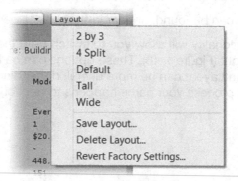

Figure 1-47. A few layout options

3. Select the "2 by 3" option.

This layout is useful for changing and checking on objects during run-time, as you get to see both views at the same time. Its tall vertical views or panels make it easier to access large numbers of assets in the Hierarchy view without resorting to the Search feature. Its main drawback is that the Project view's Two Column Layout does not lend itself to a tall vertical column very well. This is when the Single Column layout is useful.

4. Right-click over the Project tab, and select the Single Column Layout.

The Project view is now essentially the contents of the Assets folder, and the file structure has the standard operating system hierarchy (Figure 1-48).

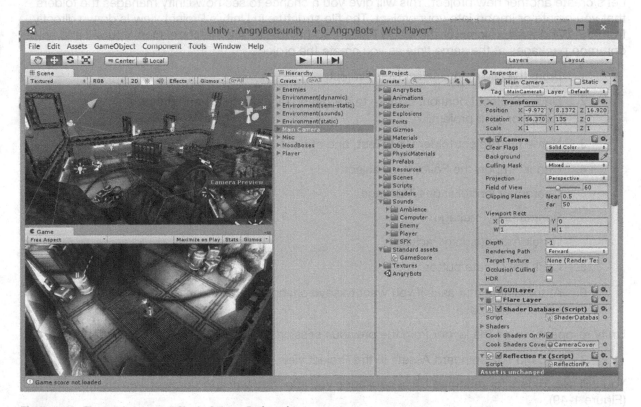

Figure 1-48. The 2x3 Layout and Single Column Project view

Besides the preset layouts, you can also float and rearrange the views manually.

5. Click and drag the Hierarchy tab around the editor.

The view snaps into various locations, ready to be dropped. If you have multiple monitors, you can even leave it floating outside the editor window. To get it back, you can choose one of the preset layouts in the Layout drop-down menu.

Project Structure

Because no job is done until the paperwork is finished, you ought to have a basic understanding of how Unity projects are organized before you jump in and start creating a game. For the most part, everything you create will reside in the Assets folder. It is up to you to keep things organized as you develop your game. And as a gentle reminder, avoid re-arranging the contents of the project view outside of the Unity editor.

File Structure

Let's create another new project. This will give you a chance to see how Unity manages the folders that you create or import into your project. The file structure in Unity's Project view is drawn directly from the Windows Explorer (or the Mac's Finder). To be able to see the correlation, you will add some common packages at the same time as you create the project.

1. From the File menu, select New Project.

2. Under Project Location, Browse to a location of your choice and create a folder for your project.

3. Name the project/folder **UnityTest**, and choose Select Folder.

4. Under "Import the Following," select:

    CharacterController.unityPackage

    Scripts.unityPackage

    TerrainAsssets.unityPackage

5. Click the Create button.

6. At the dialog that asks if you want to save changes in the AngryBots scene, select Don't Save.

Unity re-opens, using the layout from the previous session. A new, untitled scene is loaded.

7. Expand the Standard Assets in the Project view.

You will see folders for the three Unity packages you imported when the project was created (Figure 1-49).

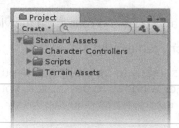

Figure 1-49. The folders containing the imported assets in the Project view

8. Now, go out to your browser (Windows) or finder (Mac), and locate the project folder to see what was generated.

Beneath the folder you created for the project, you will find an Assets folder that contains the contents of the three imported packages in a Standard Assets folder (Figure 1-50).

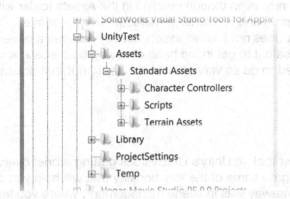

Figure 1-50. The project, UnityTest, and its folders containing the imported assets in the Explorer

9. Expand the folders to assure yourself that they are the same folders as in the Unity Project view.

Three other folders were generated besides the Assets folder: Library, where relationships between assets are stored in the large number of Metadata subfolders; Project Settings, where game-related data not contained in regular assets is stored; and Temp. You should not make any changes to these folders. You may add assets directly to the Assets folder or subfolder, but you should not rearrange the contents (and yes, that is the third time that has been mentioned!).

Project Management

As you are probably beginning to understand, Unity's file structure is fairly rigid. This ensures that assets will not go missing at crucial times.

Another important thing to know about Unity projects is that there is no quick way to back them up unless you are using a version-control system such as SVN, GIT, Perforce, PlasticSCM, or Unity's own Asset Server. There is no option to "Save Project as…" To be able to copy a project, you must first close it. You will find that as you refine scripts along the development process, earlier test scenes may no longer work. Unity project files can get quite large, so it is well worth the time and space to make occasional backup copies for emergencies, for referencing earlier functionality, or for experimenting with alternative ideas in a nondestructive way. The finished projects for each chapter of the book are included in the book's asset file, which you can download from the Apress website, www.apress.com/9781430267799. They will provide you with a means of comparing your results with a working copy at the end of each chapter. If you are already familiar with version control, you may want to do a search for Unity metadata and how the .meta files can be managed.

Load/Save

Also worth noting is the difference between saving a scene and saving a project. Changes made to the Hierarchy view will always require the scene to be saved. Changes in the Project view, because they are actually changes to the folders on the operating system, may not need to be saved. Assets that are created directly in Unity, even though residing in the Assets folder will probably need to be saved because of all of the path and relationship metadata they generate behind the scenes. Anything scene or project related that does not involve assets directly requires a project save. The bottom line is, paranoia runs deep; it is safest to get in the habit of saving both scene and project on a regular basis. You won't be reminded to do so very often in the book, but that doesn't mean you shouldn't do so on your own!

Summary

In this chapter, you got a first look at Unity's UI. Besides getting a brief overview of the major areas, you had a chance to investigate some of the functionality that will help you as the book's project progresses. The biggest takeaway was in scene management, where you learned that you could add to the Assets folder from your operating system's Finder or Explorer, but that you must not re-arrange assets outside of the Unity editor once they have been added.

If you are feeling overwhelmed at the amount of new information to digest, don't worry. Anything that is critical to know and understand will be covered again later in the book. A few of the things mentioned in this chapter are here just to give you an idea of what can be done as your knowledge of Unity increases. Feel free to revisit this chapter at a later date.

Chapter 2

Unity Basics

While you can create some assets directly inside Unity, the building blocks for your scene will usually be based on imported assets. The in-game functionality, location, and final appearance, however, will be managed and completed within the Unity Editor. For that, it is necessary that you have a good understanding of Unity's key concepts and best practices. In this chapter, you will explore and experiment with a good portion of the Unity features that don't require scripting to be able to enjoy.

Unity GameObjects

In Unity, assets can be anything from textures and materials to meshes, scripts, and physics-related components. Whether they were imported or generated inside Unity, components are combined and manipulated to bring objects to life. Unity uses the term *gameObject* to represent objects because internally they belong to a (scripting) class named GameObject. When referring to a generic gameObject, this book will use the lowercase *g*. When scripting, the uppercase and lowercase *g* will refer to either the particular gameObject (lowercase *g*) or to the GameObject class (uppercase *G*) that holds the definitions and available functionality for all gameObjects.

The most basic of GameObjects (in the formal sense of the word) consists of little more than its transform. A *transform* is an object's scale, orientation, and location in space. The gameObject itself can be used as a parent to manage multiple gameObjects, or it can be filled with components that define all manner of visual appearance and functionality. Unity provides many prebuilt gameObjects. Some are simple primitives ideal for quickly prototyping your game. Others are full-fledged systems for complex and sophisticated objects and special effects.

If you have no prior experience with 3D assets, let alone game-type functionality, don't worry, you will begin with the basics and go on from there.

Creating Primitives

In DCC (digital content creation) applications—such as 3ds Max, Maya, or Blender—a primitive object is, by definition, an object that can be defined by a set of parameters. Some examples of primitives are sphere, cube, capsule, and cylinder. A *sphere* is defined by a radius and the number

39

of longitudinal and latitudinal segments it has. A *box* or *cube* is defined by height, width, length, and its number of segments. When an object cannot be described by a set of parameters, it is called a "mesh." A mesh is a collection of vertices, edges, and faces that are used to build the object in 3D space. A primitive is a mesh, but a mesh (no parametric way to define or describe it) is not a primitive. In Unity, you have less control over the parameters, but the included 3D gameObjects are primitives, nonetheless. These primitives can be used as is or as the base for more complex gameObjects.

Let's start by using the project created in the last section of Chapter 1, the UnityTest project.

1. If Unity is not already open to the UnityTest project, click the Unity icon on your desktop.

2. In the Project Wizard, select the UnityTest project.

While the scene is small and you are not adding game play, it will be useful to use the default layout.

3. Click the Layout button at the top right of the editor to open the list of presets.

4. Select Default.

The layout reverts to having the Hierarchy view on the left, the Inspector on the right, the Scene and Game views tabbed in the center, and the Project view underneath.

The project has a default, nameless scene, but it has not yet been saved.

5. From the File menu, select "Save Scene as."

6. Save the scene as **Primitives**.

The new scene asset appears in the Project view, sporting the Unity application icon (Figure 2-1).

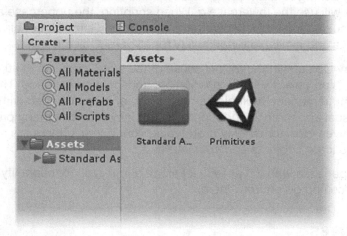

Figure 2-1. The new Unity scene asset in the Project view

7. From the GameObject menu, Create Other, select Cube (Figure 2-2).

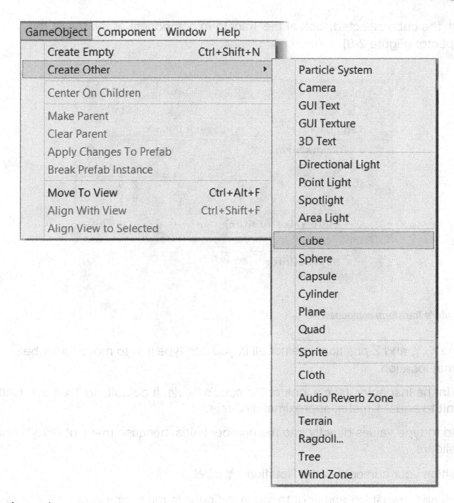

Figure 2-2. Creating a cube

A cube is created in the center of the viewport.

Transforms

All gameObjects have a Transform component. It keeps track of where the object is in space, what its orientation is, and if it has been scaled. Unlike the viewport X, Y, and Z global coordinates, gameObjects can be moved, rotated, or scaled at will. You can transform them in edit mode, and they can be animated during runtime.

If you have not navigated through the scene view since the project was created, the cube should have been created at 0, 0, 0. Unlike many Autodesk products where Z is up in the world, in Unity, Y is the upward direction. You should see your cube with its transform gizmo, specifically the Position gizmo, clearly visible. The arrows follow the convention of RGB = XYZ, or the red arrow is the X direction, the green arrow is the Y direction, and the blue arrow is the Z direction. Z is the direction Unity considers as *forward*.

1. With the cube selected, look at the Transform component at the top of the Inspector (Figure 2-3).

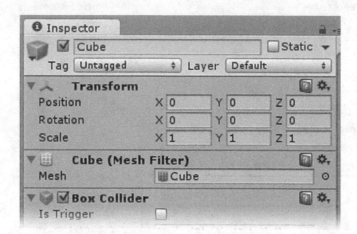

Figure 2-3. The cube's Transform component

2. If the X, Y, and Z positions are not all 0, you can type it in to move the cube to that location.

While you are in the Inspector, take a look at the cube's Scale. It defaults to 1 x 1 x 1. Unity considers 1 unit to equal 1 meter, approximately 3 feet.

You don't need to type values directly into the number fields, because many of Unity's entry box labels act as sliders.

3. Position your cursor over the Rotation's Y label.

4. Click and drag it left and right to rotate the cube in the Scene view.

5. Leave the cube at about -60 degrees.

6. At the top of the editor, make sure the coordinate system is set to Local (it is a toggle), not Global, and that the Transform is set to Move (Figure 2-4).

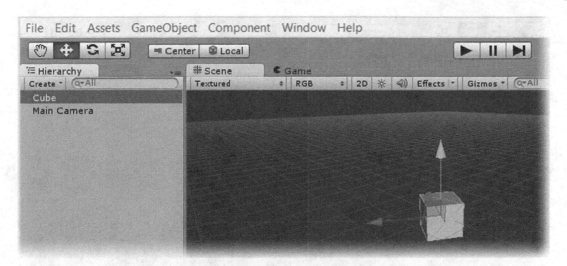

Figure 2-4. The coordinate system set to Local, Move transform active

7. Click on the Z arrow in the viewport, and drag the cube while watching the Position values in the Inspector.

The cube is moving in its local Z direction, but its X position is updated as well.

8. Change the coordinate system to Global, and pull the cube in the Global Z direction.

This time, the only value being updated in the Inspector is the Z Position. When you transform an object, its location and orientation are kept in world coordinates.

You can also rotate and scale objects using the transform modes at the top left. Just like position, rotate can use local or global coordinates.

1. Click to active Rotate mode (Figure 2-5).

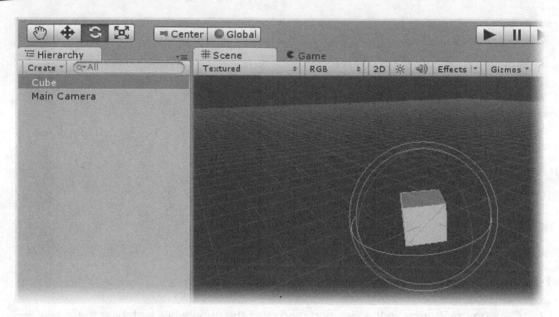

Figure 2-5. Rotate mode and the Rotate gizmo

2. Rotate the cube by placing the cursor over the circular parts of the gizmo and dragging.

3. Change the mode to Scale (Figure 2-6).

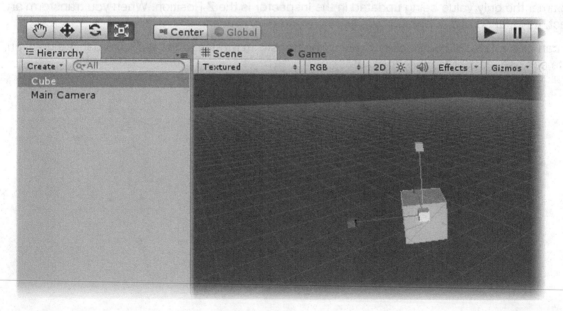

Figure 2-6. Scale mode and the Scale gizmo

Unlike position and rotation, Scale mode allows you to scale an object only on its local coordinate system. This prevents objects that have been rotated from getting skewed.

4.   Scale the cube on any of its axes.

5.   In the Inspector, set all of its Scale values back to **1**.

6.   Set the mode back to Move in the upper left corner of the editor.

7.   Set the coordinate system to Local.

So far, you have dealt with only a single object. With multiple objects, there are some tools that will help you with positioning.

1.   Hold the middle mouse button down, and pan the Scene view so that the cube is off to the left, but not out of the viewing frustum (the boundaries of the viewport window).

2.   From the GameObject menu, Create Other, select Sphere.

3.   The Sphere is created in the center of the viewport, not at 0, 0, 0 (Figure 2-7).

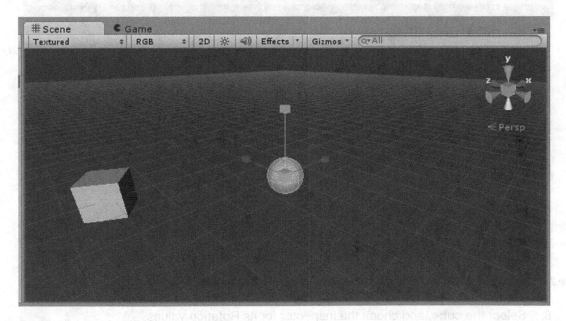

Figure 2-7. The new created Sphere, not located at 0, 0, 0

To move the sphere to the same location as the cube, you could copy and paste the values from the cube to the sphere, but that would be tedious. Instead, you will be using a typical Unity workflow where the target object is focused or framed in the viewport, then the object to move is moved to that location. Note that it will not affect the object's orientation.

4.   Select the Cube in the Hierarchy view.

5.   Double-click the cube in the Hierarchy view, or move the cursor to the Scene view and press the F key.

The Scene view zooms in to the selected object. Unity calls this action "frame selected."

6.   Now select the sphere by clicking on it in either the Hierarchy view or the Scene view.

7.   From the GameObject menu, select "Move to View."

The sphere is moved to the center of the viewport as defined by the cube's location (Figure 2-8).

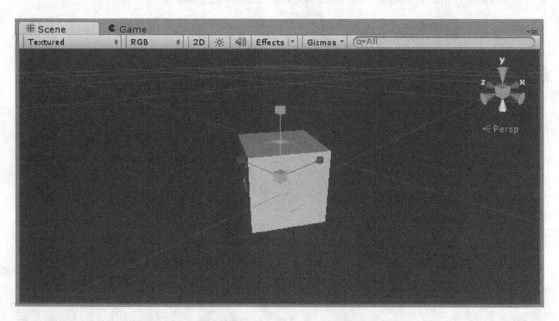

Figure 2-8. The scene focused to the cube, and the sphere moved to the scene's focus

8.   Select the cube, and check the Inspector for its Rotation values.

It should still have -60 (or whatever you left it at) as its Y Rotation value.

9.   Select the Sphere, and check its Rotation values.

The sphere was moved to the cube with "Move to View," but its rotation was not changed.

Duplicating GameObjects

In Unity, you can use Ctrl +D (⌘+ D on Mac) to duplicate objects. Some items—such as materials, textures, scripts, and many others—must have unique names and will automatically be incremented upon duplication. GameObjects, however, can share names, as you may have noticed with the AngryBots game. If you think you will need to access an object as an individual, you should give it a unique name.

In this section, you will name the duplicates for easier identification after clearing the Sphere from the Scene view.

1. Select the Sphere in the Hierarchy view.

2. At the top of the Inspector, to the left of its name, uncheck the check box to *deactivate* the Sphere in the Scene view.

The Sphere disappears from the Scene view, but its transform gizmo remains visible as long as it is selected.

3. Click in an empty spot in either the Scene or Hierarchy view to deselect the deactivated Sphere.

In the Hierarchy view, the deactivated Sphere's name is grayed out (Figure 2-9).

Figure 2-9. The deactivated Sphere in the Hierarchy view

4. Select the cube from either the Scene view or the Hierarchy view.

5. From the right-click menu, select Duplicate.

6. Rename the clone, **Cube1**.

7. Pull Cube1 away from Cube so they are at least a meter (the original size of the cubes) apart.

8. With either cube selected, press Ctrl +D (Command + D on Mac) to clone another cube.

9. Rename the new cube, **Cube2**.

In case you can't tell which is which, it doesn't matter at this point, though the one selected should be the new one.

10. Move Cube2 away from the other two.

Arranging GameObjects

Typically, when you are creating an environment with a lot of duplicate geometry, you will import the original and then make duplicates of it in the scene. Although it doesn't reduce the overhead during runtime, it does reduce disk space, or in this day and age, download time.

The end result is that the modular asset must be arranged in the scene. To help with that task, Unity has a very nice vertex snap feature.

1. Arrange the view so that you can see all three cubes easily.

2. Select Cube1.

3. Hold the v key down on your keyboard, and move the cursor around the cube.

The transform gizmo jumps to the closest vertex.

3D MESH COMPONENTS

If you are new to 3D, you might not know that mesh objects have three component parts: vertices, edges, and tris (short for *triangles*). A triangle, sometimes called a *face*, is the smallest surface that can be rendered. It is defined by three vertices and the three edges that connect them (below, left). Unless you are using a two-sided shader (a "shader" contains the code that tells the graphics hardware how an object is drawn on screen), faces are only "drawn" or "rendered" on one side, their face normal side. The "normal" is an imaginary line perpendicular to the face that indicates its "outward" or visible side (below, right).

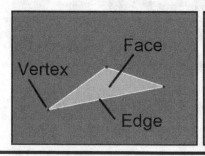 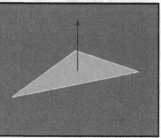

---

4. When the cursor snaps to the lower vertex closest to the next cube over, press and hold the left mouse button, and then drag it over to the next cube.

5. With the mouse button down, move the cursor around the target cube and watch the original vertex snap to its new target.

6. When you are happy with the alignment, let go of the mouse button to finalize the arrangement.

7. Repeat the process with the third cube in the row or stack you started with the first two.

You can also set objects to snap at intervals and use a rotation snap.

1. Select one of the cubes, and set its rotation values back to **0**.

2. From the Edit menu, at the very bottom, select Snap Settings.

The grid snaps are set to 1 unit. This means that the object must be within 1 unit or meter of the grid intersection before they will snap. Because the cubes' pivot points are at their centers, the cubes were originally halfway down through the scene construction grid. The first thing to do is move it up.

3. Select the cube again and, holding the Ctrl key (Windows) or the ⌘ key (Mac), move the cube up until it snaps its base to the grid floor.

4. Try snapping the cube to the grid in the Global X or Z direction.

Of interest is that the cube keeps the same offset, as it snaps 1 unit each direction. If you want it to snap to corners, you can use the buttons at the bottom of the Snap Settings dialog to center the cube on an intersection, add 0.5 to the X and Z in the Inspector, and then happily snap between corners.

Angle or Rotational snaps are set to 15 degrees as a default. You will want to set them to some number that makes sense for your needs before you snap rotate.

5. Change the mode to Rotate.

6. Hold the Ctrl (or Cmd) key down, and rotate the cube on its Y axis, noting the 15 degree increments or decrements in the Inspector.

7. Feel free to round up if the rotation value in the Inspector is infinitesimally off at the end of the rotation.

Parenting

So far, you have dealt with singular objects. It's quite typical, however, to group multiple objects together and parent them to a single gameObject for easier handling. The most important thing to know is that children inherit the transforms of their parents. If a parent is moved two meters in the Z direction, the child is moved that same two meters. If the parent is rotated, the child is rotated *relative* to the parent. If the parent is scaled, the child receives the same scale, again, relative to the parent. It sounds straightforward, but it is worth looking into further.

1. From the GameObject menu, Create Other, create a Capsule.

2. In the Inspector, set its position to 0, 0, 0.

3. Select Cube1, and position it at least a couple of meters away from the capsule.

4. Select the Capsule in the Hierarchy view, and drag and drop it onto Cube1 in the Hierarchy view.

5. Check its transforms in the Inspector, and make note of them.

They now reflect its offset from its parent rather than its location in the scene.

6. Click the arrow to the left of the new parent object to see the newly created hierarchy (Figure 2-10).

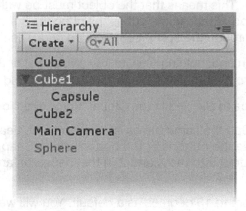

Figure 2-10. The parent, Cube1, and its new child, Capsule

7. Now select and rotate Cube1.

The capsule rotates around its parent as expected.

8. Inspect the capsule's x, y, and z Position values.

The values remain the same as when the Capsule was first parented to Cube1.

9. Double-click the capsule to frame it in the viewport.

10. Select Cube2.

11. From the GameObject menu, use "Move to View" to position it at the scene's focal point (Figure 2-11).

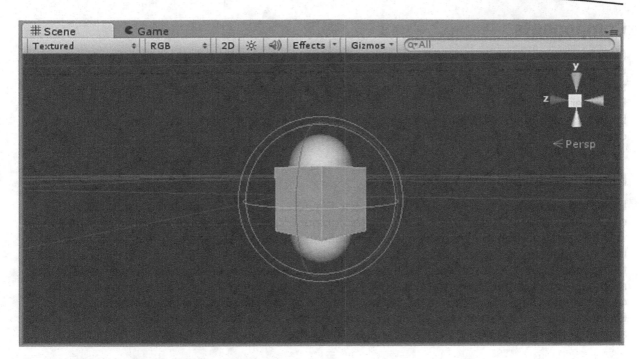

Figure 2-11. Cube2 moved to the Capsule's location

12.   Now look at Cube2's transform values.

As you may have expected, the two values do not match.

13.   Select the Capsule in the Hierarchy view, drag it out of Cube1's group, and drop it in a clear space below the other gameObjects.

14.   Now the two objects' position values match (Figure 2-12).

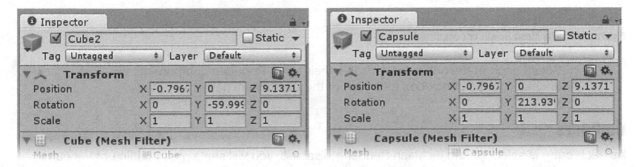

Figure 2-12. The Capsule's Position values, left, and Cube2's Position values, right

Components

Now that you've been introduced to the Transform component, let's look at a few more components. Components are the building blocks that specify the functionality for every gameObject. In addition to the mandatory Transform component, each of the primitive objects you created has a Mesh Renderer, something called a Collider of an appropriate shape for its primitive, and a Mesh Filter for its particular primitive's geometry. When you create a Unity gameObject from Create Other, it comes complete with the components that make it what it is.

Mesh Renderer

Let's begin with the Mesh Renderer component (Figure 2-13). This component is what causes the object (whose mesh is found in the Mesh Filter component) to be "rendered" or drawn into the Scene view. Its first two parameters dictate whether it can cast or receive shadows (providing there is a light in the scene set to cast shadows). It also holds an array for the material or materials assigned to the mesh. For the test objects, each has only one material, so the Material array Size is 1 and that material resides in the Element 0 slot. Arrays always start counting at 0, not 1. The material, in this case, Default-Diffuse is shown at the bottom of the Inspector, along with a preview of the material. Because this is an internally generated material, you may not adjust it. Materials dictate the visual aspect of the object's surface qualities.

Figure 2-13. The Mesh Renderer component

- Select each of the cubes, and *disable* their Mesh Renderer components by unchecking the check box to the left of the component name.

Colliders

As each cube is selected and its Mesh Renderer disabled, you will see a green outline of the cube remaining. This represents the cubes' Box Collider component. Collider components have two main types of functionality. The default is to block physics-based objects from going through the volume defined by the Collider component. The second, when the collider's Is Trigger parameter is checked, is to allow objects to pass through the object but to register the event for further evaluation and possible action. Any object that must cause an event to be triggered on pick, collision, intersection, or ray-cast must have a collider of some type. Even with their Mesh Renderer turned off (invisible in the scene), the objects are still fully active in the game.

1. Select the Capsule, and check out its Capsule Collider component in the Inspector (Figure 2-14).

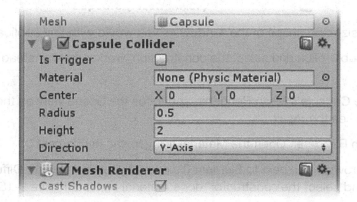

Figure 2-14. The Capsule Collider component

2. Disable the Capsule's Mesh Renderer to get a better look at its Capsule Collider in the scene view.

3. Select the Sphere in the Hierarchy view, and Activate it by clicking the check box at the top of the Inspector to activate it.

4. Disable its Mesh Renderer to get a better view of its Sphere Collider.

In addition to having the option to act as a trigger only, colliders of any shape can use a Physic Material to define how they react on collision. The Physics Material lets you set bounciness and other physics-related properties. You will be experimenting with physics in the next chapter.

Common to the collider shapes based on primitives is a set of adjustments for the shape itself, including the X, Y, and Z adjustments for its center offset. Mesh colliders can be used when the shape requires more accurate collision testing, but it is far more efficient to use one of the other shapes and adjust it to fit. Colliders are a mainstay of Unity that you will be seeing a lot more of.

Mesh Filter

The Mesh Filter component is what holds the 3D mesh for the gameObject. You will rarely need to do anything with it, but occasionally the actual mesh will go missing, so it is worth a quick look.

1. Select the Capsule object.

2. Click the little circular browse icon to the far right of the Mesh parameter's loaded Capsule mesh.

When the Browse window appears, you will see a few imported meshes at the top and several internally generated primitives that Unity includes for its own use. The Capsule is currently selected, and information about the mesh is shown at the bottom of the Browse window. The Browse window, just as with the second column of the Project view, has a scaling slider that allows you to adjust the thumbnail size or to drop down to text with a small icon. Because it is a floating window, you can also adjust its size and aspect ratio for easier browsing.

3. Adjust the thumbnail size with the slider at the top right of the Browse window.

4. Adjust the size and shape of the window as you would with any application.

5. For fun, double-click and select the construction_worker mesh instead of the capsule.

6. Turn on the Capsule's Mesh Renderer, and focus the Scene view on the Capsule to see the result.

7. In the Mesh Renderer, Open the Material array to see its Element 0.

8. Click the Browse icon next to Element 0's currently loaded Default-Diffuse material, and select the constructor_done material instead (Figure 2-15).

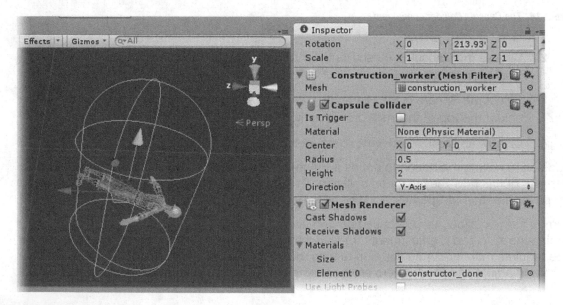

Figure 2-15. The capsule's Mesh Renderer altered

The takeaway here is that regardless of what mesh is loaded, or what material has been applied to it, or even if the mesh is not being rendered in the scene, the capsule will still act like a capsule when interacting with other objects because of its Capsule Collider. You could, of course, adjust the Capsule collider's parameters, including its up direction to better fit the new mesh. Later in the book, you will be adding and removing components as you add functionality to a variety of imported assets.

As long as you are having a first look at components, you may as well inspect the Main Camera.

9. Select the Main Camera from the Hierarchy view, and look at its components in the Inspector (Figure 2-16).

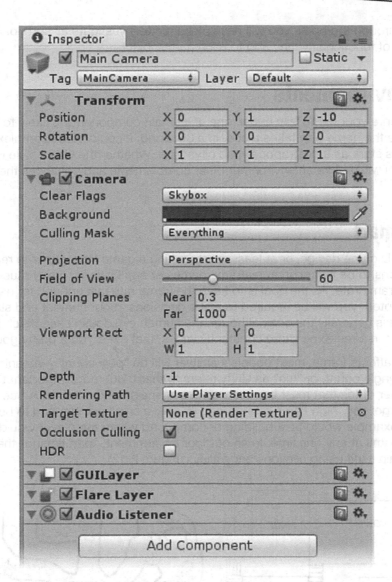

Figure 2-16. The Camera's components in the Inspector

Along with the mandatory Transform, it has a pretty robust Camera component and three components that have no parameters at all. Because there is no mesh associated with a camera, it has no Mesh Filter, Mesh Renderer, or collider components. The GUI Layer is what enables the camera to "see," and therefore render, GUI objects. These are 2D objects that are rendered in front of the 3D Scene environment. The Flare Layer component allows the camera to "see" post-process effects such as lens flares.

The Audio Listener component is a specialty component. It enables sound in the entire scene or level. Unity automatically adds one to any camera presets that are created. A default camera is created with each new scene, which ensures that your scene will be sound ready. Unfortunately, every time you create a new camera, you will get another Audio Listener. Because there can be only one Audio Listener to a scene, you will find yourself removing or at least disabling the extras.

As you progress through the book, you will have a chance to investigate all sorts of components and find out what kind of functionality they add to each gameObject.

Creating Environments

No matter what genre your game falls under, one of its main components is likely to be the environment where the game play takes place. In a 3D world, it could be as complex as a lush tropical forest or as stark as a post-apocalyptic cityscape. Whether the visual style is realistic or cartoon-like, you will require an environment that complements and enhances the game's functionality.

Designing Smart

If you are new to 3D game design, or at least new to taking a game from paper to reality, there are design limitations to be aware of. In real-time games or applications, pretty much everything adversely affects frame rate. As the goal is to keep the frame rate fast enough for game play to progress uninterrupted, you will be required to make decisions about content and staging. Sixty frames per second is generally the goal, although the human eye doesn't see much more than 30. Because frame rate in a real-time game constantly varies, that gives you a pretty good safety zone.

When asked what affects frame, most people's answer will be "poly count"—meaning polygons, or more precisely, triangle count, or "tris" as Unity refers to them. But more important than the number of tris, is the number of tris that must be rendered in a scene *at any one time*. A Scene that contains a million tris could get very high frame rate as long as only a small number had to be rendered at any one time. An example would be a building or compound where the player would never see more than one or two rooms at any one time. In an outdoor environment, "partitioning" the areas could be done with the terrain itself using canyons and valleys (Figure 2-17).

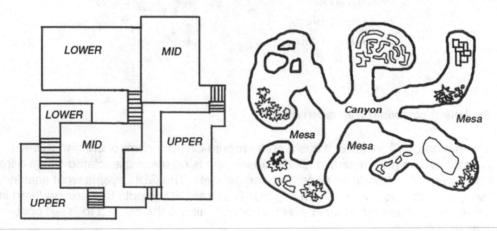

Figure 2-17. Efficient layout for indoor and outdoor scenes

Scenes where the million tris must all be rendered in the viewport at the same time—such as with the view of a complicated spacecraft, a city that can be seen from a distance as the player approaches it, or a complex piece of equipment or installation—will probably suffer from very low frame rates. There are lots of things that can be done to improve the frame rate in these cases, including the use of LOD (level of detail) stand-ins—that is, lower poly count versions of complicated meshes,—but designing to avoid problems is a better way to go.

If you think back on the Overdraw option in the Scene view you looked at in Chapter 1, you may remember that even if objects are occluded (hidden behind other objects), the engine has to determine whether they must be drawn or not. In mobile applications, especially, this can be costly. Unity Pro has an occlusion culling feature that will automatically hide occluded areas for you. If you are using the free version, you will have to manage visibility manually if your frame rate drops too low. So, with all of this in mind, whenever possible, design your environment to be able to hide large chunks of it as required.

Creating Terrain

As with most modern game editors, Unity has a terrain-building system. While not as robust as some, it covers most of the basics quite nicely, with more enhancements promised for the future. One of the more important features is a built-in LOD system. The ground mesh itself drops down in detail as it recedes into the background. 3D mesh trees are replaced with billboard (an image on a simple plane that rotates to always face the camera) versions, and smaller plants and meshes are hidden as the player move away from them. All of the distances can be adjusted.

If you are thinking that you can create and populate your terrain with abandon, you will be disappointed. Even with Unity's LOD features, it is very easy to bring your frame rate to a crawl. As with overall environmental design, it is better to keep clusters of high foliage usage localized so you can cut back the culling distances.

Enough doom and gloom! It's time to create an environment so you can get a taste of Unity's capabilities.

Defining the Bounds

The first thing you will need to do is define the size of your terrain object. Although it's tempting to work on a grand scale, remember your player will need to traverse it as the game unfolds, preferably not by placing a soda can on the keyboard and wandering off for a coffee while his character makes its way across the vast area between points of interest.

Let's begin by creating a new scene for the terrain test. The current scene has nothing worth saving, so you will abandon it.

1. From the Files menu, select New Scene.

2. At the warning dialog, choose Don't Save.

3. Save the scene as **Terrain Test**.

4. Right-click on the Assets folder in the Project view, and from the Create submenu, select Folder.

5. Name the new folder **Scenes**.

6. Drag the Terrain Test scene and the old Primitives scene into the new Scenes folder.

Now you are ready to create your new terrain.

1. From the GameObject menu, Create Other, select Terrain from near the bottom of the list (Figure 2-18).

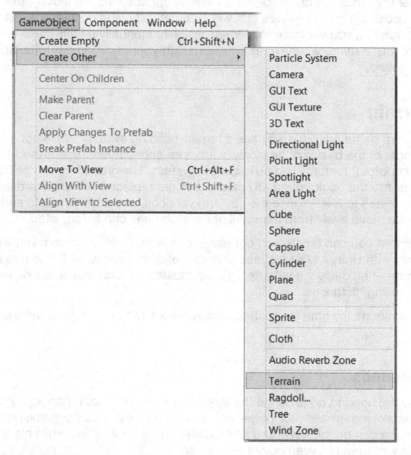

Figure 2-18. The Terrain gameObject

2. Inspect the new gameObject and its unique components in the Inspector (Figure 2-19).

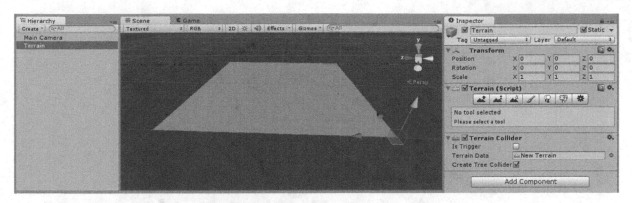

Figure 2-19. The Terrain components in the Inspector

Along with the mandatory Transform, the new gameObject has only two other components. The Terrain Collider, a specialized collider used only for terrains, and a deceptively simple-looking Terrain component. This one is a script, but you do not have access to its contents. It is, however, the place where most of the terrain building takes place—essentially, a terrain editor. In earlier versions of Unity, the terrain had its own menu that provided easy access to key features while setting up a terrain. While the re-organization make more sense for upkeep, it makes the initial setup a bit of a scavenger hunt.

1. Double-click on the new Terrain object in the Hierarchy view to focus the viewport to it.

2. Note that it was created at 0, 0, 0, but that its pivot point is at one of its corners rather than the more typical typical center location.

3. Click through the Terrain tool bar, and note the names of the various modules in the space below the tool icons (Figure 2-20).

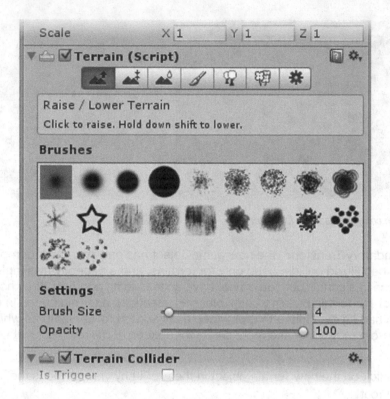

Figure 2-20. The Terrain component's modules with Raise/Lower Terrain active

The names and, in the case of the tools, a brief set of instructions for their use, are shown under the tool bar as you select each one.

4.   Select the Terrain Settings module.

5.   In the Resolution section, near the bottom, set the Terrain Width and the Terrain Length to **200 x 200** meters.

6.   Set the Height to **150** meters.

The Height consists of the lowest point—a lake bottom, for example—to the highest peak. If you want mountains that are 130 meters high from a valley floor and a lake bottom that is 20 meters deep from that same floor, you would make the Height 150 meters.

7.   Make note of the warning at the bottom of the Resolution sections.

8.   Focus the view to the Terrain's new dimensions, and then rotate the view so it is nearly a side view (Figure 2-21).

Figure 2-21. The newly sized Terrain in the viewport

Always make sure you are happy with your initial parameters before you start creating your terrain's features. The various resolutions store the information for how much detail will be used in your terrain's various features. Larger resolution for these images will, of course, take up more disk space/download time and memory. The test scene you are building will be fine with the defaults.

The next parameter that must be set is the "flatten" height. Think of it as the base level for your terrain. The topography tools allow you to paint up or down from that base level. In the earlier example, because you want your lake to be 20 meters deep, the flatten height will be 20 meters. The Flatten tool is found in the Paint Height module.

9. In the Inspector, in the Terrain's Paint Height module, set the Height to **20** and press the Flatten button (Figure 2-22).

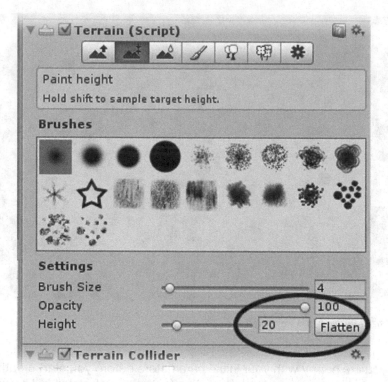

Figure 2-22. The Flatten height setting

The Terrain jumps up 20 units in the viewport, but the Y transform is not affected (Figure 2-23).

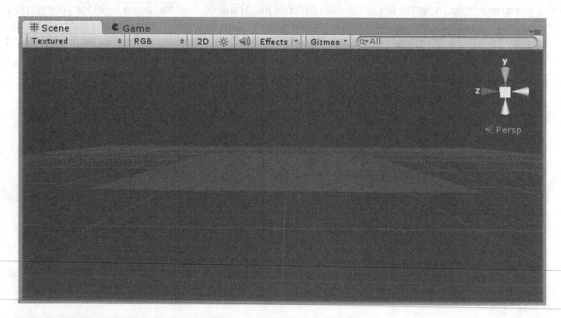

Figure 2-23. The newly sized Terrain in the viewport

With your terrain defined, you are ready to sculpt the features. The Terrain component is well covered in the Unity documentation, at `http://docs.unity3d.com/Documentation/Components/script-Terrain.html`, so you will just be covering the basics in this exercise. Painting is achieved by pressing the left mouse button down while moving the mouse.

The first of the Modules is Raise/Lower Terrain. With it, you can paint mountains and valleys using a variety of brush shapes. The two parameters are Brush Size and Opacity (strength of the effect). In this module, painting is additive.

1. Select the Raise/Lower Terrain section.

2. Rotate the view so that the terrain is closer to a top view.

3. Set the Brush Size to **100** and the Opacity to **20**.

4. Using the default brush (the soft round brush), paint some hills around the outside of the terrain.

5. Paint a couple of passes to turn them into mountains.

6. Experiment with different brushes to see the results (Figure 2-24).

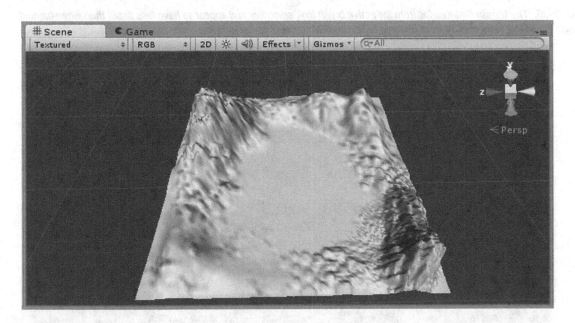

Figure 2-24. Newly formed hills and mountains around the perimeter of the terrain

Note how the detail softens as soon as you release the mouse button (Figure 2-25). This is Unity's LOD at work. If you zoom in, you will see the detail you originally saw as you painted.

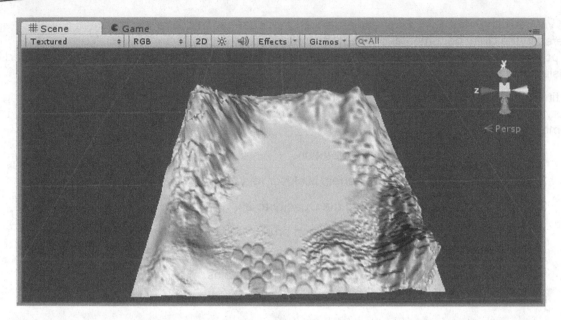

Figure 2-25. *The terrain features far from the active brush look smoother and appear to have less detail than when painted. Change the Scene view display from Textured to Textured Wire (the drop-down menu under the Scene tab)*

8.   Zoom in and out to see the detail change (Figure 2-26).

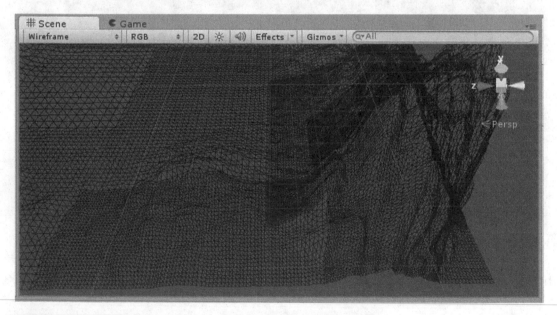

Figure 2-26. *The Textured Wire display making the resolution details more apparent*

9. Set the display back to Textured.

Most of the Terrain tools have different functionality when a specific key, usually the <shift> key, is being held down. In the Raise/Lower Terrain tool, holding the <shift> key lowers the terrain. Just as the regular painting caps out at 130 meters above the base height, painting lower will bottom out at 20 meters below base.

10. Paint a couple of depressions in the terrain by holding down the <shift> key while you paint.

11. Paint over the same depression a few times until it bottoms out (Figure 2-27).

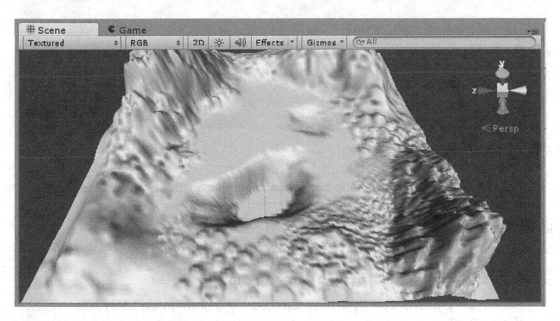

Figure 2-27. A couple of depressions in the valley floor

The next tool is the Paint Height tool. Like the Raise/Lower Terrain tool, it is also additive, but you can set the cap height to have more control when painting building pads, mesas, or even sunken walkways. Because you are already defining a target height, this time the <shift> key will sample the terrain's height at the cursor's location when you click. This is quite useful when you want to go back to a certain feature to increase its size but can no longer remember the height setting you used.

1. Click on the Paint Height button.

Note that the previous settings for Brush Size and Opacity are retained.

Let's create a plateau, slightly above the base level. The Height parameter is set to the Terrain height, 150 meters, so if base height is 20, a good height for a low plateau might be 30.

2. Set the Height to **30**.

3. Paint your plateau in a nice area in a clear spot on the valley floor (Figure 2-28).

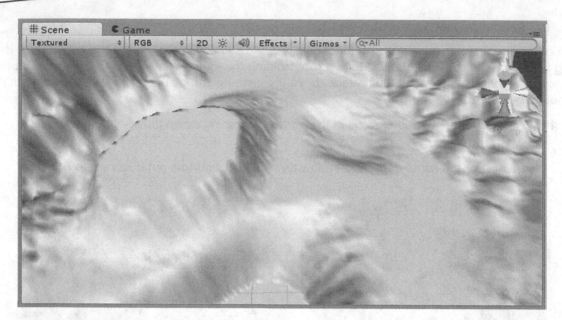

Figure 2-28. An isolated plateau on the valley floor

4. Hold the <shift> key down, and click once to sample a little way down the slope of the plateau.

The Height parameter changes to match the sampled point.

5. Reduce the brush size to something appropriate for terraced steps.

6. Paint the first step, and sample its slope to get the next height.

7. Repeat the procedure until you have terraced steps down to the valley floor (Figure 2-29).

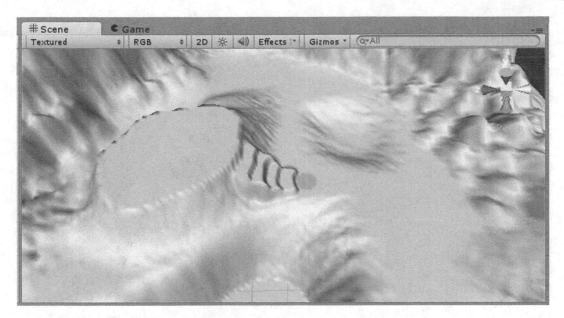

Figure 2-29. Terraced steps leading down to the valley floor

The next tool is the Smooth Height tool. Having undoubtedly experimented with several of the spottier brushes, you've probably got some pretty spiky mountains somewhere on your terrain. The Smooth Height tool will simulate some nice weathering to tame them down.

1. Click on the Smooth Height tool.

2. Set the Brush Size to **100** and the Opacity to about **30**.

3. Paint some of the jagged peaks down to simulate the passing of a few millennium (Figure 2-30).

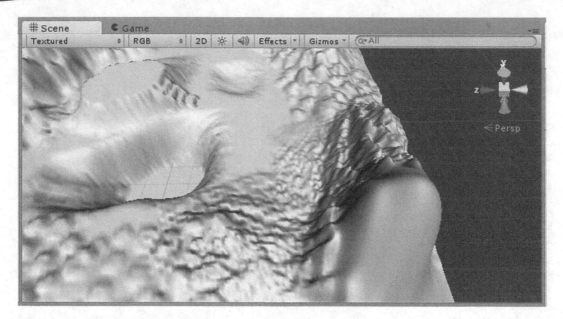

Figure 2-30. Some of the jagged peaks weathered into gentle slopes

Just as with the previous tools, the Smooth Height is also additive, so you can set the Opacity lower and make repeated passes over areas that need attention.

Adding Textures

While the terrain is certainly looking more interesting, it is in great need of some textures. Fortunately, because you imported the Terrain Assets package when you created the project, you will have some nice textures to work with. Terrain textures must be tiled, of course, to avoid seams, but they must also contain very few features that the human eye will recognize as repeated patterns. Alpha channels will be ignored.

Let's begin by looking at the textures provided by the Terrain Assets package.

1. In the Project view, Assets folder, Terrain Assets, select the Terrain Textures folder.

2. Use the size slider to see the thumbnails at their maximum.

3. Click on Grass(Hill) in the second column.

4. Adjust the Inspector's width and the preview window's height to get a good view of the texture (Figure 2-31).

Figure 2-31. The Grass(Hill) texture shown in the Inspector

5. Note the information given about the texture at the bottom of the Preview window.

The texture is 512 x 512. The compression is DXT1. Unity compresses all of the project's textures into the DDS format. If you look at the top of the Inspector, you can see that you will be able to dictate how the texture is read in and processed.

6. Click on each of the other three textures to see what is available.

7. From the Terrain Grass folder, check out Grass and Grass2, making sure to note their alpha channels by toggling the RGBA button next to the Mipmap slider (Figure 2-32).

Figure 2-32. The Grass texture not meant for a terrain texture

The two textures, Grass and Grass2, are not for the terrain texture. You will be using them later, though, to help dress up your terrain.

The first thing to know about the terrain textures is that the first one you apply to the terrain will fill it completely, so choose accordingly. Textures, as with the rest of the trees, detail meshes and grasses that must be loaded into the appropriate Terrain component module before they can be used. Let's begin by flooding the terrain with the Grass(Hill) texture.

1. Select the Terrain object again to get back to the terrain tools.

2. Click on the Paint Texture tool.

3. Under the Textures preview area, select Edit Textures.

4. From the list that appears, select Add Texture (Figure 2-33).

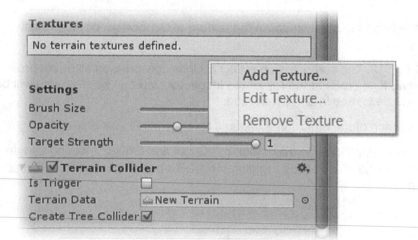

Figure 2-33. The Edit Texture list

The Add Terrain Texture dialog appears (Figure 2-34).

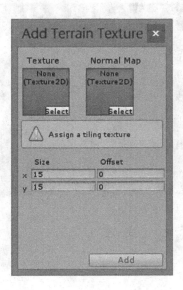

Figure 2-34. The Add Terrain Texture dialog

5. Click the Texture's Select button to bring up the Select Texture2D dialog.

6. Select Grass(Hill).

7. Click Add.

The Grass(Hill) texture is now shown in the available Textures area beneath the brushes. In the Scene view, the terrain is filled with the Grass(Hill) texture, tiled at the default 15 x 15 size (Figure 2-35). Note that this is a tiling *size*, not number. If you wanted the texture to appear smaller or more detailed on the terrain, you would decrease the Size parameters.

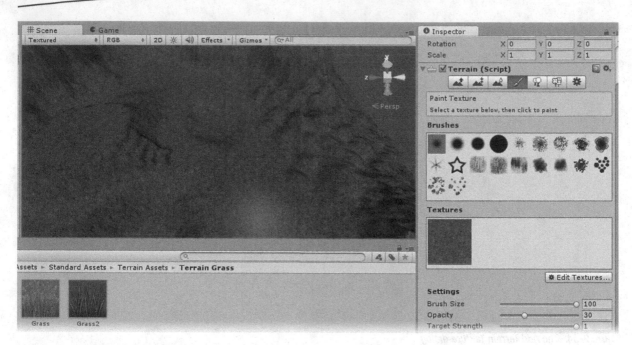

Figure 2-35. The Add Terrain Texture dialog

To get some practice painting a terrain texture, you will need to add another texture.

    8.   Click the Edit Textures button again, and select Add Texture again.

    9.   Select Grass&Rock, and click Add.

The new texture is added to the available textures (Figure 2-36). Note that the Grass(Hill) texture has a light blue strip at its base. This tells you that it is the currently active texture for painting.

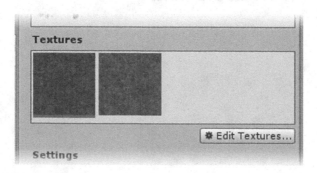

Figure 2-36. The two available terrain textures

    10.   This time, load Cliff (Layered Rock).

The thumbnail for this texture appears washed out (Figure 2-37).

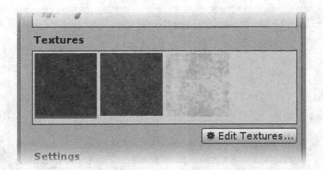

Figure 2-37. The Cliff (Layered Rock) texture added to the available terrain textures

The mystery is quickly solved if you select the texture in the Project view and then view its alpha channel in the Inspector. This texture, when used on regular scene objects, was probably designed to use its alpha channel as a glossiness map.

Now that you have loaded a few textures, it's time to start painting. Once again you have the brush choices, Brush Size and Opacity. Opacity is additive, so the more you paint an area, the more opaque the coverage is. This time, however, you have a new parameter, Target Strength. This lets you set a maximum opacity that caps the additive effect. When painting between ground and foliage, you may prefer to blend with the speckled brushes rather than opacity.

1. Select the cliff texture, set the Opacity to **100**, and paint the mountains.

2. Select the Grass & Rock texture and one of the more broken-up brushes.

3. Paint the transition between the grass and cliff textures. Try clicking rather than dragging the brush.

4. Load the GoodDirt texture.

5. Decrease the Brush Size, and paint several paths around your terrain (Figure 2-38).

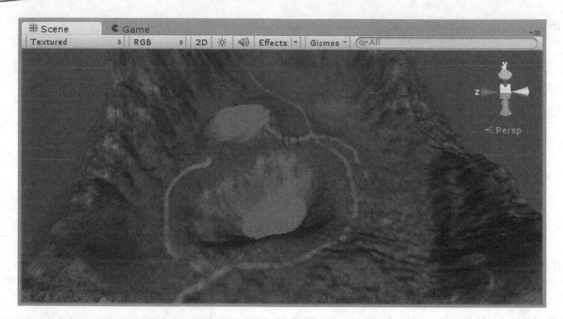

Figure 2-38. The terrain with textures painted

In earlier versions of Unity, once the scene was saved, the terrain's *splat map* would be visible in the Project view. A splat map is how Unity tracks where the textures were painted on the terrain. An RGBA texture has 4 colors available: red, green, blue, and white (Figure 2-39). The first three textures are recorded using the red, green, and blue colors. The fourth color is stored in the alpha channel as white, where black is used as a mask.

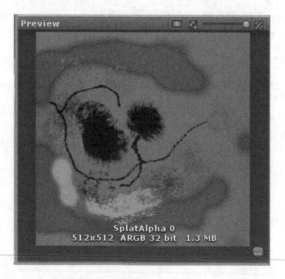

Figure 2-39. A splat map in the Inspector from an earlier version of Unity

To get a better idea of how the last "color" looks, you would have to toggle the alpha channel to see the white (Figure 2-40).

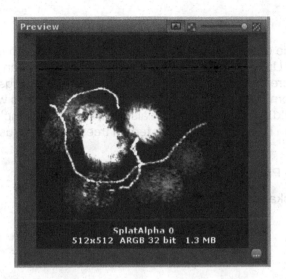

Figure 2-40. The splat map's alpha channel

You may be wondering if four textures are the most you can use on the terrain. If you note the name, *SplatAlpha 0*, the element 0 may clue you in. If you are new to scripting, you will soon find out that array elements always count from 0, indicating that there could be more splat map elements. So it turns out you *can* have multiple splat maps. Do be aware that each would be one more 1.3-MB texture added to the project and cause the terrain to be rendered again on top of the first splat map in an alpha-blended way.

Populating the Terrain

The next step in the terrain-creation process is to add some foliage. Unity handles trees differently than it handles plants. Plants also have two options, one for billboard planes and one for regular meshes. Each of the three foliage types has its own functionality and peculiarities

> **Tip**   A Billboard object is a texture map with an opacity channel that is applied to a plane. Unlike a real-life billboard, in game engines the planes always turn to face the camera. In Unity, all trees used for terrain automatically have an image generated for the planes when you load them into the Terrain component's Paint Trees section.

Unity's Terrain Assets include a single, nice palm tree you can use to populate your test scene. You can also use the BigTree that comes with the Tree Generator package. You have already seen a couple of grass textures that you can use for the "grass" style detail foliage. That leaves only the detail meshes with no samples for this test terrain. You could try your luck with some free models from the Asset Store, but because of the way the Terrain component handles these meshes, not all of the assets available will be well behaved. Fortunately, the book's project requires a few specialty plant meshes that have been set up to work well with either the Terrain system or as standalone meshes.

Trees

Let's begin by importing one of the Unity packages. When you first set up this project, you had the option of importing several Unity packages. The great thing is that you can import them at any time after the project has been created as well. The Tree Creator package brings in the assets required to create your own trees from some basic meshes and textures. Its use is well covered in the Unity documentation in case you'd like to give it a try. It also comes with a sample tree already finished. It is a higher poly count than is recommended for terrain trees, but when used sparingly it will work well for your terrain test.

1. Right-click in the Project view, or open the Assets menu.

2. From Import Package, choose Tree Creator (Figure 2-41).

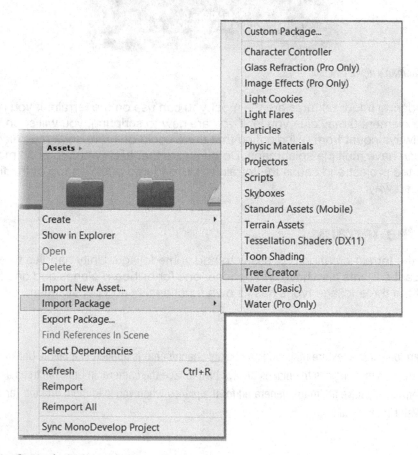

Figure 2-41. The Tree Creator in the Import Packages list

3. The Importing Package dialog will open when the package has been expanded (Figure 2-42).

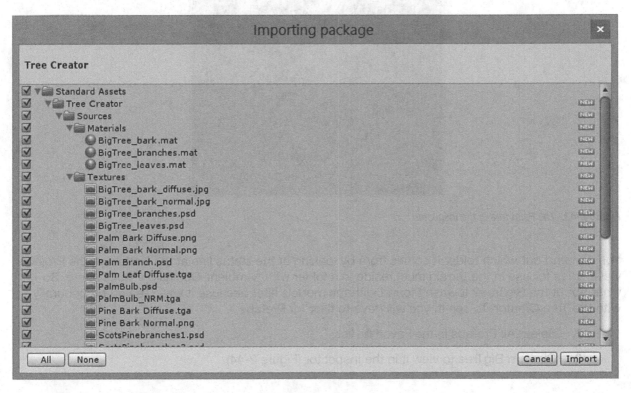

Figure 2-42. The Tree Creator package ready and waiting for import

4. Click Import.

5. In the Project view, under Favorites, click All Models.

6. The only tree model showing is the Palm tree.

7. Click on it, and click and drag in the Preview window of the Inspector to rotate the view (Figure 2-43).

Figure 2-43. The Palm tree in the Inspector

You can find out which folder it comes from by looking at the status line at the bottom of the Project view. Trees for use in the terrain must reside in a folder with "Ambient-Occlusion" in its name. So what about the BigTree? It wasn't found with the models filter because it was created procedurally with the Tree Creator. To see it, you will have to filter for Prefabs.

1.   Select All Prefabs in the Favorites list.

2.   Click on BigTree to view it in the Inspector (Figure 2-44).

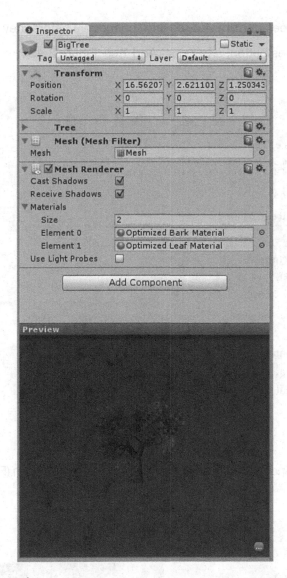

Figure 2-44. The BigTree in the Inspector

Because it's a prefab—and in this case a single gameObject, not just an imported asset—you can see its components in the Inspector along with its preview. In the Tree component, where you can see the icons for its various nodes, you can see that it has 3516 tris and two materials. Unity recommends that a terrain tree be no more than 2000 tris. It also limits terrain trees to two materials. Typically, the material for leaves and branches uses transparency, and the other material is for bark. Unity also has a few shaders designed especially for terrain trees. This tree wasn't created specifically for use in the terrain, but with a slight adjustment it will work. Let's load both trees in the Terrain's Place Trees section.

3.   Select the Terrain.

4.   Click on the Place Trees button.

Just like the textures, the trees must be loaded into the module before they are available for use.

5.   Click the Edit Trees button, and select Add Tree (Figure 2-45).

Figure 2-45. The Edit Trees list

6.   In the Add Tree window, click the Browse icon and select the Palm (Figure 2-46).

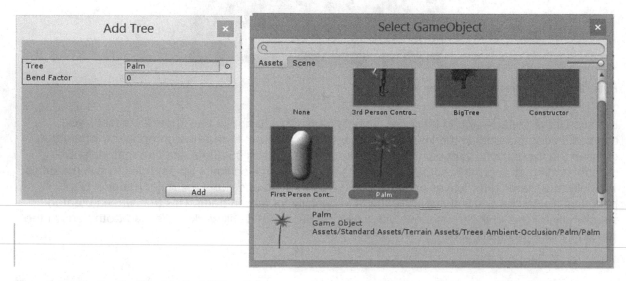

Figure 2-46. Loading the Palm into the Add Tree dialog

7. Click Add.

8. Repeat the process to load the BigTree.

9. Set the Brush Size to about **20**, and paint palm trees around the terrain.

10. Click on the BigTree to make it the active tree, and try to plant it in the same place as the Palms.

You may see a few added, but the Density parameter limits how close the trees can be planted to each other.

For the next step in your Tree exploration, you will be planting only BigTrees on the top of your plateau. If it has already been covered with palms, you can easily remove them. As the instructions for the Plant Trees tell you, you can hold Shift and paint to remove all trees, or Ctrl (Cmd on Mac) to remove the currently selected tree.

1. Hold the Shift key, and clear the palms from the Plateau.

2. Release the Shift key, and plant BigTrees on it.

3. Zoom in slowly, observing the trees of both types switch from their billboard (distance LOD) counterparts to the mesh versions.

4. Arrange the view so that you can see a few trees at a distance of about 5–10 meters (Figure 2-47).

Figure 2-47. A good view of some BigTrees

All looks good so far, but you are missing a crucial item in the scene: a light source!

5. From the GameObjects menu, Create Other, choose a Directional Light.

6. Toggle the Scene Lighting button on from the middle of the Scene view's tool bar.

The lighting improves. Directional lights cast parallel rays and are generally the choice for lighting outdoor scenes. If you are not using Unity Pro, they are the only lights that can cast shadows—which you have probably just realized are missing from the scene. Shadows of any kind tend to be costly, so they are not turned on as a default. Shadows are also set to display only as far as a specified distance from the camera.

7. In the Directional Light's Light component, set the Shadow Type to Soft Shadows.

8. Adjust the shadow Strength to about **0.6**.

Now you can see the problem with the BigTrees or, to be more accurate, their leaf material's shader (Figure 2-48). The leaf texture's alpha channel is being ignored for shadows. If you pan around the view, you will notice that the Palms' fronds cast their shadows correctly. Both are using opacity channels rather than geometry. To fix the problem, you can replace the "hidden" material with one of those already available for the Tree Creator. Generally, the easiest way to edit prefabs is to drag one into the scene view, make the changes, and then delete them from the scene.

Figure 2-48. Solid shadows for the BigTrees

9. Locate the BigTree prefab in the Project view, and drag one into the Scene view.

10. In the Project view, Assets, Standard Assets, Tree Creator, Sources, select the Materials folder.

Inside it you will see the bark, leaf, and branch materials (Figure 2-49).

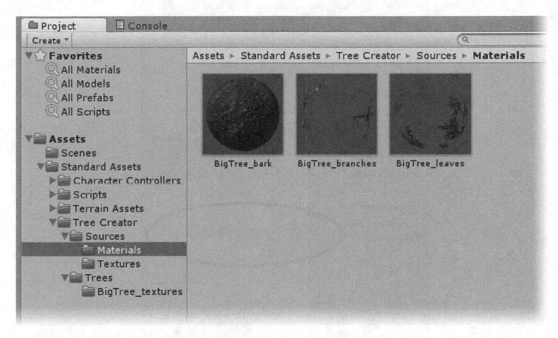

Figure 2-49. The materials found in the Tree Creator files

11. Select the BigTree in the Hierarchy view.

12. In the Inspector, in the Tree component, click on the left leaf node.

13. In its Geometry section, drag the BigTree_Leaves material into its Material field (Figure 2-50).

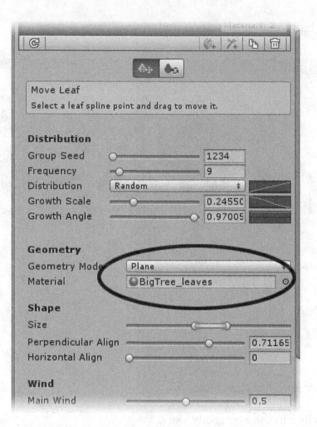

Figure 2-50. Assigning the BigTree_Leaves material to the leaf node in the Tree component

When the screen redraws, you should see proper leaf shadows below the prefab tree. Now you will have to update the tree in the Terrain's Plant Trees module.

14.   Select the Terrain, and go to the Plant Trees section.

15.   Click the Refresh button, and move the cursor over to the Scene view.

The shadows are now being drawn properly for all of the terrain trees (Figure 2-51). Any time you change a tree asset or prefab, you must use "Refresh the trees" to update them.

Figure 2-51. Terrain BigTrees now casting shadows

16.   Delete the BigTree prefab from the Hierarchy view.

For more information on setting up your own trees to use in your terrain, check out the Creating Trees section at http://docs.unity3d.com/Documentation/Components/terrain-Trees.html.

Plants

As mentioned earlier, Unity has two types of "details." The first are Grasses, which are simple billboard planes. The only asset they require is a texture with an alpha.

1.   Select the Terrain again.

2.   Open the Paint Details section.

3.   Select the Edit Details button, and select Add Grass Texture (Figure 2-52).

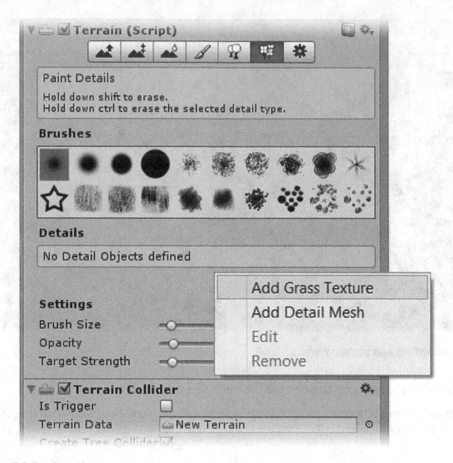

Figure 2-52. *The Edit Details options*

4. For Detail Texture, click the Browse button and load either Grass or Grass2 from the browser (Figure 2-53).

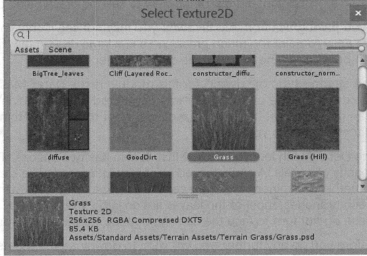

Figure 2-53. *The Add Grass Texture dialog*

5. Click Add.

6. Set the Brush size to about **50**, the Opacity to about **0.15**, and the Target Strength to about **0.125**.

7. Click once to Paint some grass close to you in the Scene view.

8. Click and drag to see how easy it is to add too much grass (Figure 2-54).

Figure 2-54. *Grass from a single click on the left, and painted on the right*

9. Zoom in and out of the view to see the grass being distance culled.

If you paint grass from too far away, you may not see it until you zoom in closer. Even with culling, it is easy to paint too much grass and see a large drop in the frame rate, so add grass carefully. This can be a good time to use some of the spottier brushes.

The second type of "detail" for this module is the Detail Mesh. With the Grass type, you loaded a texture and the planer mesh was generated for you. Obviously, you could use textures other than grass, but at some point, you will want to use something more substantial to add foliage or other features to your terrain.

The Detail Mesh lets you do just that. It also has two options. The first is used with plants that use opacity channels. A small-leaved plant with lots of twig-like stems would cost far too many tris for something so minor in your scene. You can see the idea with the BigTree's foliage. Other than a few mesh branches, most of the leaves are on large, mostly planer pieces of geometry. Unlike the grass, these do not turn to face the camera, so they are generally crossed in two or three planes.

Before you go any further, you will want to download the assets that are included with the book. To do so, go to the book's page at the Apress website (www.apress.com/9781430267799) and locate the download. The assets include asset files and source code for each chapter, along with a finished version of the project for each chapter. Unzip the assets to a location of your choice.

1. If you haven't already done so, download the book's assets for Chapter 2.

2. In Unity, right-click in the Project view to bring up the Assets menu.

3. From Import Package, choose Custom Package.

4. Navigate to the downloaded Chapter 2 Book Assets folder, and select TerrainDetailMeshes.unityPackage.

5. Click Import when the package has uncompressed and the dialog appears (Figure 2-55).

Figure 2-55. The contents of the TerrainDetailMeshes.UnityPackage

The package is imported to your scene. The file hierarchy from the original scene is retained. In the Project view, you will now find the following new folders: Imported Assets, Prefabs, and Textures. The gameObjects in the Prefabs folder are the same as the assets in the Imported Assets folder, but as prefabs they can be brought into the scene as individuals. You will be making your own prefabs later on in the project.

6.   Click on the Prefabs folder, and check out the new gameObjects (Figure 2-56).

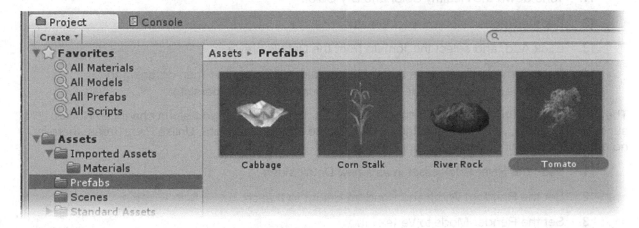

Figure 2-56. The objects from the newly imported custom UnityPackage

7. Click on the Tomato mesh to see its crossed planes in the Inspector
    (Figure 2-57).

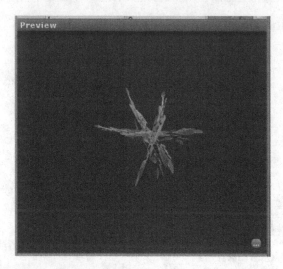

Figure 2-57. The crossed planes of the tomato mesh

8. Select the Terrain, and open the Place Details module.

9. From Edit Details, select Add Detail Mesh.

10. This time, try dragging the Tomato prefab directly into the Detail field instead
    of using the Browser.

Other than the regular parameters, you will find a new one here, Render Mode. The choices are
Vertex Lit and Grass. Vertex Lit is for meshes that do not use opacity for any of their textures. Grass
is for meshes that use opacity. Vertex Lit meshes will not be able to bend in the terrain wind that
you will try in the next section. Detail meshes like rocks or cactus are good choices for Vertex Lit.
"Grass" meshes may or may not be affected by terrain wind, depending on how they were prepared.

11. Tone down the Healthy Color and Dry Color.

12. For the Render Mode, select Grass.

13. Click Add, and select the Tomato from the Details previews.

14. Paint some tomato plants around the terrain, clicking rather than dragging to
    avoid overpopulation. (The settings for your grass should persist.)

The other Render Type in Detail Meshes is Vertex Lit. It does not support alpha channels. Rocks,
succulents, cactus, and other substantial meshes are most appropriate. Unlike Paint Trees, there is
no density restriction, so use this tool carefully.

1. Load the River Rock asset in as a new Detail Mesh.

2. Set the Random Width and Random Height to **0** each.

3. Set the Render Mode to Vertex Lit.

4. Turn the Dry Color and Healthy Color to white and grey.

5. Click Add, select the River Rock Detail mesh, and click in a few places to get a good cover of rocks (Figure 2-58, left).

6. From Edit Details, select Edit and change the Random Width and Random Height to **3** (Figure 2-58, middle).

The rocks scale in a large fractal noise pattern, with the smaller rocks around the edges.

7. Adjust the Random Height value up and down to see the results before setting it back to **3**.

8. Take the Noise Scale slowly up to **0.75** and back down to watch the scale of the noise pattern get smaller (Figure 2-58, right).

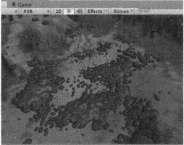

Figure 2-58. The River Rock evenly painted (left), with random Width and Height set to 3 (center), and with the Noise Scale adjusted (right)

9. Click Add to close the Edit window.

10. Hold the Ctrl or Cmd key down, and lightly paint over the rocks to thin them out.

Terrain Plants and Wind

Wind in Unity is not a simple scene addition. Wind is added to grass and detail meshes through the Terrain Settings section under Wind Settings.

1. Click Play, and switch back to the Scene view.

2. Zoom in to watch the grass and tomato plants wave back and forth.

3. Adjust the Speed, Size, Bending, and Grass Tint to see how the Grass texture and Grass Detail meshes react.

Terrain trees require a Wind object for movement. The Bend Factor setting acts as a multiplier.

4. From the GameObject menu, Create Other, select Wind Zone.

5. Select the Terrain object again.

6. In the Paint Trees section, select the Palm and click Edit Tree.

7. Adjust the Bend Factor up and down to see how the trees react.

8. Leave the Bend Factor at **2**.

Note that the distant billboard trees are not affected by the wind, so you may have to zoom in closer to the palm trees to see results.

9. Select the Wind Zone, and check out the parameters and options.

10. Stop Play mode.

The Wind Zone is deleted once you stop Play mode. Feel free to add another more permanent Wind Zone now that you are no longer in Play mode.

Terrain Bloopers

So far, you've been practicing with well-behaved assets. There are, however, a lot things that can go wrong with assets that look perfectly okay when brought into the scene on their own. It is worthwhile being familiar with a few typical problems.

The first issue is due to the way Unity calculates wind on Detail meshes. The values used to calculate the amount of movement from "wind" are stored on the object's vertices. Besides the vertices' x, y, and z locations, vertices store other types of information. Vertex color, one such piece of information, can tint the mesh to add to the texture. This can help give the Detail meshes extra depth without adding extra texture maps. With terrain wind, Unity uses the vertex alpha channel to determine how much movement each vertex receives. The bottom of the plant should have black as its vertex alpha color, and the top of the plants should grade up to gray. The lighter the alpha value, the more bend there will be. The problem comes with meshes that have had no vertex alpha assigned. A default color of white for vertex color adds no color. White for the alpha vertex colors means that the entire mesh will move back and forth. If no alpha was specified, white may be the default color for the vertex alpha, depending on what application the object was created in and how it was exported.

In the first experiment, the cabbage mesh uses an alpha channel for its outer leaves, so it must use the Grass Render Mode. The regular Cabbage object has black for its alpha vertex color, and the Fast Cabbage has the default white.

1. Load both of the cabbage objects in as Detail Meshes with Render Mode set to Grass.

2. Tint them slightly different colors, and paint a patch of each onto the terrain.

3. Click Play, and switch back to the Scene view.

4. Watch the Fast Cabbages flock back and forth across the terrain.

Another problem comes if the object's texture unwrap is not "atlased," or packed within a unit size. With regular objects, the overflow causes the texture to be tiled. With terrain objects, the texture maps are internally joined together, so the overflow ends up on a different object's texture (Figure 2-59).

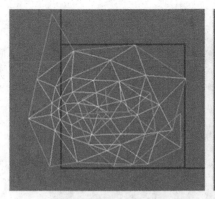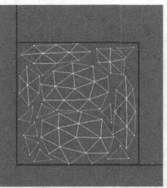

Figure 2-59. The River Rock, improperly unwrapped with its overlap inheriting part of its texture from one of the other textures

There is also a limit of one material for Detail meshes. If the limit is exceeded, the plant (or other object) will not show on the terrain. The Corn Stalk uses a regular material for its stalk and leaves, and it uses an alpha channel texture for its top tassel.

1. Load the Corn stalk as a Detail Mesh.

2. Try it as both a Grass and a Vertex Lit Render Mode.

Nothing shows on the terrain.

3. Select the Corn Stalk and from the Edit Details menu, select Remove.

Because the Corn Stalk only has two materials, it can be added to the terrain as a Tree.

4. Add the Corn Stalk as a Tree in Paint Trees.

5. If you added another Wind Zone earlier, set the Corn Stalk's Bend Factor to **2**.

6. Paint some stalks onto the terrain (Figure 2-60).

Figure 2-60. *The Corn Stalk painted as a Tree*

> 7.   Click Play, and switch back to the Scene view to see your new corn field.

The last issue you may come across is incorrect transforms on import. Depending on the application your plant was created in, its scale and orientation may be incorrect. Unity does a very good job with regular scene objects by interpreting their transforms correctly after import. The two exceptions are when the objects are used in the terrain and when they are used in Mecanim, Unity's character-animation system. When authoring in 3ds Max, for instance, where Z is up in the world, you may have to use what is commonly referred to in the 3ds Max community as the "box trick" to collapse the transform matrix in the correct orientation.

In Figure 2-61, A, a cone is created in the top viewport in 3ds Max and exported as an fbx file. With the coordinate system set to Local, you can see that its up axis is the Z axis. In Figure 2-61, B, a box is created in the front viewport so that its local Y axis is pointing up. In Figure 2-61, C, the box has been collapsed to a mesh object, the cone has been attached to it, and the box's geometry has been deleted from the resulting object. The final object is left with the cone's geometry and the box's transform matrix, where Y is pointing up.

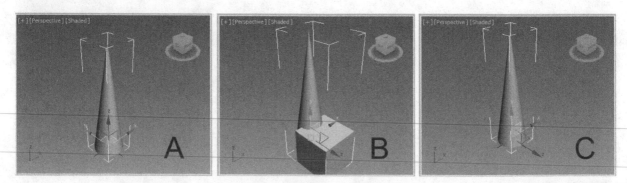

Figure 2-61. *The cone with its native orientation (left), a box created so that its up direction is Y (B), and the cone attached to the box with the box's geometry removed and the Y up orientation retained (C)*

In Figure 2-62, the first cone comes in on its side and is painted on the terrain on its side (the cones on the left). The cone with the "corrected" transform matrix comes in as a tree with the proper up direction and paints correctly, as can be seen on the right side of Figure 2-62.

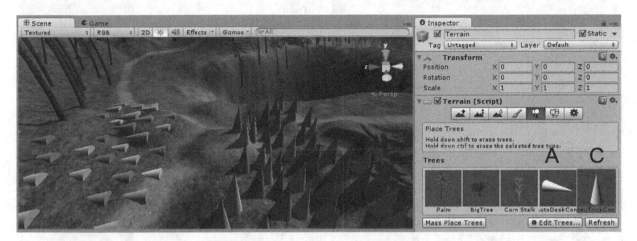

Figure 2-62. The two test "trees" loaded in the terrain library and painted in the scene, A on the left and C on the right

Environment

The plants have gone a long way toward fleshing out the terrain, but there are a few more things your scene may require.

The most obvious item is a sky. For that, you will have to import the Sky package. Unity has some nice cube maps that are utilized by special shaders to create a sky for your environment that used no mesh as a basis. This means your character will never be in danger of reaching its bounds. If you are able to generate your own cube maps from another application, you can use the six generated images to create your own cubemap inside Unity. The process is well covered in the documentation for cubemaps.

1. From the Assets menu or the Project view right-click menu, Import Packages, select Skyboxes.

2. Select the newly imported Skyboxes folder from the Standard Assets folder in the Project view.

The skybox material thumbnails are fairly useless.

3. Select Overcast1, and check out the six images that make its cubemap (Figure 2-63, left).

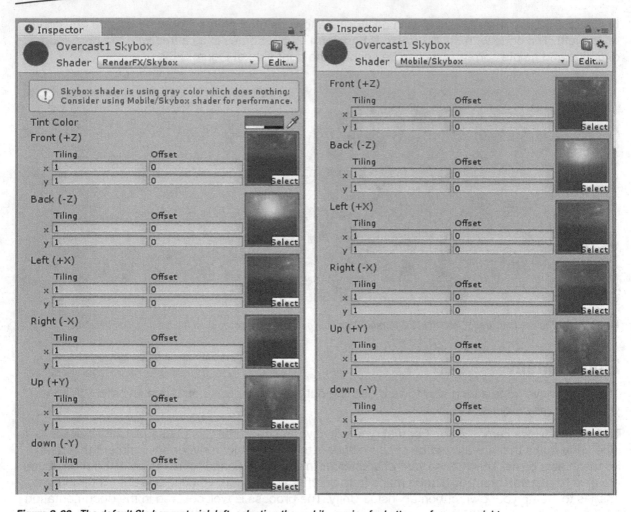

Figure 2-63. The default Skybox material, left; selecting the mobile version for better performance, right

Note the message at the top of the shader. Let's make it more efficient.

4. Click the Shader drop-down menu, and choose Skybox from the Mobile submenu (Figure 2-63, right).

Because this material is not applied to a gameObject, it gets added to the scene's settings.

5. From the Edit menu, select Render Settings.

6. In the Inspector, drag your favorite skybox material into the Skybox field or browse for it by clicking the browse icon.

The sky should now appear in the Scene view (Figure 2-64).

Figure 2-64. The sky in the test scene

7.   If the sky does not show, click the Effects drop-down arrow at the top of the Scene view and make sure Skybox is checked.

8.   Navigate the Scene view to see how the sky is presented.

As you probably noticed, Render Settings is also the place to add fog to a scene.

9.   Click the Fog check box to see fog in your scene.

10.   Adjust the color, and experiment with the Density.

Because the fog does not affect the skybox, consider using it as more of a ground mist. If you want a proper London fog, you would not use a skybox.

Shadows

With the addition of dynamic shadows for direct lights in the free version of Unity, you have probably noticed that the shadows fade off fairly close to the scene camera (Figure 2-65). The distance can be adjusted, but you may opt, depending on the type of game you want to create, to add "baked" shadows for the rest of the terrain. In Unity 5, the current lighting system, the Beast lightmapper, will be retired to Legacy status. As the date of that release is not yet known, you will do a little bit of experimenting with the current system.

Figure 2-65. Dynamic shadows fading away

1.   From the Window menu, select Lightmapping.

2.   From the Bake section, set the Mode to Dual Lightmaps (or Single Lightmaps
     if you are using the free version of Unity) and click Bake Scene.

When it is finished baking the lighting into textures, you will see the Near and Far maps (if you have
Unity Pro) in the Preview section (Figure 2-66). Inspection of your scene will show that the dynamic
close-up shadows have been replaced by the newly generated Far shadowmap and shadows are
now present beyond the dynamic shadow distance (Figure 2-67). The baked shadows from the Near
map are visible throughout the scene. To make *use* of the Dual Shadowmaps, you must switch to
Deferred Lighting and also be using Unity Pro.

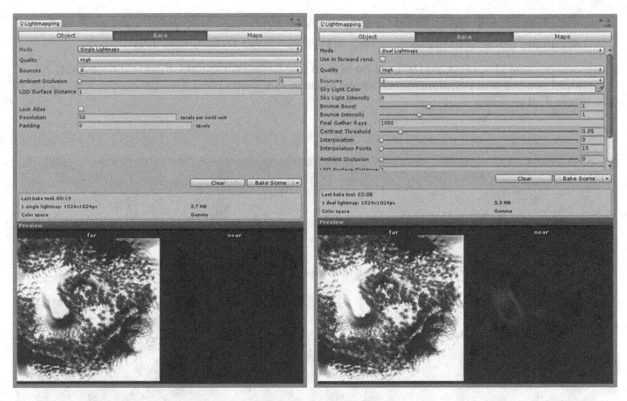

Figure 2-66.   Near and Far Baked shadows, Unity free (left), and Unity Pro (right)

Figure 2-67.   Baked shadows throughout the scene

3.   From the Edit menu, select Project Settings, Player.

4.   In the Other Settings section, Rendering Path, select Deferred Lighting.

If you do *not* have Unity Pro, you will not be able to use Deferred Lighting. If you do have Unity Pro, you should see the sharper, dynamic shadows at close range and the softer, baked shadows beyond that range (Figure 2-68).

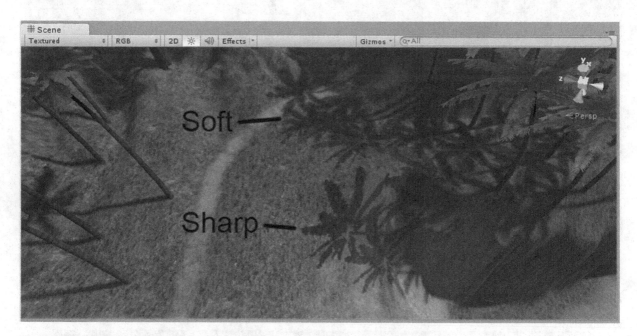

Figure 2-68. *Dynamic shadows at close range, and baked shadows beyond them, Pro Only*

Dynamic shadows are more costly than baked shadows, so Unity allows you to adjust the distance where the dynamic shadows blend into the lightmapped shadows.

If you are not using Unity Pro, you have two choices. You can have baked shadows and no dynamic shadows, or you can have dynamic shadows and no baked shadows. You will have to Clear the lightmaps in the Lightmapping view (next to the Bake Scene button) to get back to your dynamic shadows.

5.   With the Lightmapping window open, experiment with the Shadow distance, setting it to **40** when you are finished.

6.   If you are using Pro, select the Directional light from the Hierarchy view and adjust its shadow Strength to match the baked shadows.

You will be revisiting baked light later in the book after you have added static structures to your game scene.

Summary

In this chapter, you were introduced to Unity GameObjects through the use of several "primitive" objects. Having something tangible to work with, you experimented with object transforms to position, rotate, and scale objects in the scene. Making good use of Ctrl+D (Cmd on the mac), you learned how to align objects with vertex snaps, with grid snaps, and finally, through the use of "Align to View."

Parenting, you learned, gave you the *offset* from the parent's transforms in the child object's Transform component, rather than its actual transform values. Looking closer at the primitive objects, you discover several of the most common Components. You found that you could hide an object in the scene by disabling its Mesh Renderer component, or that you could fully deactivate it through the check box at the top of the Inspector. Although you have not seen them in action yet, you learned that Colliders are required to keep a player from going through other gameObjects or to trigger events when another gameObject intersects with them.

With the addition of a Terrain object (a gameObject with a Terrain component), you experimented with the generation and sculpting of a terrain. Using the Paint Terrain module, you painted textures onto the terrain and observed the splat map that recorded your endeavors. You made this more interesting by painting trees, grasses, and detail meshes, learning about some limitations and peculiarities of each. After a short introduction to wind in Unity, you were alerted in the final section to a few of the pitfalls encountered when creating terrain assets of your own or using assets not specifically created for use with Unity terrain.

Finally, you finished off your environment with a skybox, some fog, and a first look at the Beast Lightmapping system.

Scene Navigation and Physics

At this point, you have become familiar with creating, positioning, and manipulating various assets in a scene. The next logical step is to be able to experience your environment as a player. This is how you will be able to test the flow of your scene design and, as your game progresses, test functionality and game play.

Scene Navigation

Obviously, not all games will feature first-person or third-person navigation, but they are both a staple of the game industry and are important to be familiar with. In this chapter, you will be introduced to the First Person Controller and a lot of the concepts related to character navigation in general.

First Person Controller

The quickest way to get up and running in a scene is to create a First Person Controller. When you created the project, you imported the Character Controllers package. It contains scripts and assets for both a First Person Controller and a Third Person Controller. The Third Person Controller is somewhat outdated since the inclusion of the Mecanim system, but the First Person Controller is one of the most valuable assets immediately available. Let's get started.

1. Open the UnityTest project you started in the last chapter.

2. Open the Terrain Test scene, and position the Scene view to somewhere along the path you created in the second chapter.

3. Select the All Prefabs filter in the Project view.

4. Select the First Person Controller, and drag it into the scene view.

5. Drag it around, and then position it on the path.

The First Person Controller automatically is placed on the terrain. Its pivot point intersects the ground.

6. Move it up so the bottom of its capsule is just above the ground.

If it is too low, it will fall through the ground when you press Play. If it is a little high, it will fall down to ground level.

To see what the First Person Controller sees, you will have to switch to the Game view. Now would be a good time to change the UI layout so you can see both at once.

1. From the Layout drop-down menu in the top right corner, click the down arrow and select the 2 x 3 layout.

The Scene and Game views are both visible at the same time (Figure 3-1).

Figure 3-1. The Scene and Game views visible at the same time

The Project view will be easier to manage with the more compact One Column view, especially as you will have little need of the Project view for this chapter.

2. Right-click over the Project tab, and switch to the One Column Layout.

3. Select the First Person Controller in the Hierarchy view, and double-click or use Alt+F to frame the view to it.

4. Set the coordinate system to Local.

You can now see the view through the camera in the Game view The First Person Controller group contains a camera, so you will be able to see which way the First Person Controller is facing. With the coordinate system set to Local, you can also see that the First Person Controller faces in the positive Z direction, Unity's "forward" direction. With the second camera, you now also have two Audio Listeners according to the message on the status line at the bottom of the Game view and must get rid of one of them.

    5.   Delete the Main Camera from the Hierarchy view by selecting it and pressing the Delete key or selecting Delete from the right-click menu.

    6.   Orbit the Scene view so that you can see the First Person Controller from something near a top vantage point (Figure 3-2).

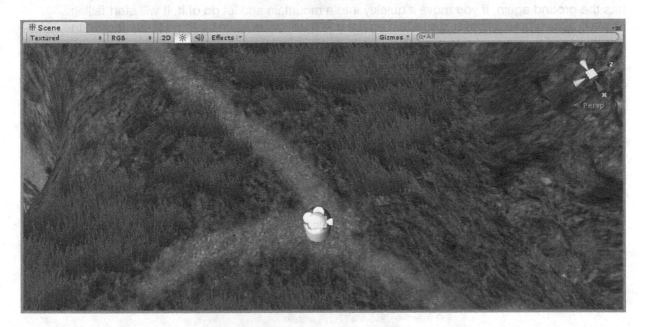

Figure 3-2. The First Person Controller seen from a near top view

    7.   Click Play, and drive the First Person Controller along your path using W for forward, S for backward, and A and D for strafe left and right, respectively.

To turn and look up and down, move the mouse around. Left/right turns the First Person Controller, and up/down movement rotates its camera up and down. Clicking the spacebar makes the First Person Controller jump. When you click Play, the focus is automatically set to the Game window.

If you click outside of the Game view, focus is moved back to the editor. This will allow you to tweak settings during game play and move objects around in the Scene view. Most of these adjustments will be lost when you stop Play mode, but it gives you a handy way to test things. Click back in the Game window.

    1.   Right-click in the Scene view to activate that view.

    2.   Select the First Person Controller from the Hierarchy view (to make sure you have selected the parent object).

When you make selections in the Scene view, Unity will first select the parent-most object; additional clicks in the same spot will select its children.

3.   Using the left mouse button, grab the transform gizmo in the yellow square that bridges the X and Z arrows, and drag the First Person Controller around the scene without releasing the button.

4.   Stop Play mode.

The First Person Controller attempts to stay grounded. If you move it over a pit, it will drop until it hits the ground again. If you move it quickly into a mountain and let go of it, it will start falling. Move it back where it is over the terrain again, and it will once again try to position itself at the terrain height.

Virtual Keys: The InputManager

Now is a good time for a first look at Unity's key mapping system. Key mapping allows the user to select their favorite keys for the various input needed throughout the game. Typically, it is for controlling a character, but it is by no means limited to that. By creating virtual keys, the scripts that make the action happen can remain generic as far as user input goes.

The First Person Controller has several alternate keys that can be used to control it. Let's take a look at the InputManager to see what they are.

1.   From the Edit menu, Project Settings, select Input.

2.   In the Inspector, click the Axes arrow to expand the list.

You will see 15 preset virtual keys or inputs (Figure 3-3).

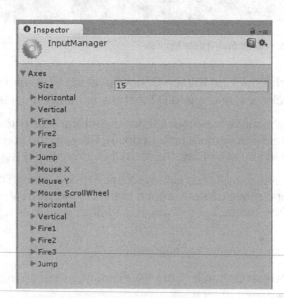

Figure 3-3. The 15 preset inputs in the InputManager

Unity uses "Horizontal" and "Vertical" as the two main directions for character control. They can be confusing unless you understand their origin. Picture a simple 2D game played in a top-down view. The character is moved forward in the up direction of your monitor and backward in the down direction, the vertical directions. Strafing, or sideways movement, is left or right, the horizontal directions. Now picture tipping the monitor down so that you are in a 3D world. "Vertical" movement is forward or backward. "Horizontal" movement is left or right.

   3.   Click to open the Vertical and Horizontal inputs at the top of the list (Figure 3-4).

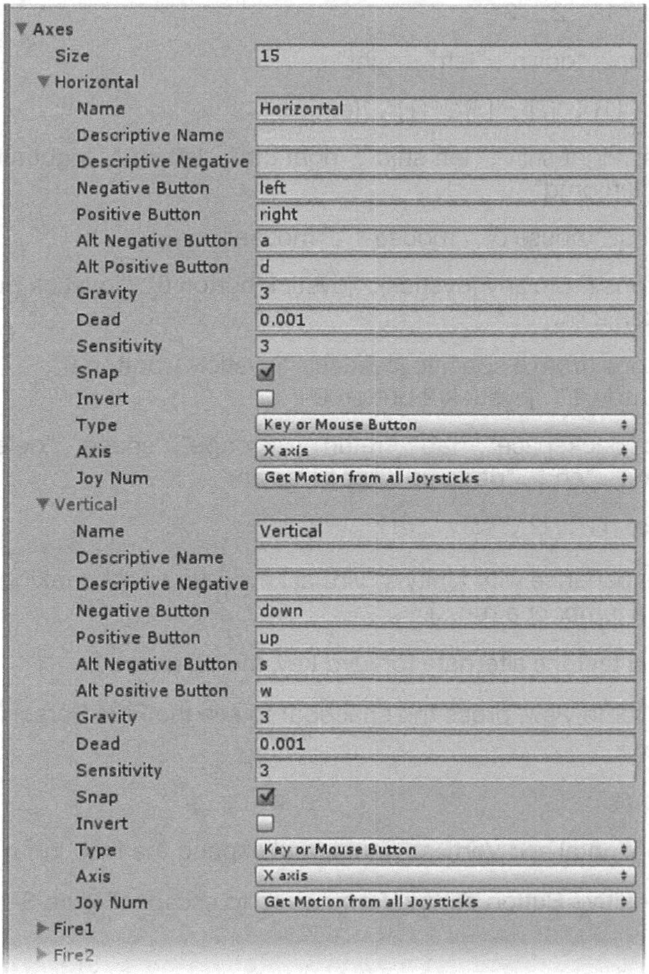

Figure 3-4. The expanded Horizontal and Vertical inputs

The Name field determines how the input is accessed through scripting. The Descriptive Name and Descriptive Negative fields will appear in the built game's configuration dialog at startup where the player can remap the keys. In case you are wondering what *Negative* refers to, take a look at the next four parameters. Instead of using separate inputs for, say, forward and reverse, Unity considers them the same input. Internally, a positive number is generated when the W key is pressed, and a negative number is generated when the S key is pressed. The second set of parameters begin with Alt, for *alternative*. The first set uses the left and right arrow keys, and the alternates use the W and S keys. Note that all key assignments are typed as lowercase.

Several key names use abbreviations. A search of the Unity Manual for "Input" will explain the Input in depth and also lists the key naming conventions.

The names of keys follow this convention:

- Normal keys: "a", "b", "c" …
- Number keys: "1", "2", "3", …
- Arrow keys: "up", "down", "left", "right"
- Keypad keys: "[1]", "[2]", "[3]", "[+]", "[equals]"
- Modifier keys: "right shift", "left shift", "right ctrl", "left ctrl", "right alt", "left alt", "right cmd", "left cmd"
- Mouse Buttons: "mouse 0", "mouse 1", "mouse 2", …
- Joystick Buttons (from any joystick): "joystick button 0", "joystick button 1", "joystick button 2", …
- Joystick Buttons (from a specific joystick): "joystick 1 button 0", "joystick 1 button 1", "joystick 2 button 0", …
- Special keys: "backspace", "tab", "return", "escape", "space", "delete", "enter", "insert", "home", "end", "page up", "page down"
- Function keys: "f1", "f2", "f3", …

To get some firsthand experience with Unity's "virtual keys," you will be taking the First Person Controller for a spin (or a jump, or a run…).

1. Click Play, and test the alternate forward key, the up arrow.
2. While in the Game view, press the spacebar to see the First Person Controller jump.
3. Stop Play mode.
4. Close the Horizontal and Vertical inputs, and expand the first Jump input.
5. Change its Positive Button setting from *space* to *escape* (Figure 3-5).

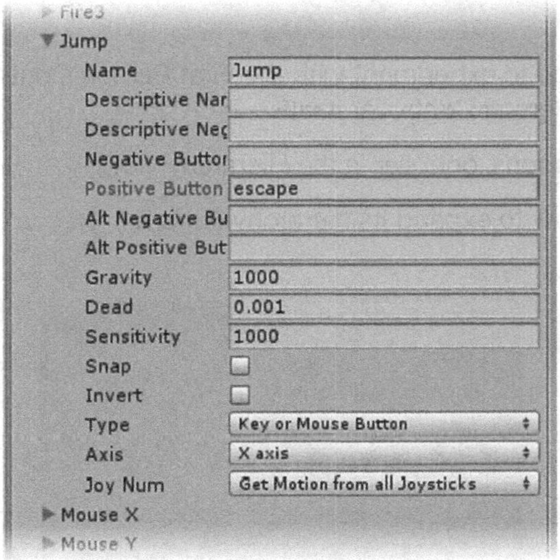

Figure 3-5. The Jump input's Positive Button mapped to the escape key

6. Click Play, and test the new jump mapping by pressing the escape key.

7. Stop Play mode, and change the Positive Button setting back to *space*.

While you were in the InputManager, you probably noticed a set of duplicate inputs for several of the keys. Two alternatives are built into the input template. If you require more alternatives for the same input, you can simply create another of the same name. The current preset duplicates add input for joysticks. To create your own input definition, you have to increase the Size value of the Axes list.

1. At the top of the InputManager in the Inspector, change Size to **16**.

A new input is added by copying the last one in the list.

Tip You can also duplicate specific array elements by right-clicking on the element parent and selecting Duplicate Array Element. This gives you a quick way to add multiple input options or to set up new inputs by starting with something close to your desired setup.

---

2. Expand it, and change its Name field to *Vertical*.

3. Set its Negative Button to *k* and its Positive Button to *j*.

4. Click Play, and test the new alternative "Vertical" input keys.

5. Test the original W and S keys and the up and down arrows to assure yourself they still work.

6. Stop Play mode.

7. In the InputManager, set the Axes array Size back to **15** to remove your extra Vertical input.

Components

Now that you've had a chance to experiment with the First Person Controller's basic functionality, it's time to inspect the First Person Controller itself.

1. Select the First Person Controller in the Hierarchy view.

2. Click its down arrow to expand its hierarchy (Figure 3-6).

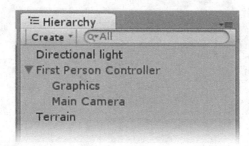

Figure 3-6. The expanded First Person Controller

You will find it has two children, Graphics and Main Camera.

3. Select Graphics.

It has only two components besides the requisite Transform component. The Mesh Filter holds an internal mesh that you do not have access to, though for all intents and purposes, it is a capsule. In the Mesh Renderer component, it is worth noting that Cast Shadows and Receive Shadows are both turned off. Shadow calculation is expensive, and this object is more of a visual placeholder, so you neither want to waste resources nor have it cast shadows into the scene.

4. Select Main Camera.

Besides the components you have already seen on the original scene camera, this has a Mouse Look script. If you are starting to catch on to the components idea, you may have wondered if one couldn't just add a Camera component to the First Person Controller directly. Let's try it and see what happens.

5. First, deactivate the Main Camera gameObject by unchecking the check box next to its name at the top of the Inspector.

With no camera in the scene, the Game view goes blank.

6. Select the First Person Controller.

7. From the Component menu, Rendering, add Camera.

The Game view is once again rendered.

8. Click Play, and drive around the scene.

The first problem is that the component functions from near the First Person Controller's bellybutton, the location of its transform pivot point (Figure 3-7). The other problem is that you've lost the ability to look up and down. If you inspect the First Person Controller's Mouse Look component, you will see that its Axes parameter is set to use Mouse X. This time, it is referring to the mouse movement. Traditionally (think graph paper), the X axis is on the horizontal and the Y axis is on the vertical. With the mouse, this means X or horizontal mouse movement. In the script, it controls rotation on the First Person Controller's Y axis, or look left/right. It turns out that the Mouse Look component *does* have the option to use both axes, but other components on the First Person Controller will keep it from tipping up or down. The bottom line here is that although you can combine specialty components, there are often good reasons to put them on separate gameObjects.

Figure 3-7. The camera component on the First Person Controller gameObject

9.   Right-click on the First Person Controller's Camera component, and select Remove Component (Figure 3-8).

Figure 3-8.   The component right-click menu, selecting Remove Component

10.   Select the Main Camera, and activate it by clicking the check box next to its
name at the top of the Inspector.

The Game view returns to its previous view. "Activate" is the term used to control a gameObjects's
state and "Enable" is the term used for components. Later, when you manipulate those parameters
from scripts, those terms will be used.

Let's take a look at the rest of the First Person Controller's components.

The Character Controller Component

The Character Controller is a specialty component that serves, more or less, to combine the
functionality of the collider and Rigidbody components. A rigidbody component is required for
using physics to drive interactions in the scene, but it is too expensive to use for the First Person
Controller, so Unity adds the most important functionality to it through the Character Controller. This,
not physics gravity, is what causes the First Person Controller to fall when you drag it or drive it off of
cliffs. It has a few parameters that can be adjusted to help or hinder your First Person Controller as it
moves around the scene.

1.   Select the First Person Controller.

2.   Click Play, and try to drive the First Person Controller into a deep pit. Then try
to get out or go up the side of a steep slope.

At some point, you can go no higher without resorting to jumping as you go up at an angle, and even that may not be enough.

3. In the Character Controller component, set the Slope Limit to **90** degrees.

4. Attempt the steep slope again.

This time you should be able to get out of the pit or up to the top of the most unlikely mountain peak (Figure 3-9).

Figure 3-9. A deep, steep-sided pit, no longer a trap for the First Person Controller

5. Set the Slope Limit back to **45** degrees.

6. Stop Play mode.

Step Offset determines how high an object is when the slope is steeper than the limit. This will allow the First Person Controller to go up steps without being blocked by the Slope Limit.

1. Focus in on the First Person Controller in the Scene view.

2. From the GameObject menu, Create Other, create a Cube.

3. In its Transform component, set its Scale parameters to **3** x **0.4** x **3** to create a nice platform.

4. Position it somewhere in front of the First Person Controller, slightly intersecting the ground on the approach side.

5. With Local coordinates set, rotate the First Person Controller on the Y axis so that it faces the cube.

6. Click Play, and drive the First Person Controller up onto the platform (Figure 3-10).

Figure 3-10.   The First Person Controller is able to drive up onto a low platform

7. Increase the cube's height to **0.6**, and lift it so it is no longer intersecting with the ground on the side that the First Person Controller will approach it.

8. Now try to drive the First Person Controller up onto it again.

This time the First Person Controller cannot drive up onto the platform. An inspection of its Step Offset parameter shows that it will not be able to "glide" up anything higher than 0.4 meters (Unity's default units) in front of it.

9. Select the First Person Controller, and change its Step Offset to **1.0**.

Once again, the First Person Controller can glide over the platform with ease.

10. Stop Play mode.

The cube returns to its original height, and the Step Offset is returned to its original amount.

The Slope Limit and Step Offset will go a long way toward establishing the difficulty and feel of the scene navigation in a first-person game, so set them up accordingly.

The Character Motor Component

The Character Motor is the script that controls the rest of the First Person Controller's functionality.

1. Select the First Person Controller again.

2. In the Character Motor script, open the Movement, Jumping, Moving Platform, and Sliding sections (Figure 3-11).

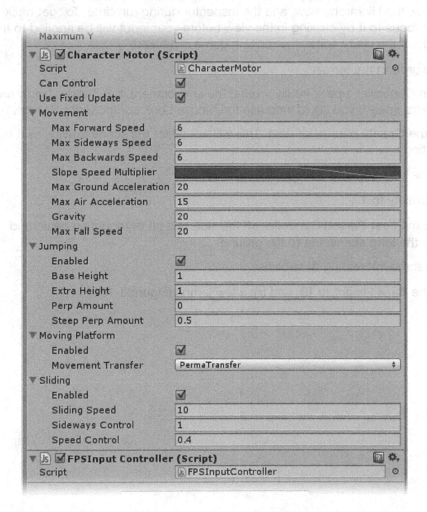

Figure 3-11. The Character Motor component, expanded

As you can see, besides the various parameters, Jumping, Moving Platform, and Sliding can be turned off individually. All of these parameters, by the way, could be exposed to the player with a GUI and some scripting. Let's test a few of them in Play mode so you won't have to remember their original values.

3. Click Play.

4. Set the Max Forward Speed to **15,** and click in the Game view to change the focus back to it.

When you first click on Play, the application focus is changed to the game window, so your input (mouse movement, keyboard entries, etc.) is applied to that view. As soon as you click *outside* of the Game view, your input no longer applies to the running game. This allows you to make adjustments in the Scene view, the Hierarchy view, and the Inspector during run-time. To "get back" to the game, you must return focus to it by clicking in the view before your input will be applied to the game. If you click outside of the Unity editor, the running game is paused.

5. Drive around the terrain.

The First Person Controller zips speedily around the environment, but it slides badly around turns. To adjust for the extra speed, you could increase the Mouse Look component's Sensitivity X if you wish.

Let's play with the Gravity parameter next. This will not affect the scene gravity, as it is controlled by the Physics settings.

6. Set the Max Forward Speed back to about **8**.

7. Set Gravity to **1**.

8. Drive the First Person Controller off the side of a pit or mountain peak, and enjoy the long scenic trip to the ground.

Jumping offers some interesting possibilities.

9. Set the Base Height to **10**, and try a few jumps (Figure 3-12).

Figure 3-12. View from the tree tops

For aggressive players, you could increase the Extra Height setting. This will add more height if the player holds down the spacebar. On the off chance your character will have a jet pack, you are out of luck with this script. It doesn't allow the player to jump again until after the First Person Controller has landed.

To test, you will import a little script to set the platform to move back and forth. This script moves the object you put it on in the z direction.

1. Right-click in the Project view, and from the right-click menu, choose Create, Folder, or click the Create down arrow at the top of the Project view and select Folder from there.

2. Name it **Test Scripts**.

3. Select it and from the right-click menu, and then select Import New Asset.

4. Locate the Hz_PositionCycler.cs script in the Chapter 3 Assets folder, and import it into your scene.

5. Drag the new script from the Test Scripts folder in the Project view to the Cube object in the Hierarchy view.

6. Click Play.

The platform moves slowly back and forth in the global z direction.

7. Select the Cube, and inspect the new component's parameters.

8. Try adjusting the Max Range to **8**.

9. Back in the Game view, drive the First Person Controller up onto the platform when it comes within range.

The First Person Controller goes for a ride on the platform.

10. Drive the First Person Controller off of the platform.

The First Person Controller can move freely around the platform because the Character Motor is adjusting its position relative to the platform. If you move the First Person Controller into the path of the platform, you will probably find that platform goes through it. If the platform is low enough, it may push the First Person Controller away.

11. Stop Play mode.

12. If the platform goes through the First Person Controller, move it lower into the ground; if it pushes the First Person Controller away, move it up higher.

13. Click Play and see if your previous results have changed.

The other possible outcome is that the platform bumps the First Person Controller and picks it up. Either way, the results are not dependable enough to use without being able to control the mounting circumstances. If you disable the Moving Platform in the Character Motor, you will see different results.

14. Select the First Person Controller.

15. Uncheck Enabled in the Moving Platform.

16. Drive the First Person Controller into the path of the platform.

The First Person Controller will be bumped up when the platform is low enough, but its position is no longer matched. There are no more free rides for the First Person Controller.

17. Select the First Person Controller.

The Sliding parameter may have suffered from version changes. Sliding, where the First Person Controller slides back down steep slopes, shows no change when enabled or disabled but is affected more by the Slope Limit. Unity has introduced a new real character controller from the new Unity Sample Assets (https://www.assetstore.unity3d.com/#/content/14474) which, unlike the old Character Controller, uses a Rigidbody to properly interact with the rest of the world. It can be downloaded from the Asset Store, but it has not yet been incorporated into the Standard Assets that ship with Unity. Feel free to give it a try.

Colliders

You've now had some firsthand experience with colliders. The platform, because it is a Cube, comes with a Collider component. Before adding the animation to the cube, the First Person Controller either was stopped by it or moved up on top of it. Once objects are animating, the rules change, but for static (or nonmoving) objects, a collider component will act as a wall, floor, or combination of both, depending on where the intersection takes place.

1. Stop Play mode.

2. Select the Cube object, and set its Y Scale to **5**.

3. Disable its Hz_Position Cycler component by unchecking the box next to the component's name.

4. Click Play, and try to drive into the side of the Cube.

5. The collider stops it.

6. Disable the Cube's Box Collider.

7. Try driving into the side of the Cube again.

With no collider, the First Person Controller goes right through the Cube. Next you will test the Is Trigger parameter.

1. Enable the Cube's Box Collider.

2. Turn on the collider component's Is Trigger parameter.

3. Drive into the side of the Cube again.

This time the Collider is on, but it no longer blocks the First Person Controller. It does, however, register the intersection, as you will find when you start scripting.

There's one other thing you can discover about colliders as long as you are in the terrain environment.

1. Drive the First Person Controller around the terrain, and drive at a few of the Palm trees.

2. Repeat the experiment with a BigTree.

The First Person Controller goes right through both types of trees. With a small-trunked tree, you might decide that stopping the First Person Controller would interfere with the game flow. With something as substantial as the BigTree, being able to drive through is not something that can be ignored.

To remedy the problem, you will start by examining the original prefab.

3. With the Project view currently in Single Column Layout, type **BigTree** in the search field at the top of the panel.

4. To quickly identify the correct asset, you can select the Prefab filter from "Search by Type," the first icon to the right of the search field.

You can also slide the thumbnail slider at the bottom of the view to the far right to see the asset icons. At the far left, you can recognize prefabs by their blue cube icons.

5. Once the BigTree prefab is selected, take a look at its components in the Inspector.

6. Collapse the Tree component so you can see the components more easily (Figure 3-13).

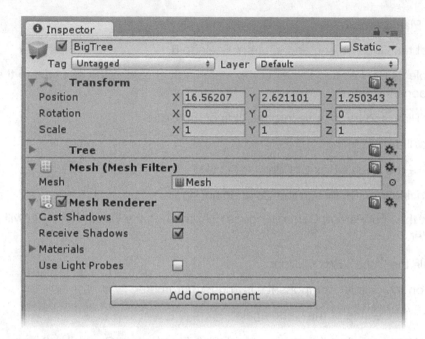

Figure 3-13. The BigTree's components in the Inspector

As you can see, there is no collider component of any type. When Colliders are added to gameObjects, they are scaled according to the object's bounding box. For a tree, you will want to adjust the collider's size to fit the trunk. The easiest way to do the adjustment is to do it in the Scene view. Let's begin by adding a collider component. Besides the Component menu, you can add components using the Add Component button at the bottom of the current components. Unlike you did in its menu counterpart, you will have to click to open the submenus.

7.   Drag the BigTree prefab into the scene.

8.   Click the Add Component button just below the Mesh Renderer component.

9.   Click to open the Physics submenu, and select Capsule collider.

The Capsule collider is scaled to fit around the entire tree (Figure 3-14).

Figure 3-14. The capsule collider added to the BigTree prefab

10. Set the Capsule Collider's Radius value to **0.7**.

11. Adjust the Height and Center values until the collider fits the tree trunk (Figure 3-15).

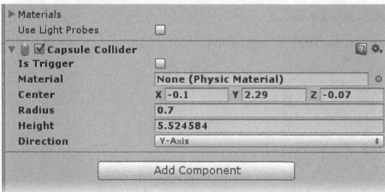

Figure 3-15. The capsule fit to the tree trunk (top), and the collider's values (bottom)

12.   Click Play, and drive the First Person Controller into the tree.

13.   Stop Play mode.

Now that you have made sure the tree will stop the First Person Controller, you have to update the prefab to include the new component before refreshing the terrain's trees.

1.   With the BigTree selected, at the top of the Inspector, click the Apply button at the right of the Prefab line (Figure 3-16).

Figure 3-16. Updating the Prefab setting

Once you have updated the prefab, it is no longer required in the scene.

2. Delete the BigTree prefab from the scene.

3. Select the Terrain object in the Hierarchy view.

4. In the Paint Trees section, click the Refresh button to the right of the Edit Trees button.

5. Click Play, and test the rest of the BigTrees by trying to drive through them.

6. Stop Play mode.

Physics

As computers have gotten faster, it has become feasible to use physics to control a lot of game action. Accurate algorithms are still too slow for real-time, however, so game physics are still only rough approximations. Because most game physics are used for mayhem and destruction, this is perfectly acceptable.

The big gain by applying physics to animation projectiles, collisions, and other actions has been to significantly reduce the need for traditional key-frame animation. It also has a side effect of automatically adding a good measure of randomness to actions. If you do need a specific result, you will be better off using a pre-made animation, though even that could be inserted into a string of physics-driven actions to preserve the illusion of randomness.

Game physics are not a silver bullet (pun intended). Physics-driven objects will not yet perform true to life. As far as frame rate goes, it continues to be too costly to do so. The most typical example of this is shooting a projectile at a wall. If the frame rate is too slow, the projectile could be in front of the wall at one frame when it is checked and beyond the wall in the next frame. Since an intersection was never detected, no reaction ever occurs. Physics intersections may be checked more often than every frame, but the concept remains the same.

Rigidbody

The two most important ingredients for using in-game physics are the collider and Rigidbody components. The collider defines the physical boundaries of the object, and the Rigidbody component handles the physics that do the work. Scenes already have default "gravity," but you can also add forces and torque to physically move or rotate objects. To make things more interesting, you can even add Physic Materials to further define the way an object reacts to the environment. Unity also provides a nice assortment of "joints" to help you combine multiple objects involved in physics-based encounters.

Let's start the investigation with a simple Cube. You will be working and observing in the Scene view, so feel free to deactivate the First Person Controller in the Hierarchy view for now and increase the Scene view size in the editor (Figure 3-17).

Figure 3-17. Rearranging the UI for the Physics tests

1.   Select the original Cube in the Hierarchy view, and rename it **Cube Platform**.

2.   Create a new Cube, and position it a couple of meters off of the ground (Figure 3-18).

Figure 3-18. The new Cube in mid-air

3. Click Play.

The Cube does nothing.

4. Stop Play Mode.

5. From the Component menu, Physics, add a Rigidbody component
    (Figure 3-19).

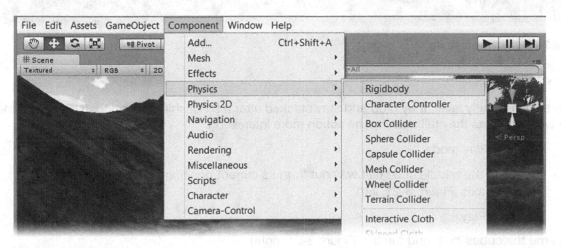

Figure 3-19. Adding a Rigidbody component

6. Click Play.

This time the Cube drops to the ground. If the ground is not level, it may even move a bit after it lands.

7. Drag the cube around, dropping it occasionally, to see how it reacts with the terrain.

8. Stop Play mode.

9. Use Ctrl+D to duplicate the first cube a couple of times, and then create a three-cube stack, leaving a little space between each (Figure 3-20).

Figure 3-20. The three-cube stack

10. Click Play.

If the terrain is fairly level, they drop and stay stacked after a bit of shifting around. If you offset them, they will tumble as they fall, making the action more interesting.

1. Stop Play mode.

2. Move the middle cube half way out from its current position, and rotate it on the Y axis (Figure 3-21, left).

3. Click Play.

This time the cubes drop and tumble (Figure 3-21, right).

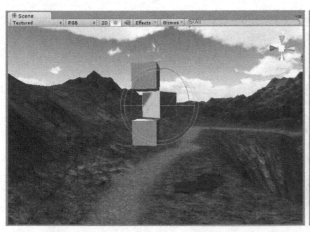

Figure 3-21. The offset cube stack (left), and the results of the adjustment in Play mode (right)

The results are more interesting, but there's something missing. They react as if they were made of concrete.

Physic Materials

The Rigidbody component controls a good part of the object's physical interaction with the scene, but not all. To have the objects interact as if they were made of different materials, you will have to assign a Physic Material. This property is assigned through the collider components.

1. Stop Play mode.

2. Right-click in the Project view, and from the Create submenu, select Physic Material.

A new Physic Material is created (Figure 3-22). It has a number of parameters that are not necessarily meaningful unless you've had a Physics class. You could, of course, do a lot of testing, but there's another option. There is a Unity package with several preset materials that you can use as is or tweak to refine.

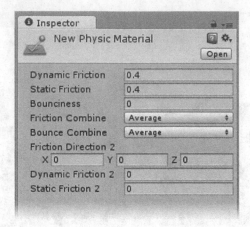

Figure 3-22. The new Physic material

3.   Once again, open the right-click menu in the Project view, or open the Assets menu and select Import Package.

4.   Choose Physic Materials.

5.   In the Import dialog, note the folder location, note the Physic Materials folder in the Standard Assets folder, and click Import.

6.   Open the folder, and click on each Physic material to see its settings in the Inspector.

Fortunately, the materials have been given nice descriptive names for those of us to whom physics remain a mystery.

7.   Drag and drop a different material directly on each cube in the Hierarchy view. Put Bouncy on the top cube, Wood on the middle cube, and Ice on the bottom cube.

8.   Select each object, and examine its collider's Material field.

The materials are added to the proper parameter automatically.

9.   Click Play.

This time the cubes react according to their individual physic materials, Bouncy bounces quite nicely. Ice, having very little Static Friction, slides off as it lands, and Wood bounces lightly before settling.

This is a good time to experiment with the Rigidbody a bit more.

1.   Stop Play mode.

2.   Select the cube with Bouncy.

3.   Set its Mass parameter to **0.1**.

4.   Click Play.

With less mass (weight/volume), you get a lot more bounce with the reaction.

   5.   Stop Play mode.

   6.   For the middle cube, turn off Use Gravity.

   7.   Click Play.

Having been clipped by the top cube, the Bouncy cube tumbles slowly downward, floating upward when it collides with the bottom cube.

The Is Kinematic Parameter

There are a few different ways to freeze an object with a Rigidbody component so it won't be affected by physics in the scene or will have limited freedom to react. The first method is using the Is Kinematic flag. This is recommended when you have objects that are not being animated by physics. In your test scene, the moving platform would qualify because a script is setting its location dynamically during runtime. Objects with key-frame animation are another use case. If the animated object has a collider and can interact with other dynamic objects in the scene, collision-detection calculations are far more efficient with a Rigidbody component set to Is Kinematic.

To develop good working habits, you can go ahead and add a Rigidbody component to the Cube Platform.

   1.   Select the Cube Platform, set its Y Scale back to **0.25,** and adjust its Y
        location so the First Person Controller will be able to get onto it again.

   2.   Enable its Hz_PositionCycler script component and its Box Collider.

   3.   Add a Rigidbody component, and turn its Is Kinematic property on.

You could activate the First Person Controller and test the platform after enabling the Moving Platform property in its Character Motor component, but you will see no difference in functionality. Instead, let's look at another means of restricting physics reactions.

   1.   Select the middle cube, and turn its Use Gravity parameter back on.

   2.   Select the bottom cube.

   3.   Check Is Kinematic, and click Play.

The bottom cube remains in place as the other two cubes interact with it. Because it is not doing anything, it would probably be better to remove the Rigidbody entirely. In this case, however, there are more experiments to run.

   4.   Stop Play mode.

   5.   Uncheck its Is Kinematic property.

   6.   Under Constraints, check the X,Y, and Z Freeze Position parameters.

   7.   Click Play.

This time the cube retains its position but spins wildly when the other cubes collide with it. You will see the Rigidbody constraints used in 3D-platform, jumper-type games where the objects may only move in the Y or Z directions and rotate on the X axis. This serves to keep them on the ramps and platforms without using invisible collider walls.

Forces

A less passive means of affecting objects with Rigidbody components is by using a physics Force. Through scripting, you will be able to add a one-time force for objects such as projectiles. The component force, Constant Force, is constant or, more accurately, continuous.

1. Select the middle cube.

2. From the Component menu, Physics, select Constant Force.

3. Give it a Z force of **10** (or **-10** if you wish) to send it off over the hills.

4. Zoom out a bit in the Scene view.

5. Click Play.

The cube goes rolling off over the terrain until it falls in a hole or goes off the edge of the terrain. Adding a local or Relative force to the bouncy cube will send it off.

1. Stop Play mode.

2. Add a Constant Force component to the top cube.

3. Set its Relative Force, Y to **-2**.

4. Click Play.

The initial downward force causes the cube to bounce more violently, causing it to spin. The force, being local, causes the cube to go off in unexpected directions.

While Force is a linear motion, Torque causes rotation.

1. Stop Play mode, and select the bottom cube.

2. In the Rigidbody Constraints, activate its X and Z Freeze Rotation parameters.

3. Add a Constant Force component to it.

4. Set its Torque, Y to **1**.

5. Click Play.

This time the cube is rotating before the other two interact with it.

6. Stop Play mode.

7. At the top of the Inspector, deactivate the top and middle cubes.

8. Click Play.

The remaining cube happily ramps up and then spins merrily around on its own.

9. Stop Play mode.

Joints

As mentioned earlier, Unity has a several Joints to allow you to combine physics objects (gameObjects with Rigidbody components). You will be doing a few tests with the Hinge Joint, the most familiar of the joint types.

1. Select the active cube, and focus the viewport to it.

2. Set its Y Torque to **30**.

3. Create a new Cube, and name it **Lid**.

4. Scale its X to 0.01, and move the Lid to the side of the Cube.

5. From the Component menu, Physics, select Hinge Joint (Figure 3-23).

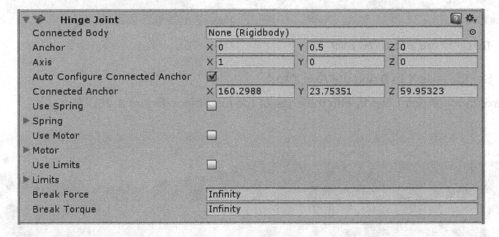

Figure 3-23. The Hinge Joint component

When the Hinge Joint is added to an object that does not already have one, a Rigidbody component will be added automatically.

As a default, the Hinge Joint's axis of rotation is set to X. You can see the small axis at the top of the Lid, pointing across (or away from, depending on the side you chose) the top face of the cube (Figure 3-24).

Figure 3-24. The Lid's X axis at its anchor point

6.   Set the Axis X to **0** and the Axis Z to **1**.

Now the axis/anchor point aligns with the edge of the Lid object (Figure 3-25).

Figure 3-25. The Lid's Z axis as the hinge

7. Click Play.

The Lid is bumped by the spinning Cube (Figure 3-26).

Figure 3-26. The Lid bumped as the Cube spins

The most logical thing to try next is to link the lid to the Cube.

8. Stop Play mode.

9. At the top of the Hinge Joint component, drag the Cube into the Connected Body field.

10. Click Play.

This time the Lid flaps open from the Cube as it spins along with it (Figure 3-27).

Figure 3-27. The Lid hinging correctly to the Cube as it spins

The flap is connected to the box at the same place as its anchor point, but that can be adjusted, giving you plenty of options for nonstandard objects. To change the anchor point, you would first have to uncheck Auto Configure Connected Anchor.

The Hinge Joint offers more options with its Spring and Motor parameters. With the right settings, the object will swing back and forth and attempt to get back to its original orientation when hit by an outside object. The flap on a Wheel of Fortune set up would make use of the spring settings as it is hit by the pegs.

The Motor lets you spin the object about its anchor.

1. Duplicate the Lid object, and rename it **Flap**.

2. Deactivate the Cube and the Lid.

3. Select the Flap, and in its Hinge Joint, click the Browse button to open the browser.

4. Select None to clear the Cube as the Connected Body (Figure 3-28).

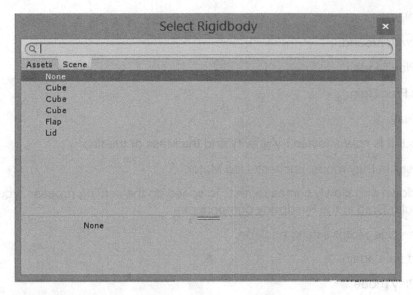

Figure 3-28. Clearing a parameter's field in the browser

5. Set the Flap's Mass to **1** in its Rigidbody component.

6. In the Hinge Joint, turn on Use Motor and open the Motor drop-down menu.

7. Set the Target Velocity to **100**, set the Force to **1**, and turn on Free Spin (Figure 3-29).

Freeze Rotation	☐X ☐Y ☐Z		
▼ ☙ **Hinge Joint**			🔲 ⚙.
Connected Body	None (Rigidbody)		⊙
Anchor	X 0	Y 0.5	Z 0
Axis	X 0	Y 0	Z 1
Auto Configure Connected Anchor	✓		
Connected Anchor	X 160.2988	Y 23.75351	Z 59.95323
Use Spring	☐		
▶ Spring			
Use Motor	✓		
▼ Motor			
Target Velocity	100		
Force	1		
Free Spin	☐		
Use Limits	☐		
▶ Limits			
Break Force	Infinity		
Break Torque	Infinity		
⬤ Default-Diffuse			🔲 ⚙.

Figure 3-29. The Flap's Hinge settings

8.   Click Play.

The flap spins slowly around.

9.   Stop Play Mode.

10.   Check Free Spin.

11.   Click Play.

The Flap spins, but it is now affected by gravity and the Mass of the flap.

12.   While still in Play mode, uncheck Use Motor.

The flap swings down and slowly comes to rest. To speed up the settling process, you could increase the Angular Drag in the Rigidbody component.

13.   Turn the Use Motor setting back on.

The Flap starts to spin again.

14.   Stop Play mode.

15.   Turn off Use Motor.

Wind

You are probably wondering how wind interacts with the physics objects. Let's try it and see what happens.

1.   Focus in on Flap in the viewport.

2.   From the GameObject menu, Create Other, select Wind Zone.

3.   From the GameObject menu, use "Move to View" to bring the Wind Zone into view.

4.   Rotate the Wind Zone so that it points at the Flap (Figure 3-30).

Figure 3-30. The Wind Zone pointing at the Flap

    5.   Click Play.

Nothing happens. The biggest hint that this is the expected behavior is that the Wind Zone is *not* found under the Physics submenu. So the takeaway here is that to get physics objects to "react" from "scene" wind, you will have to add a Constant Force component.

    6.   Stop Play mode.

    7.   Deactivate the WindZone.

Cloth

The next logical feature to take a look at is cloth. As you might guess, cloth can be costly, so use it sparingly. As a default, it uses a plane with 400 faces, but you can also load your own mesh into the Cloth component.

    1.   Focus in on the Flap.

    2.   From the GameObject menu, Create Other, select Cloth.

    3.   Rename it **Cloth**.

    4.   Rotate the Cloth 90 degrees so you can see it in the Scene view.

Default Cloth objects have no thickness, so they are only rendered on one side unless you use a two-sided shader in their material.

5. Scale the Cloth to X, **0.2**, Y, **1**, and Z, **0.12**.

6. Position it under the Flap (Figure 3-31).

Figure 3-31. The Cloth and Flap

7. Click Play.

The Cloth object crumples to the ground, but its transform does not move (Figure 3-32).

Figure 3-32. The cloth crumpled on the ground; note the location of its transform

To attach an Interactive Cloth object to another gameObject or merely prevent it from falling, you must use Attached Colliders as the connectors. The Flap object has a collider, so you can begin by using it.

1. Select the Cloth Object.

2. At the bottom of the Cloth component, click to open the Attached Colliders array and set the Size to **1**.

3. Open the new Element 0 (Figure 3-33).

Collision Response	0
Attachment Tear Facto	0.5
Attachment Response	0.2
Tear Factor	0
▼ Attached Colliders	
Size	1
▼ Element 0	
Collider	None (Collider) ⊙
Two Way Interac	☐
Tearable	☐
▼ ☑ Cloth Renderer	⚙

Figure 3-33. The Cloth component's Attached Colliders parameters

4. Drag the Flap object into the Element 0 Collider field from the Hierarchy view.

5. Click Play.

If the cloth is close enough to the Flap, it hangs quite nicely.

6. Stop Play mode.

7. Try moving the cloth farther below the Flap to see how close it must be to be held during run time.

8. Stop Play mode.

For the Attached colliders to work, the cloth's vertices must be within range of the colliders.

1. Create a new Cube, and name it **Hanger**.

2. Scale it down, and position it at one end of the flap.

3. Turn off its Mesh Renderer, and drag and drop it onto the Flap in the Hierarchy view.

4. Duplicate it, and rename it **Hanger2**.

5. Drag the new Hanger to the other side (Figure 3-34).

Figure 3-34. The new Hanger objects in position

6. Select the Cloth, and change the Attached Collider array Size to **2**.

7. Drag the two Hangers into the two elements.

8. Select the Cloth, and set the Interactive Cloth component's Stretching
    Stiffness parameter to **0.5**.

9. Click Play.

The cloth, attached only on each end, sags in the middle (Figure 3-35). The faces intersected by the
two attached colliders retain their original positions.

Figure 3-35. The cloth held by the two Hanger objects in Play mode

The cloth, like the Rigidbody objects, will not respond to Unity's Wind Zone. Like the Rigidbody
component, Interactive cloth has its own version in the External Acceleration and Random
Acceleration parameters. Both are world or global directions.

10. While in Play mode, try adjusting the two acceleration parameters.
     (Figure 3-36).

Figure 3-36. The cloth with a Random X Acceleration of 18

And finally, let's see what happens when the flap is set to spinning.

1. Stop Play mode, and make sure the Accelerations have returned to 0.

2. Select the Flap, and change its Hinge Joint's Axis Y to **1** and X and Z to **0**.

3. Turn on Use Motor in the Hinge Joint component.

4. Click Play, and watch as the cloth reacts to the torque (Figure 3-37).

Figure 3-37. The cloth reacting as the Flap spins

Because the two Attached Colliders have the Flap as their parent, the Cloth follows right along. The most notable issue you will notice is that the cloth is rendered only on one side. To use it out in the open, you would have to use a material with a two-sided shader. You could also use another cloth for the back side, but that would use twice as many resources. If you were using a custom mesh for the cloth, you could use the Self Collision check, but that also is expensive.

5.   Stop Play mode.

Cloth has many parameters that will let you fine-tune it to resemble the behavior of velvet to canvas to silk. Bending Stiffness, Thickness, and Friction are a few of the parameters that are a good starting point for customization.

Interacting with the First Person Controller

So far, your tests have been centered around objects with physics-based components. After seeing the lack of reaction with the Wind Zone, you are probably wondering how the First Person Controller will interact with the various objects. If you remember, the First Person Controller does not have a true Rigidbody component, but it does have a collider.

1.   Click Play.

2.   Drive the First Person Controller over to the Flap (Figure 3-38).

Figure 3-38. The cloth reacting as the First Person Controller moves into it

The Cloth clearly reacts to the First Person Controller's Capsule collider. You will find, however, that you may have to increase the Thickness and reduce the Friction parametersto prevent it from passing though the First Person Controller's collider.

With the Rigidbodies, you will want to try two experiments. The first is to see if moving Rigidbodies can affect the First Person Controller, and the second is to see if the First Person Controller can affect Rigidbodies.

1. Stop Play mode.

2. Deactivate the Cloth and Flap objects.

3. Duplicate the middle cube.

4. Activate the new cube, and move it so that its Constant Force will push it into the First Person Controller.

5. Click Play, and watch the result.

The cube either stops at the First Person Controller or twists and continues along its way.

6. Increase the cube's Force value to **1000** (or **-1000** if you are using a negative number).

7. In the Rigidbody component, increase the Cube's Mass to **50**.

8. Click Play.

The result is the same: the cube is unable to move the First Person Controller.

Next you will test the opposite scenario by driving the First Person Controller at the box.

1. Stop Play mode.

2. Set the Cube's Mass back to **1** and its Force back to **10** (or **-10**).

3. Click Play, and drive the First Person Controller at the moving cube.

The First Person Controller is able to push the Cube away.

4. Stop Play mode.

5. Set the Cube's Force to **0**.

6. Click Play, and drive the First Person Controller into the Cube.

When the cube is not being moved by physics, the First Person Controller is not able to influence its movement. To directly affect an object with a Rigidbody component, you would have to apply a physics force through scripting using the First Person Controller's direction to calculate the direction of a one-off force.

7. Stop Play mode.

By now, you probably realize why game physics are not comparable to real-world physics. Not only are the algorithms stripped down for speed, but the functionality itself is severely limited to control CPU usage. The important thing to remember when designing your game's functionality is not to take any physics-based functionality for granted. Some desired behavior can be enabled though the Rigidbody and other physics-related component's parameters, but other behaviors, if even feasible, may require specialized scripting.

First Build

With the addition of the First Person Controller, you were able to move around your scene and interact with a few objects. The accomplishment may be a long way from a creating a AAA title, but it is enough to let you try your first "build." Unity makes it very easy to "build," or output, your application as an executable. From Mac or Windows, you can make a game that can run either as a desktop application or in a web browser. Outputting to mobile requires extra steps, a mobile device or emulator and, in some cases, a specific operating system. It also has several more stringent guidelines and requirements for content and scripting. You will be creating a desktop application.

Creating a build takes just a few mouse clicks if you use the defaults. Before you proceed with your first build, there are a few settings worth looking at.

1. From the Edit menu, Project Settings, select Player.

2. In the Inspector, examine the top section.

You can put your name in the company Name field. The Product Name is taken from the Project name, but can be changed.

3. Change the Product Name to **MyFirstUnityApp**.

4. For the Default Icon, click the Select button and choose the Corn Tassel (Figure 3-39).

Figure 3-39. The Player Settings, top section

With Default Cursor, you have the option of using a custom hardware cursor. This means you can use an image of your choice that is directly handled by the machine's operating system. The cursor will always be drawn on top, but it has a limit of 128 x 128 pixels in size. To use a particular image, it must be marked as Cursor type in its import settings. If the Operating system can't support custom cursors, it will drop back to its own default.

1. Select the Corn Tassel image in the Project view.

2. Duplicate it, and name it **CornTasselCursor**.

3. In the Inspector, change its Texture Type to Cursor and click Apply (Figure 3-40).

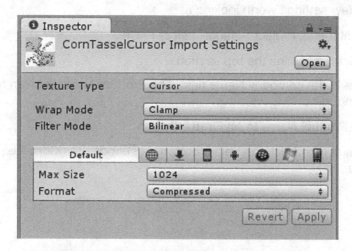

Figure 3-40. The CornTasselCursor images set to Cursor Texture Type

4. Return to the Player from Project Settings.

5. Drag the CornTasselCursor image onto the Default Cursor thumbnail.

6. Move the cursor over to the Game view to see your new cursor (Figure 3-41).

Figure 3-41. The new hardware cursor in the game view

The next section of the Player Settings allows you to customize settings according to target platform (Figure 3-42).

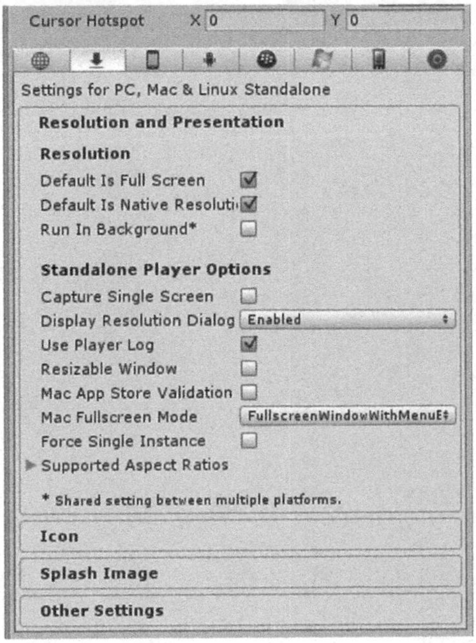

Figure 3-42. Platform settings

1. Take some time to check out each platform's settings, and then return to "Settings for PC, Mac & Linux Standalone."

2. Uncheck Default Is Full Screen.

3. Check Resizable Window.

Display Resolution Dialog, also known as the Config Dialog, is the screen that comes up on startup, allowing the user to change resolution, quality settings, and map keys. As you can see by its choices, you can block user access to this dialog.

In the Icon section, you will find that the CornTasselCursor icon has been automatically loaded for you.

The Splash Image section is available for Pro users only. There, they can set a custom image for the Config Dialog banner.

Other Settings is where you set the Render Path, among other things. If you have Pro, you have to change to Deferred Lighting to make use of dynamic shadows *and* baked lighting in your scene.

Having tweaked a few of the Player settings, you are ready to try your first build. The first thing you must do is save your work.

1. Save the scene, and save the project.

2. From the File menu, select Build Settings.

3. Click Add Current to add the currently active scene into the build (Figure 3-43).

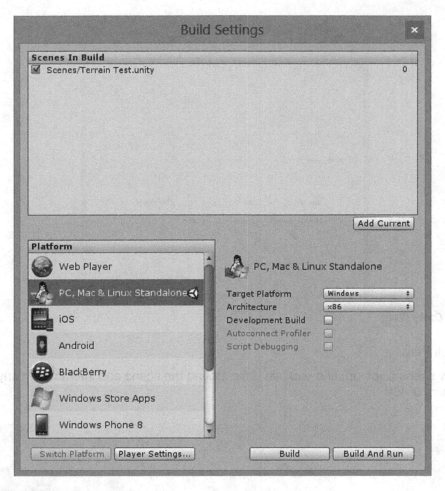

Figure 3-43. Adding the current scene to Build Settings

4. Make sure the Target Platform is correct. (It should automatically be set to your machine.)

5. Click Build And Run.

6. Save the output somewhere other than in your project folder, and name it **TestBuild**.

The project is built, and the Config Dialog pops up when it is ready to play.

7. Make sure Windowed is checked, and change any other settings as you care to (Figure 3-44).

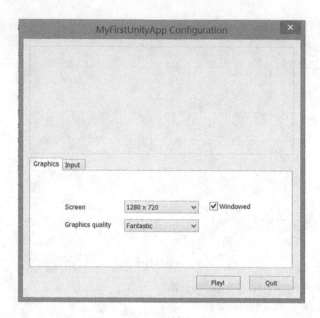

Figure 3-44. The Config Dialog

8. Click Play.

Your first Unity scene pops up, and you can drive around the scene and interact with anything you left active (Figure 3-45).

Figure 3-45. The new game running on the desktop

9. Take a minute to inspect the results.

The application name is TestBuild, but the title (as seen in the windowed title bar) is MyFirstUnityApp, which you set in the Player Settings.

10. Look in Windows Explorer (if you are on a PC) for the TestBuild application.

You will find TestBuild.exe and a folder called TestBuild_Data. When you distribute your games for the PC desktop deployment, the .exe and the data folder must be in the same location.

The content for this book was created using Windows. Other than a few keyboard differences, Unity should look and act the same on whatever platform you are authoring on. It is easy to build for other platforms.

1. Close the running game, and return to the Unity editor.

2. In the Build Settings dialog, change the Target Platform to Mac OS X (or Windows if you are already on a Mac).

3. After the changeover is complete, click Build.

4. Save the new build in the same place as the first, with the same name.

The extension type will be different (.app), so there will be no conflicts. The Mac application is contained in a single folder named TestBuild.app.

5. If you have access to the other platform, feel free to test the new version.

6. Back in the Unity editor, close the Build Settings dialog.

Summary

In this chapter, you added a First Person Controller into your terrain scene and were able to travel around in it. You discovered that several script components that made up the First Person Controller contained a lot of settings you could tweak to change the First Person Controller's behavior. You found that various functionality, such as jumping and the ability to ride on moving platforms, was optional. Moving platforms offered some interesting problems with regard to the height of the platform and how the platform could interact with the First Person Controller.

During your experiments with the First Person Controller, you had an introduction to Unity's InputManager. You were able to not only reassign input keys, but to create your own virtual keys to expand an application's versatility. At the very end of the chapter, you got to see where the player was allowed to change the key "mapping" before playing the game.

Having a means of traversing the scene, you got some firsthand experience with colliders. At some point, you realized you were able to go through the terrain trees, and then you learned how to apply colliders to assets used as terrain trees.

Moving on to physics, you experimented with the Rigidbody component and saw how it works with the colliders to provide lots of non-key-framed animation in your scene. You found that any of its position or rotation axes could be "frozen" to restrict the physics-based reactions. The Physic Material in the collider component gave you a means of tailoring the object's reactions according to a virtual material assignment. You found that you could add a Constant Force component to move or rotate (torque) your physics object. With the Hinge Joint, you discovered a means of combining physics objects. That component, you discovered, has built-in force and torque settings. One important thing you learned was that adding a Rigidbody component to objects that were animated by means other than physics was more efficient. To do so, you had to check Is Kinematic.

After a quick look at cloth, you tested your First Person Controller against the objects with Rigidbody components and the cloth object to see what reactions occurred. In the end, you found that game physics were not always predictable due to the need to keep the frame rate at acceptable levels.

Finally, you made your first build. Before doing so, you tweaked a few of the Player settings just to get a feel for what could be manipulated.

Chapter 4

Importing Static Assets

While Unity does have a handful of primitive objects, you will be importing most of the 3D art assets for your games. There are many pre-made assets available for free or for purchase at Unity's Asset Store. If you are mainly a programmer, or are just looking to prototype a game quickly to test functionality before creating assets for it, the Asset Store is invaluable. If you are a 3D artist and are looking forward to creating your own assets, or are in charge of procuring the assets from various and sundry sources, you will inevitably need to learn how to prepare them for use once imported into Unity. In this chapter, you will be exploring the importing, preparation, and management of static assets. Animated assets have different needs and will be covered in Chapter 6.

Supported Formats

Unity supports a large number of formats for imported meshes and textures. It can also read files directly from many popular DCC (digital content creation) applications, such as Max, Maya, Blender, Cinema4D, Modo, Lightwave, and Cheetah3D.

3D Assets

There are two main types of 3D models, or *mesh*, formats that Unity will read: standard export file types and proprietary application file types. The former includes .FBX, .3DS, .dxf, .obj, and .dae (Collada). The latter type can be read directly from many of the popular DCC applications, such as .max, .ma, .mb, etc. Besides containing the 3D mesh itself, these file types can store material, mapping, animation, and even the textures associated with the object's materials.

The important thing to know is that, internally, Unity converts everything to FBX on import. There are advantages and disadvantages to both import types. The export types are the most generic, as they can be used immediately by anyone. The downside is that if you update an asset in the original application, it must be exported into Unity again to be updated. If you are not using SVN or some other versioning software, this helps you by letting you keep versions of the asset to use if needed in the future. Keeping the proprietary files directly in your Unity project allows for quick

updating, but it has a few drawbacks. Most of the proprietary formats require the software to be installed and licensed in order for Unity to be able to use the content. It also is destructive. Unless you are using versioning software (where version changes are backed up and saved), if you want to revert to an earlier version of the asset, you will have no means of doing so unless you are backing up your
files externally.

The safest and most versatile file type for 3D assets is .FBX. It carries very little unneeded overhead and can be read and used by anyone.

Textures

Unity supports all image formats. Internally, most images are converted to .dds for desktop applications. For mobile, they are internally converted to the appropriate format for the selected platform. The bottom line is that you do not have to worry about the texture's original format. This allows you to work in Photoshop or other image-authoring applications, leaving layers intact. Because Photoshop layers are a means of preserving the history of an image's creation, you have the freedom of editing the image while it resides in the Unity project.

In Unity, as with any real-time engine, the optimal image size should be a power of 2. Use 32 x 32, 64 x 64, 128 x 128, 256 x 256, etc. to conserve memory. (See Figure 4-1.) Images that are over the base 2 size will take up the same amount of memory that an image of the next power of two would. The Texture Importer allows you to cap the image size, so you needn't worry about images that are too large unless you prefer to do your own size reduction manually.

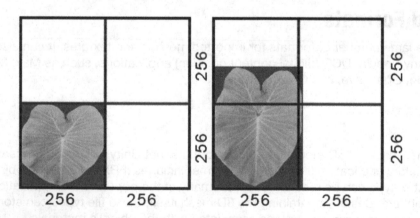

Figure 4-1. Texture memory usage

In Figure 4-1, the image on the left uses a 256 x 256 block of memory. The image on the right, retaining its original proportions and size, uses a full 512 x 512 block of memory (four 256 x 256 blocks).

Once an asset is imported, you may need to change the import settings, depending on the function of the imported texture. In Chapter 3, you had to change the import settings on a texture that was going to be used as a hardware cursor. Textures that are going to be used in 2D space only do not have to be MIP mapped. MIP mapping is the process by which an image is reduced in size, base-2 of course, and is smaller and blurrier for several iterations. The smaller, blurrier versions are used farther back in the scene to prevent "artifacting," which is the visual effect of the engine trying to decide which color from the image should be used when the object in the scene is no more than a few pixels big (Figure 4-2). A perfect example is a black-and-white checker pattern. At some point, the object with the texture is so far away that only a few pixels must represent the check. If the choices are only black and white, the color could vary from frame to frame, causing a sparkling effect. Using a blurred version of the original texture, the pixels will always be a gray color at a distance.

Figure 4-2. The checker map (left). In the three blocks to the right of the checker map, the MIP-mapped texture appears on the left and the non-MIP-mapped texture is on the right, with the quads drawn farther back in space each time

You can see the MIP map in action in the Chapter 4 project file Misc Tests, MIP Mapping scene. If you press Play, you will see the two quads move backward and forward in the Game view.

Audio

Unity reads a limited number of audio file types. Just as with Unity's other assets, they are internally converted on import. Short clips of .AIFF and .WAV are converted to uncompressed audio. MP3 and longer clips are converted to Ogg Vorbis, .ogg, an open source format heavily used in real-time applications. If you are authoring for mobile and have set the platform in the Player Settings, the audio may be compressed to MP3. If the audio clip is not already an ogg file, you can manually set the compression type for higher quality or more efficient memory usage. Ogg is an open source compression similar to MP3 that does not involve license fees. For mobile, the MP3 license fee is covered by the hardware manufacturer.

The Importer

Importing assets is one of the most ubiquitous tasks in Unity. Most of your art assets must be imported. There are a vast number of choices on import, but there are only a few that must be carefully addressed. Fortunately, the defaults are generally quite useful.

From this point on in the book, most of what you will be doing will be aimed toward the book's project, so you will begin by creating a new project.

1. From the File menu, select New Project.

2. Navigate to where you want to keep it, and create a folder named **Garden Defender**.

3. Select it, and click Select Folder.

4. Import the following packages:

    ■   CharacterControllers

    ■   Particles

    ■   Scripts

5. Click Create.

You shouldn't need to save the current project, as you saved it before creating your builds.

Because you will be dealing with assets in this chapter, it will be more useful to switch back to the default layout.

6. From Layers in the top right of the UI, select Default Layout.

Importing Assets into Your Project

There are a few different ways to bring assets into your project. You can drag them directly into Unity's Project view, drop them into the project via the Explorer or Finder, or bring them in individually through the Assets menu's Import New Asset option. When bringing in multiple assets, you will want to use either of the first two methods.

Whichever method you prefer, you will want to make some organization decisions before you go any further. The FBX exporter has the option to export materials with the files. When the file contains all of its textures, they will be grouped in the imported assets folder. This is great for assets such as characters where the texture will be used only for that character, but for more generic textures, it is generally easier to manage them if they are all in one place. To this end, you will begin by adding the texture to your project first. This is always a safer way to make sure the texture can be found when the mesh is imported and the correct material is generated. If the texture cannot be found on import, a default material is made. It is easy to add the texture after the fact, but re-importing will mean rebuilding the material, or if you created a different material, it will require that material to be applied each time the asset is updated.

Importing Textures

Let's begin by importing the textures the 3D assets will require. You used Import New Asset in the previous chapter to import a single asset, a script, but when you have multiple assets, it is easier to load them directly into the project all together.

1. Locate the Game Textures folder from the Chapter 4 Assets folder where you unzipped the book's downloaded assets.

2. Copy and paste it into your project's Assets folder in the Explorer or Finder.

3. Return to the Unity editor, and watch as it imports the textures into the project and processes them.

4. Open the new Game Textures folder, and inspect its contents with the thumbnail slider all the way to the right (Figure 4-3).

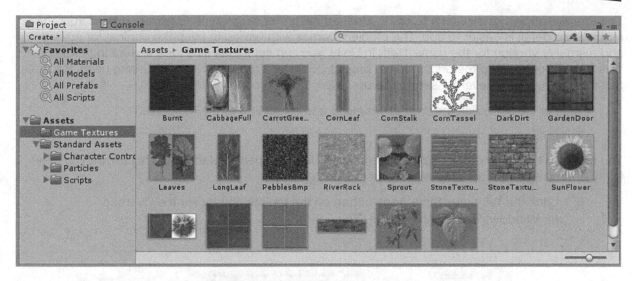

Figure 4-3. The contents of the new Game Textures folder in the Project view

5. Select the Leaves texture, and examine its import settings in the Inspector (Figure 4-4, left).

Figure 4-4. A preview of the Leaves texture's import settings (left), showing RGB colors (center), and the preview toggled to see its alpha channel (right)

6. Examine the Preview.

The color bar icon to the left of the MIP Map slider indicates that the texture contains an alpha channel (Figure 4-4, center).

7. Click the icon to toggle the alpha channel in the preview (Figure 4-4, right).

The Preview shows its size as 512 x 512. Most artists prefer to create their texture maps larger than required so detail is easier to add. The problem comes with having to keep the original for editing and a smaller version for the game itself. In Unity, you can set a max size for a texture in the game. This allows you to keep the original in the project but have it reduced when it is being used. Because these two leaves will never be seen close up, 512 x 512 is probably unnecessary.

1. For Default, click the drop-down menu and select 256 as the Max Size.

2. Click Apply.

You can also leave the default size large and override it for specific platforms. This allows you to let Unity optimize the texture automatically on build.

3. Click the Windows Store Apps button on the toolbar and locate the Override for Windows Store Apps option (Figure 4-5).

Figure 4-5. The Override for Windows Store Apps option for the Windows Store Apps platform

The Texture Type defaults to Texture when you import an image. This is a quick preset that adds compression of the appropriate type for the .dds format—in the case of the Leaves texture, DXT5. If you are a graphics guru and find the preset types to be less than acceptable, you can choose Advanced and tweak the various settings manually.

1. Click the Texture Type drop-down menu, (Figure 4-6) and select Advanced.

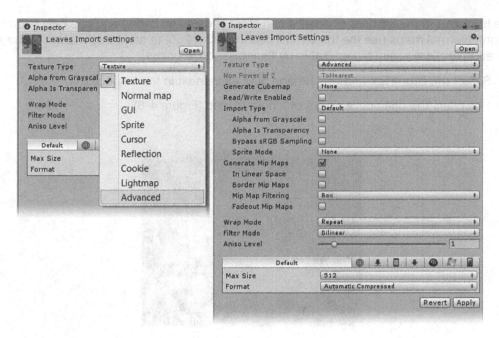

Figure 4-6. The Advanced option for the texture importer

2.   Reset the Texture Type to Texture.

Let's look next at bump maps. If you are new to the term, *bump maps* add information that is used by the renderer to make 3D meshes look like they have more detail than they actually do have. They use the bump colors to determine where the light and shadows would go if the mesh *did* have the extra triangles or faces. As you may guess, it does add to the frame rate, but far less than if the mesh itself had the detail. Traditionally, a bump map was grayscale. White was bump forward, and black was bump backward.

Modern shaders now use what is called a *normal map*. The "normal" is a direction perpendicular to the face or triangle, pointing the direction that the face will be rendered (Figure 4-7).

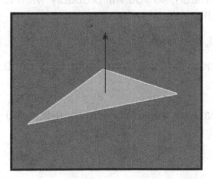

Figure 4-7. The face normal of a triangle

Grayscale is limited in the amount of detail it can store (it uses256 bytes) and has only information about height. Normal maps use the three RGB channels (3 x 256) to store information for three times the information and are easily recognizable by their distinctive colors.

3.   Select the StoneTextureBump image, and examine it in the Inspector.

The texture displays the distinctive colors of a normal map (Figure 4-8).

Figure 4-8. *The distinctive lavender, cyan, and pinkish colors of a typical normal map*

The terra cotta tile image you will be using in the game comes with a traditional grayscale bump map, TerraCottaBump. You can easily convert it using the Normal Map option from the Texture Type drop-down menu.

4.   Select the TerraCotta texture.

5.   Set its Max Size to **512**, and click Apply.

6.   Select the TerraCottaBump texture.

7.   Change its Texture Type to Normal Map in the Inspector, and click Apply.

The default settings are often too harsh, so you will probably want to tone it down a bit. Reducing the Max Size will also help smooth it out.

8.   Set its Max Size to **256**, and click Apply.

9.   Set the Filtering to Smooth and the Bumpiness to about **0.1**.

10.   Click Apply.

The normal map is more appropriate for a tile floor (Figure 4-9, right).

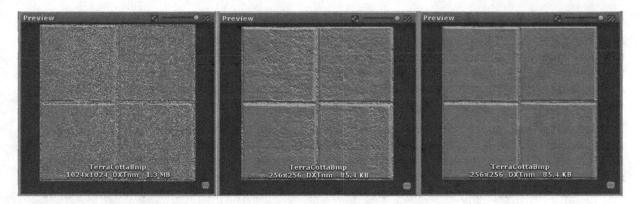

Figure 4-9. *The TerraCottaBump normal map using default settings (left), reduced to 256 Max Size (middle), and adjusted for more subtlety (right)*

Earlier in the book, it was mentioned that Unity shaders quite often commandeer a Texture's alpha channel for other purposes. For textures that have no need of transparency, using the alpha channel for a different purpose saves on resources. RGB uses 256 x 3 bytes. RGBA uses 4 x 256. By storing some other grayscale information in a texture's alpha channel instead of another RGB texture, you save 2 x 256 bytes plus the overhead of keeping track of the second texture. If an asset doesn't come with the extra information, Unity can generate an alpha channel from the texture's grayscale. For the terra cotta tile, it might be nice to have a glossiness map.

1.   Select the TerraCotta texture.

2.   Click Alpha From Grayscale, and click Apply.

The Preview now shows the color bar icon.

3.   Toggle the RBG icon to show the new alpha channel (Figure 4-10).

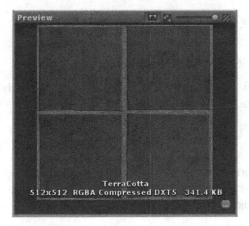

Figure 4-10. *The TerraCotta texture's new alpha channel*

For glossiness, white is glossy and black is not, so the grout will be glossier than the tiles.

Atlasing is the combining of multiple objects' textures on the same image or texture sheet. It doesn't necessarily mean you will be using less *memory*, but it does mean there will be fewer "draw calls" made when a scene is rendered. There is also less overhead when there are fewer maps to manage. Among the textures you imported for the game, a few have been combined. The Sprout texture contains two different sprout images. The Leaves texture contains a kale leaf and a radish leaf.

To atlas some textures, you may not be able to keep a square texture. With the exception of some mobile platforms, this is not a problem as long as they remain base-2 dimensions. The SunFlowerLeaf texture, for example, is not square, but it does use base-2 sizes. It is not, strictly speaking, an atlased texture because the leaf, stem, and flower head meshes all are part of the same mesh, but it definitely cuts down on the number of textures and materials when they can be combined.

1. Select the SunFlowerLeaf texture.

2. Toggle the RGB/A icon to see its alpha channel (Figure 4-11).

Figure 4-11. The SunFlowerLeaf texture's alpha channel

3. In the Inspector, set its Max Size to **256** and click Apply.

The Size in the Preview window now reports 256 x 128, showing that the maximum dimension is affected when limiting Max Size.

Importing Meshes

With the Textures already imported, it is now safe to import the meshes that use them. On import, not only will the meshes come in, but materials will be generated for each object using the main texture that was used in the object's native material.

1. Locate the Imported Assets folder from the Chapter 4 Assets folder where you unzipped the book's downloaded assets.

2. This time, with the Explorer (or Finder) open and Unity windowed on your desktop, drag the Imported Assets folder directly onto the Assets folder in the Project view.

This method only works the first time you import an asset. If you try use it to replace an existing asset, it will import the asset as a copy and increment the name. Replacing an existing asset should be done through the operating system, where you can specify *replace*.

3. Select the folder in the Project view to see what came in (Figure 4-12).

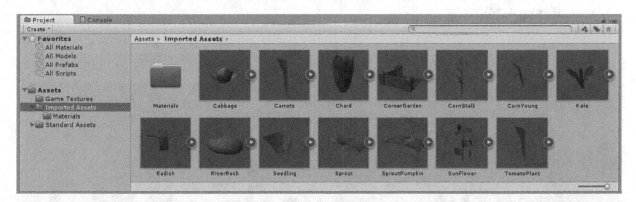

Figure 4-12. The newly imported mesh assets

When the meshes were imported, a material was generated for each using the main texture. As a default, the material is named after the texture (Figure 4-13).

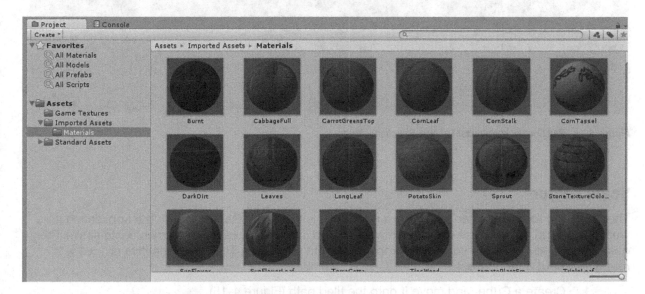

Figure 4-13. The materials generated for the meshes, using their main textures

The first thing you will notice is that the materials are rather dull and lifeless. The next is that most of the plants require both a shader that uses the texture's alpha channel as transparency and that most will also require a two-sided shader. Before dealing with the plants' materials, let's examine the garden structures that also came in.

1. From The Imported Assets folder, drag the CornerGarden asset into the Hierarchy view.

2. Add a Directional light to the scene, and set Shadow Type to Soft Shadows.

3. Set the shadow Strength to about **0.8**.

4. Adjust it so the garden is nicely visible, and toggle on Scene Lights (Figure 4-14).

Figure 4-14. The CornerGarden asset lit by a Directional light

Scale Factor

The first thing to check when importing a new asset is the scale. Depending on the application it was built in and the purpose for which it was created, it may require an adjustment in its scale. The quickest way to check the scale is to drop a cube into the scene. The Cube primitive is 1 x 1 x 1 meter, or about 3 feet cubed.

1. Create a Cube, and move it onto the tiled path (Figure 4-15).

Figure 4-15. A Cube put in the scene to check for scale

If the Cube is 1 meter, the garden looks to be a bit on the large size. You could scale it in the scene, but if it needed to be re-imported or used in another scene, you would have to rescale it. Also, changing it in the scene view costs more in performance and can break batching if the scale is not uniform. The best practice is to adjust the scale of imported assets in the Importer itself.

   2.   Select the CornerGarden asset in the Project view.

   3.   In the Inspector, Model section, set the Scale Factor to **0.005** and click Apply.

The individual meshes shrink in the Preview window but will recover the next time you select the asset in the Project view. In the Scene view, you can position the Cube near the doorway to see the improvement (Figure 4-16).

Figure 4-16.   The scaled CornerGarden more in keeping with the size of the Cube

4.   Deactivate the Cube in the Inspector.

Asset Optimization

No matter what platform or platforms you plan to author for, optimization is always something to be aware of. Besides file size (important for deploying mobile apps), optimization also applies to all types of asset management with the ultimate goal of faster frame rate. Some types of optimization, such as batching, model creation, and mapping must be designed into the assets before import. Other optimizations, such as the type of colliders used on an object are more flexible.

Batching Textures and Objects

The CornerGarden asset is made up of several separate meshes so that you can mix and match them to create many different configurations. In case it occurred to you that several objects will cost extra frame rate, don't worry. Unity "batches" objects that use the same material and have less than 300 vertices each. Another requirement is that stored vertex information is limited to three types. Typically, this is the x, y, and z location, normal (the direction it faces), and UV (its mapping coordinate). This means that each mesh is limited to 900 vertex attributes. If the requirements are met, instead of making separate draw calls for each object at render time, it can combine them into a single draw call.

Although Unity has a script that virtually "combines children" into a single object, batching is preferable because it is done after it is determined which objects are within the viewing frustum. Combining objects in different areas of the scene would cause a slowdown in frustum culling. An object's bounding box is checked first; if any part of the box is within the frustum, each face or triangle is then checked to see if it is within the frustum and must be drawn. An object that has meshes in and out of scene at any one time must always have each face checked, costing frame rate while doing so.

Static batching, available in Unity Pro only, is significantly more efficient because it can batch objects of any size as long as they are static and share the same material.

If you have Unity Pro, you have the option to use Dynamic Batching.

1. In the Project view, open the CornerGarden asset and inspect each of the meshes used to create the garden enclosure (Figure 4-17).

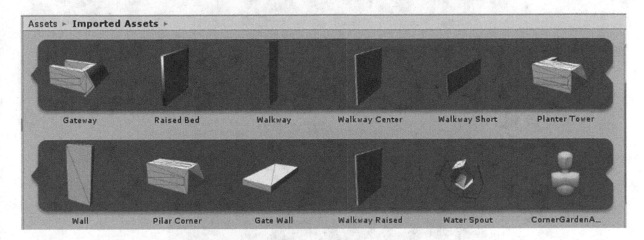

Figure 4-17. The meshes that make up the CornerGarden asset

As you select each one, note the vertex count shown in the Preview window of the Inspector.

To get accurate results for the batching, all of the objects must be within the viewing frustum (the screen's bounds) in Play mode. You had a First Person Controller to direct the camera in your terrain test scene. At present, you have a camera but no means of directing it at runtime, so you will have to set it up before you press Play.

2. Arrange the Scene view to be able to see all of the objects.

3. Select the Main Camera.

4. From the GameObject menu, select Align With View.

The camera's view now matches the Scene's view (Figure 4-18).

Figure 4-18. *The camera aligned to match the Scene view*

5.   Click Play, and turn on Stats at the top right of the Game view (Figure 4-19).

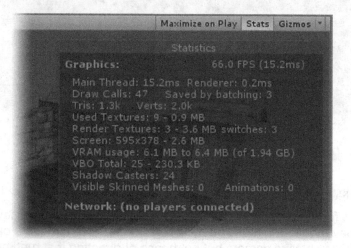

Figure 4-19. *The Stats dialog in the Game view*

If you have Pro, the Stats report 47 draw calls and only three saved by batching. If you don't have Pro and Dynamic Batching, your numbers may be different.

6.   In the Hierarchy view, select the Raised Bed object and deactivate it in the Inspector.

The Stats now report 42 draw calls and 0 saved by batching. The Raised Bed is the only object with two materials, so it appears that Unity can save some draw calls when objects with different materials are combined into one mesh. To test this further, you can drag a couple of the multiple material-using plants into the scene and watch the numbers.

7. Drag the Sunflower into the Hierarchy view. (It should show up in the Game view at the corner of the walkways.)

The draw calls go up to 47, and three are saved by batching. The Sunflower also uses two materials.

8. Delete the Sunflower from the Hierarchy, and drag the CornStalk into it.

The draw calls go up to 48 and six are saved by batching. The CornStalk uses three materials. The tassel at the top requires an alpha channel, but the CornStalk would probably be more efficient by one draw call if the stalk and leaf materials had been atlased onto a single texture sheet.

9. Stop Play mode.

The garden returns to the way it was. The Sunflower is gone, and the Raised Bed it once again active in the scene.

So you've seen a bit of batching done on objects that use multiple materials, but so far, you've yet to see any batching on the objects that share a single material. It turns out you need to mark the objects as *static* before you will see any results. Static objects are objects that will not move in the scene. There are several Unity features that can make use of this setting to improve performance, and each can be handled separately if needed.

1. Select the CornerGarden in the Hierarchy view.

2. At the top right of the Inspector, check Static.

3. Click "Yes, change children" in the dialog.

4. Click the down arrow to see all of the features that were marked as Static (Figure 4-20).

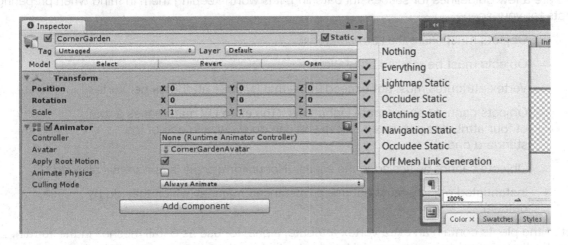

Figure 4-20. Marking the CornerGarden (and its children) as Static

A few of the settings that make use of the Static flag are lightmapping, occlusion culling, batching, and path finding.

5.   Click Play, and examine the changes in the Stats dialog (Figure 4-21).

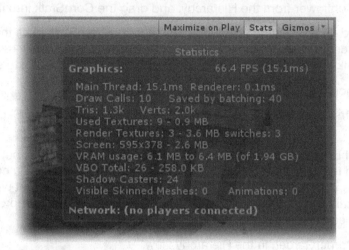

Figure 4-21. The Stats dialog after setting the CornerGarden objects to Static

This time the draw calls drop to 10, and 40 are reported saved by batching!

6.   Stop Play mode.

There are a few guidelines for successful batching. It is worth keeping them in mind when preparing objects for your scene.

- Objects must share the same Material.

- Objects must be marked as Static.

- Vertex attributes must not exceed 900—that is, three attributes per vertex.

- Objects cannot use separate Lightmaps. (The extra UV map makes a total of four attributes per vertex unless you can do away with one of the standard ones.)

- Objects cannot be scaled in the scene. (Nonuniform scale is apparently allowed.)

- Instantiated objects must not use an instanced material (which they do by default).

Most of the plants contain an extra vertex attribute, alpha, for use as detail meshes in the Terrain. Currently, they are not using the special terrain shaders, so they can also be batched.

Vertex Count

If vertex count seems to be a mystery to you, there's good reason to be confused. There are two main reasons the count may not add up to what it looks like it should be. Lighting and UV mapping are the primary culprits. Besides containing location, diffuse, and alpha color information, vertices also hold lighting and mapping information.

The simple spheres in Figure 4-22 all have 120 tris, or faces. Their vertex number varies greatly. As long as the sphere is smooth and requires no mapping coordinates, what you see is what you get. Sphere 1 has 62 vertices, with the tris sharing a vertex where the edges meet. When the model is not smooth, as in sphere 2, vertices can no longer share the vertex normal (lighting) information unless they are also coplanar. Sphere 2, faceted (nonsmoothed or shared vertices), has a count of 264 vertices.

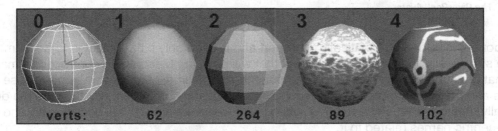

Figure 4-22. Several spheres with the same triangle count of 120, but vastly different vertex counts

If it requires simple mapping coordinates, as with sphere 3, it will require more vertices because the same vertex cannot exist at more than one position on the map. Figure 4-23, far left, shows a typical automatic mapping where a texture is wrapped around its circumference. As long as the texture is solid at the top and bottom, it may be okay. If it is Unwrapped, as with sphere 4, it may have an even higher count to accommodate the extra pieces (Figure 4-23, left center). For this reason, unwrapping a model becomes a study in compromise. Bigger pieces are easier to paint and will dictate a lower vertex count. The downside is that they tend to be more distorted on organic models, and they may not make efficient use of the texture map, so you will get less detail per pixel. Smaller pieces give you the opposite pros and cons. The spheres can be inspected in the Chapter 4 assets, the Misc Tests project, Mapping Spheres scene.

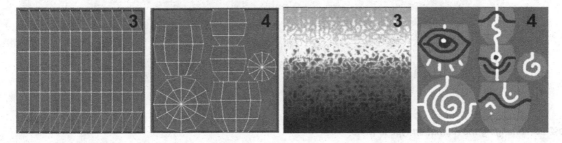

Figure 4-23. The unwrap UVs of spheres 3 and 4 and their respective texture maps

Before going any further, you can solve a small importer-based mystery. You've probably noticed a small human torso icon in the Project view (Figure 4-24), and an Animator component on each of the imported assets.

Figure 4-24. *The RiverRock Avatar*

This component is added automatically on import and is used only if the object is to be animated and, more specifically, is a character or object that will be using Mecanim to control its animations. Objects that are static do not require the component. At one time, Mecanim was only for use with characters and the Animator component was called the *Avatar component*. Unity made the decision to eventually replace its legacy animation system with Mecanim, so you will occasionally find character-centric names related to it.

You will be importing a few characters later in the book, but the current assets should be corrected.

1. Select the CornerGarden asset in the Project View.

2. In the Inspector, go to the Rig tab.

3. Set the Animation Type to None (Figure 4-25).

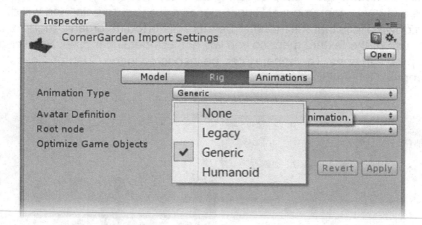

Figure 4-25. *Changing the Animation Type to None*

4. Click Apply.

The Avatar icon disappears and, if you check the CornerGarden in the Hierarchy view, you will see that the Animator component has been removed.

5. Select each of the other imported assets, and change their Animation Type to None.

6. Select the CornerGarden in the Project view once again.

Adding Colliders to Imported Meshes

Switching back to the Model section of the importer, you will notice an option to Generate Colliders automatically (Figure 4-26). This can be useful for quickly checking objects like structures to see how well a character or First Person Controller can navigate through or around them. The problem is that automatically-generated colliders are Mesh colliders.

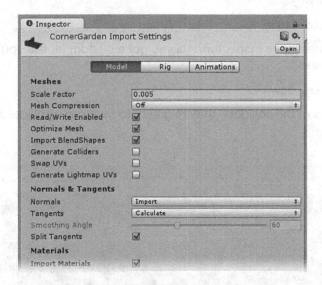

Figure 4-26. The Generate Colliders option in the Importer's Model section

These are the least efficient of the colliders because they use the object's actual mesh as the collider. Instead of doing a simple distance check for a primitive shape, each face must be tested. Not only does this take more resources, it will fail if the object has too many tris. Another problem is that most collision detection is performed with no more than one object having a Mesh Collider. If they both have Mesh Colliders, one will be dropped back down to something simpler.

With this in mind, let's look at the CornerGarden objects and decide what sort of collider is most efficient for each. To do that, you will need a bit more information about the game. The character will not be able to go into the Raised Bed and will never be able to get close enough to a wall to interact with it. With that information, you might want to put a simple Box collider on everything but the gate. The game, however, will also have plant-devouring vermin that will be dropped into the scene with physics, so two pieces (the Raised Bed and the Planter Tower) should have Mesh colliders to allow the NPCs (non-player characters) to land and move around on the visible mesh surfaces. The player will get to shoot projectiles around the garden that shouldn't be able to go through walls, so you can use Box colliders on those.

1. Select the Raised Bed in the Hierarchy view, and from the Components, Physics menu, add a Mesh Collider.

2. Repeat step 1 for the Planter Tower.

3. Select the Gate Wall, and add a Box Collider to it.

4. Repeat for the Wall, Pillar Corner, and all four walkway objects.

The Gateway is a special case. Obviously, the character tasked with eradicating the vermin will have to come through the doorway, but the mesh itself is too complicated to waste a mesh collider on if you consider that most of the tris are up in the roof area. For that object, you will use two simple box colliders. Using multiple, simple colliders is a common and efficient solution in many cases.

5. Select the Gateway.

6. Add a Box Collider to it.

You could change its values in the Inspector until you got a custom fit, but you can use a shortcut key to speed up the process.

7. Hold the Shift key down.

Grips appear on the sides of the collider—they're green, to match the collider's wire color (Figure 4-27).

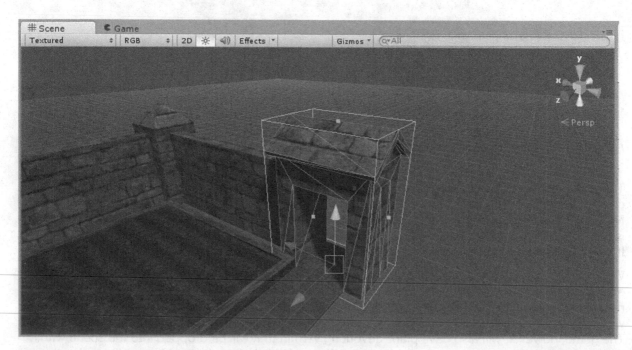

Figure 4-27. *Grips appearing on the collider when the Shift key is pressed*

8. Tip the view so you can access the grip on the underside of the collider.

9. Select the Rotation button so the gizmo won't get in the way of the bottom grip.

10. Holding the Shift key down, grab the grip and move the bottom of the collider up to the top of the door opening (Figure 4-28).

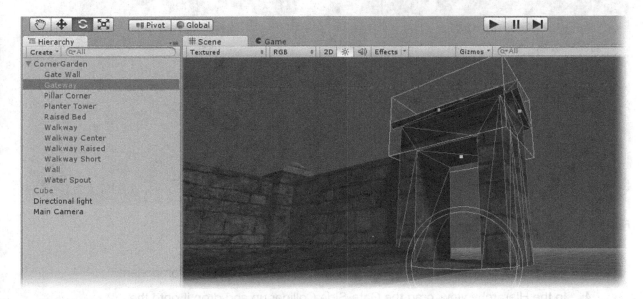

Figure 4-28. Moving the collider's base up with the bottom grip

Even with the grips, the scaling and positioning of collider components is not as easy as manipulating their parent objects. For the side colliders, you will begin with a Cube object. You could add a Box Collider to an empty gameObject, but a Cube will be quicker to set up.

1. Create a Cube, and name it **Gate-Side Collider**.

2. Position and scale it to fit one side of the Gateway (Figure 4-29).

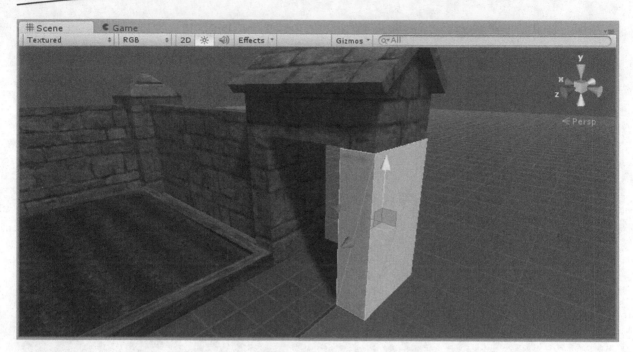

Figure 4-29. *Scaling a Cube to the Gateway side*

3. Right-click over the Cube's Mesh Renderer, and select Remove Component.

4. In the Hierarchy view, drag the Gate-Side Collider up and drop it onto the Gateway object.

5. Use Ctrl+D (CMD+D) to duplicate the new collider object.

6. Move the clone to the other side of the Gateway.

7. Select the Gateway object (Figure 4-30).

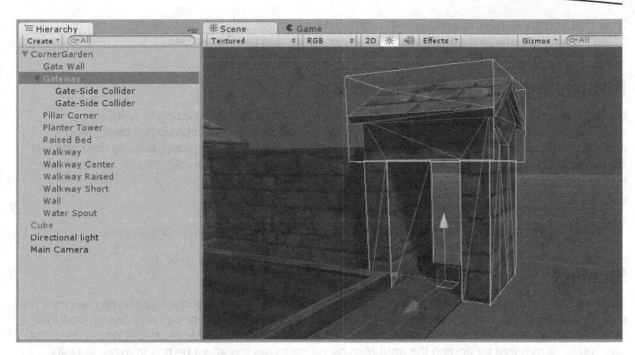

Figure 4-30. The Gateway's colliders

If you wanted to get fancy, you could add two more Cubes for their Box Colliders and rotate them for the top section instead of the adjusted Box Collider currently on the Gateway (Figure 4-31).

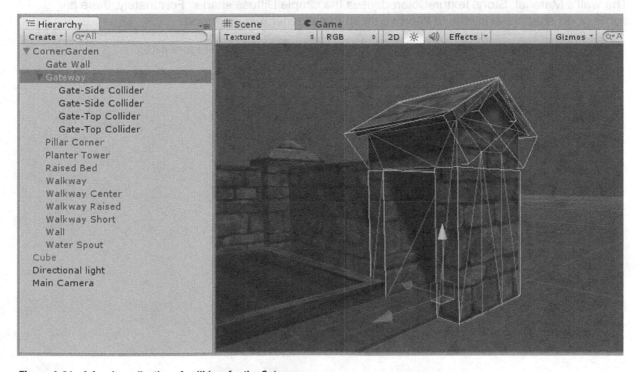

Figure 4-31. A fancier collection of colliders for the Gateway

Now that you know how to add multiple colliders to an object, you can probably figure out how you could make more efficient colliders for the Planter Tower and the Raised Bed.

Improving Generated Materials

Earlier in the chapter, you improved and added to the textures that were going to be used by the imported assets. When the assets came in, materials using the most basic (for basic, read *economical*) shader were generated. Let's go ahead and make some improvements to the materials. Be aware that using more complicated shaders may decrease frame rate. As always, use the fancy stuff sparingly.

1. Select one of the wall objects.

2. At the bottom of the Inspector, you will find its material, StoneTextureColored.

Shaders

Shaders are the code that tells the graphics hardware how an object's surface properties will look on screen. Materials in Unity are assigned prebuilt shaders, where the author can only assign textures or adjust parameters that already exist in the shader. Unlike many DCC applications where the artist can "build" a material by adding the attributes he wants to get the affect he has in mind, in Unity, you must look for the shader that best suits your needs. Writing custom shaders requires a different coding language and is beyond the scope of this book. There are custom shaders available at the Asset Store if you can't find what you want in the standard shaders.

The wall's Material, StoneTextureColored, uses the simple Diffuse shader. Fortunately, there are some good shaders available to improve the material generated on import.

1. Click the Shader drop-down list to see the shader choices (Figure 4-32).

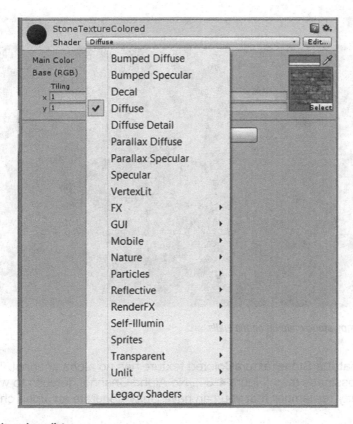

Figure 4-32. The Shader drop-down list

2. Select Bumped Specular.

3. Drag the StoneTexturebump texture from the GameTextures folder in the Project view onto the Normal Map thumbnail.

A warning appears telling you that the imported texture is not marked as a normal map.

4. Select the texture by clicking on the thumbnail to locate it in the Project view, and then clicking on it in the Project view.

You will see that it is set to the default import Texture Type, Texture.

5. Select one of the walls again.

6. Click the Fix Now button next to the warning message.

If you check the texture now, you will see that it has been changed to a Normal map texture type. The bump now appears correctly in the viewport (Figure 4-33).

Figure 4-33. The glossy bumpy stone material on the walls

The problem now is that the StoneTextureColored texture has no alpha channel. The shader uses the Alpha channel as a glossiness map (Figure 4-34). No Alpha Channel defaults to white, so the walls are fully glossy. You may remember that you can have Unity generate an alpha channel for you.

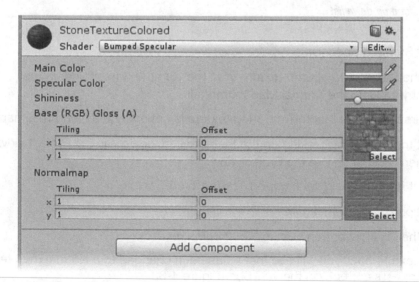

Figure 4-34. The shader using the alpha channel as glossiness

7. Select the StoneTextureColored texture in the Project view, and check Alpha from Grayscale.

8. Click Apply.

The Stone's glossiness is toned down to a more believable amount.

With the gloss reduced, you might decide the mapping on the walls is a bit off. You can adjust the Offset to get rid of the thin ledge at the top of the wall.

9. Select a wall again to gain access to the StoneTextureColored material, or select it from the Project view by filtering for materials to help locate it.

10. Set the y Offset for both the Base and Normal map textures to **0.04**.

The top of the wall looks much better (Figure 4-35).

Figure 4-35. The results of adjusting the two stone textures' y Offset

Earlier in the chapter, you generated a normal map from a grayscale bump map for the TerraCotta texture. You also created an alpha channel using the TerraCotta's grayscale, so you should be ready to go on the TerraCotta material.

1. Select one of the walkway objects.

2. In its TerraCotta material, change the shader to Bumped Specular.

3. Drag the TerraCottaBump into the Normalmap thumbnail.

The tiling is obviously different (Figure 4-36).

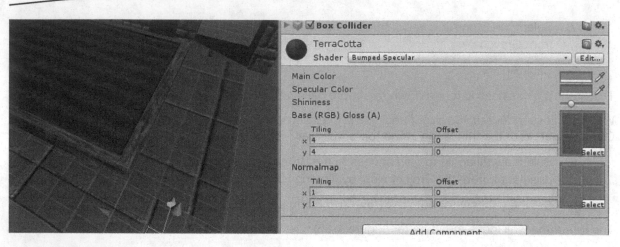

Figure 4-36. Tiling mismatch between Base and Normalmap

4.   Set the x and y tiling to **4** to match the Base texture's tiling.

5.   Adjust the Shininess until you like the result.

The last two materials belong to the Raised Bed. The wood texture probably has enough detail that it doesn't warrant a normal map. The DarkDirt material could stand to be a little brighter.

1.   Select the Raised Bed.

2.   In the Inspector, make its Main Color a bit lighter.

You may have noticed that the Main Color is a neutral (150,150,150) gray. In 3ds Max, where these assets were made, a diffuse texture overrides the default Diffuse color, gray. On import, Unity blends the color and the texture by adding them together. The color *could* have been changed before export, but leaving it a light gray can be a time saver. With the light gray darkening the texture slightly, you have a means of "highlighting" an object on mouseover or some other event. By temporarily changing the Main Color to white through scripting, the texture becomes brighter without the more resource intensive use of a second texture. While this is probably not very useful for a first-person shooter, it is a mainstay of adventure or exploration type games.

The Plants

Typical plants require special shaders. If the textures have alpha channels for transparency, they will require a shader that uses the alpha channel for transparency and possibly renders two-sided. For substantially sized plants, you may also want shadows. These three requirements limit the shaders for the plants.

Because the CornerGarden objects now have colliders, you can quickly "plant" the plants by dragging them onto the walkways or Raised Bed. You've also got a directional light in the scene, so you will be able to check on shadows. You may not use all of the plants in the basic game, but you will want to see what they look like in the scene before you make any decisions about which to use.

1. Drag each of the plants from the Project view into the garden in the scene.

2. Create an Empty GameObject, and name it **Garden Plants**.

3. Drag all of the plants onto the new parent object.

4. Select Garden Plants, and check Static in the Inspector.

5. Choose "Yes, change children" in the dialog.

6. Rotate the Sunflower and CornStalk to face the view (Figure 4-37).

Figure 4-37. The plant assets

Upon examination, you will find three types of plants in the collection. The simplest are little more than crossed planes. Besides the Tomato (which you saw in your terrain test), you have Carrots. Both of these two use images to simulate thick bushy foliage. Because there are basically only two or three crossed planes, you will not want the plants to receive shadows, and they must render the image on both sides of the planes. The Soft Occlusion shaders used for the terrain plants will be a good choice.

1. Move the TomatoPlant near the Carrots so you will be able to compare shaders.

2. Change the shader on the Carrot to Nature/Tree Soft Occlusion Leaves.

3. Adjust its Base Light value to make it slightly brighter.

4. Change the shader on the TomatoPlant to Transparent/Cutout/Soft Edge Unlit.

Both shaders have a slider to control the alpha cutoff in case the texture's alpha map is showing some background bleeding.

5.   Try adjusting the Alpha cutoff in both shaders.

6.   Orbit the view to make sure both sides of the planes are rendered for both plants.

The Transparent shader does not cast shadows, but both *do* render two-sided (Figure 4-38).

Figure 4-38. Carrot and TomatoPlant; the Carrot casts a dynamic shadow

Because shadow casting can be costly, and even if you are using Unity Pro and Deferred lighting, you may decide that minor plants do not warrant dynamic shadows. Let's see what happens with baked lighting. First you will need to set all of the plants as Static so they will be capable of generating shadows during the baking process. You should also save the scene to make sure you don't lose all of the setup you've done.

1.   Select all of the plants in the Hierarchy view, and check Static at the top of the Inspector.

2.   From Files, choose Save Scene.

3.   Name it **Garden**.

4.   From the Windows menu, open the Lightmapping window.

5.   Click Bake Scene from just above the Preview window.

6.   When the baking is finished, turn the Shadow Distance to **0** in the Lightmapping dialog (Figure 4-39) so you will see only the baked shadows.

Figure 4-39. Shadow Distance set to 0 to show only lightmapped shadows

Besides the expected absence of the dynamic shadows, there seems to be very little change. Looking at the generated maps in the Lightmapping, you can see a few pixels' worth of something at the lower left (Figure 4-40). If you do not have Pro, you will only have a far map.

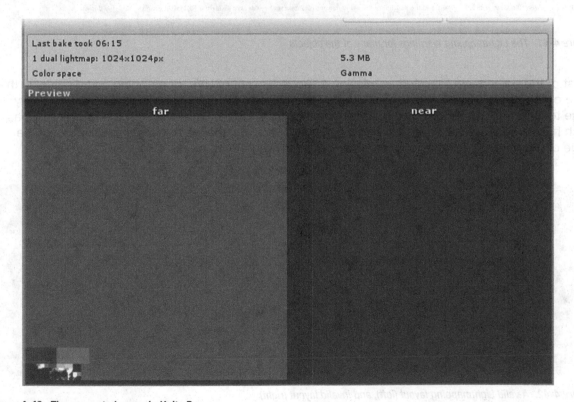

Figure 4-40. The generated maps in Unity Pro

If you toggle the Use Lightmaps option off and on in the Lightmap Display, you might notice a slight change in a few of the plants where they have cast shadows on themselves. None of the structures are receiving shadows, and the Carrots are missing. The status line (below the Project view) reports a problem. This one is just the tip of the iceberg.

7.   Click the Console tab (next to the Project tab) to examine the warnings (Figure 4-41).

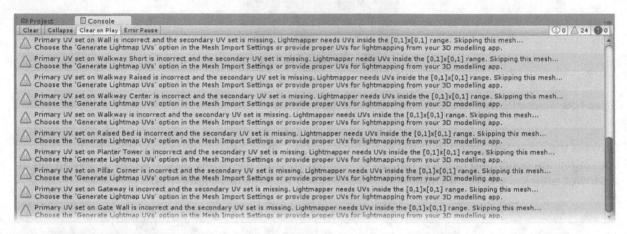

Figure 4-41. The Lightmapping warnings for many of the objects

Most of the objects are reported as missing a secondary set of UVs, or mapping coordinates. In the case of the garden structures, the texture has been tiled to increase detail without creating a very large texture map. In Lightmapping, each face must occupy a unique place on the texture map, as each has its lighting calculated individually (Figure 4-42, left). Pieces that overlap or spill over the edge of the map will fail this requirement (Figure 4-42, right).

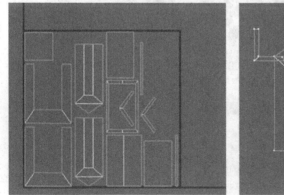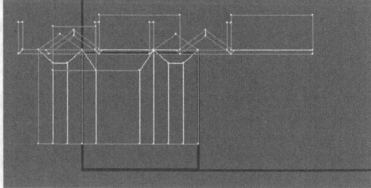

Figure 4-42. A valid Lightmapping layout (left), and invalid layout (right)

If you are a 3D artist, you may be familiar with the unwrapping process and UV unwraps in general. If not, don't worry. One of the import options is to generate a second set of UVs. These will automatically be laid out correctly for Lightmapping. Unity, in case you are interested, supports only two sets of mapping coordinates. Let's see about fixing the CornerGarden asset.

1. Click Clear in the Console to get rid of the warnings, and select the Project view again.

2. Select the Corner Garden asset in the Project view.

3. In the Model section, check Generate Lightmap UVs (Figure 4-43).

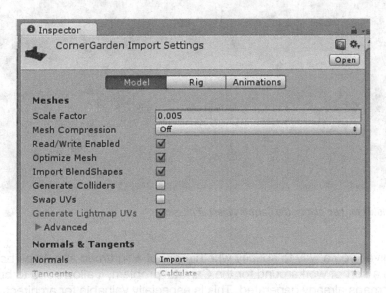

Figure 4-43. The Generate Lightmap UVs option in the Importer

4. Click Apply.

5. Rebake the lights in the Lightmapping window.

This time you should see shadows from the Carrots, TomatoPlant, and Radish objects and see several objects atlased in the lightmap (or maps if you have Pro). The Carrots object itself, however, is conspicuously missing (Figure 4-44). It turns out that the Nature shaders use the second UV map for adding wind on terrain plants, so Carrots comes up short one set of UVs . . . in this case, the one used for its regular texture map.

Figure 4-44. Three shadows for two plants; the Carrots object is missing

Fortunately, Unity gives you a way to specify whether or not a lightmap should be baked for any given object. While this is a sort of workaround for the Carrots' problem, it allows you to bring in objects with their own Lightmaps already generated. This is especially valuable for architectural models where the lighting is far more complex than you could create in Unity. If you do opt to create Lightmaps outside of Unity, the Lightmaps must be in .ext format. The no-bake flag is also useful for any object that does not have to receive baked shadows. Let's suppress the lightmap on the Carrots.

1.   Select the Carrots object in the Hierarchy view.

2.   In the Lightmapper, Object section, set the Scale in Lightmap to **0**.

3.   Bake the Lights again.

The Carrots object appears along with its shadow (Figure 4-45).

Figure 4-45. The three plants and their baked shadows

4. Set the TomatoPlant's Scale in Lightmap to **0** as well and rebake.

If you are using Pro, it's time for some decisions. With Deferred Lighting, objects within the Shadow Distance will have dynamic shadows. Anything outside of the distance uses the baked shadows. The problem is that Transparent shaders do not cast dynamic shadows.

1. If you have Pro, switch to Deferred Lighting for a moment with Edit, Project Settings, Player, Other Settings, and select Deferred Lighting for Rendering Path.

2. In the Lightmapping Display in the Scene view, turn the Shadow Distance back up to **20** or so until you can see dynamic shadows from the other objects.

The Tomato shadow disappears. If you remember, it is using the Transparent shader. So you have two options. You can change the TomatoPlant's shader to the Nature/Soft Occlusion Leaves shader, or you can use the Forward Rendering Path and give up dynamic shadows. For this very small garden area, the dual lightmaps and transition between dynamic and baked shadows are hardly worthwhile. Because you will have a large population of transient objects, you will do away with baked shadows altogether and rely on dynamic shadows.

3. Return Rendering Path to Forward if you are using Pro.

4. In the Lightmapper, clear the lightmaps to get back to dynamic shadows.

5. Change the TomatoPlant's shader to Nature/Tree Soft Occlusion Leaves.

There are six more plants that must use a two-sided, Transparent shader: Carrots, Kale, Radish, Seedling, Sprout, and the CornStalk's CornTassel material.

6. Change those objects' materials to use the Nature/Tree Soft Occlusion Leaves shader.

When you use any of the the Nature shaders, the objects' assets would have to be added to a folder with "Ambient-Occlusion" in its name in order for shadows to be calculated on them if they were being used as terrain Trees or Detail Meshes. Those shadows are added as vertex color, darkening the object when its vertices lie within a shadow cast by another object. Because the garden plants will be dynamically planted at run-time and are not Detail Meshes or Trees, they will not be receiving shadows, so you can turn the ambient occlusion settings down for each. If the term "ambient occlusion" is unfamiliar to you, think of it as the darkness in cracks, small holes, and other surface areas where light is occluded. The ambient occlusion settings will produce undesirable results on plants that are not being used as terrain Trees or Detail Meshes.

7. Turn the Ambient Occlusion and Direct Occlusion values to 0 on each of the materials using the Nature/Tree Soft Occlusion Leaves shader, and adjust the Base light values until you are happy with them.

The remainder of the objects don't require opacity but a few should have a double-sided shader. At this point, however, you may decide that a bit of specular highlight has a better visual impact than having all of the leaves render on both sides. The corn leaves in particular may be better off. The SunFlower has duplicate geometry for the backside of its foliage to work around the shortcomings of the Specular shader.

8. Assign the Specular shader to the Cabbage, CornStalk, CornYoung, and SunFlower.

9. Adjust the Specular Color and Amount to your taste.

Specular shader helps to give the plants a more realistic look than the Nature shaders and can also receive and cast dynamic shadows. To have a shader that includes double-sided, transparency-respecting, specular highlighting *and* casts shadows requires a lot of resources to render, so it's not surprising that Unity doesn't ship with one.

10. Clear the console.

Creating Prefabs

Having spent a bit of time processing your imported assets, both textures and models, you've probably realized that a lot of the setup, because it was done in the Hierarchy view, will have to be redone if you wish to re-use the objects in a different scene. To avoid doing so, you can create *prefabs* from all of the objects you are likely to use again. Prefabs can contain almost all information an object or objects require to function correctly in your scene. They allow you to quickly re-use assets in multiple scenes or levels and also to instantiate them into a scene at any given time.

1. Switch the layout to the 2 by 3 setting, and change the Project view back to Single Column Layout.

2. In the Project view, create a new folder and name it **Prefabs**.

3. In the Hierarchy view, open the CornerGarden group and drag the Water Spout onto the Planter Tower.

4. Agree to losing the prefab.

5. Now drag the Planter Tower into the Prefab folder in the Project view, and open the Prefabs folder to see the new Planter Tower prefab with its blue cube icon.

In the Inspector, you will see that the object and its child have come in with collider and materials just as they were in the scene (Figure 4-46).

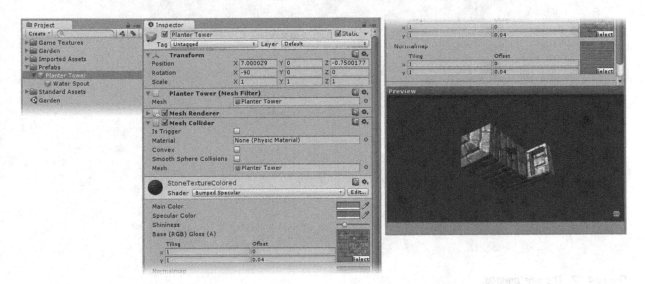

Figure 4-46. The new PlanterTower prefab

6. Make two folders in the Prefabs folder, **Structures** and **Plants**.

7. Drag the Planter Tower into the Structures folder.

8. Drag each of the other CornerGarden objects into the Structures folder.

9. Drag each of the plants into the Plants folder.

Notice that as you drag the objects in, the names go blue in the Hierarchy view, indicating they are prefabs (Figure 4-47).

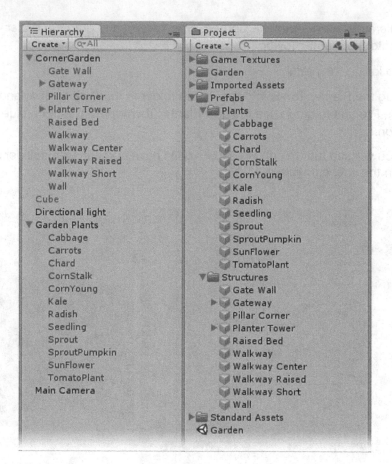

Figure 4-47. The new prefabs

Unity's Asset Store

These days, no chapter on assets would be complete without a trip to Unity's Asset Store. If you are artistically challenged, you may find a wealth of assets, both free and for purchase. If you are at the prototyping stage of your game, you may find it advantageous to spend a small amount of money for proxy objects to test ideas and functionality. This can help save days of work by artists.

The drawback, of course, to buying assets available to anyone is that your game will not look unique. Worse yet, if the art assets you chose to use were already used on a less-than-stellar game, it could impact the sales and reception of your own game just by association. A prototype using recognizable, existing assets may give the impression that you lack imagination, so always be sure to make it clear where and why they were used.

Scripting assets, on the other hand, can be a big help when there is no need to re-invent the wheel. The caveat to this one is that if you don't know enough scripting to understand how they work in the first place, you may have problems integrating them into your own project.

All warnings aside, the fun part about the Asset Store is that you can shop for assets directly in the Unity editor. Because "free" rarely includes the rights to redistribute other people's work (in any field), you won't be directly using assets from the Asset Store in the book's project. You will, however, have the opportunity to test out the asset acquisition process without worrying about impacting the finished chapters included in the book's resource downloads.

The Asset Acquisition Process

To use the in-editor functionality, you will want to switch to the default layout again.

1. Switch the layout to the Default layout.

2. From Favorites, select All Models and click on the Asset Store text (Figure 4-48).

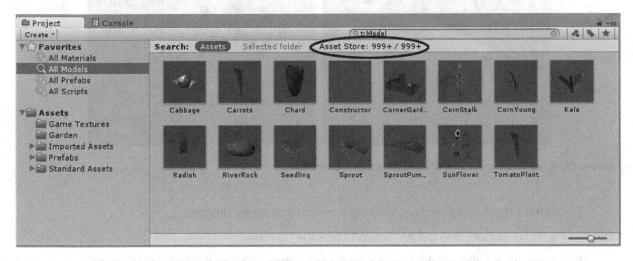

Figure 4-48. Accessing the Asset Store through the Project view's Favorites

3. In the search field, type in **'bench'**.

You may or may not see anything useful turn up.

4. Type in **'bench t: Model'**.

This time you should see several models in the Free Assets section and a few hundred in the Paid Assets section.

5. Further refine the search by typing **'stone_bench t:Model'**.

6. In the Paid Assets, click on the thumbnail.

In the inspector, you will see the asset's relevant information (Figure 4-49). If you click the Open Asset Store button, you will find that the curved stone bench is part of a collection that contains several textures and two different configurations of the bench.

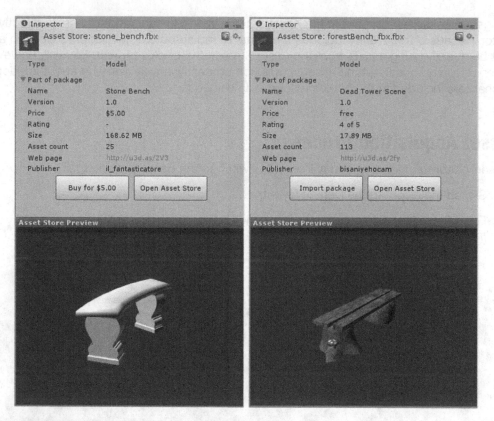

Figure 4-49. A Paid Asset in the Inspector (left), and a Free Asset (right)

7.   In the Free Assets section, click on a bench that looks promising.

Instead of a "buy" button, you get an "Import package" button.

8.   If you wish, click on the "Import package" button to bring the free assets into your scene.

The asset will be downloaded, and you will then get the familiar Import dialog.

9.   Click Import if you wish to see how the assets are brought into your package.

Due to Unity's current policy favoring "collections" rather than individual items, you may end up bloating your project file just to use one or two items from a large collection. You may be able to separate them out if they have individual FBX files. The procedure would be to make a new prefab of just the items you want, export it as a Unity package, delete the Asset Store assets, and import the stripped-down package. If you have access to a DCC program, you could open the FBX file and further separate just the assets you want.

Once you've checked them out, feel free to delete the Asset Store assets. To avoid further file bloat, you will use the stone bench provided for you in the Chapter 4 Assets folder.

10.   Import the StoneGardenAccessories.unitypackage from the Chapter 4 Assets folder.

You will find a folder for the Stone Garden Accessories that contains a bench and various pots (Figure 4-50).

Assets ► **Stone Garden Accessories** ►

Materials   Textures   Stone Planter   Stone Round Pot   Stone Vase Large   StoneGardenBench   StoneGardenBench

Figure 4-50. *The new Stone Garden Accessories in the Project view*

    11.   Drag the Stone Garden Bench prefab into the scene (Figure 4-51).

Figure 4-51. *The new bench asset in the scene*

There will be a few more assets to bring into your scene as the game progresses, but they will come in as Unity packages and will not require extra processing.

Summary

In this chapter, you learned that although Unity supports many file types, both generic and application-specific, the underlying format is .fbx. You found that there are trade-offs to importing directly from your DCC applications such as 3dMax, Maya, or Blender. Saving files directly into Unity is quick, but unless you are using versioning software, you risk not being able to revert to earlier versions of your assets. Files created in proprietary applications may also require licensed versions installed on the machines before Unity can read them. To make sure the assets can be used by anyone for Unity, model assets files should be saved in .fbx format.

With Imported texture assets, you found that Unity can add grayscale alpha channels and generate normal maps. You discovered that it was easy to keep the textures in your favorite format and size because Unity lets you specify a maximum size in scene, and it automatically converts textures to an appropriate .dds format for in-game use.

Once your textures were safely in the project, you brought the model assets in. You found that Unity generated materials using the main texture for the various models. Scale Factor is the first thing to check when importing assets. A quick way to do that is to create a Cube with its default size of 1 meter cubed, for comparison. You discovered that models come in with generic Animator rigs that can be removed by setting the Animation Type to None. Colliders you found, when auto-generated by Unity on import, were always Mesh Colliders. After examining each of the structures included in the CornerGarden asset, you determined that most would be more efficient with standard primitive colliders.

Next you learned how Unity batches" objects to be able to combine draw calls. The main requirement was that the objects be marked as Static. This, you discovered, was used for both batching and Lightmapping. With the structures, you had the chance to see how Unity shaders often use a texture's alpha channel for parameters other than transparency. Upon processing the plants, you had to decide between several shaders, but found that plants that required double-sided shaders and transparency were limited to only two choices. Of the two, only one cast dynamic shadows, and the other was likely to disappear when using Deferred Lighting (a Pro-only feature).

With all of the processing for the imported objects finished, you created prefabs of each of the objects. This, you found out, would insure that you would not have to go through the setup each time you wanted to use them in other scenes or instantiate them during runtime. Finally, you learned how to locate and load an asset directly into your scene via the Unity Asset Store.

Chapter **5**

Introduction to Scripting with C#

To bring your games to life in Unity, you will be adding scripts to trigger and manage the desired functionality. Scripting is about equal parts syntax, logic, and Unity functionality, with a good dose of math thrown into the mix. If math skills are part of your distant past, the Unity community is a good source for specialty scripts. If you already have programming skills, you will be able to tap the community for detailed advice, suggestions, and solutions.

Whether you are already familiar with programming or are a complete beginner, you will require a basic understanding of scripting in Unity to set you on your way. If this sounds daunting, don't worry. Scripting is a bit like a subset of the English language in that the syntax and vocabulary are familiar enough that you will be able to read through and figure out what a lot of it will do. Unity's Scripting Reference is full of helpful examples once you grasp how and where to implement them. You will also find that, just as with automobiles, you don't have to understand the inner workings of some of the code in order to use it.

Scripting for Unity

Unity supports three scripting languages directly: C# (C sharp), UnityScript (Unity's version of JavaScript), and Boo (a Python-like language). In the early days of Unity, UnityScript/JavaScript was used in most of the tutorials, documentation, and sample code. It is a very forgiving language that is easier for beginners and made the transition for users of Flash (where ActionScript is a JavaScript derivative) relatively painless. Today, however, C# has become increasing popular within the Unity community, as it is more powerful than UnityScript and well suited for mobile. There are now C# examples for most of the code in the documentation, and a lot of the code samples you will find online are C#. The syntax is very similar to Unity script, and as you become more familiar with Unity and scripting, you will often find yourself converting one to the other.

In Unity, the scripting languages are based on a Mono framework (an open source version of .NET). Mono is a cross-operating-system software platform that comprises language compilers (C#, etc.), a runtime (a distributable program that manages memory, threading, and operating-system differences and executes compiled code) and a set of class libraries for things like networking, user interface, openGL (graphics handling), etc. This is what allows you to "author once and deploy to multiple platforms."

With scripting, you will be creating custom components that will act as templates that you can reuse, not only on different objects, but in different projects as well. Unlike the imported art assets, scripts are created inside Unity with the help of an editor. Theoretically, you could write the scripts in any simple text editor, but using a conventional text editor designed specifically for scripting provides you with all sorts of advantages that will help you problem-solve or debug your scripts. Unity ships with the MonoDevelop text editor.

The Script Editor

The easiest way to create a script is through the Create menu, either from the Assets menu or by right-clicking in the Project view. As with all project assets, it is up to you to keep them organized. The first few scripts will be experimental, so it will be well worth making a folder to keep them separate from the rest of your game assets.

1.   Create a new folder in the Project view with the right-click menu, or from the Create drop-down list, "Create a Folder" option.

2.   Name the folder **Test Scripts**.

3.   Right-click over the new folder and, from Create, select C# Script.

A new script is created and is put immediately into rename mode (Figure 5-1).

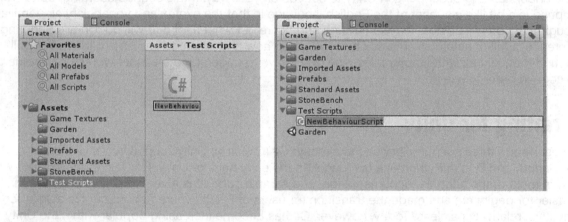

Figure 5-1. The new script in the two-column view (left) or the one-column view (right)

4.   Name the new script **VariablesTest**.

The new script comes with a default name of NewBehaviourScript. According to the documents, "A script makes its connection with the internal workings of Unity by implementing a class which derives from the built-in class called MonoBehaviour"—hence, "NewBehaviourScript." A class is a kind of blueprint or template that allows you to define parameters and functionality in a generic way. Because it is a component, you can then customize the object it resides on by changing the values of its parameters.

Unlike UnityScript or Boo, the scripting template generated with C# contains the script or class name as part of the script itself. For that reason, you should always name the script as soon as you create it. Also, Unity will allow you to use spaces in the name, but internally, they will be removed. So a best practice is to use "CamelCase," where the first letter of each word is capitalized or use underscores. This will help prevent confusion when you have assets, scripts, and variables of the same name by allowing you to reserve spaces for asset names.

5.   Open the new script by double-clicking on it in the Project view.

The MonoDevelop script editor opens, showing your newly created script (Figure 5-2).

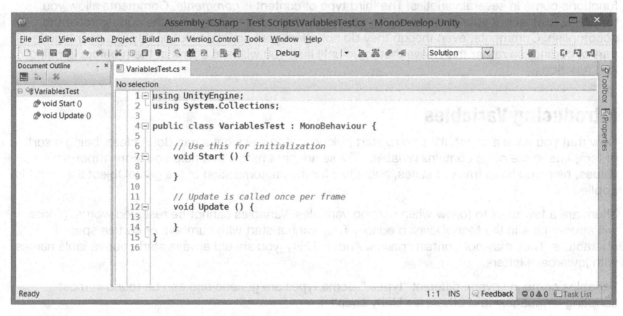

Figure 5-2.   The new script in the MonoDevelop script editor

In the regular Unity editor, the icon shows that the script is a C# script. In the script editor, you can see by its name in the tab that the extension for a C# script is *.cs*. The left pane shows the Document Outline area. This is where a list of functions and variables can be seen as long as there are no syntax errors in your code.

In the code section, you will notice that a lot of the text is color coded. Words in blue such as "using" and "void" are reserved words. Comments are in green and are ignored when the script is evaluated. The first two lines tell the engine where to find most of the functions. At line 4, you will see that in C# the class name *must* be explicitly declared. The name is the name of the class, the name of the script and, once applied to a gameObject, the name of the script as a component—unlike UnityScript, where the name of the class is assumed to be the name of the script. Inside the class declaration, you will see the two blocked-in functions, Start and Update. Functions, as you will find later in this chapter, are where the functionality for your game gets carried out.

The MonoDevelop editor has a lot of nice features that you will be introduced to throughout this chapter. In case you are feeling a bit overwhelmed by all of its menus and tools, you needn't worry. There are really only a handful that you will use on a regular basis.

If you are already a programmer, by the way, you can use an editor of your own choosing by accessing the External Tools panel in Unity's preferences from the Edit menu.

Writing Scripts

With a bit of general information about scripts under your belt, you are probably ready to learn how to start filling them up with code. Basic scripts usually have three types of content: variables, functions, and comments. *Variables* are the means of storing information that is used and often changed throughout your game. *Functions* are where all the action happens. Both variables and functions come in several varieties. The third type of content is *comments*. Comments allow you to make notes about your code so you or someone else can decipher what the code is meant to accomplish. Comments, even though they do not affect your script's functionality, are an integral part of coding, so rather than leave that topic until last, you will take a look at them before jumping into functions.

Introducing Variables

Now that you have a script, it's time to start poking at it to see what it can do. A class, being a sort of template, quite often contains *variables*. These are parameters that help you store important values, help you keep track of states, and allow for the customization of the gameObject the script is applied to.

There are a few rules to follow when naming variables. Variables cannot be reserved words. (Those will appear blue in the MonoDevelop editor.) They cannot start with numbers or certain special characters. They may not contain spaces. And, in Unity, you should always start your variable names with lowercase letters.

Variables come in several different "types." Some types are generic and can be found in most scripting languages, and others are Unity specific.

Defining Variable Types

Variables have types. In Unity's version of JavaScript, if you do not declare the type of variable, it will do its best to try to figure out what type of variable it is. Not only is this a slow process, it is also not allowed in most mobile platforms. In C#, the type *must* be declared when the variable is first introduced into the code. The most common types are numbers, strings, and Booleans.

A classic example using various variable types is a script, or class, for describing an animal. It might have a parameter for blood type (warm or cold), number of legs, type of teeth, coat type, or any other number of parameters that let you define a particular type of animal.

So the first thing you have to do with your variable is to decide what *type* it is.

Numbers come in a few different types. Integers are whole numbers that can be negative or positive. Fractional numbers come in several different varieties in C#. Floats or floating point numbers are 32-bit, floating-point values. Doubles store 64-bit, floating-point values. Integers and floats are the most commonly used types of numbers in Unity.

Strings, or character strings, are strings of characters that can be letters, numbers, or other characters. They are identified by always being enclosed in quotation marks. Beware of trailing or leading spaces when referring to strings. the string "This is a string" is different than "This is a string " because of the trailing space at its end. Note also that the number 4 has a value of *4*, while the string "4" is merely the character 4 and has no value.

Booleans, named after George Boole, an English mathematician and logician, have a value that is either true or false. The Boolean type uses the least amount of memory. It is typically used as a flag for keeping track of the state of an object or objects.

As you get more familiar with how Unity handles communication between various gameObjects and their components, you will discover that they can be defined as types as well.

Also worth noting is that variable and function names are case-sensitive. If your code is not working, the first place to look is in your naming. A variable named myVar is a different variable than myvar.

Now that you've had a quick rundown of types, it's time to see how to implement some variables in your new script. At this point, the variables won't do anything, they will just serve as a place to store values of the appropriate type.

Besides the actual syntax, you will have to know where to put the variables. In C#, the "scope" of the variable is determined by its location. The variables you will be adding now will be available to anything within the class itself.

1. In the script editor, below the class declaration, press <enter> a couple of times, and then tab over until you are even with the rest of the class's contents.

Indentation and extra line feeds or carriage returns are optional in C#, but they are invaluable for keeping code neat and easy to read.

2. Add the following:

```
int legs;
```

At its simplest, your first line of code contains the type int, or integer, the name of the variable, legs, and a semi-colon signifying the end of the instruction (Figure 5-3).

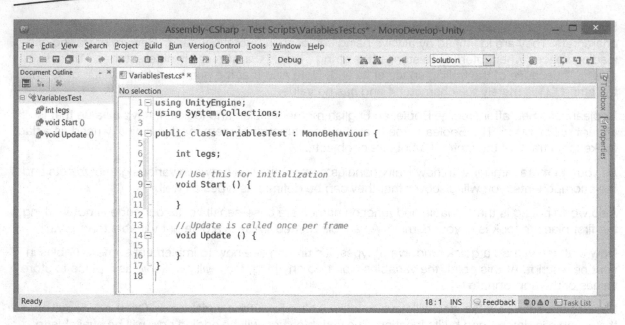

Figure 5-3. The legs variable inside the script's class declaration

In the Document Outline area, on the left, you will see the new variable and its type. The next thing you will have to do is make the addition permanent. If you look at the tab, you will see an asterisk next to the script's name. This means there have been changes that must be saved before they can be recognized.

3. Click the Save icon on the toolbar, press Ctrl+S on the keyboard, or select Save from the File menu.

Now the script has not only been saved, but it has been *compiled* into a form that the engine can use.

Currently, the script resides only in the Project view as a template. To put it into use, you will have to put it on an object in the scene. For fun, you can add it to the bench. There's one more thing you will need to do before you can.

4. Drag the VariablesTest script from the Project view to the StoneGardenBench in the Hierarchy view.

5. Select the StoneGardenBench.

The new script component appears in the Inspector with the rest of the bench's components (Figure 5-4).

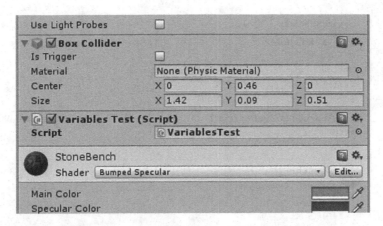

Figure 5-4. The new Variables Test component on the StoneGardenBench object

Note that the "CamelCase" script name now sports a space between the two words and "(Script)" reminds you what kind of component it is. Conspicuously missing, however, is the variable you added to the script.

Exposing Variables to the Inspector

As a default, C# variables are automatically "private." Not only are they not accessible by other scripts, they are not exposed to the Inspector. With Unity's version of JavaScript, the *default* is publicly accessible. With both JavaScript and C# in Unity, you have the option of making it accessible to other scripts but not exposed to the Inspector by marking it as *internal*. Let's see about exposing the variable to the Inspector.

6. Change your variable line to read as follows:

    ```
    public int legs;
    ```

7. Save the script.

8. Click back in the Unity editor to change the focus.

The Inspector updates, and the legs variable is now exposed (Figure 5-5).

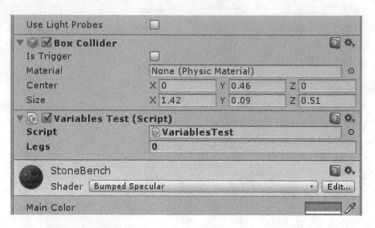

Figure 5-5. The Legs variable exposed to the Inspector

With the variable name, note how the first letter has been capitalized for easier reading in the Inspector. Also note that a default value of 0 has been assigned to it as well. When you declared the variable, you did not initialize it to any value, so the default was assigned to it. Let's go ahead and initialize the value to something other than 0. Going back to the Animal class, 4 would probably be a good value to start with.

9.   Change your variable line to the following:

```
public int legs = 4;
```

10.   Save the script.

11.   Click back in the Unity editor to change the focus.

This time, the Inspector doesn't update to reflect the new default value. Values set in the Inspector always override the values that were initialized when a variable was declared. There is, however, a way to force an update.

12.   Right-click over the Variables Test component label.

13.   Select Reset.

14.   Now the default value for the Legs parameter reads as 4, the value that was initialized in the script.

The only problem now is that the bench has only two legs. This is where the concept of an instance script comes in. When you modify the script, you are modifying the master template. It doesn't matter where you access it from—the Project view or an object in the scene—there is just one master. The same script can be used on many different objects and will be the same until the variables exposed to the Inspector are changed during edit mode.

1.   Drag the VariablesTest script onto the Sunflower and onto the Walkway (the long walkway in front of the gateway).

The Sunflower could be said to have one leg, and the walkway definitely has none.

2. Set the Sunflower's Legs parameter to **1** and the Walkway's Legs parameter to **0**.

Now you have three gameObjects using an instance of the VariablesTest script, yet the script is customized to each one.

3. Click Play.

4. Change each of the object's Legs parameters to a different integer.

5. Stop Play mode.

The values return to their original Inspector values. Most, but not all, parameters exposed in the Inspector cannot be permanently changed during runtime. This allows you to test parameters during runtime without the fear of breaking functionality. For times when you are experimenting to get optimal values during runtime, you will have to remember or make note of the values you wish to make permanent. If you find yourself forgetting you are in Play mode too often while setting values, you can change the tint of the editor. As a default, it goes slightly darker in Play mode.

1. From the Edit menu, Preferences, select Colors.

2. Under General, locate Playmode Tint.

3. Change the color to something more obvious, and click Play.

Much of the editor, with the notable exception of the Game view and Scene view, is tinted to reflect your color choice.

4. Back in the Preferences window, click the Use Defaults button to return the default color.

5. Stop Play mode.

The default color, restored during runtime, does not revert back to the color you set before you pressed Play. Feel free to reset the color to its default or to use a color of your own choosing.

With a bit of typical Unity variable functionality investigated, it's time to check out a few more variable types.

6. Under your existing variable line, add the following:

```
public float earLength = 2.5;
public string description = "";
public bool isWarmBlooded;
public GameObject favoriteFood;
```

7. Save the script.

8. Click Play.

A message appears in the Scene view (Figure 5-6).

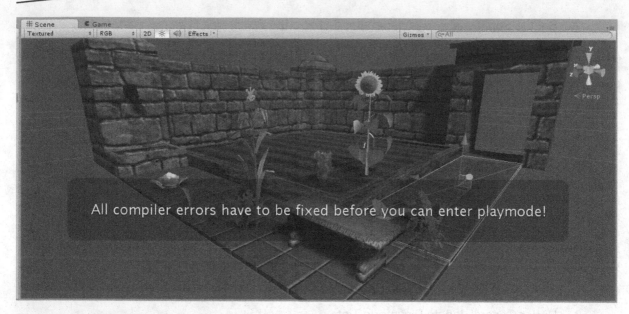

Figure 5-6. A compiler error blocking Play mode

If you take a look at the script editor, you will see that the Document Outline is not blank. If it was, you could expect a syntax error. Instead, the message tells you that there is a compiler error. The script was saved but was not able to compile, so the game cannot run. You will get this error whether or not the script is being used in the scene.

The trick here is to figure out where the problem lies. The console will often provide clues and occasionally even suggest a solution.

The Console and Error Messages

The *console* is where Unity will communicate with you. It will tell you when your code has errors and often make suggestions about what it thinks you meant to write. The message may be cryptic, but it will also tell you where it was generated in the code. The console is also a place where you can have messages of your own printed out, as you will find later in the chapter.

1. Look at the status line, and check out the message it holds (Figure 5-7).

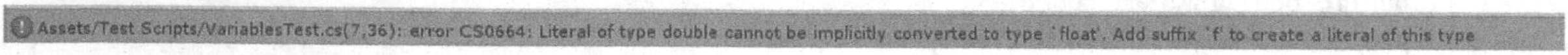

Assets/Test Scripts/VariablesTest.cs(7,36): error CS0664: Literal of type double cannot be implicitly converted to type 'float'. Add suffix 'f' to create a literal of this type

Figure 5-7. The error message in the status line

It tells you which script has the problem, VariablesTest.cs. It gives the line number and column number (7, 36). It gives the error, "Literal of type double cannot be implicitly converted to type 'float.'" And, in this case, it offers a suggestion for fixing the problem.

2. Click on the status line to open the console, or click on the Console tab.

> **Tip**   You can easily tear off the Console tab to float the Console window. If you are working in the 2x3 layout, it will automatically be floated when you double-click the message on the status line. You can also open the console through the Window menu.

3. Double-click on the error message in the console.

4. Switch focus to the script editor.

The line in question is highlighted in the script editor (Figure 5-8).

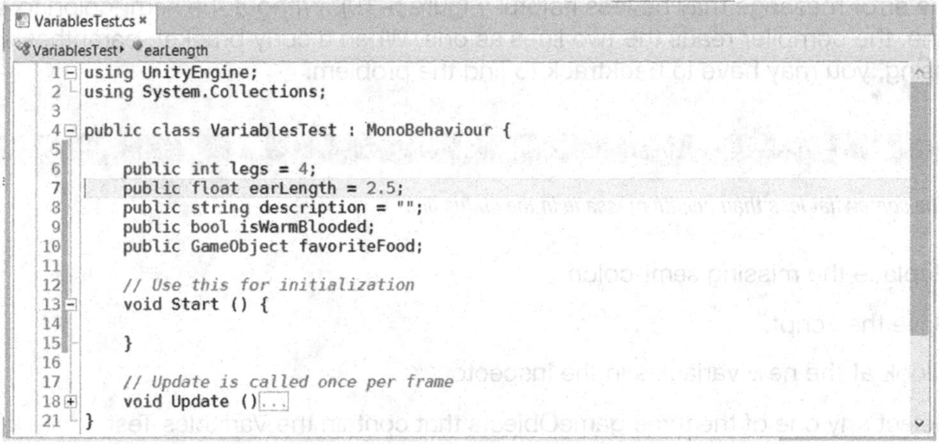

```
VariablesTest.cs ×
VariablesTest ▸   earLength
  1 ⊟ using UnityEngine;
  2 └ using System.Collections;
  3
  4 ⊟ public class VariablesTest : MonoBehaviour {
  5
  6       public int legs = 4;
  7 |     public float earLength = 2.5;
  8       public string description = "";
  9       public bool isWarmBlooded;
 10       public GameObject favoriteFood;
 11
 12       // Use this for initialization
 13 ⊟    void Start () {
 14
 15 └    }
 16
 17       // Update is called once per frame
 18 ⊞    void Update () ...
 21 └ }
```

Figure 5-8. The line in question, highlighted in the code window

Let's append the number with *f* as suggested in the console.

5. Change the line as follows:

    ```
    public float earLength = 2.5f;
    ```

6. Save the script.

The error message in the console goes away. Floats require a lower case f after the number.

7. Click Play.

This time, Play mode turns on.

8. Turn off Play mode.

9. Delete the semi-colon at the end of the line.

Before you even save the script, the script editor draws a squiggly line under the line that will generate an error (Figure 5-9).

```
VariablesTest ▸ earLength
 1 ⊟ using UnityEngine;
 2 └ using System.Collections;
 3
 4 ⊟ public class VariablesTest : MonoBehaviour {
 5
 6      public int legs = 4;
 7      public float earLength = 2.5f
 8      public string description = "";
 9      public bool isWarmBlooded;
10      public GameObject favoriteFood;
11
```

Figure 5-9. The script editor after removing the semi-colon from line 7

This time, the error message may be less helpful (Figure 5-10). Without the semi-colon to signify the end of the line, the compiler reads the two lines as one. When a curly bracket, parenthesis, or semi-colon is missing, you may have to backtrack to find the problem.

⊗ Assets/Test Scripts/VariablesTest.cs(8,14): error CS1519: Unexpected symbol `public' in class, struct, or interface member declaration

Figure 5-10. The somewhat less than helpful message in the status line

10.   Replace the missing semi-colon.

11.   Save the script.

Let's take a look at the new variables in the Inspector.

1.   Select any one of the three gameObjects that contain the Variables Test component.

2.   Check out the new variables in the Inspector (Figure 5-11).

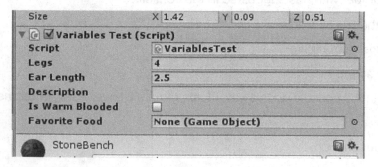

Figure 5-11. The new variables exposed in the Inspector

The variable names that used CamelCase have had spaces inserted and, just like the legs variable have had the first character capitalized. A convention in Unity is to use lowercase characters for variable names' first character. They cannot start with a number or certain special characters. Variable names may also not contain spaces. Just as with the script names, use CamelCase or underscores to make the variable names more readable. Ideally, variable names should be meaningful without being too long or difficult to read.

Next, take a look at the values for the parameters. The Ear Length's value, a float number, does not require an f after the number in the Inspector. The description variable was initialized as an empty string, "". The value for the isWarmBlooded variable, of Boolean type, appears as a check box. Because it was not initialized in the script, it defaults to false, or off.

Introducing Unity-Specific Variables

The last variable is a type uniquely available in Unity. Because a gameObject is an instance of the GameObject class, it is also a type. The big difference between Unity-specific types and the usual types found in most programming languages is that they cannot be initialized when the variable is declared. They can be "found" in a function during runtime, or they can be loaded in the inspector manually. The former is best when all of the instances of the script will be using the same gameObject. The latter is easy when you only have to do it once or twice. Let's load something into that parameter.

1. Make sure you are not in Play mode.

2. Open the Garden Plants object in the Hierarchy view.

3. Locate the Cabbage.

4. Select the StoneGardenBench.

5. Locate the Favorite Food parameter in its Variables Test component.

Whenever you declare a variable as any of the available Unity types, the parameter will show that "none" has been assigned and it will show the type that is expected (Figure 5-12).

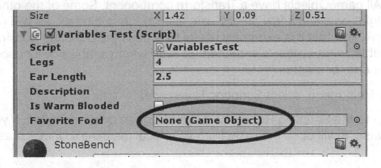

Figure 5-12. *The Favorite Food parameter waiting for a value of type Game Object*

6. Drag the Cabbage from the Hierarchy view into the StoneGardenBench's Favorite Food parameter (Figure 5-13).

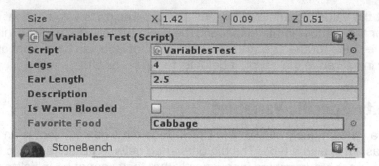

Figure 5-13. The Cabbage gameObject loaded into the bench's Favorite Food parameter

You may be wondering why you couldn't just type "Cabbage" into the field. The word "Cabbage" is just a string of characters that has no connection with the Cabbage gameObject. By dragging the Cabbage gameObject into the Favorite Food field, you have given your script access to the Cabbage's components and their exposed parameters. You have, in effect, "introduced" the Cabbage gameObject to the bench's Variables Test script so that they will be able to exchange information. This is a key concept in Unity because each object in the scene will have its own scripts and may need to communicate with other objects throughout the game. You can also load the Cabbage gameObject into the parameter by clicking on the Browse icon at the right of the value field and selecting it from the Browser.

Accessing Unity's Scripting Reference

Let's add two more variables before jumping into functions. This time, you will add a couple of component types. All gameObjects have a Transform component. Some of the other components— such as Camera, Rigidbody, and a few others—are already internal types. As you get farther along with scripting, you will find that it is extremely useful to access the Scripting docs on a regular basis to see what is available, what syntax is expected, or even what variables or functions are associated with various components or classes.

1.   From the Help menu, select Scripting Reference.

A browser opens up to the Scripting Reference page of Unity's documentation. If you are online, it will be live; otherwise, it will open the page from your local machine's Unity install (Figure 5-14).

Figure 5-14. The Scripting Reference opened in the browser

The first thing to do is to specify the scripting language you are using.

> 2. Just under the Scripting tab, click to open the drop-down menu and select C# (Figure 5-15).

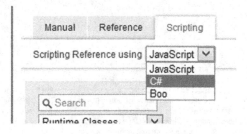

Figure 5-15. Specifying C#

> 3. In the Search field, type in **GameObject** and press Enter.

A long list of matches is generated (Figure 5-16).

Scripting Reference

Your search for "*GameObject*" resulted in 119 matches:

GameObject
Base class for all entities in Unity scenes.
GameObject.activeInHierarchy
Is the GameObject active in the scene?
GameObject.activeSelf
The local active state of this GameObject. (Read Only)
GameObject.AddComponent
Adds a component class named className to the game object.
GameObject.animation
The Animation attached to this GameObject (Read Only). (null if there is none attached).
GameObject.audio
The AudioSource attached to this GameObject (Read Only). (null if there is none attached).
GameObject.BroadcastMessage
Calls the method named methodName on every MonoBehaviour in this game object or any of its chil

Figure 5-16. The matches for "GameObject"

4.   Select the top one, GameObject.

A page opens for the GameObject class (Figure 5-17).

GameObject

Namespace: UnityEngine
Parent class: Object

Description
Base class for all entities in Unity scenes.

See Also: Component.

Variables

activeInHierarchy	Is the GameObject active in the scene?
activeSelf	The local active state of this GameObject. (Read Only)
animation	The Animation attached to this GameObject (Read Only). (null if there is none attached).
audio	The AudioSource attached to this GameObject (Read Only). (null if there is none attached).
camera	The Camera attached to this GameObject (Read Only). (null if there is none attached).
collider	The Collider attached to this GameObject (Read Only). (null if there is none attached).
collider2D	The Collider2D component attached to this object.
constantForce	The ConstantForce attached to this GameObject (Read Only). (null if there is none attached).
guiText	The GUIText attached to this GameObject (Read Only). (null if there is none attached).
guiTexture	The GUITexture attached to this GameObject (Read Only). (null if there is none attached).
hingeJoint	The HingeJoint attached to this GameObject (Read Only). (null if there is none attached).
isStatic	Editor only API that specifies if a game object is static.
layer	The layer the game object is in. A layer is in the range [0...31].
light	The Light attached to this GameObject (Read Only). (null if there is none attached).
networkView	The NetworkView attached to this GameObject (Read Only). (null if there is none attached).
particleEmitter	The ParticleEmitter attached to this GameObject (Read Only). (null if there is none attached).
particleSystem	The ParticleSystem attached to this GameObject (Read Only). (null if there is none attached).
renderer	The Renderer attached to this GameObject (Read Only). (null if there is none attached).
rigidbody	The Rigidbody attached to this GameObject (Read Only). (null if there is none attached).
rigidbody2D	The Rigidbody2D component attached to this GameObject. (Read Only)
tag	The tag of this game object.
transform	The Transform attached to this GameObject. (null if there is none attached).

Constructors

GameObject	Creates a new game object, named name.

Figure 5-17. The GameObject class in the Scripting Reference

At the top of the page is the name of the class, GameObject. As you become more familiar with scripting, you will see both GameObject and gameObject. If the first character is capitalized, it refers to the class. If not, it will be referring to a specific instance of the class, e.g., a particular gameObject.

The next line states the Namespace as UnityEngine. If you remember, when you first created the script, it came with 'using UnityEngine' at the top of the page. A namespace is a type of shortcut to tell the script where to find things, or more specifically which one it is referring to. An example could be two people named John Smith. The first John Smith lives on Baker Street. The second one lives on Maple Avenue. By declaring a namespace of BakerStreet, you are saying that every time you refer to johnSmith, you are referring to the one on Baker Street, it implies BakerStreet.johnSmith. So if you need to refer to the other person, you must explicitly say MapleAvenue.johnSmith. In C#, the period denotes inheritance and is called dot notation. The part following could be a sub-class, a property, or a function available for the preceding part.

Let's skip the Parent class for a minute and look at the description, GameObject is the "Base class for all entities in Unity scenes." This means that every object in the Hierarchy is a gameObject, an instance of the class, GameObject.

Going back up to Parent class, that line tells you what class GameObject inherits from, Object

5.   Click on the Object link.

This time, the description says "Base class for all objects Unity can reference." This includes things that are not put in the scene (Hierarchy view), such as window size, inputs, ambient light, and pretty much any other Render or Project settings that are accessed through the Edit menu. The Object class has only a few variables and functions, but you will use a few of them on a regular basis. Of note are the name variable and the Destroy and Instantiate functions. Because GameObject inherits from Object, you can find the selected instance of its name, destroy the current instance of it, or instantiate a new instance of it.

6.   Take the browser back to the GameObject class.

7.   Note the large number of variables the GameObject class includes.

Any variable that has "attached" in its description is referring to a component on the gameObject that can be easily accessed by your scripts. The newer entry for Collider2D is more descriptive: "The Collider2D component attached to this object." So if you see a component in this list, it is automatically a type. Let's add a new variable for a Camera component. Component types, because they are classes, are always capitalized and will turn blue in the script editor.

1.   Add the following new variable to your script, beneath the others:

    public Camera theView;

2.   Save the script, and check out the new parameter on the bench in the Inspector.

As you probably anticipated, this one is expecting a gameObject with a Camera component. The only object in the scene with a Camera component is the Main Camera gameObject. If you try to drag any other gameObject onto the The View field, it will not let you drop it.

3. Select the Main Camera, and reassure yourself that it has a Camera component.

4. Select the bench or any of the other objects with the Variables Test component.

5. Drag the Main Camera onto its The View field.

This time, the objects drops nicely into place (Figure 5-18).

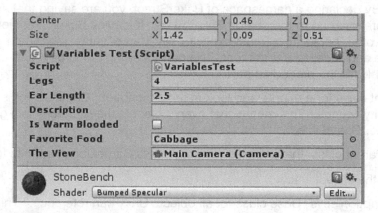

Figure 5-18. Main Camera as the value of the The View parameter

You will notice that the difference between the GameObject and the Camera variable type is that because the name of the gameObject (which, you may remember, is a variable of the parent class, Object) is what is shown in the field, the component type, Camera, is also shown in parentheses for clarification.

So now you have one piece of the variable type puzzle left. You have created a script which is essentially a class and becomes a component when it is added to a gameObject. But because it is a new class that you have created, it does not exist in the Unity engine class libraries. To use it, you will specify the name of the script, but it will not turn blue as the known Unity types do.

6. Add the following variable beneath the others, and save the script:

```
public VariablesTest myCustomScript;
```

The custom type in the script (Figure 5-19).

```
VariablesTest.cs ×
VariablesTest ▸  myCustomScript
  1 ⊟ using UnityEngine;
  2 └ using System.Collections;
  3
  4 ⊟ public class VariablesTest : MonoBehaviour {
  5
  6       public int legs = 4;
  7       public float earLength = 2.5f;
  8       public string description = "";
  9       public bool IsWarmBlooded;
 10       public GameObject favoriteFood;
 11       public Camera theView;
 12       public VariablesTest myCustomScript;|
 13
 14       // Use this for initialization
 15 ⊟    void Start () {
 16
 17 ⊦    }
 18
 19       // Update is called once per frame
```

Figure 5-19. The variable named myCustomScript of type VariablesTest

The type does not turn blue for the custom type.

7. Drag the Sunflower (that also has the Variables Test component on it) onto
    the bench's My Custom Script parameter.

If you are wondering why you might want access to the Sunflower's VariablesTest script, imagine
the following scenario: An alien zombie ray strikes the bench, causing it to give off a toxic essence
that turns Sunflowers into carnivorous monsters. At this point, the VariablesTest script on the bench
would change the Sunflower's Variables Test's Favorite Food value to something more fauna than
flora. It's a silly scenario, but it illustrates the concept of one object's script communicating with
another.

Creating Comments

There's one last thing to add to your first scripting efforts. Sometimes you can name a variable so
that it perfectly describes what it is for and what is done with it. Most of the time, that is not fully
possible without creating long and unwieldy names. It is also not unusual to revisit old code or
maybe even someone else's code and have to try and figure out what it is meant to do. This is where
comments come in.

Comments allow you to make notes and add explanations to your code. They may be strictly for
your own benefit, or they might be necessary when working with other people on a project where
they will want to understand how the code is designed to work. Typically, you make comments to
explain specific variables, to describe what functions are meant to do, or to make general notes
about what is happening in your code.

The double backslash at the front of any text tells the engine not to evaluate anything after the // on the line. The text in the script editor goes green to indicate to you that the text will be ignored.

Another typical use for the double backslash is to "comment out" code during testing. This gives you a quick way to disable code without deleting it.

Let's go ahead and add a few comments to the variables in your script. The existing comments are designed to introduce functions below them, but comments can also be put at the end of a line of code. You will see them in both places, but the goal is to keep things easy to read.

1. Add comments so your variables code reads as follows:

```
public int legs = 4;                 // number of legs, will need to calculate speed
public float earLength = 2.5f;       // will need to calculate hearing distance
public string description = "";      // will need for mouseover text
public bool IsWarmBlooded;           // also needed for speed calculation
public GameObject favoriteFood;      // objects that will be eaten within range
public Camera theView;               // a test for a Unity component
public VariablesTest myCustomScript; // a test for a custom component
```

2. Save the script.

The new addition will not affect the functionality of the script, but now makes it more understandable (Figure 5-20).

```
VariablesTest.cs ×
VariablesTest ▶ No selection
1  using UnityEngine;
2  using System.Collections;
3
4  public class VariablesTest : MonoBehaviour {
5
6      public int legs = 4; // number of legs, will need to calculate speed
7      public float earLength = 2.5f; // will need to calculate hearing distance
8      public string description = ""; // will need for mouseover text
9      public bool IsWarmBlooded; // also needed for speed calculation
10     public GameObject favoriteFood; // objects that will be eaten within range
11     public Camera theView; // a test for a Unity component
12     public VariablesTest myCustomScript; // a test for a custom component
13
14     // Use this for initialization
15     void Start () {
16
17     }
18
19     // Update is called once per frame
20     void Update (){...}
23  }
24
```

Figure 5-20. The new comments in the script

Exploring Functions

Variables are pretty much useless unless you do something with them. This is where functions come into play. Functions come in a few different varieties, differentiated by how and when they are called. Some are called or evaluated continually. Some are called only when triggered by certain events, and some are called on demand from inside other functions. Their contents contain instructions to carry out the functionality in your game.

Introducing the Start Function

The two most common functions, and therefore included in the C# template, are the Start and Update functions. Let's begin by examining the Start function. It is one of a small number of functions that are called only at the start of the game or when an object is instantiated or created during runtime (e.g., when it is started). The Awake function, another, is called before the Start function and is often where you will have to find and identify objects that are inactive at the start of a game, You will use it later in the book as the game progresses. Generally, the Start function is the one you will use most often.

Function syntax is fairly simple. There are basically four parts (Figure 5-21). The return type, the function name, the argument list (inside the parentheses), and the code that does the work between the curly brackets.

```
15      void Start () {
16
17      }
```

Figure 5-21. The Start *function on lines 15–17*

In the Start function, the first word is void. It is a reserved word (you may not use it as a variable or function name), and it tells you if a function will return a value. If it is void, that means that no value will be returned.

The next word is the name of the function. In Unity, the convention is to capitalize the first character of function names. Just as with variable and script names, you may not use spaces but may use CamelCase or underscores. Reserved words may not be used either—if it turns blue, add an extra character to the name to change it slightly.

In the parentheses, you will find arguments if the function uses them, The parentheses are mandatory, but the arguments in side them are optional. An example of use of an argument could be a function named PaintMe. It could take an argument of type Color and would change the color of an object (Figure 5-22). An argument is a variable whose *scope* will only be within that particular function.

```
void ColorMe (Color newColor) {
    // some code to change the color of some object to newColor
}
```

Figure 5-22. A function with an argument of type Color*, where the value is assigned to a local variable named newColor*

In the example, the variable newColor is *local* to that function. It is created when the function is called and a Color value is passed into it. When the function has been evaluated, the variable is destroyed, freeing up memory. Your earlier variables' scope makes them available to any functions within the class at any time because they were declared outside of the functions and will exist as long as the instance of the script exists.

The final part of the function syntax is the pair of curly brackets or braces. Like parentheses, they must always exist in pairs. The opening one follows the argument parentheses. It can be on the same line, or even the following line. The formatting style makes no difference to the code but can be an important convention in some companies. You will see it both ways in Unity scripts, so it is worth being aware of (Figure 5-23). The closing bracket aligns with the function on the left. The code between the curly brackets is carried out or evaluated (and acted upon) when and only when the function is called.

```
void Start ()
{

}
```

Figure 5-23. Another valid layout style for curly brackets

Because many syntax errors are caused by orphaned parentheses and curly brackets, the MonoDevelop script editor will automatically show the mate to the selected character.

1. In the script editor, click before or after the opening curly bracket for the Start function. (Do not highlight it.)

The mate to the selected curly bracket is highlighted (Figure 5-24).

```
void Start ()
{

}
```

Figure 5-24. The mate to the opening curly bracket selected when the focus is next to the opening one

2. Repeat the process for one of the parentheses (Figure 5-25).

```
void Start ()
{

}
```

Figure 5-25. The opening parenthesis selected when focus is at the closing one

While it is obvious where the pairs are in this very small and simple script, it is easy to get layers of nested curly brackets in more complicated scripts, so this is a good bit of script editor functionality to remember.

As mentioned earlier, spaces and Tab-overs are optional, but by convention they are used to keep code more readable.

Adding Contents to Functions

Functions generally contain instructions that are used to move the game forward. They may be as simple as assigning a variable's value, or as complex as the instructions that must be carried out if a particular condition is met. They may be equations used to calculate values for variables, or they may be calls to other functions that can be called from several different places. Whatever the purpose of the contents of a function, one of the most valuable means of checking your code is to have values involved printed out to the console as the code is evaluated.

Using "Print to Console"

Earlier in the chapter, you received a few error messages from the console. Now you will put the console to another use by having it print out messages of your own choice. The easiest way to get feedback from your script is to have it print something out to the console. The official way to do that is with Debug.Log(). If you put that line inside the Start function, it will get called once, when the game starts.

1. Add the following inside the curly brackets for the Start function (Figure 5-26):

```
Debug.Log("Hello");
```

```
// Use this for initialization
void Start ()
{
    Debug.Log("Hello");|
}
```

Figure 5-26. The new line in the Start function

Note how the string, *Hello*, is inside quotation marks and is color-coded a nice magenta. If several lines go magenta colored, it's a good indication that you've forgotten a closing quotation mark.

2. Save the script, and click Play.

3. Open the console by clicking the Console tab or double-clicking the status line.

The message was printed out three times, one for each of the objects that has the script on it (Figure 5-27).

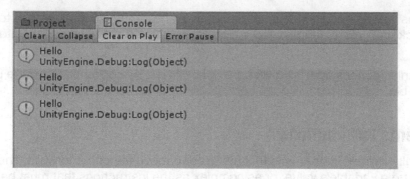

Figure 5-27. The three messages in the console

If you left off the quotation marks around the message and saved the script, you would get an error message that reads "The name 'Hello' does not exist in the current context." But if you replace it with one of your variables, everything is good.

4.   Replace the Debug.Log line with

        Debug.Log(legs);

5.   Save the script, and click Play.

This time you can see the different legs values you entered in the Inspector for each of the three gameObjects (Figure 5-28).

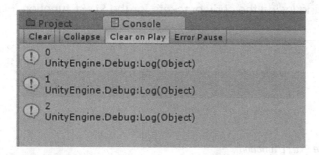

Figure 5-28. The three Legs parameter values

The problem with having the value of the variable printed out is that it is rather cryptic. Fortunately, you can have the best of both character strings and variables.

6.   Change the line to

        Debug.Log("This object has " + legs + " legs.");

7.   Save the script, and click Play.

This time, it is less cryptic (Figure 5-29), but it could be better.

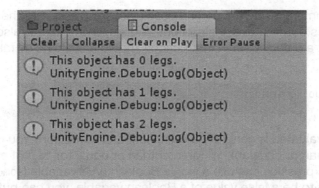

Figure 5-29. The message as a combination of strings and variables

Instead of "object," it would be much better if it used the name of the object the script is on. If you remember, the Object class has a variable called "name." The GameObject class inherits from Object, so you can get the name of the gameObject the script resides on.

8. Change the line to the following:

```
Debug.Log("The " + gameObject.name + " has " + legs + " legs.");
```

9. Save the script, and click Play.

The message is now customized for the object that each instance of the VariablesTest script is on (Figure 5-30).

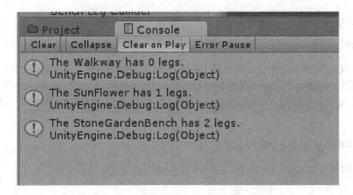

Figure 5-30. The message telling you the name of the object as well as its Legs value

The Conditional

Besides instructions, another extremely common element inside a function will be the *conditional*. The conditional is the logic that often decides how your game will function under differing circumstances.

Two of the messages are perfect, but the Sunflower, with only 1 leg, would be better if the message said *leg* instead of *legs*. Obviously, for a printout in the console it's not an issue, but changing the grammer according to the value of the variable will give you a good opportunity to get familiar with one of the most useful bits of code in a game, the *conditional*, or `if`, statement. The conditional checks to see if the statement inside the parentheses evaluates as `true`. If the statement does evaluate to `true`, it carries out whatever instructions you set for it. There is also an optional `else` clause that can carry out a different set of instructions should it evaluate as false. The syntax roughly is as follows:

```
if (<some expression>) <do something>
else <do something else>
```

The expression that is evaluated is generally a comparison of some sort. You can use < (less than), > (greater than), <= (less than or equal to), >= (greater than or equal to), != (not equal to), == (equivalent to). At its simplest, the expression can use a single Boolean type variable (`someBooleanVariable`). If you want the condition to be a false value of a Boolean variable, you can put a "not" in front of it (`!aBooleanVariable`), which is the exclamation point.

For the message, you will want to check for a `legs` value equivalent to 1. If that condition is met, you may have to do more than one thing. To do that, you can put all of the instructions inside their own "shopping bag," a set of curly brackets. You can do the same for the `else` clause.

1. Replace the line with

```
if (legs == 1) {
    Debug.Log("The " + gameObject.name + " has " + legs + " leg.");
}
else {
    Debug.Log("The " + gameObject.name + " has " + legs + " legs.");
}
```

2. Save the script, and click Play.

This time the message is grammatically correct for any number of legs.

One of the most common tasks carried out in the `Start` function is the initialization of variables, particularly the types than cannot be initialized before the game has begun. Let's take the opportunity to try setting and also initializing a variable in the `Start` function. Setting a non-Unity type variable is easy.

1. Select the code you added in the last section.

2. Right-click and choose Toggle Line Comment(s) (Figure 5-31).

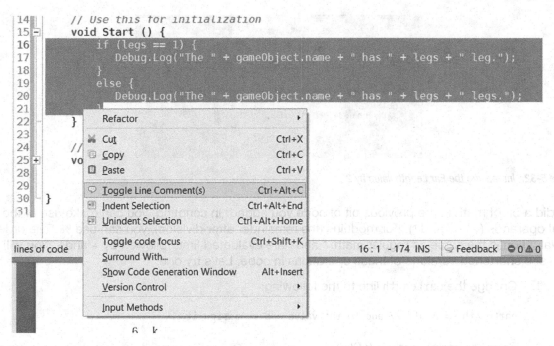

```
14   // Use this for initialization
15 = void Start () {
16       if (legs == 1) {
17           Debug.Log("The " + gameObject.name + " has " + legs + " leg.");
18       }
19       else {
20           Debug.Log("The " + gameObject.name + " has " + legs + " legs.");
21       }
22   }
23
24   //
25 + vo
28
29
30
31 }
```

Refactor ▶

✂ Cut   Ctrl+X
▣ Copy   Ctrl+C
▯ Paste   Ctrl+V

💬 Toggle Line Comment(s)   Ctrl+Alt+C
▦ Indent Selection   Ctrl+Alt+End
▤ Unindent Selection   Ctrl+Alt+Home

Toggle code focus   Ctrl+Shift+K
Surround With...
Show Code Generation Window   Alt+Insert
Version Control   ▶

Input Methods   ▶

lines of code   16 : 1 - 174 INS   💬 Feedback   ⊖0⚠0

Figure 5-31. Commenting out the message code in the Start *function*

Be sure you haven't commented out the closing curly bracket for the Start function.

You will often see an alternate way to print to the console. Instead of using Debug,Log(), you can use print(). Let's use it for the next test.

1. Select each of the three objects with the script, and set their Ear Length parameter to different values.

2. Add a few blank lines above the commented section, and then add the following to re-assign the value of the earLength variable:

```
earLength = earLength + 2.0f; // add to the value and re-assign it
print (earlength);
```

Once the variable has been declared in the script, you only refer to it by its name. For the value, a float, you still must add the *f*. When assigning a value, the item receiving the value is always on the left, the value is on the right, and the assignment operator, =, is used.

3. Save the script, and click Play.

The amounts you set in the inspector have each been incremented by 2 at startup (Figure 5-32). So the order of evaluation is initialized and the variable is overwritten by value set in Inspector, which in turn is overwritten by the value assigned in the Start function. Note that during Play mode, the new values can be seen in the Inspector.

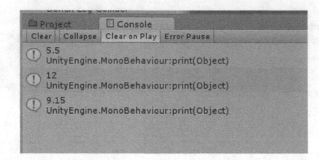

Figure 5-32. Increasing the Ear Length value by 2

You did a bit of math in the previous bit of code you added. In scripting, you can make use of the usual operands (+, -, / and *). For modulus (the remainder after division), you can use %. The order of evaluation is the same as regular math: * and / are evaluated first, followed by + and -. You will often see shortened versions of these operations in code. Let's try one.

1. Change the earLength line to the following:

    ```
    earLength += 2.0f; // add to the value and re-assign it
    ```

2. Save the script, and click Play.

The results are the same.

While numbers, strings, and Booleans are easy to initialize or set up in the Inspector, Unity-specific types take a bit more work. Dragging a single gameObject into a parameter's value field is easy enough, but if you had multiple objects with the same script component that all required the same gameObject, it would become quite tedious. For this scenario, you can let Unity "find" the object by name. This process is relatively slow, so it should be used only in the Start function or after one-off-type events, where speed is not an issue. Let's assign the same gameObject as the Favorite Food to all of the gameObjects with the test script.

1. Select the earLength and print lines, and apply Toggle Line Comments from the right-click menu so they will be ignored.

2. Add the following lines below them:

    ```
    favoriteFood = GameObject.Find("Carrots");
    ```

This time, GameObject is capitalized because you are using the GameObject class's Find() function. Also, because you are using a string to identify the object of the search, the name must be *exactly* as it is in the Hierarchy view. Be especially careful with spaces and capitalization.

3. Now add the following line to print the results:

    ```
    print("The " + gameObject.name + "'s favorite food is " + favoriteFood.name + ".");
    ```

In this line, you are referring to specific gameObjects, so gameObject is not capitalized.

4. Save the script, and click Play.

The messages show that the new value assignment was successful (Figure 5-33).

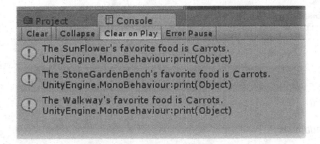

Figure 5-33. The message reflecting the new value for favoriteFood

Identifying a component of known type, such as the Camera, is a matter of adding the component with dot notation. Let's assign the Main Camera to the three test objects.

5.   Add the following code beneath the `print` line:

```
theView = GameObject.Find("Main Camera").camera;
```

Assigning a component that is not listed as a variable for the GameObject class (see Figure 5-17) is handled using `GetComponent()`, a generic function. But because everything must be "typed" in C#, you will have to specify the type rather than just provide the class name. As before, you must also specify which gameObject's component you want. Let's use the Walkway object for this example.

6.   Add the following code beneath the `theView` line:

```
myCustomScript = GameObject.Find("Walkway").GetComponent<VariablesTest>();
```

7.   And now, add a print statement to check the results:

```
print ("The view uses " + theView.gameObject.name);
print ("The script is from the " + myCustomScript.gameObject.name + " object");
```

Note that this time you start with the script, but it's the gameObject's name you want, not the script's name, so you traverse the object hierarchy up to the parent using dot notation before asking for its name, `myCustomScript.gameObject.name`.

8.   Save the script, (Figure 5-34).

```
20  //      favoriteFood = GameObject.Find("Carrots");
21  //      print("The " + gameObject.name + "'s favorite food is " + favoriteFood.name + ".");
22
23          theView = GameObject.Find("Main Camera").camera;
24          myCustomScript = GameObject.Find("Walkway").GetComponent<VariablesTest>();
25
26          print ("The view uses " + theView.gameObject.name);
27          print ("The script is from the " + myCustomScript.gameObject.name + " object");
28
29  //      if (legs == 1) {
30  //          Debug.Log("The " + gameObject.name + " has " + legs + " leg.");
```

Figure 5-34. The script's new additions

9. Click Play.

The messages correctly report the parent object of the components used by the variables (Figure 5-35).

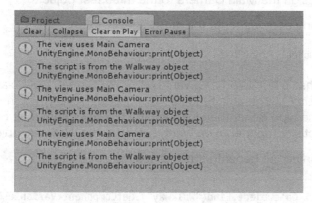

Figure 5-35. The message reporting the camera component's parent, Main Camera, and the specified VariablesTest script component's parent, Walkway

In using GetComponent, you may occasionally come across Unity functions that do not have generic counterparts yet. The nongeneric variant, with typeof([*the component name here*]) may be required. A search of the Unity Manual for "Generic Functions" will give you a C# example of the syntax. In this form, your GetComponent line would look as follows:

```
myCustomScript = (VariablesTest) GameObject.Find("Walkway").GetComponent(typeof(VariablesTest));
```

There are plenty of other things you can do in the Start function, but as with the tests you have just performed, most have to do with identification and initialization.

Using the Update Function

The Update function, also included in the scripting template, is called at least every frame. This is where you will manage things like generic input—a key press, for example. It is also where you can set things to happen over a period of time. As you may expect, code in this function should be kept as efficient as possible.

Let's begin by seeing what happens when you print something to the console from the Update function. The VariablesTest script is on three objects, so you would get everything in triplicate. Now would be a good time to create a new script.

1. Right-click over the Test Scripts folder in the Project view and, from Create, select C# Script.

2. Name it **UpdateTests**.

3. Double-click on it to open it in the script editor.

The new script gets its own tab in the script editor (Figure 5-36).

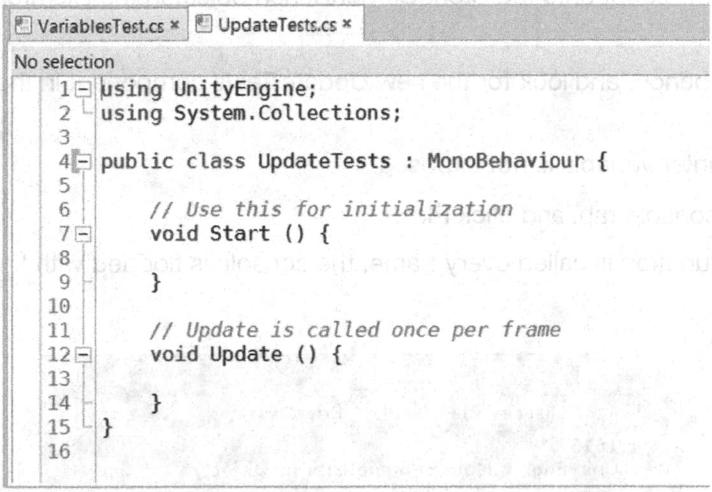

```
VariablesTest.cs ×   UpdateTests.cs ×
No selection
 1  using UnityEngine;
 2  using System.Collections;
 3
 4  public class UpdateTests : MonoBehaviour {
 5
 6      // Use this for initialization
 7      void Start () {
 8
 9      }
10
11      // Update is called once per frame
12      void Update () {
13
14      }
15  }
16
```

Figure 5-36. The new script in the MonoDevelop editor

4. Just below the class declaration, create the following variable:

```
int counter = 1;
```

Note that this variable is not public, so it will not appear in the Inspector.

5. Inside the Update function's opening and closing curly brackets, add the following:

```
counter++; // increment the counter by 1
print (counter);
```

Using ++ to increment a value by one is the most abbreviated way to get the job done (Figure 5-37). You will see it used quite often.

```
    // Update is called once per frame
    void Update () {

        counter++; // increment the counter by 1
        print (counter);

    }
```

Figure 5-37. The new code in the Update function, nicely indented for readability

6. Save the script.

7. Drag the new script onto the StoneGardenBench object in the Hierarchy view.

8. Select the bench, and look for the new Update Tests component in the Inspector.

As expected, the counter variable is not exposed.

9. Open the console tab, and click Play.

Because the Update function is called every frame, the console is flooded with the printouts (Figure 5-38).

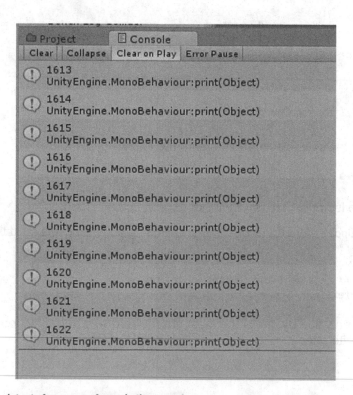

Figure 5-38. The counter printouts from every frame in the console

10. Stop Play mode.

11. Comment out the `counter` and `print` lines in the `Update` function by adding two backslashes in front of them:

```
//counter++; // increment the counter by 1
//print (counter);
```

Having commented out the two counter lines, you will soon discover that Unity will warn you, via the console, that the variable `counter` is never used. For efficiency, you should comment it out as well.

12. Comment out the `int counter = 1` line as well:

```
// int counter = 1;
```

13. Save the script.

A common task to perform in the `Update` function is a *transform*. Remember transforms are move, rotate, and scale. Let's have some fun with the bench.

1. Set the coordinate system to Local.

2. Select the bench, and set its Y Rotation to 180 degrees so that its local Z points toward the gate opening (Figure 5-39).

Figure 5-39. The bench "facing" the opening

In Unity, Z is considered "forward."

3. Add the following lines to the Update function:

```
// Move the object forward along its z axis 1 unit/frame
transform.Translate(Vector3.forward);
```

4. Save the script, and click Play.

The bench quickly scoots out through the gateway. Let's slow it down.

5. Change the transform line as follows:

```
transform.Translate(Vector3.forward * 0.1f);
```

The transform.Translate() function expects floats for its argument, so you must add the *f* to the speed adjustment.

6. Save the script, and click Play.

The bench isn't in quite as much of a hurry to leave the scene this time. But the problem is that it is moving 0.1 units per *frame*. And frame rate varies throughout a game and from device to device. You could put the code in a FixedUpdate function to ensure a constant speed across platforms and throughout the game, but a more common solution is to use Time.deltaTime. This essentially tells the engine to divide the task so that it uses seconds rather than frames. The variable deltaTime is a member of the Time class, so Time (the first one) is capitalized.

7. Change the transform lines as follows:

```
// Move the object forward along its z axis 1 unit/second
transform.Translate(Vector3.forward * Time.deltaTime);
```

8. Save the script, and click Play.

The bench moves at a nice stately pace and heads out the gateway. Typically, though, speed is something that is exposed to let the author adjust at will. Where you had a float number earlier, you can add a variable.

1. Create the new speed variable beneath the counter variable:

```
public float speed = 0.5f;
```

This one is public, so it will be exposed to the Inspector.

1. Change the transform lines as follows:

```
// Move the object forward along its z axis 1 unit/second * speed.
transform.Translate(Vector3.forward * Time.deltaTime * speed);
```

Before you test, remember that most number fields in Unity usually have slider functionality. By positioning the cursor in front of the text box or over its label, you will see the cursor change to include a couple of horizontal arrows. At that point, you can mouse down and move the mouse left and right to increase or decrease the value quickly.

2. Save the script, and click Play.

3. Adjust the Speed parameter in the Inspector with the slider functionality.

This time, you can set the bench to moving back and forth at varying speeds.

Game scripting consists of a lot of problem solving. No matter how detailed the design docs (formal, or a bunch of scribbled notes) are, there are bound to be surprises. In this little exercise, you may have noticed that the bench intersects the gateway as it leaves the garden. Let's try a couple of solutions.

The first uses physics to prevent the intersection. It's not a very good solution for this scenario, but it is entertaining.

1. Stop Play mode.

2. In the Inspector, set the Speed to about 2 to liven things up a bit.

3. From Components, Physics, add a Rigidbody component to the bench.

4. Move the bench group over so its trajectory will cause it to hit the corner of the Raised Bed.

5. Click Play.

The poor bench struggles to get past the corner of the raised bed. Increasing the speed bounces it quickly out of the scene.

6. Stop Play mode.

7. Right-click over the Rigidbody label in the Inspector, and remove Component.

This time, you will get a chance to use a "flag" to control which code gets evaluated in the Update function. You will first have the bench rotate into position, and then allow it to move off. You will start by creating a Boolean variable that functions as a flag or keeper of state. A Boolean-type variable can be true or false. It is the most economical, as it takes up only 1 byte of memory.

1. Add the following variable to your script:

```
bool allClear = false; // flag to activate the translate
```

The Bench's y Rotation value is currently 180 degrees, so as soon as it goes past 270, it should stop rotating:

2. In the Update function, *above* the Translate code, add the code that will rotate the bench:

```
//rotate the object on the world Y or up axis if the y rotation is less than 270 degrees
if(transform.localEulerAngles.y < 270) {
    transform.Rotate(Vector3.up * Time.deltaTime * 20f, Space.World); // speed it up by 20f
}
```

Once the bench has rotated 180 degrees, the `allClear` variable will eventually be set to true, so the bench will once again move. Having been rotated, though, it will have to move on its X axis, or `Vector3.Right`. Left is the negative, `-Vector3.Right`. The bench will have to move to its left unless you want to reverse the direction it turns in.

3.   "Wrap" the `Translate` line with a conditional to check the state of the `allClear` variable:

```
if (allClear) {
    transform.Translate(-Vector3.right * Time.deltaTime * speed);
}
```

The `allClear` variable, because it is a Boolean type of true or false, is all you need in the conditional. The conditional, if you remember, evaluates the contents to see if they return `true` or `false`.

4.   Click Play, and watch the bench's y Rotation in the Inspector or in the console.

The y Rotation is slightly past 270 degrees when it stops, which gives you a good condition to meet to set the `allClear` flag to `true` and set the y Rotation exactly to 270 at the same time. While this may sound simple, rotation is actually fairly complicated. If your bench falls off of the walkway just as it completes its rotation, feel free to move it forward slightly when you are not in Play mode.

It can be managed using quaternion math, where the direction is a simple vector or direction, or it can be handled with Euler angles where it is split into x, y, and z rotations. The latter option is generally easier for most people to deal with, but it comes with several issues, such as order of evaluation and gimble lock. (That's a good term to Google if you've never heard it before.).

Another problem comes with *setting* a transform value (as opposed to *animating*, which is what you have been doing so far). In C#, you must create a temporary variable to manage the transform. In Unity's version of JavaScript, you can set a value directly (e.g., `transform.position.y = 5.5`), but apparently it is doing the same process under the hood. Let's add the code and then examine it closer.

5.   Below the rotation code and above the translate code, add the following:

```
// adjust the rotation and set the allClear flag if over 270
if(transform.localEulerAngles.y > 270) {
    Vector3 rot = transform.localEulerAngles; // create a temp variable to store the rotation
    rot.y = 270f;                             // change the y part of the variable
    transform.localEulerAngles = rot;         // update the rotation to the temp variable's value
    allClear = true;                          // set the flag to true
}
```

The two new bits that aren't covered by the comments are the first line of instructions for when the condition is met. The `transform.localEulerAngles` is how you handle the object's rotation using the local x, y, z values. Another version, `transform.rotation`, uses quaternion rotation, and under the hood, that is what Unity uses regardless of which type of rotation you use. The other new bit here is the Vextor3 type. This is a three-part variable where the component parts (x,y,z) can be accessed and changed using dot notation. So the first line uses the temporary variable to store the object's current Euler rotation values, and then the next line changes only the y value. The last line feeds the updated value back to the object. Now that you have set the bench straight, it is now safe to set the allClear flag to true so the Translate code can send the bench on its merry way.

6. Save the script, and click Play.

This time, the bench rotates into position and then heads out through the gate (Figure 5-40).

Figure 5-40. The bench, showing local coordinates, leaving the garden (Scene view)

At this point, you can add the Rigidbody component again and watch it fall as it goes out the gate. Feel free to adjust the bench's position for a better trajectory out of the gateway.

1. Add a Rigidbody component to the bench.

2. Click Play, and watch (or help) it head out the gateway.

Making Use of Event-Based Functions

So far you've checked out common functionality in the Start function, where the code is evaluated only on startup, and in the Update function, where it is evaluated every frame. Event-based functions, however, make up the bulk of predefined functions available for use.

1. Search the Scripting Reference for MonoBehaviour.

The Messages list shows what functions will receive "messages" or be *called* when their condition is met (Figure 5-41).

Messages	
Awake	Awake is called when the script instance is being loaded.
FixedUpdate	This function is called every fixed framerate frame, if the MonoBehaviour is enabled.
LateUpdate	LateUpdate is called every frame, if the Behaviour is enabled.
OnAnimatorIK	Callback for setting up animation IK (inverse kinematics).
OnAnimatorMove	Callback for processing animation movements for modifying root motion.
OnApplicationFocus	Sent to all game objects when the player gets or loses focus.
OnApplicationPause	Sent to all game objects when the player pauses.
OnApplicationQuit	Sent to all game objects before the application is quit.
OnAudioFilterRead	If OnAudioFilterRead is implemented, Unity will insert a custom filter into the audio DSP chain.
OnBecameInvisible	OnBecameInvisible is called when the renderer is no longer visible by any camera.
OnBecameVisible	OnBecameVisible is called when the renderer became visible by any camera.
OnCollisionEnter	OnCollisionEnter is called when this collider/rigidbody has begun touching another rigidbody/collider.
OnCollisionEnter2D	Sent when an incoming collider makes contact with this object's collider (2D physics only).
OnCollisionExit	OnCollisionExit is called when this collider/rigidbody has stopped touching another rigidbody/collider.
OnCollisionExit2D	Sent when a collider on another object stops touching this object's collider (2D physics only).
OnCollisionStay	OnCollisionStay is called once per frame for every collider/rigidbody that is touching rigidbody/collider

Figure 5-41. *A few of the "Messages" that are used as functions*

Different types of games will use different callbacks. A classic adventure game will use OnMouseDown() to track the user picking various items in the scene. First-person shooters, will make heavy use of OnCollisionEnter(), where physics control a lot of the action. Let's do a few tests to see how they work.

Using Collisions to Call Functions

OnCollisionEnter() and its close relative OnTriggerEnter() are a mainstay of most 3D games. The first allows you to set off events like explosions, audio, and special effects when objects collide. The second is a bit more subtle, letting you trigger events or change states when the object passes through the (usually invisible) object.

The trickiest part about using either function is that the triggering object, at least, must contain a Rigidbody component. This may not sound like an issue—after all, projectiles usually contain Rigidbody components. When they hit something, a lot of events can be triggered. The problem comes when trying to use, say, the First Person Controller to trigger something. The First Person Controller doesn't contain a true Rigidbody component, as several of its physics-type properties are rolled into its Character Controller component. The newer First Person Character prefab (not yet available as a standard asset) will help to solve this issue, as it contains an actual Rigidbody component. The important thing to remember is that at least one of the objects must contain a Rigidbody component.

The bench will serve nicely for some preliminary tests, so let's begin.

1. Right-click over the Test Scripts folder in the Project view and, from Create, select C# Script.

2. Name it **ColliderTests**.

3. Double-click on it to open it in the script editor.

4. Below the Update function, add the following:

```csharp
void OnCollisionEnter () {
    print ("Ouch!");
}
```

With C#, it doesn't really matter what order your functions are in the script, but the convention is to put event-driven and custom functions below the Start and Update functions.

5.   Save the script, and drag it onto the bench.

6.   Comment out the 3 print lines in the VariablesTest script, and save the script.

7.   Center the bench on the Walkway Center object.

8.   Click Play.

The console will print "ouch" once on startup, once as it hits the long walkway, and once when it goes onto the slightly raised walkway piece under the Gateway. It would be better if you could tell what it collided with so you could customize the message. Fortunately, it turns out that you can. Many functions can be used in different configurations.

9.   Search the Scripting Reference for MonoBehaviour.OnCollisionEnter.

The function can take an *argument* of type Collision (Figure 5-42).

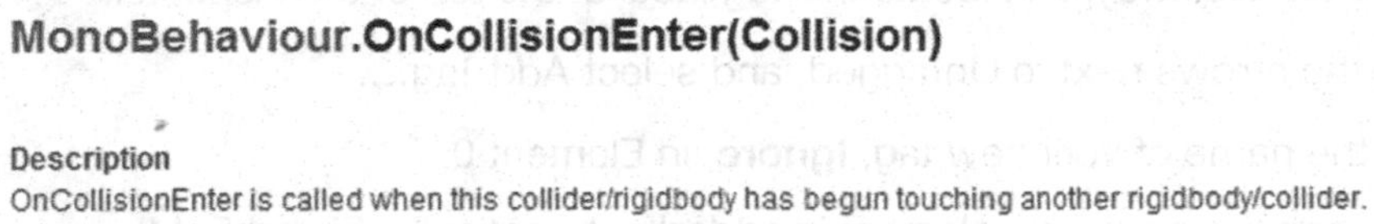

MonoBehaviour.OnCollisionEnter(Collision)

Description
OnCollisionEnter is called when this collider/rigidbody has begun touching another rigidbody/collider.

Figure 5-42. OnCollisionEnter's argument type

10. Click on the Collision type in the example (or search for collision) to see what information it stores.

Among the variables, you will see gameObject. This means you can get the object, and therefore, its name property.

11. Return to the ColliderTests script.

12. Change the OnCollisionEnter code as follows:

```
void OnCollisionEnter (Collision theVictim) {
    print (theVictim.gameObject.name + " got hit");
}
```

The variable, theVictim, of type Collision, is used to get the name of the gameObject the bench hits.

13. Save the script, and click Play.

This time, you can see that it is the collider-containing walkway objects that are triggering the print statement (Figure 5-43). Ideally, you would like to be able to exclude certain objects from causing any reactions. If there was only one object, you could check it by name, but there are three different objects that it would be nice to exclude.

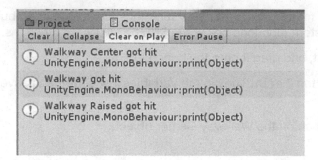

Figure 5-43. The more specific collision report

Using Tags

Unity has a way of marking, or "tagging," gameObjects so you can filter results from events like collisions. If you look at the top left of the Inspector, just below the name, with an object from the Hierarchy selected, you will see a property called Tag.

1. Select the Walkway, and locate the Tag label at the top of the Inspector.

2. Click the arrows next to Untagged, and select Add Tag….

3. Type the name of your new tag, **Ignore**, in Element 0.

As soon as you start typing, a new element is added automatically (Figure 5-44).

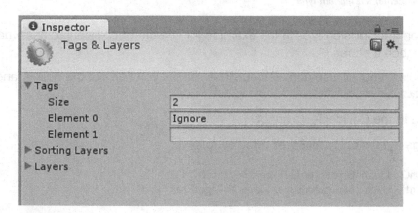

Figure 5-44. The newly created tab, Ignore

4. Select each of the walkway objects and the Raised Bed, and select Ignore for each from the Tag drop-down menu.

5. Activate the Cube that should be blocking the Gateway. If it's not blocking the Gateway, move it into place (Figure 5-45).

Figure 5-45. The Cube reactivated and blocking the doorway

6. In the script, change the code to filter for the tag:

```
void OnCollisionEnter (Collision theVictim) {
    if (theVictim.gameObject.tag != "Ignore") {
        print (theVictim.gameObject.name + " got hit");
    }
}
```

Now the message will print only if the hit object does *not* (!=) have the *Ignore* tag.

7. Save the script.

8. Set the bench's Speed back to **0.5**.

9. Click Play, and watch the console.

This time, only the Cube is reported as being hit.

Creating User-Defined Functions

You may wonder why the bench is not moving the Cube. The reason is that the Cube does not have a Rigidbody component but does contain a collider. Once the bench runs into the Cube, it is no longer able to go forward even though its code is telling it to do so.

Ideally, it would be more efficient to turn off the code that tells the bench to go forward when it can no longer go forward. The great thing is that all you will have to do is set the allClear flag back to false. But that will mean contacting the other script. That is the essence of interaction in Unity: the communication between scripts, whether they are on the same gameObject or on other gameObjects.

There are several ways to accomplish the communication, but for this example, you will be using SendMessage(). It sends a message to (or calls) a function on another script and can take an argument to send on as well.

For the function it calls, you will make a user-defined function that will change the value of a new flag in the UpdateTests script.

1. In the script editor, switch to the UpdateTests script.

2. Create a new variable beneath the existing variable declarations:

    ```
    public bool stopIt = false; // flag to stop translate after object is underway
    ```

3. Below the Update function, just above the closing curly bracket for the class, add the following:

    ```
    void ToggleStopIt (bool newState) {

        stopIt = newState; // update the variable's state
    }
    ```

Function naming conventions are similar to variable naming conventions except that, in Unity, you should always capitalize the first character of the name. As with variable names, you cannot use a number or most special characters for its first character, and you cannot have any spaces in the name.

4. Add the new variable as another condition to the Translate conditional:

    ```
    // Move the object forward along its z axis 1 unit/second.
    if (allClear && !stopIt) {
        transform.Translate(-Vector3.right * Time.deltaTime * speed);
    }
    ```

The && means "and," so *each* condition must be true for the entire expression to evaluate as true. The exclamation point negates the value of the variable it precedes. In this conditional, allClear must be true *and* stopIt must be false (which makes !stopIt true). Conditionals can also use the or operator, ||. The statements in between the && and || are always evaluated first.

5. Save the script.

6. Return to the ColliderTests script.

7. Search for SendMessage in the Scripting Reference.

The description says "Calls the method named methodName on every MonoBehaviour in this game object." *Method* is another name for *function*, and a MonoBehaviour is a script. (Remember the default name of newly created scripts.) Both of the scripts are on the bench, so you won't have to specify a different gameObject than the one the script is on.

8. Inside the OnCollisionEnter function, under the print statement, add the following:

   gameObject.SendMessage("ToggleStopIt", true);

9. Save the script.

10. Click Play.

11. Switch to the Scene view, and select the Cube.

12. When the bench stops at it, move it up clear of the bench.

13. Do not exit Play mode yet.

The bench does not move forward when the Cube is moved out of the way.

14. Now select the bench in the Hierarchy view.

15. In the Inspector, toggle the Stop It parameter off.

The bench moves forward once again and goes over the edge.

As a last little test, you can try the OnTriggerExit function. You may remember the Is Trigger parameter in the collider components. It lets the object detect intersection without functioning as a barrier. Because the script stops the forward movement, let's use OnTriggerExit() instead of OnTriggerEnter(). That way, you can see the bench going through the collider instead of being blocked by it at first touch.

1. In the ColliderTests script, copy the entire OnCollisionEnter block of code and paste it below the original.

2. Modify the first line as follows:

   void OnTriggerExit (Collider theVictim) {

Note the *Collider* type for the argument instead of *Collision*.

3. Save the script.

4. Select the Cube.

5. Check Is Trigger in its Box Collider component.

6. Disable its Mesh Renderer.

7. Click Play, and turn on Gizmos on the right side of the Game view's tool bar.

The bench trundles through the Cube's collider and stops just as it starts to leave on the other side (Figure 5-46).

Figure 5-46. The OnTriggerExit event triggering the code that stops the bench from moving

       8.   Save the Scene, and save the project.

With a few scripting basics under your belt, most of the rest of the scripting you do will be for the game.

Summary

In this chapter, you got your first look at scripting in Unity with C#. You found that when you created a new script, it came partially set up with the class it represented already defined and the two most common functions blocked in and ready to use. You learned that all Unity scripts derived from a built-in class named MonoBehaviour and that scripts are where you will control most of the functionality in your games. Scripts, you discovered, when added to gameObjects, became components.

Your first experiments were with variables, where you learned that besides the regular types (number, strings, and Booleans), Unity gameObjects and components could also be types. You learned the rules and Unity conventions for naming scripts, variables, and, later, functions. You discovered that variables could be hidden or exposed in the Inspector and that values added there replaced any that were initialized with the variable declarations. With Unity-specific types, you learned to assign the values; you either had to drag the gameObject onto the parameter in the Inspector or let the engine "find" the one you wanted in the Start function. Some components, you found, came already predefined as accessible from your gameObjects, while others, especially any custom scripts, had to be defined by type before they could be identified for later access.

The Start function, you learned, was a great place to initialize and even override values in the Inspector because it is only read once—at start up. As you experimented with the variables, you made use of the console, both to help troubleshoot errors and to report on the state of your variables through the use of the print and Debug.Out functions. Comments, you found, could be used to leave notes about your code and to disable code.

Continuing with functions, you discovered the MonoDevelop script editor helped you with both syntax and layout as you began to write code that made use of your earlier variables. You got quite a bit of practice with the if conditional as you learned how to control which code was used in the Update function that is called or evaluated every frame. Variables storing the state of things were especially useful as flags in that particular scenario. You also discovered Time.deltaTime, the main ingredient to turn frame time into seconds when animating things in the Update function.

Finally, using SendMessage, you were able to send a message from one script after an event-driven function was triggered, to affect the functionality of the parent gameObject from another script. In doing so, you also designed your first user-defined function. The main concept, you found, was that it was crucial for scripts to be able to communicate with other scripts, both on the same gameObject and on any others, to control functionality in your game.

Mecanim and Animation

While some games have no characters whatsoever, a great number feature compelling characters that drive both story and game play. A major part of their appeal and entertainment value comes from their animation. Unity's Mecanim character-animation system is arguably one of the features that pushes it seriously toward the realm of AAA title game development. In this chapter, you will delve into some character set up and control, as well as traditional mechanical animation of non-character objects.

The Story

To give you an idea where this odd collection of assets is leading, it's time to review the game's little scenario. It's simple. You have a garden where you have a delicious selection of vegetables. But you have a problem. The garden is being overrun by a horde of voracious zombie bunnies. As a last resort, you've ordered a kit from the Internet that will turn a simple plaster garden gnome into a potato-gun-wielding Garden Defender. Potatoes for ammunition are no problem, but the car battery that runs your first line of defense has limited juice. The zombie bunnies multiply at will, so you must make the best use of the "Gnomatic" device to eradicate them before the charge runs out on the battery. The appearance of a psychedelic slug speeding through the garden heralds the chance of extending the life of the battery.

Importing Animated Assets

You've already imported several static assets for your game and have a basic understanding of scale factor, managing textures, and adding colliders. This time, however, you will also be defining animation clips and preparing animated characters for use in your scene. Let's begin by importing the new assets. As before, the safest way to ensure proper material generation is to bring the textures in first.

1. Open the Garden scene from the previous chapter.

2. Save the scene as **GardenSetUp**.

3. From the Chapter 6 Assets folder, drag the Character Textures folder into the Project view or the Assets folder in the Explorer or Finder.

4. Using either method, bring the Animated Assets folder in next.

5. Open the Animated Assets folder in the Project view to inspect the new additions (Figure 6-1).

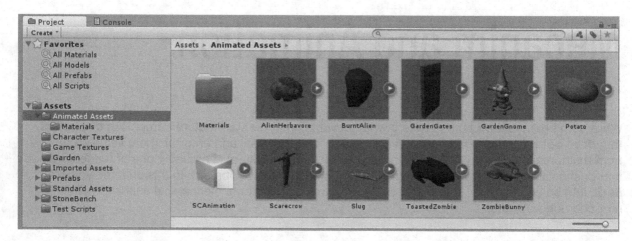

Figure 6-1. *The new assets*

You will find a garden gnome, a scarecrow, a zombie bunny, a psychedelic slug, some garden gates, and a couple of dead replacement meshes.

Legacy Animation

Unity offers several different options for animation. For mechanical-type animation where the object doesn't have an idle animation but is occasionally triggered, like a door opening, Legacy is the quickest to set up and use. Eventually, Unity may phase this one out, but for now it remains the animation type of choice for simple, one-off mechanical animations.

1. Select the GardenGates object in the Animated Assets folder.

2. In the Inspector, select the Rig section.

3. For Animation Type, select Legacy and click Apply.

4. Select the Animations tab.

The default animation from the object, Take 001, is already loaded as an animation clip (Figure 6-2).

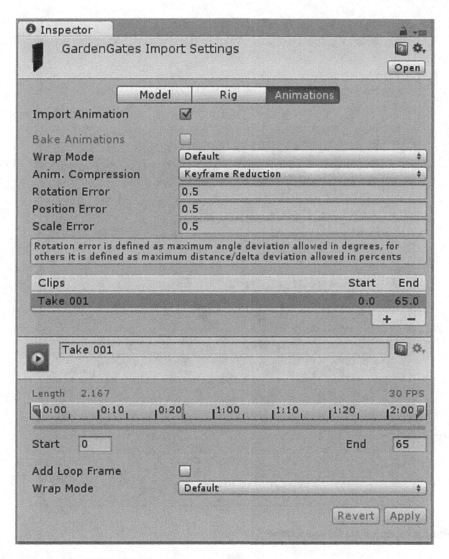

Figure 6-2. The imported asset's default animation clip

5.   Click Play in the Preview window to see the animation (Figure 6-3).

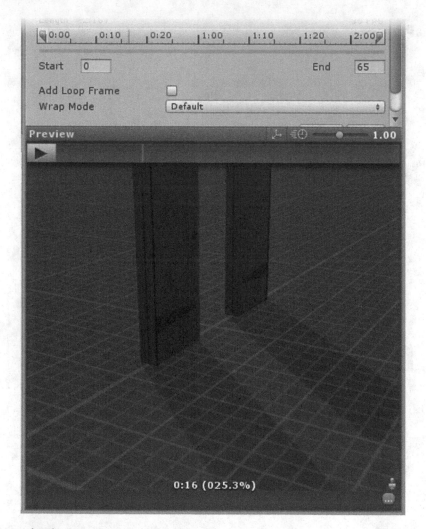

Figure 6-3. The doors animating in the Preview window

The doors start out closed and are fully open at frame 30. At frame 35, they start to close and are fully closed at frame 65. When you drag the time slider in either the time bar or the Preview window, the time (in seconds) of the current clip segment is shown with the remainder in frames. When Unity imports a file, it keeps track of the frames per second used in the application it was animated in. The assets you just imported were animated using 30 frames per second.

6.   Rename Take 001 to **door open**.

7.   Just below the time line, set the End value to **30**.

8.   Click the plus sign at the lower right of the Clip section to add a new clip (Figure 6-4).

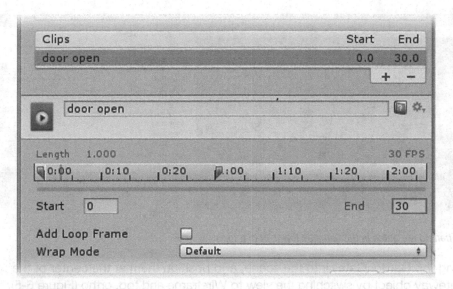

Figure 6-4. The Clip list, adding a new clip

9. Name the new clip **door close**.

10. Set its Start value to **35** and leave its End value at **65**.

11. Click Apply to finish the setup.

Tip Always name your clips with unique names, as there will be times when you will be required to choose from all available clips. Most characters will have an idle and a walk or run. Make sure you will be able to identify the correct one.

The legacy animation automatically adds an Animation component to the object (Figure 6-5). The first clip is loaded as the default clip, and the clip is set to Play Automatically when the scene starts.

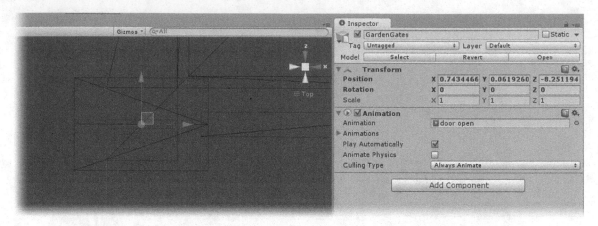

Figure 6-5. Positioning the gates in the Gateway tower from a top view

1. Drag the GardenGates into the scene, and position them at the center of the Gateway object by switching the view to Wireframe and top, ortho (Figure 6-5).

2. Return the Scene view to "perspective" and "Textured."

3. Click Play, and watch the *door open* animation play on start up.

With the Animation component, the object defaults to its position at frame 0.

4. Stop Play mode.

5. Select the GardenGates, and expand its hierarchy.

6. Uncheck Play Automatically.

7. In the Hierarchy view, add a Box collider to Gate 1, Gate 2, and the GardenGates.

8. Adjust the GardenGates collider until it fills the opening and protrudes slightly beyond the opening (Figure 6-6).

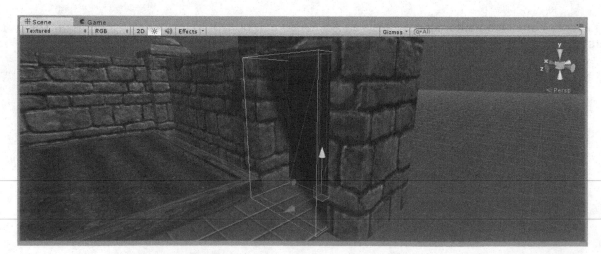

Figure 6-6. The GardenGates collider adjusted

9. Turn on the GardenGates collider component's `Is Trigger` parameter.

Next you will create a small script to trigger the gates' animation so the doors will open and close when the garden defender enters and exits the collider. It is very similar to the last script you created in Chapter 5. Once it confirms that the object triggering it is tagged as Player, it will trigger the animation.

1. Create a new folder in the Assets folder, and name it **Game Scripts**.

2. Create a new C# script in it, and name it **SensorDoors**.

3. Open it in the script editor, and add the following two variables below the class declaration:

```
public AnimationClip clipOpen; // the open animation
public AnimationClip clipClose; // the close animation
```

4. Below the `Update` function, add an `OnTriggerEnter()` function:

```
// open the gates
void OnTriggerEnter (Collider defender) {
   if (defender.gameObject.tag == "Player") {
      animation.Play(clipOpen.name);
   }
}
```

5. Duplicate the `OnTriggerEnter` code, and adjust it for an `OnTriggerExit`:

```
// close the gates
void OnTriggerExit (Collider defender) {
   if (defender.gameObject.tag == "Player") {
      animation.Play(clipClose.name);
   }
}
```

This script will go on the GardenGates object that also contains the Animation component, so you can trigger the animation clip you want with only the component name and the `Play()` function. The clip is actually accessed by name, so you must use `.name`. Feel free to look up "animation.Play" in the Scripting Reference.

1. Save the script, and drag it onto the GardenGates object.

2. Change the bench's tag to Player from the drop-down Tag list.

3. To prevent the bench from stopping at the gateway, delete the Cube.

You might think that disabling the ColliderTests script will keep it from doing anything, but the only things it turns off for certain are `Start` and `Awake` functions.

4. Remove the ColliderTests script from the StoneGardenBench object.

5. Select the GardenGates object, and load the two animation clips into the Clip Open and Clip Close parameters using the browse icon at the far right of each.

6. Set the Speed parameter on the bench to about **3** to ensure that the bench won't get stuck on the walkway.

7. Click Play, and watch as the doors open to let the bench through and close after it leaves.

Adding Audio

If you are a *Star Trek* fan, you are probably thinking that the animation needs a nice sound effect to top it off. Playing an audio clip is similar to playing an animation clip, and an audio clip usually accompanies an animation.

1. Select the GardenGates object, and add an Audio Source component to it from the Component, Audio menu (Figure 6-7).

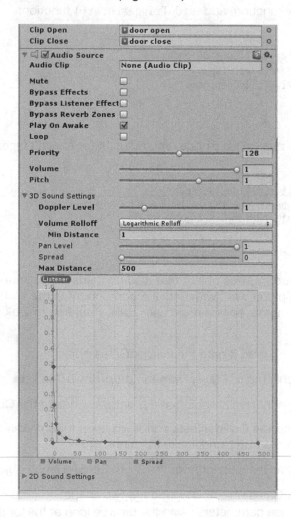

Figure 6-7. The new Audio component

Audio clips are imported into Unity as 3D sounds by default. With the Volume Rolloff set to Logarithmic Rolloff, the clip will be pretty much gone at 50 meters. (See the bottom of the graph in Figure 6-7.) It should be audible in this small scene, but if not, you can increase the Max Distance, adjust the curve, or change the Volume Rolloff to Linear Rolloff.

2.   Just to make sure you can hear the clip, change the Volume Rolloff to Linear Rolloff.

3.   Uncheck the "Play on Awake" option.

4.   Drag the Sound FX folder into the Project view from the Chapter 6 Assets folder.

5.   Load the Chest Open audio clip into the Audio Clip parameter.

Unity converts most sound clips into the .ogg format for desktop and web deployments. Ogg files are an open source mpeg-like format. For mobile, Unity generally uses mpeg format. The mpeg license is covered for mobile by the hardware manufacturers and is hardware accelerated.

Feel free to add more sound effects to the project. Many are free to use but cannot be redistributed, so the project only comes with a few. You must have one Audio Listener in the scene to be able to play audio clips. Remember to remove extra Audio Listeners whenever you add Cameras to your scenes. You can click on the audio clips in the Project view to hear the clips play.

Next you will add a few lines of code to include your sound effect. In this case, you can use the same sound for open and close.

6.   In the SensorDoors script, beneath the `animation.Play()` code in each of the `OnTrigger...` functions, add the following:

```
audio.Play(); // play the clip loaded in the audio component
```

7.   Save the script, and click Play.

The bench heads through the gateway accompanied by the new sound effect. With the animated gates working well, you will want to create a prefab to go with the rest of your modular garden pieces.

8.   Drag the GardenGates object into the Prefabs, Structures folder.

9.   Deactivate the bench.

Mecanim

With Unity's Mecanim animation system, character animation is the main focus. There are three main parts of Mecanim: The importer, where you can manipulate the animation clips to alter or refine the raw imported animation, the Rig section, where you can 'map', or retarget animation from one character to another as long as they are both humanoid, and the Animator Controller, Mecanim's state engine, where animation states are set up to blend between each other according to various criteria. Additionally, Mecanim's masking system lets you isolate body parts and blend animations between multiple sources for complex combinations on demand. If you are a Pro user, you can even set up IK (inverse kinematics) to override baked animations so the characters can interact with other objects in the scene dynamically.

> ## KINEMATICS
>
> Kinematics, for those of you without a background in character animation, is the means of posing the character at key positions to create the animation. With inverse kinematics, a child object in the hierarchy controls the position and rotation of the parent objects in the hierarchy. In FK (forward kinematics), the parents control the children's location and orientation. An example would be an arm hierarchy. To position the your hand at a particular place using FK, you would individually rotate your upper arm, lower arm and wrist into position. With an IK linkage, if you use your other hand to position your wrist, your forearm and upper arm will automatically be adjusted into place according to the the rotational constraints on their joints.

Generic Rigs

While the full power of Mecanim is realized only with humanoid characters, you will still be able to benefit from many of Mecanim's features by using Generic rigs. To use the Humanoid Animation Type, a character must have at least 11 bones and be roughly humanoid. Anything else will have to use the Generic Animation Type option. This is useful for minimal characters, animals, and anything else that has at least an idle animation.

For your introduction to Mecanim, you will set up a ZombieBunny from the Animation Imports folder. These brainless eating machines have one goal: to eat all the plants in your garden! They have a very simple animation: they chew and they move forward as they chew. The ZombieBunny asset is a good size for a real bunny, but a zombie bunny should be larger and more of a threat (and an easier target). If you can't bring yourself to destroy even zombie bunnies, feel free to substitute the AlienHerbavore for the ZombieBunny for the book's project.

1. Select the ZombieBunny from the Character Imports folder.

2. In the Model section, increase its Scale Factor to **.015**.

3. In the Rig section, set the Root Node to Bunny Motion Root (Figure 6-8).

Figure 6-8. The Root node of the ZombieBunny

The Root node is the node of the object that moves it in the scene. With Mecanim, that velocity can be used to move the object or turned off to let outside sources move the object. Transforms on children of the node will continue to work as animated.

4. Click Apply.

5. In the Animations section, rename Take 001 to **Bunny Eat**.

6. Click Play in the Preview window to watch the animation.

In the Legacy animation, objects go into the scene at the first frame of their imported animation. Mecanim is just the opposite; those objects will go into the scene at their final frame's position. If the object has a run or walk behavior and the final frame was at the end of that transform, the object will be offset to that location when you put it into the scene. The problem comes when you try to fit a collider to it. The collider will be (and must be) at the start location, making it difficult to get it properly aligned. To avoid this problem, the final five or so frames of the total animation should putting the character or object back to its starting position.

In the ZombieBunny's animation, the last 10 frames are used to return it to its start position, so they must be cropped from the animation for it to loop properly.

7. Set the End value of the clip to **110**.

8. Check Loop Time to set the clip's wrap mode to loop.

9. Check "Bake Into Pose" for "Root Transform Position (Y)" (Figure 6-9).

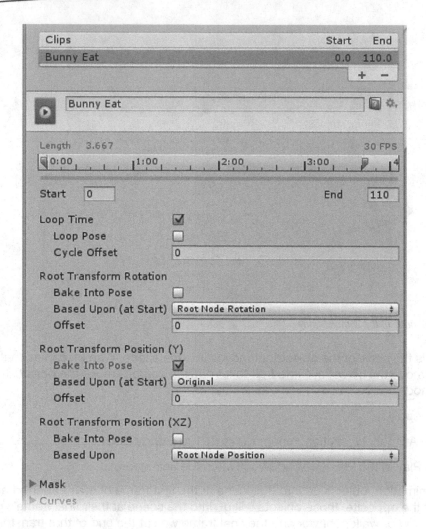

Figure 6-9. The new clip parameters with Mecanim and a Generic rig

When the transforms are used to move the character through the scene, they are relative repeats—they are additive. If there is even a small upward movement (the Y direction) in the animation, the character will start to drift upwards. This setting blocks the Y direction from being additive. For a jump animation, it would not be checked.

10.   Click Apply at the bottom of the panel.

The next part of setting up for Mecanim is done with the object in the scene. Before doing that, it's worth looking in the Project view to see what makes up the asset.

1.   In the Project view, slide the thumbnail slider to the far left to see icons instead of thumbnails.

2.   Click the arrow to open the ZombieBunny asset in the project view (Figure 6-10).

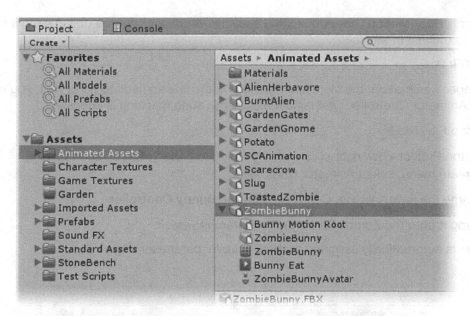

Figure 6-10. The contents of the ZombieBunny asset, including the new clip and a ZombieBunny Avatar

The avatar was generated with the Generic Mecanim rig.

    3.   Drag the ZombieBunny asset into the scene.

    4.   In the Inspector, you will see the Animator component that was also generated (Figure 6-11).

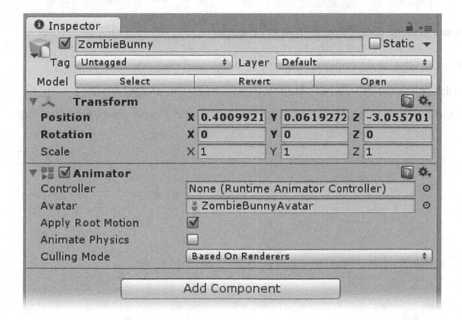

Figure 6-11. The Animator component with the avatar preloaded

Note the "Apply Root Motion" check box. This specifies whether or not the object's roots transforms will be used to move it in the scene.

5. Click Play.

Unlike the Legacy animation, the Mecanim rigs do not animate immediately. For that, you will need to create an Animator Controller. That is how Mecanim's state machine is accessed.

6. Stop Play Mode.

7. In the Project view, right-click over the Animated Assets folder, and from the Create menu, select Animator Controller.

8. Name the new Animator Controller **Zombie Bunny Controller**.

9. Drag it onto the ZombieBunny in the Hierarchy view.

The controller is automatically assigned to the Controller parameter (Figure 6-12).

Figure 6-12. The new Animator Controller in the Animator component

Now you can set up the state engine. This one is easy, as it only has one state.

1. Double-click on the Zombie Bunny Controller in the project view.

The Animator view opens in a new tab next to the Scene and Game views (Figure 6-13).

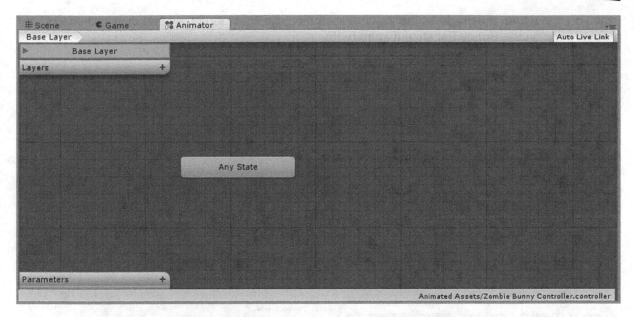

Figure 6-13. The Animator view of the Mecanim state machine

The controller currently showing is listed at the lower right of the window.

To add a state, you can right-click and choose Add New State, or you can drag a clip directly into the window. The latter approach sets the name for you and will save a few steps.

   2.   Drag the Bunny Eat clip into the Animator view.

A default state (it is orange colored) is created, named, and preloaded with the Bunny Eat animation (Figure 6-14).

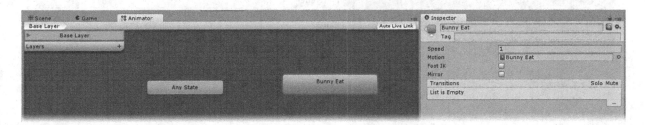

Figure 6-14. The default Bunny Eat state

The Speed, 1, denotes the original speed of the clip. A speed of .5 would be half as fast, and 2 would be twice as fast.

   3.   Click Play, and watch the ZombieBunny in the Game view.

The ZombieBunny will slowly work its way along the walkway, munching as it goes.

   4.   Select it in the Hierarchy view, and switch back to the Animator view.

Now you can watch the progress through the animation clip as it loops over and over in the blue progress bar on the Bunny Eat state (Figure 6-15).

Figure 6-15. The Bunny Eat clip's progress showing in the state

Before you turn the ZombieBunny into a prefab, he'll need a collider. You will add more to him later, but this is a good start.

1. Stop Play mode.

2. Add a Box collider, and size it to fit the character (Figure 6-16).

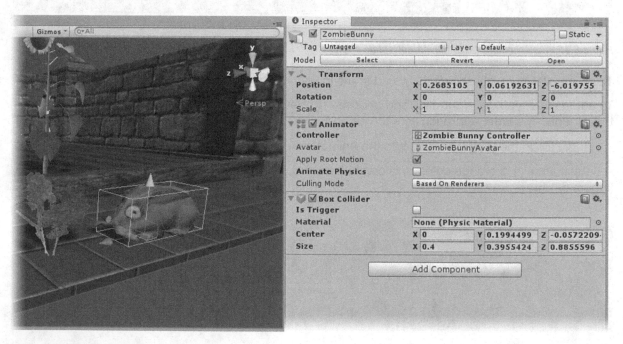

Figure 6-16. The ZombieBunny with a collider sized to fit

3. Make a **Characters** folder in the Prefabs folder in the Project view.

4. Drag the ZombieBunny into the new folder.

The next character is the garden gnome with his various modifications. The ZombieBunny character has a simple bone system to deform its mesh. If you locate the mesh object in the hierarchy, you will see that it has a Skinned Mesh Renderer component instead of the regular Mesh Renderer. The garden gnome, on the other hand, is just a collection of parts, some of which will be animated with Mecanim, and others though scripting.

1. Select the GardenGnome in the Animated Assets folder.

2. Spin the Preview window to check him out (Figure 6-17).

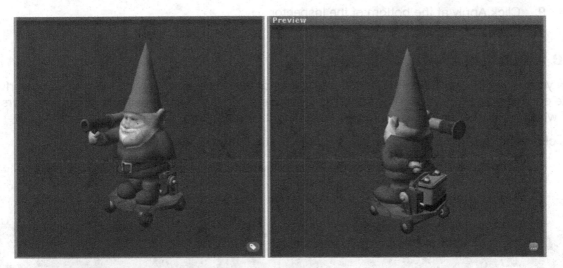

Figure 6-17. *The GardenGnome with his "Garden Defender" modifications*

3. In the Rig section, set "Gnome Motion Root" as the Root Node and click Apply.

4. In the Animations section, in the Preview window, turn the gnome so you can see the battery from his left side.

5. Click the play button to see the full 270-frame animation.

In the idle behavior, the gnome contraption vibrates as the pulley spins. When he goes forward. the switch is on and the wheels turn as he moves forward. After a short strafe (a sideways movement), the gnome's hat hinges down to reveal a laser device.

6. Set the clips with the following names and Start and End values (Figure 6-18):

Clips	Start	End
Gnome idle	0.0	90.0
Gnome travel	95.0	150.0
Gnome strafe	165.0	175.0
Gnome arming	185.0	230.0
Gnome armed	231.0	235.0
Gnobe disarming	235.0	270.0

Figure 6-18. *The gnome's animation clip values*

7. Set the Loop Time *on* for idle, travel, strafe, and armed.

8. Check "Bake Into Pose" for "Root Transform Position (Y)" for all of the clips.

9. Click Apply at the bottom of the Inspector.

The Mecanim State Engine

Now you will create an Animator controller for the gnome and get serious with Mecanim's powerful state engine. This time, you will be taking full advantage of the states, transitions, and parameters that will connect the scripts to the engine to control the character in the scene.

This character has two states he will go between for the time being.

1. Drag the GardenGnome into the Scene view onto the walkway (Figure 6-19).

Figure 6-19. The GardenGnome in the Scene view

2. Select the Animated Assets folder, and create a new Animation Controller in it.

3. Name it **Gnome Controller**, and drag it onto the GardenGnome in the Hierarchy view.

4. Double-click the Gnome Controller in the Project view or from the gnome's Animator component to open it in the Animator view.

5. Expand the GardenGnome asset in the Project view, and drag the Gnome travel and Gnome idle clips into the Animator view in that order.

6. Click Play.

The gnome does a *relative position repeat* thanks to Mecanim and heads out of the view instead of jumping back to the same position every time the clip loops.

Because the travel clip was dropped in first, it became the default clip. The gnome goes right through the other objects because he does not have a collider. You will get him hooked up so he can be player-controlled in the game shortly. Let's go ahead and change the default state to the idle animation.

7. Right-click over the Gnome idle state control, and choose Set As Default.

8. Click Play again, and switch to the Scene view to get a close view of the gnome.

This time the gnome vibrates expectantly in place as the pulley spins around.

To see how Mecanim transitions between states, you will have to add a couple of Transitions. You won't really need them for the gnome, but it will be a first look to get an idea about how powerful Mecanim can be.

1. Stop Play mode.

2. Right-click over the Gnome idle control/label in the Animator view, and choose Make Transition (Figure 6-20).

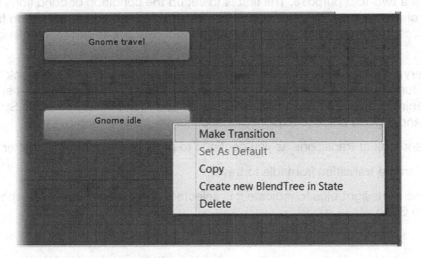

Figure 6-20. The Make Transition option in the right-click menu

3. Click on the Gnome travel control to finish the transition.

4. Click on "Gnome travel," and create a transition back to "Gnome idle" (Figure 6-21).

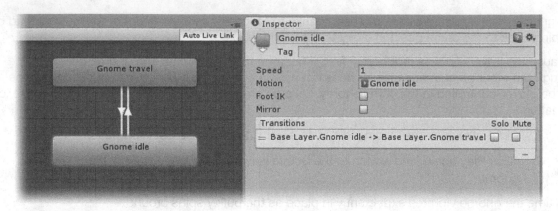

Figure 6-21. The states connected by transitions

If you select a state, such as the Gnome idle, you will now see the transition for it listed in the Inspector. You can rearrange the state controls in the view by dragging them around, and you can navigate the view by holding the middle mouse button down and moving the mouse. The Any State, by the way, is for a state that can be reached at any time from any state. A "die" behavior would be a good example, where, when finished, it could only transition to a "dead" state.

Transitions serve a two-fold purpose. The first is to set up the condition or conditions that must be met to take the character into the other states. The second is to blend the animation from the current state smoothly into the target state. Here you have control over the length of the blending between the two clips.

Mecanim is a very powerful and complex system. It is beyond the scope of this book to cover all of its features and functionality. There are two very good sample projects on the asset store that are full of sample Mecanim scenes: Mecanim Example Scenes and Mecanim Locomotion Starter Kit. The assets are free and a good place to explore Mecanim functionality in depth.

Let's take a closer look at transitions as you continue to prepare the gnome character.

1.   Click on the transition from idle to travel.

The transition line turns light blue to indicate it is selected, and the transition itself shows in the Inspector (Figure 6-22).

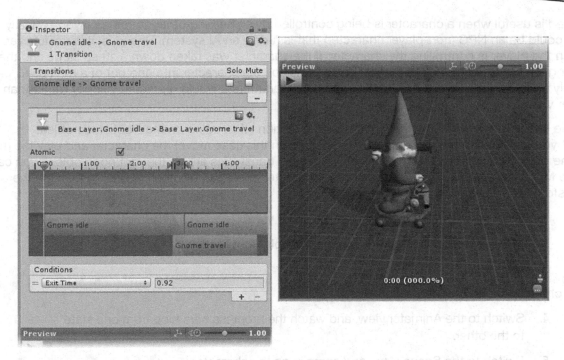

Figure 6-22. The Gnome idle to Gnome travel transition, including the Preview window

The top section tells you what transition is showing. The next section lets you selectively disable transitions during testing. The next section tells you what layer you are working in. Layers will allow you to control parts of the character with totally different clips though the use of masks. If you were to create a mask for the hinging part of the hat, for example, you could control it independently of the rest of the body, even though in that clip the character does not have any other animations.

The next section is for the blending of the two clips as they transition from one to the other. Atomic prevents the transition from being interrupted once started. The timeline shows the time overlap where one animation is blended with another. This can be adjusted to suit your preference. With the gnome, the transition is not very apparent. If you looked closely, you would see the switch going up and the vibrating lessen as the gnome goes forward.

2. Click Play in the Preview window to observe the transition.

The idle transition plays until it is 92% along, at which point it transitions fully into the travel state for the remainder of its length.

The last section of the transition is where you set the conditions that trigger the transition. As a default, it uses Exit Time, the length of the clip minus a percentage for the blending of the two clips.

3. Click Play, and watch the gnome.

He idles until that clip ends, and then goes forward until that clip ends, and then idles again, etc.

Typically, one-off animations such as a jump—or for the gnome, the arming and disarming animations—will use the exit time to automatically put them back to what the character was doing when they were triggered. Looping animations such as idle, walk, run, and strafe are generally set to trigger and un-trigger on a parameter change or speed change.

Speed is useful when a character is being controlled by something other than the player. Typically this could be an NPC (non-player character) that is run by an AI system. Speed is also useful even when the player is controlling the character. If the character was taken down a steep slope and the sliding effect added to the speed, you could transition the character into and out of a run based solely on its forward velocity. In that scenario, the parameters would represent velocity rather than input values.

In the last test, you saw how Mecanim uses the motion information on the Root Node object (that you specified in the Rig section) to transform (in this case move) the character *and* play the rest of the objects' animations. As long as only the base transforms are on the root node object, you can have Mecanim suppress them and allow the character controller, or other scripts, to manage the transforms.

1. Select the GardenGnome in the Hierarchy view.

2. In the Animator component, uncheck Apply Root Motion.

3. Click Play.

The character no longer moves forward.

4. Switch to the Animator view, and watch the progress bars loop from one state to the other.

5. Switch to the Scene view, and zoom in on the character.

You will see that the two clips are still being triggered just as before. The main indicator is the switch position on the motor. When you finish setting up the character in Chapter 7, you will be using the First Person Controller to control the main movement, so you will be suppressing the root node motion that came in with the animations.

6. Stop Play mode.

7. Drag the GardenGnome into the Prefab's Characters folder.

Humanoids

The driving force behind Mecanim development is humanoid characters. With them, you can take advantage of Mecanim's powerful retargeting system by starting with a rigged character and using a large variety of animation clips. A short, broad character can easily use the same animation as a tall lanky character. The only caveat is that the animation clips must all come from a character of the same build.

To qualify as a Humanoid Animation Type, your character must have at least 11 bones and be roughly humanoid—a bipedal creature with no extra limbs, tails, wings, or other accessories. You can have the extras, but you would be required to animate them with masks and layers if they required controls. The character must also be rigged. Rigging is the process of associating a skeleton, a hierarchy of bones, with a mesh. Each vertex on the mesh is controlled by at least one bone. The more bones controlling the position of a vertex, the higher the overhead. Unity lets you select the maximum number of bones allowed to affect a vertex in its Quality Settings.

If you can create or have access to character models without rigging, you can use Mixamo, www.mixamo.com,to rig them. At the time of this writing, as long as the character is less than 4,000 faces, you can have two characters rigged for free. For more information on Mixamo's rigging service, please see Appendix A.

For the game, you will have the option to include a scarecrow. He won't do much, but he will give you an excellent test case for the Humanoid rig. The character was rigged in Mixamo and is roughly based on Unity's "Dude" character, the humanoid that is used on animations that have no mesh of their own. You will be using some animations from a different character, or rather just an animated skeleton. It was quickly generated with 3ds Max's CAT (Character Animation Tools) system.

The Unity Mecanim sample files mentioned earlier in the chapter come with several motion capture-based files that are free to use in your own projects. If character animation is your specialty, be aware that the Humanoid rig may not use all of your character's bones during animation. If that is a problem, you can drop back to the Generic rig to retain the animation as you created it. In doing so, however, you will lose access to the retargeting system.

1. From the Animated Assets folder, select the Scarecrow and check it out in the Inspector (Figure 6-23).

Figure 6-23. The Scarecrow character

2. In the Rig section, select Humanoid for the Animation Type.

3. Click on the newly added Configure button.

You will first be asked if you wish to save the scene, as Mecanim makes use of the Scene view for the configuring process. You will be able to get back to it after you press the Done button.

4. Agree to saving the scene and also to Applying the settings.

The Inspector now shows the character and the bones that have been successfully mapped as green (Figure 6-24). Objects such as the Chest and Shoulders are optional, as indicated by the broken circle of dots. For the Scarecrow, the hands are not green but gray, indicating that there are no finger bones to be assigned.

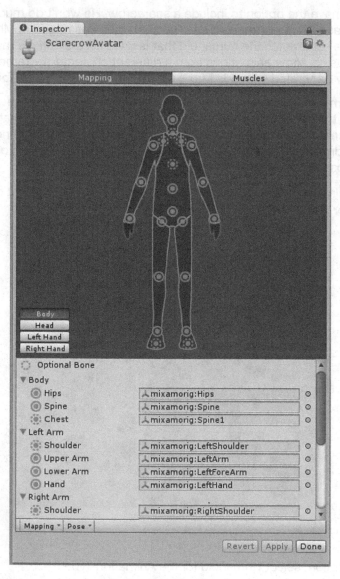

Figure 6-24. The Mapping panel; green parts have been successfully mapped

If any of the parts are red instead of green, it means the automapper was not able to find the missing bones. Bones are identified both by naming conventions and by location in the hierarchy. If you have to manually assign bones, you can select them in any of the three locations: in the Scene view, in the Hierarchy view (Figure 6-25), or in the Inspector in the mapping list. At the bottom of the Mapping section, you will find the Mapping and Pose drop-downs that may be able to help you if your character has too much red showing.

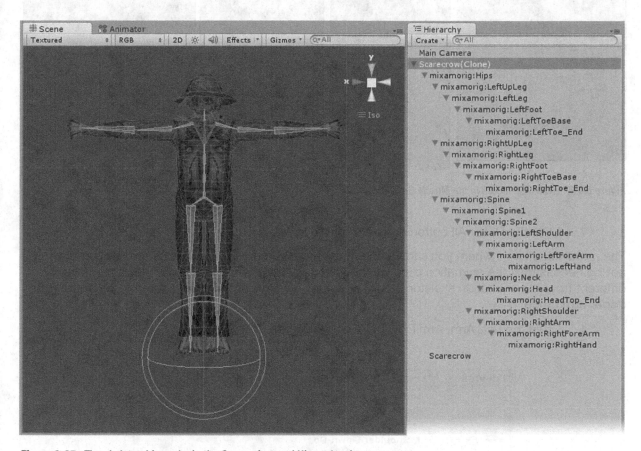

Figure 6-25. The skeleton hierarchy in the Scene view and Hierarchy view

Next to the Mapping section is the Muscles section. This is where you can set the limits of the character's movement and also adjust the mapping to account for characters of vastly different body types (short and stocky, tall and thin, extra long legs or arms, etc.).

5. Click the Muscles tab.

6. Try adjusting the sliders in the Muscle Group Preview to see how the character's rigging holds up (Figure 6-26).

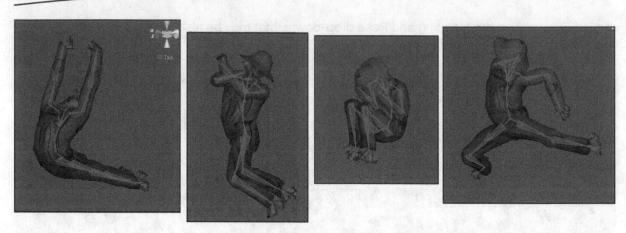

Figure 6-26. Tweaking sliders in the Muscle Group Preview

7.   Click the Reset All button at the top of the sliders.

The middle section is where you can set the range of movement for the various bones, This may not be necessary if the animation clips you are using are fairly tame, but if your character is vastly different from the animation skeleton's build, you may have to do some adjustments. Let's limit the upper arm range.

1.   Open the Left Arm, Arm Down-Up setting (Figure 6-27).

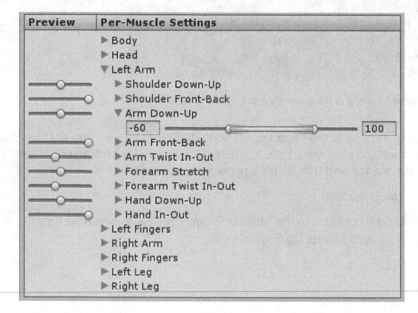

Figure 6-27. Adjusting the Arm Down-Up range

> **Tip**   If you don't see the number fields for the range slider, you will have to widen the Inspector.

   2.   Push the Arm Down/Up Preview slider all the way to the left, and then adjust the left knob slider to about **-44** to move the arm out from the body a bit.

   3.   Push the Arm Down/Up Preview slider all the way to the right, and then adjust the right knob slider to about **95** to move the arm away from the hat a bit.

The arm is prevented from going too close to the body and too close to the hat (Figure 6-28).

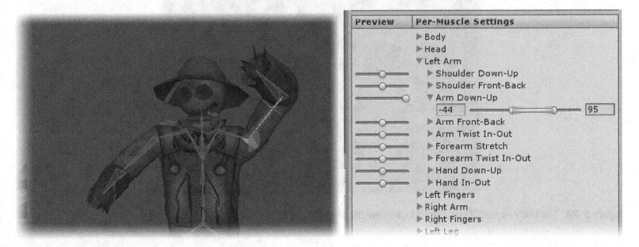

Figure 6-28.   The limits set for the left arm, down-up

   4.   Repeat the process for the right arm.

The last section is for adjusting miscellaneous settings. They don't offer immediate feedback, so you will have to go back and forth until they are correct.

   5.   At the bottom of the Inspector, click Apply and Done to get back to the Rig section.

The Scene view is restored.

   6.   Click on the Animations Section.

It reports that there is no animation on the Scarecrow. So now you will find some animation to put on it.

   1.   Select the SCAnimation asset in the Animated Assets folder.

It has no mesh, so there is no preview.

   2.   In the Rig section, set it to Humanoid.

   3.   Click Apply.

The Configure button has a check mark to its left indicating that is was able to auto-map with no problems.

4.   In The Animations section, check out the Preview window (Figure 6-29).

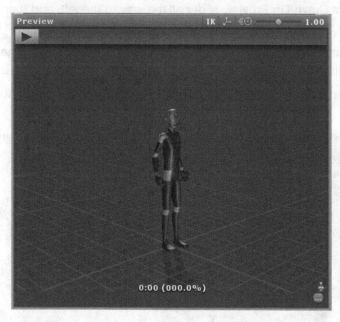

Figure 6-29. The Unity avatar, "Dude," used to preview the skeleton's animations

When an animation is imported without a mesh, in the Animations window, the default avatar mesh, "Dude," is used to show the animations.

5.   Click the Play button to preview the animations.

The idle is pretty boring, the walk is a bit odd (what did you expect for a scarecrow?), the hanging-out behavior is obviously the one you'll use in the game, and there's a half way down jump pose.

6.   Set the clips as per Figure 6-30.

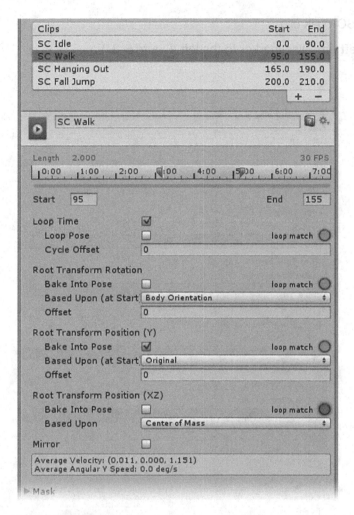

Figure 6-30. The animation clips for the SCAnimations asset

With the Humanoid rig, you got a lot of extra goodies. Most noticeable are the loop indicator dots: green for good loop and red for no loop. In the walk behavior, the XZ will not loop because Z is the forward direction. Note especially the Z Velocity for the walk clip, 1.151.

7. Set the idle, walk, and hanging out clips to Loop Time.

Loop Pose is useful for motion-capture files where the start and end of the clips must be made to match up.

8. Set Root Transform Position (Y) to Bake Into Pose for the idle and walk.

There's one other very nice feature available for Humanoids. If you move the markers for the clips on the time line, a mini graph appears, helping you identify the looping points on the graph. There again, this is especially useful for mo-cap data.

1. Select the SC Walk clip.

2. Move the left time-line marker to the left (Figure 6-31).

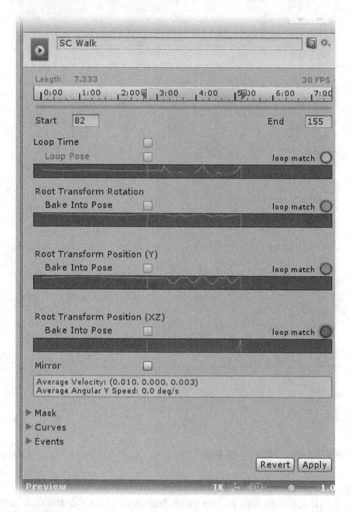

Figure 6-31. Adjusting the clip time segment

The graphs appear below the transforms so you can see where they will loop. As the marker gets farther away from the loop time, the dot goes yellow.

3. Set the Start back to **95**.

4. Click Apply.

Next you will set the Scarecrow up to use the SCAnimations's clips.

1. Deactivate the GardenGnome in the Hierarchy view.

2. Drag the Scarecrow into its place.

At its current scale, this thing won't scare a ladybug. Fortunately, Unity is very good at adjusting scale on rigged characters.

3.   Select the Scarecrow in the Project view.

4.   In the Model section, set the Scale Factor to **0.1** and click Apply.

The Scarecrow is scaled to fit the scene (Figure 6-32).

Figure 6-32. The Scarecrow in the scene

Next you will create an Animator controller for the Scarecrow.

1.   Create a new Animator controller in the Animated Assets folder.

2.   Name it **Scarecrow Controller**.

3.   Drag it onto the Scarecrow in the Scene view.

4.   Open the Scarecrow Controller in the Animator view.

5.   Expand the SCAnimation asset in the Project view.

6.   Drag the SC Idle, SC Walk, and SC Hanging Out clips into the Animator view.

7.   Create transitions to and from the idle and walk states.

8.   Click Play, and watch the scarecrow idle and toddle off into the scene using animations from the other asset.

Let's create a very simple script to run the scarecrow with Mecanim. To communicate with the Animator state machine, you will have to create a *parameter* inside the Animator first.

1.   In the lower left of the Animator view, click the + at the right of the Parameters bar.

2.   Select Float for the type (Figure 6-33).

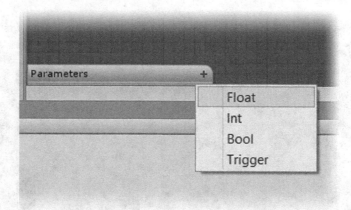

Figure 6-33. The Parameter types

3.   Name it **Input V** (Figure 6-34).

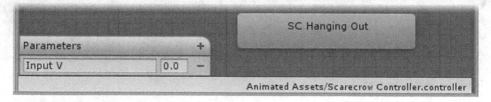

Figure 6-34. The new float parameter

4.   Select the transition from idle to walk, and set its Conditions to Input V Greater than **0.1** (Figure 6-35).

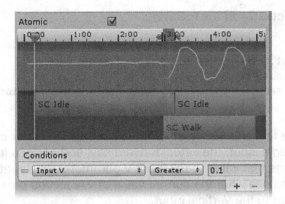

Figure 6-35. The condition for the idle-to-walk transition

The Input value from the Input manager for the vertical or forward goes from 0, no input, to 1, with the W or up arrow pressed.

5. Select the transition from the walk to the idle, and set its Conditions to Input V Less than **0.1** (Figure 6-36).

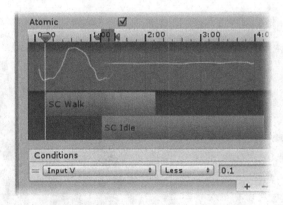

Figure 6-36. The condition for the walk-to-idle transition

1. Create a new C# script in the Game Scripts Folder, and name it **SimpleCharacterController**.

2. Open the new script in the script editor.

3. Add the following variable under the class definition:

```
Animator animator; // the Animator component/ state engine
```

4. In the Start function, locate and assign the Animator:

```
animator = GetComponent<Animator>(); // assign the animator
```

5. In the `Update` function, add the following:

```
if (animator) {
    float v = Input.GetAxis("Vertical");
    animator.SetFloat("Input V", v);
    print (v); // see what the v input value sent to the animator
}
```

In this conditional, the code first checks for the existence of the Animator component. It then gets the current value of the vertical input, the virtual forward key, and assigns it to a variable, v. Using `animator.SetFloat`, it assigns that value to the Input V parameter you created in the Animator. The print line will let you watch to see what the current value of v is as you press and release the forward and backward keys assigned to the Vertical input.

6. Save the script.

7. Add it to the Scarecrow in the Hierarchy view.

8. Press Play and then press the w or up key to move the scarecrow forward, watching the console's output as you do.

The scarecrow walks forward while the key is down (Figure 6-37).

Figure 6-37. The Scarecrow walking away

To add a little more control, you can make the character go backwards with minimal effort. The Vertical input generates a -1 when the player presses the s or down arrow keys. To make him go backwards without a back-up animation, you simply set the [playback] speed of the clip to a negative number.

1. Press the s key or down arrow, and look at the value reported in the console.

Note that the value ramps up and down rather than going directly to 1, 0, or -1.

2. Right-click over the SC Walk state in the Animator view, and select Copy.

3. Right-click again, and select Paste.

4. Rename the new state **SC Walk Backward** in the Inspector, and set the Speed to **-0.5**.

5. Create transitions to and from the backwards and the idle states (Figure 6-38).

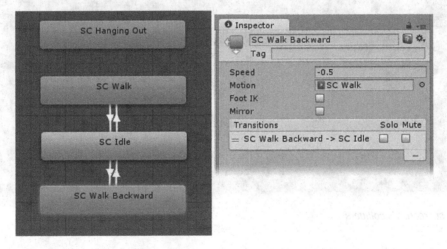

Figure 6-38. The new backwards state using the SC Walk clip with a negative Speed value

6. Set the transition from idle to backwards to Input V Less than **-0.1**.

7. Set the transition from backwards to idle to Input V Greater than **-0.1**.

8. Click Play, and walk the Scarecrow forward and backwards in the scene.

The controls are extremely minimal, but you can now see one means of moving a character with Mecanim and some animations. To turn the character, you could add an animation with the turn built into the Root motion, or you could let the mouse do the rotation and send the turning velocity back to Mecanim. Using a Blend tree, it would time the animation to match the velocity. Although the functionality is beyond the scope of this book, it is something worth exploring at some point.

Meanwhile, the Scarecrow really doesn't have to do anything in this scene other than hang around.

1. In the Animator view, right-click over the SC Hanging Out state and select Set As Default.

2. Press Play.

The Scarecrow is now hard at work in his traditional role. It's a little creepy at the regular speed.

3.   Select the SC Hanging Out state, and set its Speed to **0.2**.

4.   Add a Capsule collider component to fit his body.

5.   Add a Box collider as well, and fit the collider to his arms (Figure 6-39).

Figure 6-39. *The scarecrow's colliders*

It turns out you can add more than one collider component to an object as long as they are not the same type.

6.   Drag the Scarecrow into the Prefabs, Characters folder in the Project view.

7.   Comment out the print line in the script, and save the script.

BlendShapes

With Unity 4.3 came support for BlendShapes, also known as *morph targets*. Morph targets are a means of animating the vertex positions without the use of bones. The procedure is to create several "target" configurations of the mesh and then blend between them to animate the mesh. This technique is very useful for very organic creatures that have no bone system. It is also used for facial animation, although the results may be more suited to cartoon characters than those derived from traditional methods. For the game, you will have a slug character that shoots through the garden from time to time. The majority of its body animation was created through the use of morph targets (Figure 6-40).

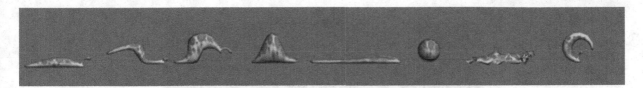

Figure 6-40. *The slug's morph targets*

1. Select the Slug in the Animated Assets folder.

In the Preview window, the slug looks a bit dingy (Figure 6-41). A better shader will improve things.

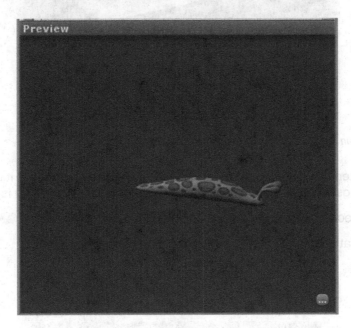

Figure 6-41. *The imported slug*

2. Open the Animated Assets' Material folder, and locate the Slug material.

3. Change the shader to Unlit/Texture (Figure 6-42).

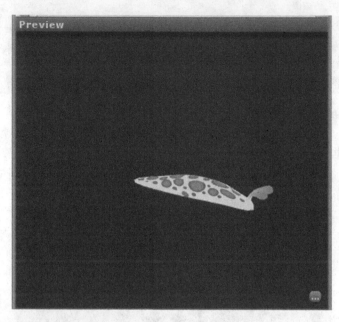

Figure 6-42. The slug with an Unlit/Texture shader to brighten it up

"Unlit" means the material is not affected by scene lighting, which also means it uses less resources. To continue that savings, you will also turn off Receive Shadows once the slug is in the scene.

4. In the Rig section, select Slug Root for Root Node and click Apply.

5. In the Animations section, set up the clips as follows (Figure 6-43):

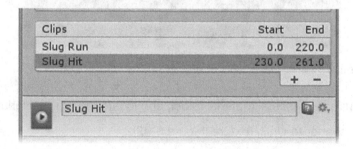

Figure 6-43. The Slug clips

6. Set the Slug Run to Loop Time and Root Transform Position (Y), Bake Into Pose.

7. Click Play in the Preview window to see the slug's boneless animation.

If you are still struggling to understand Bake Into Pose, the Slug Hit clip may give you some enlightenment.

1. Select the Slug Hit clip.

2. In the Preview window, just to the right of the Speed slider, turn on the transform gizmo.

3. Click Play in the Preview window.

The Preview window stays focused on the object's transform root. The slug pops up into the air and the camera stays focused on it.

4. For Root Transform Position (Y), check Bake Into Pose and click Play again.

This time, the slug jumps up out of sight because the slug's transform remains on the ground (Figure 6-44).

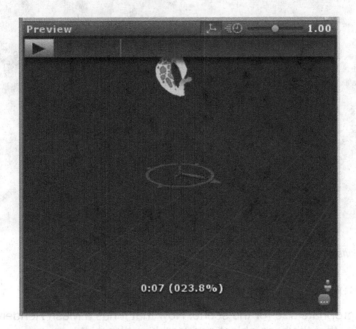

Figure 6-44. The Slug mesh jumping out of its transform root

The jump part, has been removed from the root node object and baked into the regular animation. Another way to think about this is to think about a collider. If a collider is added to the root node and the jump is put on the rest of the animation, the mesh will leave the collider behind during the jump. If the jump is left on the root node, the root node, along with the mesh and collider, goes upwards and can interact with other colliders.

So why does one tend to use Bake Into Pose (Y) for most looping poses? The answer is simple. If there is even a small bit of upward movement, the relative repeat that moves a character forward (or sideways) would also keep adding to the Y position so that, eventually, the character will be floating above the ground! If your character slowly turns (and shouldn't) while in idle or forward motion, you can bake the Root Transform Rotation. If your character wanders off to the left or right when he should only move forward, you're out of luck. The other Transform Position Bake Into Pose lumps forward and sideways (X and Z) together. It is useful if your character wanders off during an idle.

5.   Leave Root Transform Position (Y), Bake Into Pose checked.

6.   Click Apply, and drag the slug into the scene.

At his current size, this thing could be seriously dangerous (Figure 6-45).

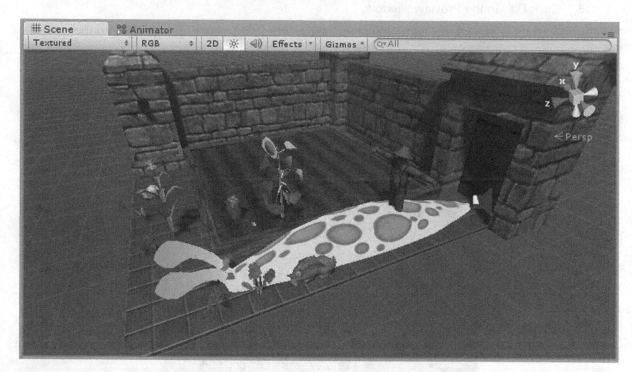

Figure 6-45. The Slug in scene, at the default size

7.   Select the Slug asset in the Project view, and change its Scale Factor to **0.002**.

The slug is a more appropriate size for the scene. Now that it has a Mesh Renderer component, you can see the shapes that the base object can morph or blend into.

1.   Select the child Slug in the Slug's hierarchy in the Hierarchy view (Figure 6-46).

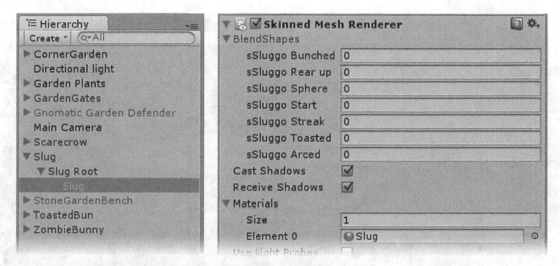

Figure 6-46. The Slug's BlendShapes in the Slug's Mesh Renderer component

2. Try adjusting the BlendShapes values for the various targets—they range from 0-100.

3. In the Scene view, expand the Slug's hierarchy.

4. Select the child Slug that contains the Skinned Mesh Renderer.

5. Turn off the Cast and Receive Shadows parameters.

Because they are exposed in a component, you could change or animate the BlendShapes in-game. There are a few systems available to make this easier on the Asset Store. For now you will be using the imported animations.

1. Create a new Animator Controller, and name it **Slug Controller**.

2. Expand the Slug Controller in the Project view.

3. Drag Slug Run and Slug Hit into the Animator view in that order. Do not create transitions between them.

4. Drag the Slug Controller onto the Slug parent object in the Hierarchy view.

5. Add a Box collider component, and size it to fit the slug (Figure 6-47).

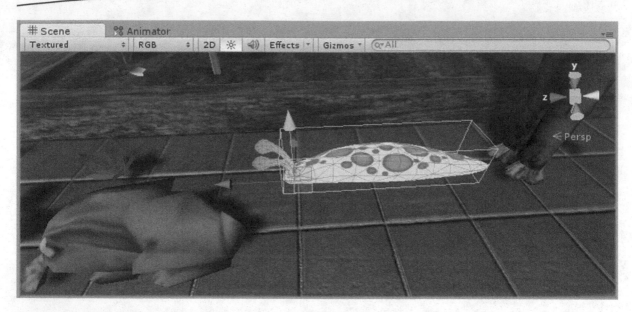

Figure 6-47. The Slug with Box collider

6.   Drag the Slug into the Prefabs' Characters folder to create a prefab for it.

You will revisit the Slug in Chapter 11 to finish setting it up.

The Animated Assets folder is getting cluttered. Let's take a moment to get organized.

1.   Create a new folder in the Animated Assets folder, and name it **Animator Controllers**.

2.   Drag the animator controllers into the new folder.

Native Animation

For simple animations, you may prefer to create the clips directly in Unity. Unity has an Animation editor, where you can create key-frame animation for almost any settable parameter. You may create animation clips for Humanoid rigs and Legacy rigs, but not Generic rigs.

For your game, when the gnome character blasts a zombie bunny, it will be replaced by a burn-up replacement mesh. That object will not have a bone system, but to keep from littering the scene with the "dead replacements," you will scale the object down to almost nothing before deleting it from the scene.

1.   Create a new folder in the Project view, and name it **Animation Clips**.

2.   Select the ToastedZombie from the Animated Assets folder.

On import, the ToastedZombie was given a Generic Rig even though it had no animation. You will be creating an animation clip for it, but there is something you must understand about animations. Animations use absolute values. If an object's position transform is animated at point A and you position it to a different location, it will return to point A to animate. You should always parent the object to an empty gameObject *before you start animating*. Children inherit the transforms of their parents. Their animations are always relative to their parent's location, so you will be able to position the parents without disturbing the children's animations.

3. Drag the ToastedZombie (or the BurntAlien if you are using the AlienHerbavore instead of the ZombieBunny) into the Scene view.

4. Frame the Scene view to the ToastedZombie.

5. Create an Empty gameObject, and name it **Toasted Zombie Parent**.

The new gameObject should be in the same spot as the ToastedZombie (using Center, not Pivot).

6. Drag the ToastedZombie onto the new Toasted Zombie Parent.

7. Select the ToastedZombie.

8. From the Window menu, select Animation (Ctrl + 6) (Figure 6-48).

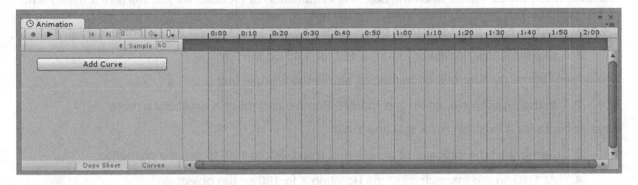

Figure 6-48. The Animation view or editor

9. In the Animation editor, click on the Add Curve button.

Because you don't yet have an animation clip to add a curve to, you are redirected to create one first.

10. Create a new animation clip named **Jump Shrink** in the Animation Clips folder.

When you have created a clip, its name appears as the selected clip and the list of available parameters appears to the button's right. You will not see curves because the view opens to the Dope Sheet rather than the Curves view. Either can be selected at the bottom of the Animation view.

Rather than manually adding the animation tracks you want one at a time, you can animate the gameObject directly in the viewport or from its parameters in the Inspector. The tracks will automatically be created.

The red Record button should now be active (Figure 6-49).

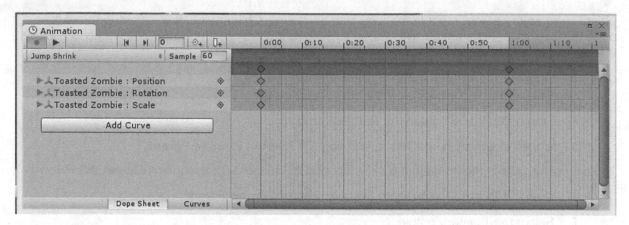

Figure 6-49. *The new "curves" showing keys at 0 and 60 (1:00 second) in the Dope Sheet*

This animation will be called when the object is instantiated or created, so you will give it a lead time of 1 second before anything happens so the player can watch the pyrotechnics you will be adding in the next chapter. Note that Unity uses 60 samples or frames per second for its native animations.

1. Move the time indicator to frame **100**, or **1:40** on the timeline.

The current frame number can be found just above the Sample text.

2. In the Scene view, select the Toasted Zombie and move it up about a meter.

Keys appears for a Position track at 0 and 1:40.

3. Scrub the time indicator to time 0, and then back to 1:40 to see the animation.

4. At 1:40, in the Inspector, set the Rotation X to **180** so the object is upside down.

A Rotation track has been added. If you had attempted to use the gizmo to directly rotate the object in the scene, you would have discovered that the rotation goes onto all three axes because of the rotation being handled internally as quaternions. If you get unexpected results with rotations, try typing the numbers into the Inspector, where they are handled as local x, y, and z rotations [Euler rotation] instead.

5. Now Scale the object down until the x, y, and z gizmo end markers are within the center gizmo marker.

A Scale track has been added.

6. Drag the time indicator back and forth to see the animation.

The animation looks okay when you drag the time indicator manually, but you need to see it at its correct rate of speed.

7. Click the Play button next to the red Record button in the Animation view.

The timing is sluggish.

8. Stop Play mode, and move the top key at frame 0 to frame **60**, time **1:00** to move all of the keys at frame 0 at once.

9. Move the end Position key back to frame 80 (Figure 6-50).

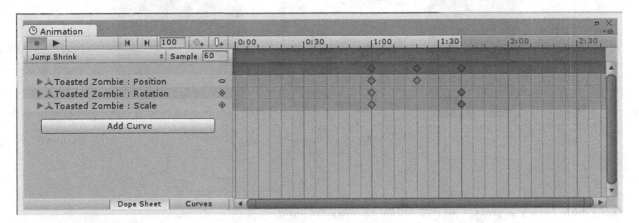

Figure 6-50. The adjusted keys

If you are familiar with curve editors, you can switch to the Curves view and adjust the curves. As a default, they are linear, which tends to be rather boring.

1. From the bottom of the view, switch from the Dope Sheet to the Curves display.

2. Open the Position track, and select the Position.y track.

3. Frame its two keys by selecting the two keys, putting the cursor in the curve window, and pressing the F key.

4. Right-click to bring up the tangency options (Figure 6-51, left).

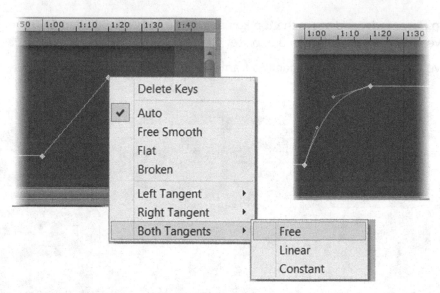

Figure 6-51. The key tangent options (left), and the adjusted curve (right)

5. Select Both Tangents, Free.

6. Tweak the handles for a fast out (steep) and slow in (flat) curve (Figure 6-51, right).

7. Open the Rotation.x track, move the indicator to 1:40, and type in **750** to increase the rotation (Figure 6-52).

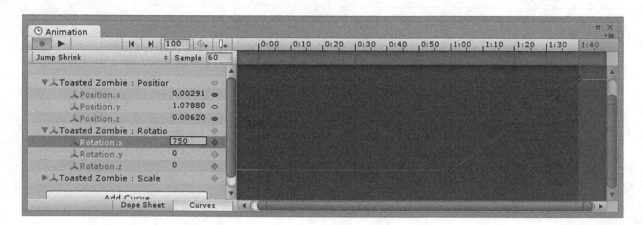

Figure 6-52. Increasing rotation

8. Feel free to tweak any of the other curves to improve the animation.

9. Close the Animation view when you are finished; the clip is automatically saved every time you make a change to it.

Click Play, and watch the results of your efforts.

The ToastedZombie animation loops when it should be a one-off. Also, you may be wondering why it is playing at all. The mystery is quickly solved.

1.   Stop Play mode.

2.   Open the Animation Clips folder in the Project view.

Inside it you can see the Jump Shrink clip you created, but a ToastedZombie Animator controller was automatically generated at the same time as the clip!

3.   Double-click to see what is in the newly created Animator Controller.

It is no surprise that it is a state for the Jump Shrink clip.

4.   Select the Jump Shrink clip.

5.   In the Inspector, uncheck Loop Time.

Now is a good time to make sure the object can be moved in the scene with no ill effects.

6.   Move the Toasted Zombie Parent to a different location in the scene.

7.   Click Play.

The ToastedZombie animates correctly from its parent's new location.

8.   Drag the Toasted Zombie Parent (or Burnt Alien Parent) from the Hierarchy view into the Prefabs' Characters folder.

9.   Save the scene, and save the project.

You will finish setting up the functionality on the characters later in the book, but you should now have the beginnings of your game off to a good start.

Summary

In this chapter, along with an odd assortment of imported characters, you got your first peek at the game's premise. Invaded by voracious zombie bunnies, your mission will be to eradicate the threat with the help of a repurposed garden gnome statuette. Among the cast of characters, you got to explore setting up several different animation types.

You began with Legacy animation, the Rig type that works well with mechanical animation where the object is only asked to animate occasionally. Using the OnTriggerEnter code you learned in Chapter 5, you set up a set of sensor-activated garden gates. Legacy, you discovered, has an option to Play Automatically on start-up. You got your first experience with setting up animation clips when the animation comes in as a single "take." Using frames to specify individual clips, you learned that Unity acknowledges the frames per second used when the animation was created. While there was no particular naming conventions for animation clips, you did learn that it was important to give clips unique names that identified their source. With the clips in place, you added two simple animation.Play lines to the script to trigger the appropriate clips. Audio, you discovered, was even easier to add with audio.Play for sound effects.

With the Generic Rig type, you got your first look at Mecanim and a basic Animator set up to get the Zombie Bunny chewing its way through the scene. Mecanim, you discovered, turns clips into states and was designed especially for looping animations that are always active. Generic rigs, you discovered, are used for characters with fewer than 11 bones and non-humanoid characters. With the zombie bunny, you found that to access Mecanim's state engine, you had to create an Animator controller. Unlike the process you used for the Legacy animation, you had to set up the Animator before you could see the character animate in the scene, but for a simple looping animation, it required no coding.

The second character also used the Generic rig and had no bones at all in its hierarchy. You left the gnome transitioning between two clips using their "Exit Times" to trigger the states. By designating a clip as the Default state, you could control the state that was used first. The most important concept you experienced was that the root node animation, if separated from the rest of the animation, can be used to move the character about the scene. Root node animation, whether translation or rotation, you learned, was additive—the character kept moving forward rather than jumping back to its start point.

With the Scarecrow character, you got a first look at a Humanoid Animation Type rig. Although the character had no animation of its own, its rigging allowed it to be configured by Mecanim's retargeting system, where its bones were identified and you could set up limits for the limbs' range of movement. With the Scarecrow prepared, you looked into the SCAnimation object that had no mesh, but a humanoid skeleton and some animations. With the help of Dude, Unity's default avatar, you discovered the extra features to help define the frames for looping animation behaviors. You also discovered that the velocity of clips could be seen for clips of Humanoid rigs.

With a Humanoid to control, you learned the basics of setting up conditionals using "Parameters," which are variables used to communicate with scripts. In the script, you used the values returned by the virtual Input keys as conditions to trigger the transitions between states.

Returning to a Generic rig for the Slug character, you saw how Unity can use BlendShapes (a.k.a., morph targets). By changing the slug's shader to Unlit, you found you could save a few resources. The slug also provided a nice example to help understand the concept of Bake Into Pose. You discovered that the morph shapes reside as parameters on the Skinned Mesh Renderer and can be adjusted in percents added to the original mesh.

With the last "character," you got a chance to create your own animations in Unity's Animation view. The first thing you learned was that objects with position animations must be parented to an empty gameObject *before* you create animation clips for it. Beginning with the Dope Sheet, you learned how to set keys and adjust the timing of the clip. Switching to the curve editor, you learned how to manipulate the tangents to fine-tune the animation. Once a clip was created for an object with the Generic Rig, you discovered that an Animator Controller was generated and the new clip was automatically added to it.

Chapter **7**

Populating the Game Environment

Before you can finish setting up the characters, you will have to get the game environment blocked in and ready for testing. Game flow, how readily the player can move through the game environment and accomplish tasks or goals, may look good on paper, but once implemented, it might not work as well as expected. In a larger game, you would probably use proxy geometry and simple primitives for characters to mock up the relevant features of the environment so you could test the functionality of the game early on. Even for something as simple as the game you are creating with the book, much of the early testing was done exclusively with Unity primitive objects (Figure 7-1). As issues were encountered, workarounds or solutions were developed, often leading to design changes in the garden structure assets.

Figure 7-1. An early test version of the game using proxy objects

Design Strategies

As mentioned in Chapter 2, one of the goals to designing a game environment is to be able to hide, or *occlusion cull*, objects that are covered up or occluded by other objects, preferably on a large-scale basis. It's not by chance that the garden walls are high and the gates fully block the entryway. Once the layout of the modular pieces of the garden is finished, you will have a fully self-contained section of the scene. When the character is inside it, you will safely be able to deactivate other garden modules. For the book's project, you will start the game in a staging area where the player can get used to controlling the Gnomatic Garden defender before the game play begins in earnest.

Besides the concept of occlusion culling, there is another issue that comes with a third-person point of view, and that is camera management. If the game was set in a large open area with nothing higher than a corn stalk, there would be nothing that the camera could collide with. In the walled area, every time the character gets near a wall and turns around, the camera will go through the wall. Besides the visual interruption of the game's "suspension of disbelief," it could put the view in a position to see places that are fully empty of environment.

To avoid the camera issue for most of the garden, the GGD (Gnomatic Garden Defender) is constrained to the walkways. Paths that do not lead to other garden modules can use the Planter Tower that blocks the character from getting too close to the wall, or they could use some other device, such as a wheelbarrow or stack of potting-soil bags, as a logical barrier. While it is easy to drop in an invisible collider for a barrier, the player is likely to resent having the character's movement blocked for no logical reason. Unless, of course, it is part of the game play, in which case there would probably be some sort of audio or visual effect to go with the character colliding with the barrier.

1. Open the GardenSetUp scene from the previous chapter.

2. Save the scene as **GardenLevel1**.

Although there is no naming convention used particularly for scenes, keeping the names clear of spaces will allow you to use the name itself as a value available from a drop-down list later on.

With three scenes cluttering the Project view, now would be a good time to create a folder for them.

3. Create a new folder, and name it **Scenes**.

4. Move the three scenes into it.

Creating the Environment

You already have almost everything you will require to build your game environment. In this section, you will start bringing the pieces together and learn how to manage them for more efficiency. To begin, you will be using the prefabs you have created in the earlier chapters to quickly fabricate your game environment. Because an environment must be tested for flow before it can truly be called a *game* environment, you will have to finish more of the Gnomatic Garden Defender's functionality so you can move through the scene as a player. Once the character is mobile in the scene, you will be able to improve the efficiency of the environment with some basic occlusion culling.

Utilizing the Prefabs

It is quite typical to put an asset into the scene long enough to get it set up and functioning correctly, and then create a prefab from it and delete it from the scene. Many objects, such as projectiles, are created and destroyed on demand throughout the game. Others are reused in different levels. Either way, when using prefabs, you only have to set them up once.

If you have made changes to any of the scene objects since you created their prefabs, you can "apply" the changes made to the object to the prefabs or revert the objects back to the prefab's configuration. Once you make changes to a prefab in the Project view, all instances of the object, regardless of scene, will reflect the changes. Let's test the functionality on the bench. Most garden benches do not drive themselves around people's gardens.

1. Open the GardenSetUp scene again by double-clicking on it in the Scenes folder.

2. Select the StoneGardenBench in the Hierarchy view, and activate it.

3. From the GameObject menu, select Break Prefab Instance.

4. Save the scene.

The lettering is no longer blue (indicating an instance) in the Hierarchy view. The bench will now retain its functionality in this scene.

1. Open the GardenLevel1 scene.

The bench's prefab does not reside in the Prefabs folder with the rest of the imported objects, so you may have trouble locating it.

2. Select the StoneGardenBench in the Hierarchy view and, from the right-click menu, choose Select Prefab.

The prefab is temporarily highlighted yellow in the Project view.

3. Select the StoneGardenBench prefab in the Project view, and inspect its components.

4. Select the StoneGardenBench in the Hierarchy view, and note the differences.

5. In the Inspector, near the top, press Revert on the Prefab line.

The bench in the Hierarchy view loses the scripts and Rigidbody components that caused it to turn and head out of the garden. It also becomes active in the scene again.

6. Deactivate the bench in the scene.

7. In the Inspector, click Apply at the far right of the Prefab line to update the prefab in the Project view to match the one in the Hierarchy view.

8. Select the StoneGardenBench in the Project view, and note that it is now inactive.

9. Reactivate the prefab in the Project view.

The instance of it in the scene is also activated.

10. Check the Prefabs folder to make sure that all of the plants, characters, and structures have prefabs and are up to date.

11. Delete the characters, plants, and the bench from the scene.

12. Open the Lightmapping view, and press Clear to delete the Lightmaps associated with the previous scene.

13. Save the GardenLevel1 scene.

In the this section, you will be setting up the garden environment using the prefab modules. Set the two garden areas up as instructed so the values used later on in the game will be valid. Feel free to use the modules to set up more custom areas if you wish.

1. Switch to Default layout or tear off the Scene view to get a nice large window for it.

2. Select the Gate Wall Pillar Corner, Planter Tower, Raised Bed Walkway Short, and Wall.

3. Use Ctrl+D to duplicate them.

4. Move the new objects over to the other side of the center (nonduplicated) walkway (Figure 7-2).

Figure 7-2. The duplicated garden objects

Although the scene is not yet cluttered with non-mesh objects, you may have noticed the gizmos associated with the camera, light, and audio components intruding on the view of the scene's contents. You may wish to turn them off or adjust their size. Feel free to switch from 3D to 2D if you prefer them to be a consistent size. You may want to turn the icons off entirely for some of the components.

5.   Click the Gizmos drop-down list on the Scene view's title bar (Figure 7-3).

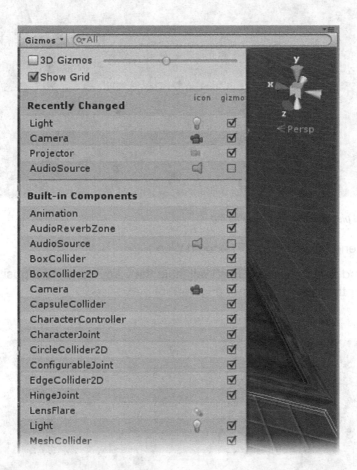

Figure 7-3. The Gizmos drop-down list, where icon visibility and style can be affected

6.   Click on the Audio Source, Camera, and Light gizmos to disable them in the scene for now.

With the icons suppressed in the Scene view, you have a clear view and can begin arranging the duplicate objects.

1.   Move the Pillar Corner, Planter Tower, and Wall to the far side of the other assets (Figure 7-4).

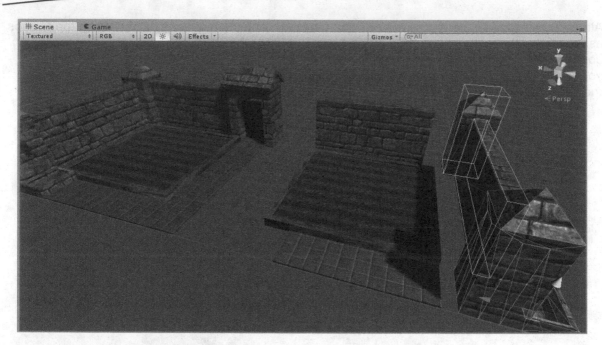

Figure 7-4. The duplicated pieces before final positioning

2. Set the Scene View display to Textured Wire.

3. Zoom in and select the new Gate Wall, hold the v key down, and position the cursor over the lower left corner (Figure 7-5).

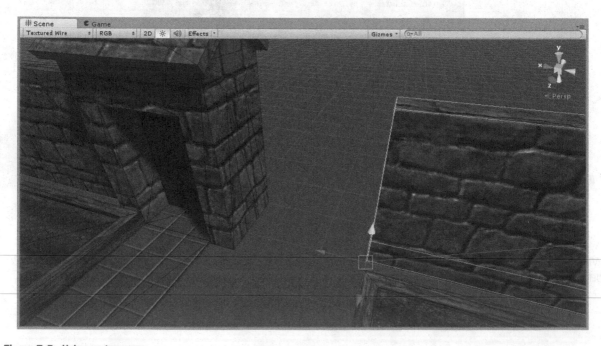

Figure 7-5. Using vertex snap

4. Holding the v key down, move the Wall over until it snaps to the corresponding vertex on the Gateway.

5. Set the Planter Tower group's rotation y to **180** degrees.

6. Rotate the new Raised Bed 90 degrees, using vertex snapping if necessary for final positioning.

7. Using the v key to snap to vertices, snap the various parts of the garden into position (Figure 7-6).

Figure 7-6. Half of the garden in place

8. Change the coordinate system to Center/Local.

9. Select all but the two Planter Towers, two Walkway Shorts, and the Walkway Center.

10. Add the GardenGates Group to the selection.

11. Duplicate and rotate 180 degrees *in the viewport* while holding the Ctrl (Cmd on the Mac) key down to enable rotation snap.

Rotation snap may leave a value not quite 180 degrees in the Inspector, but you can manually type that in to correct any variation. The values will all be changed on a local basis.

12. Deselect just the duplicate GardenGates object and its children. (It will be in the CornerGarden group.) It uses the coordinate system it had on import, z up, and will fall over if included.

13. With the remainder of the objects still selected, set the Rotation y to **180** degrees.

14. Add the gate back into the selection, and use vertex snap to snap the entire selection into place (Figure 7-7).

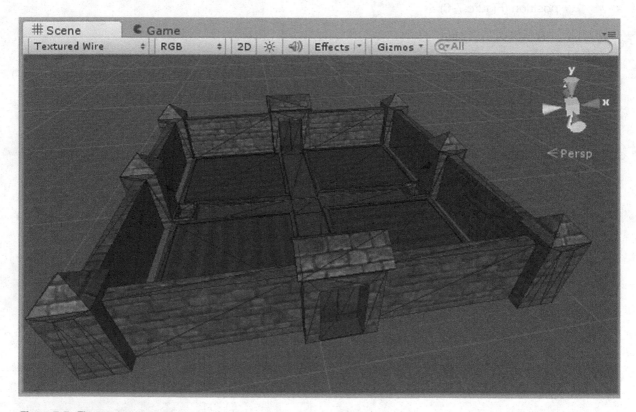

Figure 7-7. The two halves of the garden in place

Next you will be adding a staging area. As you've probably realized, you can build a complex of gardens with walls that will be shared between them, making culling a little trickier.

1. Create a new Empty GameObject, and name it **Staging Area**.

2. Select all but the Raised Beds and the objects comprising the connecting walls.

3. Duplicate them, and move them over to make the next enclosure (Figure 7-8).

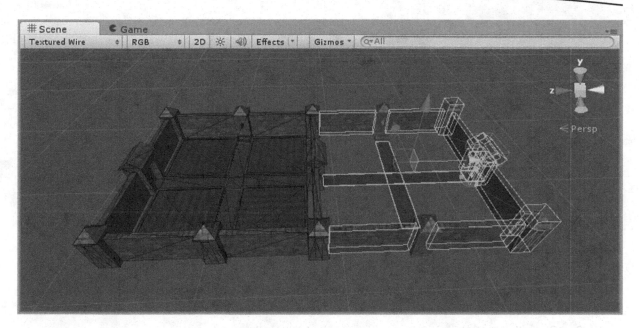

Figure 7-8. The Staging area

Because you will want to be able to turn off the staging area when the character is in the garden, you have to group the new objects together. Fortunately, you can create a group with your selection.

4. While they remain selected, drag them into the Staging Area group.

5. Agree to Losing the Prefab.

Because the staging area won't have any vegetable beds, you should find something to prevent the GGD from getting close to the walls. There is a Unity package in your Chapter 7 Assets folder that should do the job.

6. Import the custom package, StagingExtras, from the Chapter 7 Assets folder.

7. Drag the StagingExtras prefab from the Prefabs, Structures folder into the scene (Figure 7-9).

Figure 7-9. The StagingExtras object

Prefabs come complete with their location in the Project view. If a folder doesn't exist, one will be created for the asset or assets.

8. Snap the two objects into position against the walkways.

9. Duplicate the StagingExtra object three times, and rotate and snap them into position.

10. Set the Scene display back to Textured.

11. From the StoneBench folder, drag the prefabs into the staging area to flesh it out (Figure 7-10).

Figure 7-10. The StagingExtras object (left), and the staging area, neatly arranged (right)

12. Drag all of the new additions into the Staging Area.

13. Set all of the StoneBench assets to Static, and update their prefabs by clicking Apply.

14. Select the Staging Area, and deactivate and reactivate it to make sure all of the Staging Area objects are handled together.

To fill in all of those blank spaces, you will create a small terrain object. Besides providing a ground object for the gaps, it will allow you to paint trees and detail meshes to add to the scene. If you wish, you can add a pond or a mound or two.

1. From the GameObject, Create Other menu, select Terrain.

2. In the Terrain's Terrain component, Terrain Settings section, set it up as shown in Figure 7-11.

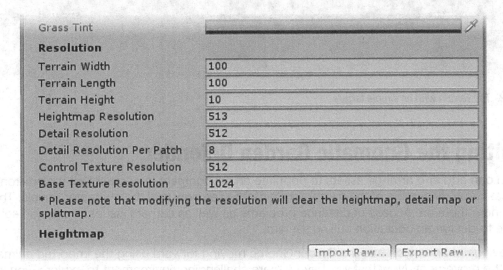

Figure 7-11. *The settings for the terrain set up*

3. In the Paint height section, set the Height to **5** and click Flatten.

4. In the Transforms component, set the Position Y to **-5** to compensate for the flatten height.

5. Move the Terrain over to the garden.

6. Import the TerrainAssets package, but uncheck the assets pertaining to the Palm tree before clicking Import.

7. In the Paint terrain section From Edit Texture, Add Texture and select the Grass&Rock texture.

8. Set the X and Y Size to **5** so the texture size will be smaller on the terrain, and click Apply (Figure 7-12).

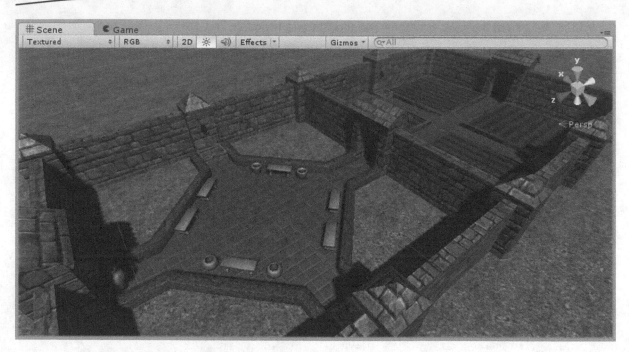

Figure 7-12. The Terrain with its simple texture

Revisiting the Gnomatic Garden Defender

While you can add and arrange assets to populate an environment, you must test the environment with at least a proxy version of the game's character to see how well the character travels. This will tell you where there are access or distance problems as well as camera issues. It will also set you up to be able to design an occlusion-culling system.

In the previous chapter, you had the GardenGnome moving forward using the imported animation to direct the movement. Now that you have a more challenging environment to explore, you will be turning control of the little gnome over to the player. When you last tinkered with the little fellow, you had just turned off Apply Root Motion in the Animator component.

With the root transforms deactivated, you will use the First Person Controller component as a quick means to drive the character around the garden.

1. Drag the GardenGnome prefab into the staging area.

2. Focus in on the GardenGnome.

3. From the Standard Assets folder, Character Controllers, drag the First Person Controller prefab into the Hierarchy view.

4. Assign the Player tag to it so it will be able to activate the garden gates.

5. From the GameObjects menu, use "Move to View" to position it over the gnome.

6. Delete the Graphics object from its hierarchy.

7. Select its Main Camera, and rename it Arm Group.

8. Remove its Audio Listener, Flare Layer, and GUILayer components.

9. Remove the Camera component.

10. While holding the Alt key down, click the Gnomatic Garden Defender's down arrow to expand its hierarchy.

Now you will merge the two objects. The gnome's Bazooka Arm will be parented to the repurposed Arm Group. It has the Mouse Look component that will rotate the Bazooka/Potato gun up and down, just at it previously rotated its Camera component.

1. Change the vlew to an ortho right view, and toggle off Scene lights.

2. Set the coordinate system to Pivot and Global (Figure 7-13).

Figure 7-13. The coordinate system

3. Locate the Bazooka Arm, and focus the view to it (Figure 7-14).

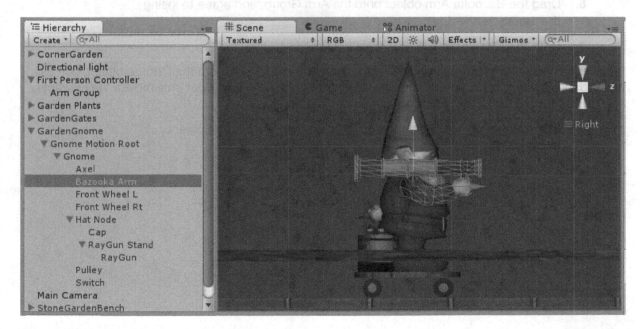

Figure 7-14. The view focused on the Bazooka arm

4. Now select the Arm Group, and use "Move to View" to center it on the Bazooka Arm.

5. Manually adjust it so it is in about the same place as the arm's pivot point (Figure 7-15).

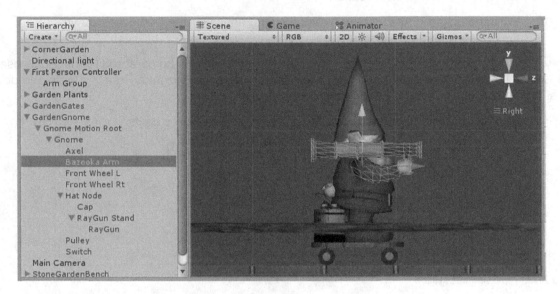

Figure 7-15. The Arm Group moved to the Bazooka Arm's pivot point

6. Drag the Bazooka Arm object onto the Arm Group, and agree to losing the prefab.

7. Drag the GardenGnome onto the First Person Controller.

In order for the Arm group to inherit the extra bouncing movement from the Gnome object, you will have to move the Arm Group into the Gnome group. Gnome Motion Root only moves the character around the scene, and it is currently bypassed by Mecanim.

8. In the Hierarchy view, drag the Arm Group onto the Gnome object (Figure 7-16).

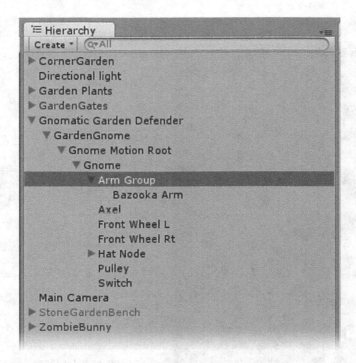

Figure 7-16. The restructured hierarchy

Before you can test the character, you will need to adjust the First Person Controller's collider. It resides in the First Person Controller's Character Controller component. That component contains a capsule collider combined with some Rigidbody features.

1. Set the Character Controller's Height to **1.43** (Figure 7-17).

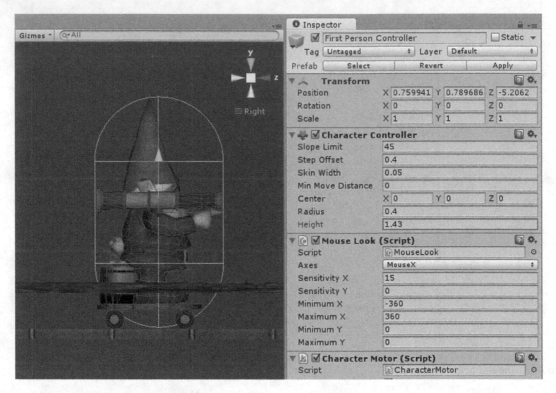

Figure 7-17. The adjusted Character Controller

2.   In the Character Motor component, set the Forward and Sideways Speed to **2**.

3.   Set the Backwards Speed to **1.5**.

Because the little garden defender's wheeled platform doesn't have a jet pack, he shouldn't be allowed to jump.

4.   Turn off Jumping, Moving Platform, and Sliding.

5.   Switch the layout to 2 x 3 or tear off the Scene or game view so you can see both at the same time.

6.   Set the Coordinate system to Local, and select the First Person Controller.

7.   Click Play, and try driving the character around using WASD; the up, down, left, and right arrows; and the mouse to turn and raise and lower the Bazooka Arm.

8.   Drive into the garden area, and drive at the raised bed.

The gnome drives up and into the garden beds with ease. Chances are he could do as much damage as a zombie bunny. You will want to turn the Step Offset down.

1.   Stop Play mode.

2.   In the Character Controller component, set the Step Offset to **0**.

3. Click Play, and try driving to make sure the gnome can't drive up onto the raised beds.

4. Deselect the First Person Controller in the Hierarchy view, refocus to the Game view, and move the mouse to watch the bazooka arm control.

5. Stop Play mode.

6. Rename the First Person Controller to **Gnomatic Garden Defender**.

7. Drag the new combo character onto the GardenGnome prefab in the Prefab's Characters folder.

8. Agree to the "Possible unwanted replacement" warning, and rename the prefab **Gnomatic Garden Defender**.

The character's controls are more in keeping with the environment. There is, however, one obvious problem. The camera should follow the character as a third person so you will be able to see where to aim once the weaponry has been activated. Fortunately, there is a script in the Standard Assets that will work for you.

1. Select the original Main Camera.

2. From the Component menu, Camera-Control, select Smooth Follow.

3. Drag the Gnomatic Garden Defender in as its Target.

4. Set the Distance to **2.8** and the Height to **1.8**.

5. Click Play and test.

6. Stop Play mode.

7. Click Play again, and carefully move the mouse straight up until you can click out of the Game view.

8. Select the Main Camera.

9. From the GameObject menu, select Align View to Selected.

10. Stop Play mode.

11. With the Main Camera selected, in the GameObject menu, choose Align With View.

The camera now starts fairly close to its starting position and orientation when it calculates the Gnomatic Garden Defender's location.

Occlusion Culling

Now that you have a couple of distinct areas in your scene and a means to traverse them, you can consider some occlusion culling. The areas cannot be seen from one to the other except when the character is going through the gates. Unity Pro includes Umbra's Occlusion Culling system, rewritten for Unity 4.3. If you don't have Pro, you can script your own culling when your environment has logical culling areas.

In the current set up, you will use colliders to turn the two areas off and on at either side of the gate. Because the gate walls can be common to multiple areas, you will begin by putting them in their own groups.

1.   Create 3 Empty gameObjects, and name them **Common Wall 1**, **Common Wall 2**, and **Common Wall 3**.

Although the order doesn't really matter, let's consider Common Wall 1 to be the far side of the Staging Area, Common Wall 2 to be the wall between the garden and staging area, and Common Wall 3 to be the far side of the garden.

2.   In a top view, position the empty gameObjects with their future contents.

3.   For each gate wall, select the Garden Gates, Gateway, Raised Walkway, and the two Pillar Corners and Gate Walls.

4.   Put them into the appropriate group (Figure 7-18).

Figure 7-18. Common Wall 2 selected

5.   Rename CornerGarden to **Garden 1**.

Occluder Logic

The logic and layout is simple, but you may have to go through it in your head a few times to reassure yourself that it will work. There will be two colliders on either side of each gateway. They will be set to Is Trigger. As you approach a gateway and go through the outer collider, the area on the other side will be deactivated. (It is already deactivated at this point.) When you go through the inner collider, it will be activated. Next, you go through the collider that opens and closes the gates. You then go through the inner occlusion collider on the other side. The area you just left is turned on (it has remained on), and as you go through the outer collider, it is turned off (Figure 7-19).

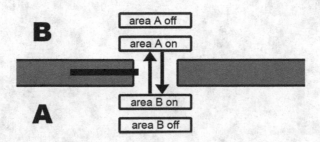

Figure 7-19. An Area/Door/Area occlusion scheme

Arrays and Looping

With the script, you will be introduced to a new concept, that of arrays. *Arrays* are a means of storing multiple objects. In C#, the contents must all be of the same type. To perform your occlusion culling, you will be activating and deactivating the various areas and walls. A deactivated gameObject cannot be "found" with GameObject.Find(<object name>), so it must be identified to the script before the Start function, where you typically set the active state of an object. Because each instance of the script will have to turn different gameObjects off and on, you will keep a list of the objects to be turned on and a list of objects to be turned off.

1. Create a Cube, **2** x **2.5** x **0.5**, about a meter in front of Common Wall 2 on the garden side (Figure 7-20).

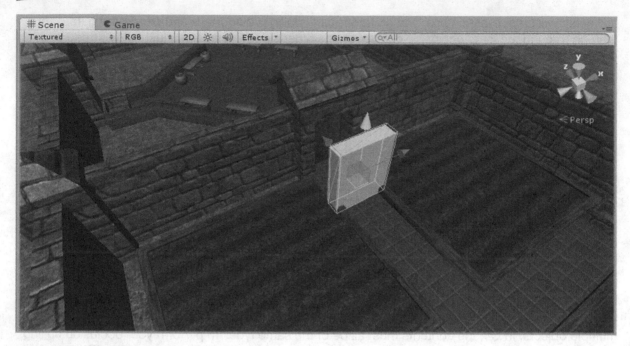

Figure 7-20. The occlusion trigger

2. Name it **Occluder**, and check Is Trigger on its collider.

3. Create a new C# Script in the Game Scripts folder, and name it **OcclusionManager**.

4. Open the script.

5. Beneath the class declaration, create the following variables:

    ```
    public bool state; //active state to put the array elements into
    public GameObject[] newArea; // array for the other side of the gate
    ```

6. Save the script, and put it on the Occlusion object.

7. In the Inspector, open the New Area array.

The New Area array will include Common Wall 1 and the Staging Area, the objects on the *other* side of the wall. So its Size will be 2.

8. Set the array Size to **2**.

9. Drag the appropriate gameObjects into the array elements (Figure 7-21).

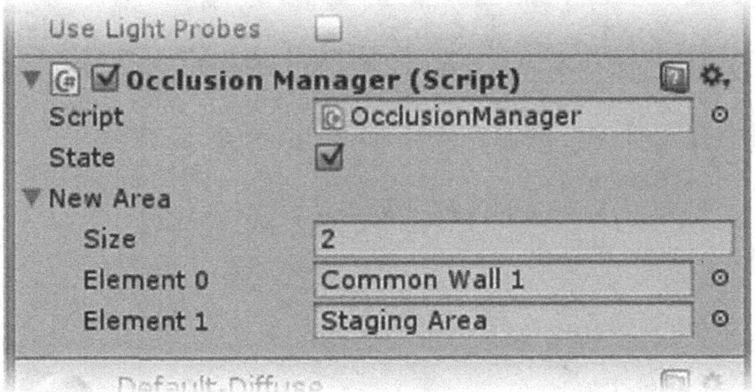

Figure 7-21. The New Area array

The code will use the same OnTriggerEnter function that you used for the SensorDoors script, including the check for the "Player" tag. Anything that can trigger the doors also must trigger the occlusion culling.

1. Open the SensorDoors script, and copy the OnTriggerEnter function.

2. Paste it into the OcclusionManager script in the same location.

3. Delete the animation and audio lines, and clear the comments above the function.

Inside the function, you will iterate through the array, setting the objects to active or inactive. The difference between the inner and outer colliders will be the state that the array elements are put into.

To iterate through an array, you have a couple of options. Arrays must have their size declared before they can be used. By making this one public and filling it out in the Inspector, you have met this requirement. Because their size must be declared and cannot change during runtime, arrays have a length parameter. Knowing that, you can iterate through them with a for loop. To test the code, you will have it print out the contents of the array from the Start function.

4. Inside the Start function, add the following:

```
for (int i = 0; i < newArea.Length; i++) {
    print (newArea [i].name); // print the name of element number i
}
```

Note the capital *L* on *Length*. The for loop iterates through an array by element number, a temporary int type variable named i in this example, as long as i is less than the length of the array. Arrays always start at 0, so the last element number is 1 less than the length. The counter, i, is incremented by 1 (i++) after whatever is inside the curly brackets is evaluated. The for loop is especially useful when you don't want to go through the entire array or when you require the element number for a particular operation.

5. Save the script, and click Play.

The contents of the New Area array are printed in the console (Figure 7-22).

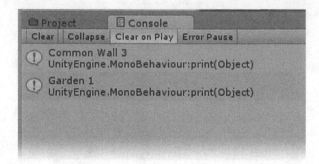

Figure 7-22. The contents of the New Area array on Occluder

A more abbreviated way to iterate through an array is the foreach loop. Because foreach loops do not require a *length* to know when to stop, they have the advantage of being able to iterate through lists. Lists are a close relative of arrays. Unlike arrays, you cannot get their length, but their length *can* be dynamically changed during run time. Let's get the contents of the newArea array with the foreach loop.

6. Below the closing curly bracket for the for loop, add the following:

```
print (""); // do a carriage return

foreach(GameObject theElement in newArea) {
    print (theElement.name); // print the name of the current element
}
```

7. Save the script, and click Play.

The results are the same. The foreach loop goes through the array, assigning each to a temporary variable of type GameObject, prints its name, and continues going through the array until it has come to the end of the array. The foreach is perfect for doing something to each element in an array. Let's use the foreach loop to change the active state on the array elements.

8. Delete or comment out the contents of the Start function.

9. Add the following to the OnTriggerEnter function, inside the if clause:

```
foreach(GameObject theElement in newArea) {
    theElement.SetActive(state); // set the object's active parameter to state
}
```

The SetActive function or method will set the object and all of its children on or off according to whether you use true or false as its argument.

10. Save the script.

You will require four occluder triggers for each gate, so this will be a good candidate for a prefab.

1. In the Prefabs folder, create a new folder and name it **Misc**.

2. Drop the Occluder object into the new folder.

3. Rename Occluder in the Hierarchy to **Occluder 2a Off**.

4. Duplicate the Occluder 2a Off object, and name it **Occluder 2a On.**

5. Turn its State on by checking it in the Inspector.

6. Move the Occluder 2a Off object back away from the gateway.

Before you can test the new code, you must make occluder objects for the other side of the gate.

1. Duplicate the two occluder objects, and move them to the other side of the gate, putting the On version close to the gate and the Off version farther from it.

You may have to adjust the spacing if you back through the gateway, and the area disappears before the doors have finished closing.

2. Name them **Occluder 2b On** and **Occluder 2b Off** (Figure 7-23).

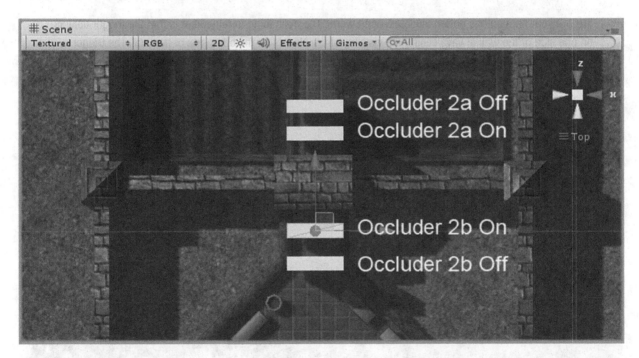

Figure 7-23. The occluder boxes

3. Change the "b" versions' New Area array element assignments as per Figure 7-24.

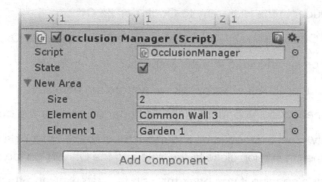

Figure 7-24. The contents of the New Area array on Occluder 2b On

> **Tip** If your naming has gotten muddled, don't worry. The main thing to remember is that the trigger objects on one side of the wall always control the visibility of the objects on the other side of the wall. The trigger closest to the door always turns things on, and the one furthest away always turns things off.

4. Disable the Mesh Renderer component on the Occluder prefab in the Hierarchy view.

To test the occluders, you will require something to drive through the gate. It's time to bring the GGD back into the scene.

1. Click Play, and drive the Gnomatic Garden Defender backwards and forward through the gate.

The areas disappear and reappear as the Gnomatic Garden Defender goes through the gateway (Figure 7-25).

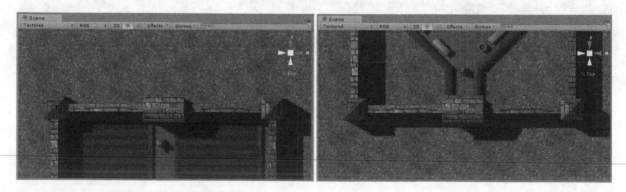

Figure 7-25. The occlusion system in action

It would be nice to see if you can turn off the garden area before the game starts to see if the deactivated objects will continue to function properly.

2. Deactivate the Common Wall 3 and the Garden 1 objects in the Inspector.

3. Click Play, and drive the GGD back and forth through the gate.

The objects continue to work as expected. The problem is that it will be difficult to work on the scene with half of it hidden. A better solution is to turn the objects off in the Start function.

4. Reactivate the Common Wall 3 and the Garden 1 objects.

5. Create a new C# Script in the Game Scripts folder, and name it **HideAtStart**.

6. In its Start function, add the following:

```
gameObject.SetActive(false); //deactivate the object this script is on
```

7. Save the script, and drop it on the Common Wall 3 and the Garden 1 objects.

8. Click Play, and test the new functionality.

The objects disappear on startup and reappear when you exit Play mode. Feel free to set up the other GardenGates for occlusion culling or disable the box collider that opens the doors.

Game Functionality

With the static part of the environment working well, you can concentrate on the dynamic elements. The most obvious is the main character, the Gnomatic Garden Defender. The drawback to using objects that can occlude sections of the environment is that third-person cameras will usually go through them at some point, as you probably noticed as you drove the d back and forth.

You will also be adding the protagonists of the story as well as fleshing out the environment with the help of a few more scripts.

Camera Refinements

You probably noticed that the third-person camera is fine until the Gnomatic Garden Defender goes through the gateway. At that point, it clips the top of the Gateway. One solution is to change Distance and Height values on the Smooth Follow component when the Gnomatic Garden Defender triggers the gates. It's a bit abrupt, but it is a simple solution. The first thing to do is get access to the Camera's SmoothFollow component.

1. Open the SensorDoors script.

2. Add the following variable below the existing ones:

```
public SmoothFollow follow; // the camera' SmoothFollow script
```

3. In the `OnTriggerEnter` function below the `if` function, add

```
follow.distance = 1.15f; // change the SmoothFollow distance
follow.height = 0.5f;    // change the SmoothFollow height
```

4. In the `OnTriggerExit` function below the `if` function, add

```
follow.distance = 2.8f; // revert the SmoothFollow distance
follow.height = 1.8f;   // revert the SmoothFollow height
```

5. Save the script.

6. Select Common Wall 2's GardenGates object, and drag the Main Camera onto the Follow parameter.

7. Click Play, and test the new functionality.

It's an improvement, but you would have more control if you could adjust the camera relative to how close the gnome was to the gate. The closer the gnome is to the gateway, the closer to the gnome the camera should be. While this solution also has some "gotchas," it will give you a chance to try another extremely useful bit of scripting, the `Distance()` function.

1. Comment out or delete the `follow` lines you added to the SensorDoors script (including the variable declaration).

2. Save the script.

3. Create a new C# Script in the Game Scripts, and name it **DistanceDetector**.

The `Distance()` function can use `Vector2`, `Vector3`, and `Vector4` data to calculate distance. `Vector2` is (x,y), `Vector3` is (x,y,z), and `Vector4` is (x,y,z,w). Color, a 3 or 4 part *struct*, can be (r,g,b) or (r,g,b,a). For the gateway, the `Vector2` variety will give better results, as it can ignore the distance from the ground.

4. Just below the class declaration, add the following variables:

```
public Transform targetTransform; // the gnome's transform
public Transform theCamera;       // the camera's transform
Vector2 source; // the gateway
Vector2 target; // the gnome
```

Using a `Vector2` means you will have to assign the x and z values from the transform manually.

5. In the `Start` function, add the following:

```
// assign the x and z position to the source var
source = new Vector2(transform.position.x,transform.position.z);
```

A *Struct*, or structure, is a value type that is typically used to encapsulate small groups of related variables. To access the elements of the struct, one uses dot notation.

The target, the Gnomatic Garden Defender, because it may be moving, must be updated every frame. To begin with, you will have the distance printed out in the console.

6. In the Update function, add the following:

```
// update the target's location
target = new Vector2(targetTransform.position.x,targetTransform.position.z);
// get the distance between the target and source
float dist = Vector3.Distance(source, target);
print (dist);
```

7. Save the script, and add it to the Common Wall 2's GardenGates object.

8. Drag the Gnomatic Garden Defender onto its Target Transform parameter.

9. Drag the Main Camera onto its Camera parameter.

10. Click Play, and watch the distance in the console as you drive back and forth through the gateway.

The distance should be at about 0 when the gnome goes through the doors (Figure 7-26).

Figure 7-26. Almost at doors, distance nearing 0

Before you go any farther, there is a logic problem to solve. The camera is currently controlled by the SmoothFollow script. A solution is to link the camera to a dummy object that has the SmoothFollow so that the camera distance can always be adjusted relative to the dummy's position. While this sounds like a painful adjustment, because of Unity's component architecture, it will actually be quick and easy.

1. Duplicate the Main Camera, and drag one onto the other.

2. Name the parent **Main Camera Target**.

3. Remove its Camera, Audio Listener, GUILayer, and Flare Layer components.

4. Select the child, Main Camera, remove its Smooth Follow component, and set its tag to Untagged.

5. Look at Main Camera's Transforms.

When Main Camera was parented, its transforms were all set to 0 because transforms in the Inspector are always "local." When an object has a parent, its transforms are relative to its parent. Because they were just duplicated, the offsets between the parent (with the SmoothFollow component) and child (with the Camera component) are all 0.

6. In the Garden Gates' Distance Detector component, assign the Main Camera as its The Camera parameter.

7. Click Play, and test to make sure the camera works as it did before the changeover.

The results should be the same, but now the object with the camera component can be moved independently of the object that is used to calculate the distance. You will be setting its local z, or forward direction, to an offset derived from the distance between the gnome and the Gateway center.

Logically, you only want to adjust the camera's position when it is close to the gateway, without letting it get too close to the character. A range of 3.0 to 1.0 is a good starting point. When the gnome gets within 3.0 meters of the center of the gateway, the camera will start getting closer to the character. When the gnome is 1 meter from the gateway center, the camera will not be able to get any closer to the gnome. Let's add a condition for the range and watch the printouts to see if it looks okay.

1. Change the `print` statement so it is wrapped in conditional as follows:

```
if (dist < 3.0f && dist > 0.5f) {
   print (dist);
}
else print (""); // clear the status line
```

2. Save the script, and test to make sure the values reported are always within the stipulated range.

You could get fancy with the distance calculations, but in this script you will just use the total range minus the current range. For example, when the gnome is 2 meters from the gateway's center, the camera will be 3.0 - 2.0, or 1.5 closer to the gnome on its local Z, or forward, direction. At 1 meter away, the camera will be 2.5 meters closer to the gnome than its base distance.

3. Replace the `print` statement with the following:

```
Vector3 pos = theCamera.transform.localPosition; // make a variable to hold the current
local position of the camera
pos.z = 3.0f - dist; // assign the inverse of the distance to the z part of the temporary
variable
theCamera.transform.localPosition = pos; // assign the new position
```

4. Comment out the `else` line.

5. Save the script, and test the new code.

This time the camera sucks down to the character as you head through the gate (Figure 7-27) and comes back up as you leave it behind. You could get some clipping if you turn the character in the center of the gate, especially if the character is off to one side. To avoid it, you could tighten the minimum distance, add colliders that would funnel the character to the center, increase the character's collider while in the gateway, or even prevent the character from turning while in the gateway. Because it is far too easy to get bogged down in details early in a game's development, you will be leaving it as is.

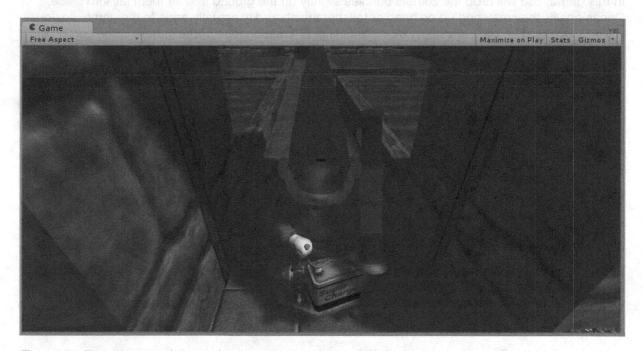

Figure 7-27. The camera moved close to the character as he passed through the gateway

Even if you have disabled the door functionality to prevent the Gnomatic Garden Defender from leaving the compound completely, you will want the camera to avoid intersecting the gateway structures and doors when the character is too close to them.

1. Right-click over the Distance Detector component, and select Copy Component.

2. Select one of the other GardenGate objects.

3. Right-click over any of its component labels, and select "Paste Component as New."

4. Repeat for the other GardenGates object.

Adding the Zombie Bunnies

The Gnomatic Garden Defender's main task will be to obliterate the ravening hoards of zombie bunnies from your garden. To make things interesting, you will be dropping the varmints randomly around the garden in random numbers and adding to the population at random times. In case you haven't guessed yet, the key word here is "random." Randomness is a staple of most games, but especially casual games that are meant to be played over and over as the player refines his skill and cunning.

In this game, you will drop the zombie bunnies slightly off the ground and let them fall into place. Occasionally, they may end up on head or tail, but the absurdity actually adds to the game, so you will let them land at will. Let's begin by *instantiating*, or creating, one of the critters in the garden area during runtime. The trick to instantiation is that you are not creating everything from scratch, you are re-creating existing prefabs.

1. Create a new C# Script, and name it **SpawnBunnies**.

2. Add the following variable under the class declaration:

   ```
   public GameObject zombieBunny; // the zombieBunny prefab
   ```

3. In the Start function, instantiate the prefab:

   ```
   Instantiate (zombieBunny); // create a new zombie bunny prefab in the scene
   ```

4. Save the script.

Before you can test the script, you will have to put it on an object in the scene. You will be defining an area where the zombie bunnies can be instantiated, but you will want to keep the script abstracted from any particular garden in case you eventually have multiple gardens or levels.

5. Create a new Empty GameObject, and name it **Zombie Spawn Manager**.

6. Add the SpawnBunnies script to it.

7. Drag the ZombieBunny prefab from the Prefabs' Characters folder in the Project view to the Zombie Spawn Manager's Spawn Bunnies component's Zombie Bunny parameter.

8. Move the Gnomatic Garden Defender into the garden area, and disable the Hide At Start component on the Garden 1 and Common Wall 3.

9. Click Play, and look around the garden to find the new instantiated zombie bunny.

The zombie bunny is instantiated in the scene at the last position he was in when you created or updated his prefab (Figure 7-28).

Figure 7-28. The instantiated zombie bunny

Investigating Instantiation

Many functions can be "overloaded," that is they can take different arguments. When you use the Instantiate function with only the prefab to be instantiated in it, it will use the transform stored on the prefab to position and orient it. But this function can also set the new object at a specified location and orientation.

■ Do a search for GameObject.Instantiate in the Scripting Reference.

You will see that it shows both argument options or overloads (Figure 7-29).

Object.Instantiate

static Object **Instantiate**(Object **original**, Vector3 **position**, Quaternion **rotation**);
static Object **Instantiate**(Object **original**);

Parameters

original	An existing object that you want to make a copy of.
position	Position for the new object.
rotation	Orientation of the new object.

Description
Clones the object original and returns the clone.

Figure 7-29. The Instantiate function options

This is where you will make use of a "Zombie Zone" to come up with a random location and orientation for the critters. You could hard-code the location, of course, but set up will be easier and more flexible if you create a bounding box from which to pull the location and dimensions.

1. Create a cube in the garden area, and name it **Zombie Zone**.

2. Set its collider to Is Trigger.

3. Turn off its Mesh Renderer, and scale it to cover the inside garden area, just inside the walls (Figure 7-30).

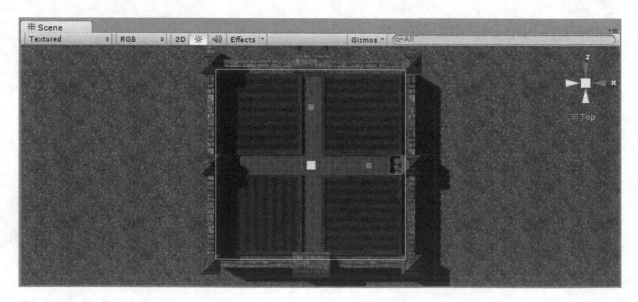

Figure 7-30. The Zombie Zone

The height doesn't matter, as you will only be using its x and z dimensions.

4. In the SpawnBunnies script, add the following new variable declarations:

```
public Transform currentZone; // the drop zone
float minX; // variables to hold the object's bounding box location
float maxX;
float minZ;
float maxZ;
```

Rather than calculate the corner locations manually, you can let Unity do the math in the Start function. This has the added advantage of being able to clone the zone, move it, or resize it at will.

5. Add the following in the Start function above the Instantiate line to calculate the bounds:

```
minX = currentZone. position.x - currentZone. localScale.x/2;
maxX = currentZone. position.x + currentZone. localScale.x/2;
minZ = currentZone. position.z - currentZone. localScale.z/2;
maxZ = currentZone. position.z + currentZone. localScale.z/2;
```

Because you defined the currentZone variable as a Transform, you need only add .position instead of transform.position when accessing its x and z values.

Randomization

To make use of the data, you will use Random.Range() to choose the locations to spawn the varmints. To set the location, you will construct a new Vector3 to hold the x, y, and z values. For y you will use 1.0 so the prefab can drop and settle.

1. Change the Instantiate line as follows:

```
// create a new zombie bunny prefab in the scene
Instantiate(zombieBunny, new Vector3(Random.Range(minX,maxX), 1.0f, Random.
Range(minZ,maxZ)), Quaternion.identity);
```

Quaternion.identity means that the object will have no rotation, it will be perfectly aligned with the world or parent axes, which all have rotation values at 0.

When using Random.Range with integers, the max number is *exclusive*. That means it will not use the maximum range number when generating. This is useful if you are randomizing anything in an array where the element numbers start at 0 and the last element number is 1 less than the array Length. For floats, the maximum number is *inclusive*. It can be one (or more) of the generated numbers. One thing to be aware of is that random numbers may occur more than once in a list generated by Random.Range. In case of the zombie bunnies, dropping them with the physics' rigid body will deal with any duplicate locations.

Before you test the new additions to the script, you will have to make a change to the zombie bunny prefab. To drop and settle, the zombie bunny will require a Rigidbody component.

2. Add a Rigidbody component to the zombie bunny prefab in the Project view.

3. Save the script.

4. Assign the Zombie Zone object to the Current Zone parameter.

5. Click Play several times to see the random locations each time the prefab is instantiated.

If you are having trouble locating the object in the scene, it will be named ZombieBunny(Clone) in the Hierarchy view. You can click on it in the Hierarchy view to help locate it (Figure 7-31). You will be randomizing its rotation later on.

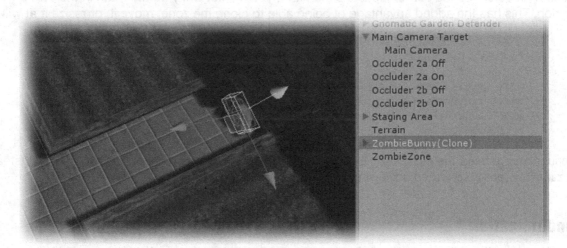

Figure 7-31. The clone showing in the scene and Hierarchy view

With the location randomization working, let's see about adding more critters to the scene. But first, since you will be populating gardens at different times, let's see about putting it in its own function.

1. Create a new function below the Update function:

```
void PopulateGardenBunnies (int count) {

}
```

By having it take an argument, count, you can use it to populate gardens of different sizes or difficulties.

2. Move the Instantiate lines from the Start function, and add them to the new function.

3. Add a new variable to allow the difficulty to be changed more easily:

```
int litterSize = 10; // max base number of zombie bunnies to instantiate
```

4. In the Start function, after the min/max assignments, call your newly created function and pass it an argument using the litterSize variable, 10 in this case:

```
PopulateGardenBunnies (litterSize);
```

Next you will use the count number to generate some bunnies. You've used a foreach loop to manage the areas in your OcclusionManager script, but this time you have no pre-existing arrays to iterate through. You just want to do something a finite number of times, so you will use a standard for loop.

5. Wrap the Instantiate code as follows:

```
for (int i = 0; i < count; i++) {
    // create new zombie bunny prefabs in the scene
    Instantiate(zombieBunny, new Vector3(Random.Range(minX,maxX), 1.0f, Random.
Range(minZ,maxZ)), Quaternion.identity);

}
```

6. Save the script, and press Play.

The ravening hoard creeps slowly forward (Figure 7-32).

Figure 7-32. The randomly placed zombie bunnies creeping slowly forward through the garden

You may have noticed that with the addition of the Rigidbody component, the zombie bunnies are no longer as mobile as they originally were. You could decrease their Mass and Angular Drag, but the result would not quite be the same. In this case, if they were to continue moving at their animated pace, many would just end up clustered around the edges of the garden. As zombies aren't terribly mobile at the best of times, the reduced forward momentum is more of a bonus than a hindrance.

Let's get some more practice with random numbers. Because you never know how many zombie bunnies might be devouring your garden, it would be fun to populate it with a random number based on the number that was passed in, count. A good range might be 3/4 of the count to a full count.

7.   At the top of the PopulateGardenBunnies() function, add the following:

```
count = Random.Range(count*3/4,count +1); // randomize the count number
print("zombie Bunnies = " + count);
```

8.   Set the litterSize value to **8.**

9.   In the Start function, change the call to PopulateBunnies as follows:

```
int tempLitterSize = litterSize * 3; // increased for first drop only
PopulateGardenBunnies (tempLitterSize);  // create new zombie bunny prefabs in the scene
```

Setting a temporary variable based on the normal litter size keeps the variables that would have to be changed to a minimum if you were going to adjust the difficulty of the game at a later stage. This way, you will get a higher number of zombie bunnies the first time the garden is populated.

10.   Click Play a few times to see the adjusted count in the console and in the scene.

With more critters in the scene, it's time to change a few things. If you want to change things that can't be set directly in the Instantiate method, you will need a means of identifying the clone right after it was created. If you look back to the description of Instantiate, you will see that it "returns" a value, the instantiated prefab of type GameObject. That means you can assign the new prefab as a value to a new variable of the same type.

11.   Preface the Instantiate line with the following:

```
GameObject zBunny = (GameObject)
```

The instantiated object has to be cast as a GameObject before you can assign it to a type GameObject.

12.   Add the following after the Instantiate line:

```
Vector3 rot = zBunny.transform.localEulerAngles; // make a variable to hold the current
local Euler (x,y,z) rotation
rot.y = Random.Range(1,361); // assign a random rotation to the y part of the temporary
variable
zBunny.transform.localEulerAngles = rot; // assign the new rotation
```

13.   Save the script, and click Play.

The critters are nicely random in their orientation (Figure 7-33).

Figure 7-33. The critters randomly overrunning the garden

Now the main problem appears to be that they all start the animation clip at the same place. Let's see about randomizing that as well. The clip length is referred to as a unit size, so 1 is 100% of the animation clip. You will require access to each individual clone's Animator component and will get it on the fly.

14.   Beneath the rotation code, add the following:

```
// randomize the animation clip starting point zBunny.GetComponent<Animator>().
Play("Bunny Eat", 0, Random.Range(0.0f,1.0f));
```

Here you are accessing the Animator component, referring to its Bunny Eat state/clip on the base layer, 0, and choosing a random place on its (normalized) timeline to start the animation clip.

15.   Save the script, and click Play.

Now the zombie bunnies happily overrun the garden in a much more random state. But wait, there's more…

Coroutines as Timers

Everyone knows rabbits are famous for their rapid rate of reproduction. Part of the challenge of the game will be to destroy the zombie hoard before it can reproduce beyond the Gnomatic Garden Defender 's ability to stop it. As you probably guessed, the number of zombie bunnies added each time will be random within a small range. This is the beauty of having created the PopulateGardenBunnies() function to take a count as an argument. Here's the new part; this time, you will create a timer that, yes, you guessed it, randomly calls the PopulateGardenBunnies() function to add to the current zombie bunny population.

This timer is very simple. It doesn't require any GUI printout, so for it, you will use a `yield`. Using yield in C# is a lot more complicated than in JavaScript, but it is a very handy thing to know how to do. Yield sets a pause before the lines of code following it are evaluated. Most code is evaluated in a linear fashion: *b* follows *a*, *c* follows *b*, etc. A *coroutine* does not pause the evaluation of the functions; it merely delays what happens after the time has elapsed, by running in *conjunction* with the rest of the code until it has finished. To call it from any function, you must use `StartCoroutine()`. The function it calls from there is an iEnumerator. You will let the Gnomatic Garden Defender do his job for 25–30 seconds before the zombie bunnies start multiplying. Once they start multiplying, they will multiply every 10–15 seconds thereafter. In case you are wondering if there will be any way to stop the ravening hoards from reproducing and overrunning the garden and the world, you will create a flag, canReproduce, that will be able to stop the vicious cycle!

1. Create a new variable to store the rate of reproduction:

```
float reproRate = 12f; // base time before respawning
```

2. In the `Start` function, after the call to `PopulateGardenBunnies`, add the following:

```
float tempRate = reproRate * 2; // allow extra time before the first drop
StartCoroutine(StartReproducing(tempRate)); // start the first timer; pass in reproRate
seconds
```

The first respawn is longer to give the player time to settle in. It uses a temporary variable, local to the `Start` function, derived from the regular reproduction rate. It may seem like a lot of extra work to add variables instead of hard-coding numbers, but if you wanted to make things easier or harder for the player, just as with the `litterSize`, you would have to change the `reproRate` in only one place.

3. And now create the `StartReproducing()` iEnumerator (a different kind of function):

```
IEnumerator StartReproducing(float minTime) {
    // wait for this much time before going on
    float adjustedTime = Random.Range(minTime, minTime + 5f);
    yield return new WaitForSeconds(adjustedTime);
    // having waited, make more zombie bunnies
    PopulateGardenBunnies (litterSize);
    //and start the coroutine again to minTime, but only if there are enough left to reproduce...
    if (canReproduce) StartCoroutine(StartReproducing(reproRate));
}
```

4. Up with the variable declarations, add the flag to control the reproduction:

```
bool canReproduce = true; // flag to control reproduction of zombie bunnies
```

5. Save the script.

6. Click Play, and sit back and watch the show.

The zombie bunnies quickly overrun the garden (Figure 7-34).

Figure 7-34. The ravening hoards overrunning the garden

It would be fun to stress out the player by triggering an audio cue that the zombie bunnies are about to multiply. Because you calculated the random number before it was fed into the for loop, you can delay the reproducing by a few seconds to give the audio cue.

1. Change the yield return new WaitForSeconds(adjustedTime) line to:

    ```
    yield return new WaitForSeconds(adjustedTime-3f); // pause 3 seconds before time's up
    audio.Play(); // play the sound effect that signals the repro populating
    yield return new WaitForSeconds(3f); // finish the adjusted time
    ```

2. Save the script.

3. From Components, Audio, add an AudioSource component to the Zombie Spawn Manager object.

4. Set its Volume Rolloff to Linear Rolloff.

5. Uncheck "Play on Awake."

6. From the Sound FX folder, load the Stork audio clip in as its default clip.

Storks communicate by using a lot of beak clacking. This will tell the player that a new batch of zombie bunnies are about to be deposited in the garden.

7. Click Play, and listen for the stork heralding the arrival of more zombie bunnies.

It would also be useful to know the current number of zombie bunnies…to put more pressure on the player! Let's create a variable to keep count. In Chapter 9, you will incorporate the count in the GUI.

1. Create a new variable with the other variables:

```
int currentBunCount = 0; // current number of zombie bunnies
```

To be able to add all of those random amounts, you need only track the PopulateGardenBunnies function.

2. In the PopulateGardenBunnies() function, directly above the print statement, add the following:

```
currentBunCount += count; // add the lastest count to the current total
```

3. In the print statement, replace count with currentBunCount.

4. Save the script.

5. Click Play, and watch current count being incremented in the console as new zombie bunnies are instantiated into the scene.

Spring Planting

Now that the zombie bunnies are under control, or out of control in this case, you may want to find room for some of the vegetable prefabs you created in Chapter 4. Unlike with the zombie bunnies, you will want these laid out in neat rows.

Nested Loops

Once again, you will make use of a for loop, but this time, to get nice evenly spaced rows, you will embed or nest one for loop inside the other. Think of one loop for the rows and the other for the columns. Just as with the Zombie Zone, you can define a Bed Zone with a cube. This time, however, you will be using its y value to determine ground level.

1. In an overhead ortho view, create a cube to cover the inner part of one of the Raised Bed objects (Figure 7-35).

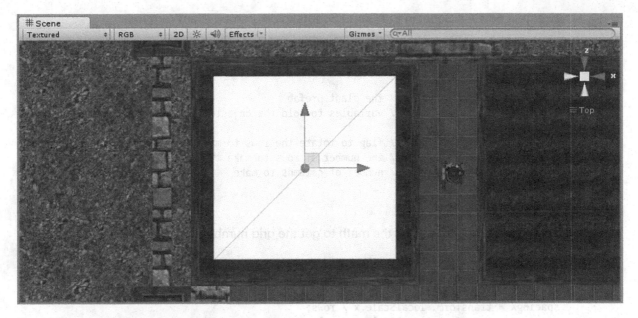

Figure 7-35. The Plant Zone, smaller than the ground area

2. Name it **Plant Zone**.

3. Set its collider to Is Trigger, and disable its Mesh Renderer.

4. Switch to a side ortho view and Wireframe, and move it up so its pivot point is level with the ground in the Raised Bed (Figure 7-36).

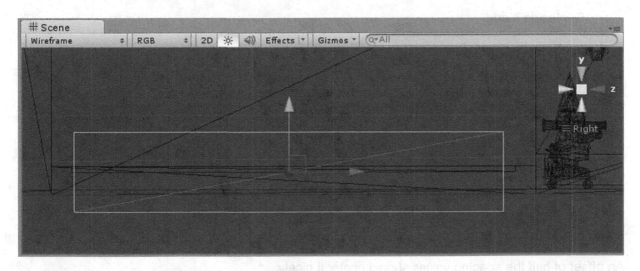

Figure 7-36. The Plant Zone on top of the ground in the Raised Bed

1. Create a new C# Script in the Game Scripts folder named **PlantVeggies**.

Some of the code is the same as in the SpawnBunnies script. Feel free to copy and paste.

2. Below its class declaration, add the following variables:

```
public GameObject veggie; // the plant prefab
float minX;               // variables to hold the object's bounding box location
float minZ;
public bool rotate;       // flag to rotate the rows to match the bed
public int rows = 6;      // the number of rows to make
public int columns = 6;   // number of columns to make
float spacingX;
float spacingZ;
```

3. In the Start function, do all the math to get the grid numbers:

```
// calculate box position
minX = transform.position.x - transform.localScale.x/2;
minZ = transform.position.z - transform.localScale.z/2;
spacingX = transform. localScale.x / rows;
spacingZ = transform. localScale.z / columns;

PopulateBed(); // plant the Veggies
```

4. Create the function:

```
void PopulateBed () {

}
```

5. Inside it add

```
float y = transform.position.y; // ground level
for (int x = 0; x < columns; x++) {
   for (int z = 0; z < rows; z++) {
      Vector3 pos = new Vector3(x * spacingX + minX, y, z * spacingZ + minZ);
      GameObject newVeggie = (GameObject) Instantiate(veggie, pos, Quaternion.identity);
   }
}
```

6. Save the script.

7. Drag it onto the Plant Zone object.

8. Drag one of the smaller plant prefabs in as its Veggie.

9. Click Play, and note the positioning of the plants.

An offset of half the spacing values should center it nicely.

10. Change the `Vector3` pos line to include the offset amounts:

    ```
    Vector3 pos = new Vector3(x * spacingX + minX + spacingX / 2, y, z * spacingZ + minZ +
    spacingZ / 2);
    ```

11. Click Play, and check the positioning (Figure 7-37).

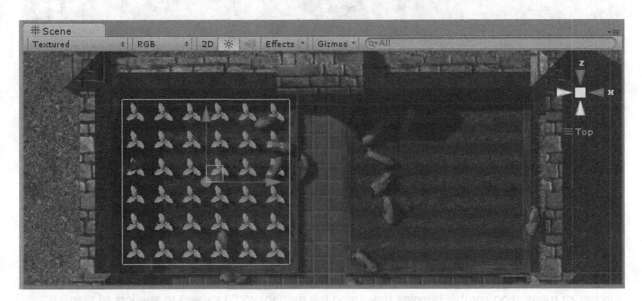

Figure 7-37. The veggies auto-planted

With the computer doing all the hard work in your garden, you might want to make use of the code from the SpawnBunnies script to add some rotation variation. And you may as well do a bit of scale randomizing as well because the code is very similar.

1. Add the following code for random rotation beneath the `GameObject` `newVeggie` line:

    ```
    // assign a random rotation to the clone
    Vector3 rot = newVeggie.transform.localEulerAngles; // make a variable to hold the
    current local Euler (x,y,z) rotation
    rot.y = Random.Range(1,361); // assign a random rotation to the y part of the temporary
    variable
    newVeggie.transform.localEulerAngles = rot; // assign the new rotation
    ```

2. Save the script, and click Play to see the results.

3. Add the following code for random scale:

    ```
    // assign a random scale to the clone
    Vector3 scale = newVeggie.transform.localScale; // variable to hold the current local
    scale
    float rScale =  Random.Range(0.5f,1.2f);
    scale = new Vector3(rScale,rScale,rScale);
    newVeggie.transform.localScale = scale; // assign the new rotation
    ```

4.   Save the script, and click Play to see the results (Figure 7-38).

Figure 7-38. The randomized veggies

The plants a looking pretty good. But there's one more thing you could do to them. Given the number of marauding zombie bunnies devouring the garden, you'd expect to see lots of plants missing. So the final refinement will be to remove random plants, or better yet, prevent them from being instantiated. To do that, you will wrap all of the Instantiation and customization code in an `if` statement. The condition will be a percent specified in the bed's set up. If the random number is less than that percent, the plant is skipped over during planting.

1.   Add one more variable to the rest of the regular variables:

```
public int percent = 20; // percent of missing plants
```

2.   Below the `Vector3 pos = new Vector3` line, add

```
int rPercent = Random.Range (1,101); // 1-100%
if (rPercent > percent) { // plant the plant
```

3.   Add the closing curly bracket below the randomize scale section, and indent the contents of the new conditional.

4.   Save the script, and click Play to see the results.

The plants now look authentically decimated by the zombie bunnies (Figure 7-39).

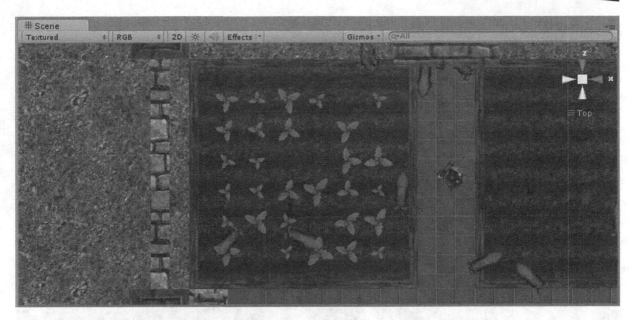

Figure 7-39. The veggies ravaged by zombie bunnies

Parenting

There's one last thing to be done to wrap up this chapter. Between the plants and the zombie bunnies, you've added quite a bit of geometry that should eventually be hidden by your occlusion system. This means you will want to see about getting all of the clones parented. The most obvious parent is the object that defines the zone. Fortunately, parenting is a simple operation performed on the object's transform, not the gameObject itself.

1. Open the SpawnBunnies script again.

The SpawnBunnies script uses the Zombie Zone object to place the zombie bunnies, but due to their mobile nature, you won't want any mishaps with inherited scale distorting them. The safest parent will be an empty gameObject with its default scale of 1 x 1 x 1.

2. Create a new Empty GameObject, and name it Bun Holder.

3. In the SpawnBunnies script, add a variable to store the object's transform:

    ```
    public Transform bunHolder; // to parent the instantiated zombie bunnies to
    ```

4. Add the following line below the zBunny.GetComponent<Animator> line of the SpawnBunnies script:

    ```
    zBunny.transform.parent = bunHolder; // assign the clone to this object's transform
    ```

5. Save the script.

6. Drag the new Bun Holder object onto the Bun Holder parameter in the Spawn Bunnies component.

7. In the PlantVeggies script, just below the GameObject newVeggie = line, add

    newVeggie.transform.parent = transform; // assign the clone to this object

8. Save the script.

9. Click Play, and inspect the Hierarchy view.

The clones are neatly stashed with their zones in the Hierarchy view during runtime (Figure 7-40).

Figure 7-40. The clones neatly parented to the zone objects that generated them

One little problem. Children inherit the transforms of their parents. The plants are scaled *after* they are parented, so the plants pick up the Plant Zone's scale. Fortunately, if you assign the parent *after* the random scaling, everything is good.

10. Move the parenting line *below* the scaling line in the PlantVeggies script.

11. Save the script.

12. Click Play, and make sure everything is working properly.

13. Duplicate the Plant zone, and fill out the plants to suit your fancy.

Now you can move the zones so that the plants and zombie bunnies are hidden when the rest of the garden is out of sight.

14. Drag the Plant Zone, Zombie Zone, and Bun Holder objects onto the Garden 1 object.

15. Click Play, and drive the gnome into the staging area.

16. Check the Scene view to confirm that all the "extras" disappear when the garden area is deactivated.

17. Save the scene, and save the project.

Summary

In this chapter, you got a chance to expand your working knowledge of prefabs as you created a couple of enclosed areas for the game's environment using the assets you set up in earlier chapters. By enclosing the areas so that each was occluded when the player was in the other area, you got to create a small system for occlusion culling. In doing so, you were introduced to the concept of arrays to store and manage multiple objects of the same type.

With two areas for the player to travel between, you discovered a drawback of third-person camera navigation. Any time the character goes into a tight spot or turns too close to a barrier, the camera could go through the geometry. While the garden's design helped to prevent the latter, the former needed a solution. To help you solve the problem, you turned to the `Distance()` function. It allowed you to set the camera's local z position relative to how close the character was to a gate.

Having worked out the structure and flow of the environment, you turned your efforts to populating the garden. Using `Instantiate`, you discovered the joys of `Random,Range` as you dropped zombie bunnies into the scene with abandon. You discovered that you could randomize everything from position, rotation, and even the starting location in the motion clip for each of the instantiated critters.

Repurposing the instantiating code, you learned how to use a *coroutine* to delay events while allowing the rest of the game to go forward. `Yield` and `WaitForSeconds` allowed you to add to the varmint population throughout the game automatically. Splitting up the delay even gave you the opportunity to warn the player when a population explosion was imminent.

Using nested loops, you discovered that you could let the computer plant the garden for you. The liberal use of `Random.Range` once again helped break the monotony of a computer-generated layout.

Finally, to tidy up the large number of clones instantiated into your scene, you learned how to dynamically parent them so that all could be tucked away in the proper area for occlusion culling when the Gnomatic Garden Defender traveled from one area to the other.

Chapter 8

Weaponry and Special Effects

With the garden currently being overrun by ravenous zombie bunnies, you will be thankful to get some weapon-craft knowledge under your belt. Hand in hand with the rocket launchers, death rays, and other weapons of mass—or even subtle—destruction are special effects. Mayhem and destruction, as Hollywood can tell you, is just massively more entertaining with a liberal dose of smoke, sparks, fireballs, the sound of exploding structure, and dying monsters. While your little Garden Defender game is nowhere near to being a triple-A title, you will be learning the basics of weaponry and special effects in this chapter to help with whatever your end goal may be.

Weaponry

No matter what your favorite game genre happens to be, there seems to be a strangely attractive addiction to destroying things. Shooting them to make it happen is even more satisfying. It's probably hardwired into us as part of the survival instinct. Regardless of its root, the functionality it makes use of in game design is also useful for more passive scenarios.

Simple Projectiles

The mainstay of many weapon systems is the projectile. In Unity, it is generally brought to life and controlled with physics. For this game, it seemed fitting that the garden gnome's bazooka be used as a potato gun. For those of you who have had the opportunity to witness a real potato gun in action, you will know that while they are loads of fun, potatoes are a bit lacking in pyrotechnics upon collision. Fortunately, you will be taking some liberties with reality.

Let's get started by deactivating zombie bunny production while you build the weapon's functionality.

1. Open the Garden 1 object.

2. Select the Zombie Zone and Plant Zone, and deactivate them.

3. Select the Zombie Spawn Manager, and deactivate it.

4. Create a new C# Script in the Game Scripts folder, and name it **PotatoLauncher**.

The launcher script at its most basic will require a variable to hold a projectile, a means of tracking user input, and some code to instantiate and push (with physics) a projectile. Let's begin with the variables. Besides the projectile, you will have a variable to dictate the speed of the push. By having it exposed to the Inspector, you will be able to fine tune the action at runtime.

5. Below the class declaration, add the following variables:

```
public GameObject projectile; // the projectile prefab
public float speed = 20f; // give speed a default of 20
```

6. In the Update function, add the following to get the player input:

```
// if the Fire1 button (default is left ctrl) is pressed ...
if (Input.GetButton ("Fire1")) {
    ShootProjectile(); // ...shoot the projectile
}
```

You can open the Input manager from Edit, Project Settings, to see what keys belong to the virtual "Fire1" key. On a Windows machine, it is the left mouse button, "mouse 0" and the "left ctrl" keys.

Next you will create the function that instantiates and fires the projectile.

7. Create the following function below the Update function:

```
void ShootProjectile () {
    // create a clone of the projectile at the location & orientation of the script's parent
    GameObject potato = (GameObject) Instantiate (projectile, transform.position, transform.rotation);
    // add some force to send the projectile off in its forward direction
    potato.rigidbody.velocity = transform.TransformDirection(new Vector3 (0,0,speed));
}
```

The last line gives the object a push via its rigidbody component. It gets the direction from the script's object's transform using TransformDirection(). The Vector3 argument says no velocity in the x or y direction, but a velocity of speed in the z direction. The projectile is instantiated at the position and orientation of the object that will hold the script.

8. Save the script.

The script will go on either the weapon or an empty gameObject parented to it. With imported assets, the weapon may not always point in the z direction (forward in Unity). By creating an empty gameObject to hold the script, you can control both the forward direction and the actual point of instantiation.

1. Hold the Alt key down, and click on the Gnomatic Garden Defender to expand its hierarchy.

2. Select the Bazooka Arm, and focus the viewport to it.

3. From the GameObject menu, select Create Empty.

4. Name it **Fire Point**.

5. Set the coordinate system to Local so you can see the object's z direction.

6. Rotate it **180** degrees on the y axis if necessary so that the z points forward with the gnome's orientation.

7. Toggle off the scene lighting.

The z arrow should point forward.

8. Using the ortho views, position the Fire Point at the front of the bazooka (Figure 8-1).

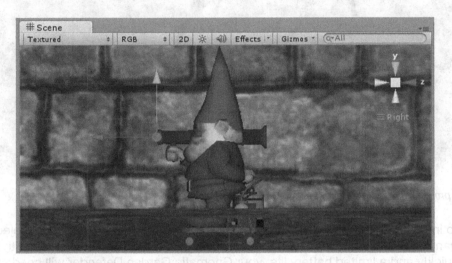

Figure 8-1. The Fire Point positioned at the front of the bazooka

9. Drag the PotatoLauncher script onto the Fire Point object.

10. Drag the Fire Point onto the Bazooka Arm in the Hierarchy view.

Let's use a simple sphere for some quick experiments. The key component is the Rigidbody.

1. Create a new Sphere, and scale it to **0.2 x 0.2 x 0.2**.

2. Add a Rigidbody component to it.

3. Drag it into the root Prefabs folder.

4. Select the Fire Point, and drag the Sphere prefab onto its Projectile parameter.

5. Delete the Sphere in the scene.

6. Click Play, and press the left mouse button, the left ctrl key or the Mac equivalent.

The spheres fly out in a steady stream while the "Fire1" input is held down (Figure 8-2). Besides making it too easy to obliterate the zombie bunny population, this many projectiles will quickly kill the frame rate.

Figure 8-2. The projectiles firing in a steady stream when Fire1 is held down

The next step in scripting the projectile functionality is to limit the rate at which the projectiles can be fired. Many games will also limit the amount of ammunition the player will have, but with the enemies multiplying quickly and a limited battery life, your Gnomatic Garden Defender will need all the help he can get. And potatoes are rarely in short supply.

To gain control over the assault, you will be making a little timer. Unlike the coroutine used to spawn the zombie bunnies, for the projectiles, you will be tapping into the system time, Time.time, to specify the exact time the next projectile will be available. To make the timer, you will create a variable for the reload rate and for the target time.

1. Create the following variables in the PotatoLauncher script:

    ```
    float loadRate = 0.5f; // how often a new projectile can be fired
    float timeRemaining;   // how much time before the next shot can happen
    ```

2. Change the contents of the Update function as follows:

    ```
    timeRemaining -= Time.deltaTime; //
    // if the Fire1 button (default is left ctrl) is pressed and the alloted time has passed
    if (Input.GetButton ("Fire1") && timeRemaining <= 0) {
        timeRemaining = loadRate; // reset the time remaining
        ShootProjectile ();// ...shoot the projectile
    }
    ```

Here is how it works: timeRemaining is the default 0 [seconds] the first time through, so the player can shoot immediately. Time.deltaTime is approximately 1 second divided by the frame rate—so for 60 frames per second, or *fps*, it would be 1/60th of a second. If the player doesn't shoot, Time.deltaTime, the duration of a frame, is *subtracted* each frame, so it will remain less than 0. As long as `timeRemaining` is less than 0, the player may shoot when ready. When the player *does* shoot, the `timeRemaining` is set to the `loadRate` and he must wait for it to drop back down before he can shoot again.

`Time.time` is started when the game starts, so at any time during the game, you can use it to find how much time has elapsed since the start of the game. In this code, to "set" the timer, you are getting the current time since the start of the game and adding the rate or amount of time between firing. It's like saying it's 3:05 now and in 15 minutes I want something to be able to happen. 3:05 + 15 makes the target time 3:20. When the player presses the Fire1 key or button, a new target time is set and until that time has been reached, the condition to shoot another projectile is not met.

3.   Save the script, and test the new limitation by continuously holding down the Fire1 button.

This time, the number of projectiles littering the scene is greatly reduced. The overload rate for filling the scene with projectiles is lower, but the possibility of that happening remains. With the projectiles under control, you might wish to add a nice little sound effect to go along with the gun firing.

4.   Add an Audio Source component to the Fire Point object, and uncheck "Play on Awake."

5.   Load GunPop as its Audio Clip.

6.   Back in the PotatoLauncher script, add the following after the line:

```
audio.Play (); // play the default audio clip on this component's gameObject
```

7.   Save the script.

8.   Click Play, and test the potato gun.

Unlike conventional ammunition that is designed to explode on contact, at most, potatoes might break apart on contact. Fortunately, your varmint invasion consists of zombie bunnies, so the rules of nature no longer apply!

You will begin by destroying the projectile at a set time after it is instantiated. With a normal projectile, such as a bullet, it would be destroyed on first contact through an `OnCollisionEnter` function. Potatoes, lacking an explosive charge, aren't so easy to get rid of. Typically, you will set the projectile to be destroyed in the `Start` function in case it never hits anything, and also in an `OnCollisionEnter` function in case of a valid hit. Later you will spice up the collision event with some special effects. The good news is that the `Destroy()` function has a built-in timer, so you won't have to fuss with coroutines to activate it after a given amount of time.

9.   Create a new C# Script in the Game Scripts folder, and name it **Projectile**.

10.   Add the following to its `Start` function:

```
//destroy the object this script is on 3 seconds after instantiation
Destroy(gameObject, 3f);
```

Remembering that the `Start` function is called when the gameObject is activated in the scene, not when the game itself is started, you can see that the destroy method's timer starts as soon as the projectile is instantiated.

If it does hit an object with a collider, you will have it destroyed sooner. Because the potato should roll or bounce a little first, it will have a delay also.

11.   Create the OnCollisionEnter function:

```
void OnCollisionEnter () {
    //destroy the object this script is on 2 seconds after collision
    Destroy(gameObject, 2f);
}
```

12.   Save the script.

13.   Add the script to the Sphere prefab in the Project view.

14.   Click Play, and test the new functionality.

The spheres now disappear 3 seconds after they are shot unless they hit something first.

With the basics sorted out, you may as well bring in the real ammo.

1.   From the right-click menu in the Project view, choose Import New Package, Custom Package, and load Potato.unitypackage from the Chapter 8 Assets folder.

The package includes a lone potato and a pile of potatoes that conveniently fit into the garden pots from a previous import (Figure 8-3). The assets are added to the Imported Assets folder. You will also find a prefab for each object in the Prefabs folder. Rather than using the default Diffuse shader, the PotatoSkin material is using a Self Illuminated Diffuse shader to brighten the object slightly through the use of the BoxHedge texture's alpha channel. To brighten the potatoes even more, you could create an alpha channel on the Potato Skin texture and use it in place of the BoxHedge texture. No texture, or a texture that has no alpha channel, defaults to white or fully self-illuminated and will appear very flat.

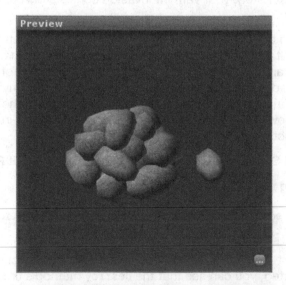

Figure 8-3. *The imported potato assets—looks like the Yukon Gold variety*

2. Drag the Potato and the Pile O' Potatoes into the Staging Area from the Prefabs folder.

3. Add a Sphere Collider to the Pile O' Potatoes, and adjust it to fit.

4. At the top of the Inspector, click Apply to update the Prefab.

5. Duplicate the pile and single potato around the staging area for effect (Figure 8-4).

Figure 8-4. The potatoes artfully deployed around the staging area

6. Create an Empty GameObject, and name it **Lots of Potatoes**.

7. Drag the new potatoes into the group, and drag it into the Staging Area object.

To allow the ammunition potato to be affected by gravity and to register collisions, it must have a `Rigidbody` component. You will be adjusting its Mass and the projectile's Speed parameter to make the game more challenging.

1. Focus in on the Gnomatic Garden Defender—it should be in the left or right ortho view you used to set up the Fire Point object.

2. Drag the new potato into the Scene view, and rename the Potato **PotatoAmmo**.

3. With the help of the "flat" ortho views, position it at the end of the Bazooka (Figure 8-5).

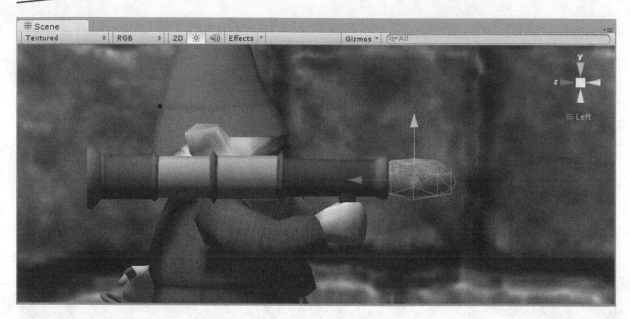

Figure 8-5. The single potato in position in the bazooka

4.   Focus the scene to the PotatoAmmo.

5.   Select the Fire Point, and use "Move to View" from the GameObject menu to move it to the potato.

6.   Reselect PotatoAmmo, and add a Capsule Collider to it.

7.   Adjust its size and orientation as necessary.

A Radius of **0.05** and Height of **0.2** on the Z axis should work well.

8.   Add a `Rigidbody` component to PotatoAmmo.

9.   Drag the Projectile script onto it as well.

10. Drag PotatoAmmo into the Prefabs' Misc folder to create a prefab for it.

11. Delete the Sphere prefab while you are there.

12. Delete PotatoAmmo from the scene.

13. Select the Fire Point object, and assign PotatoAmmo prefab as the Projectile.

14. Click Play, and test the new projectile.

Because the potato is instantiated slightly in front of the bazooka's muzzle, the potato should not interfere with the parent object's colliders. When parent-child collision is a problem, you can use `Physics.IgnoreCollision(<the projectile's collider>, <the weapon's collider>)`. That line would go just below the `rigidbody.velocity` line.

The PotatoAmmo could stand to be more visible in the scene when fired.

15. Select the PotatoAmmo prefab object in the Project view, and set its x, y, and z scales to **1.1** each.

For traditional ammunition, where the velocity is high enough to overcome gravity, you would not use gravity. Currently, the potato is moving too fast to make the game challenging. The player could keep the Gnomatic Garden Defender near the gateway and the potatoes would easily reach to all corners of the garden. If you give the potato more mass, it will slow down but pack a bigger wallop when it hits something. The drag will make it harder to aim, as the potato will have to be shot up so it will come down in the right place.

1. In the prefab's `Rigidbody` component, give it a Mass of **20** and a Drag of **1.2**.

2. Click Play, and check out the difference (Figure 8-6).

Figure 8-6. The new range for the potato gun

With the adjusted range, the player will be forced to drive the Gnomatic Garden Defender through the scene to reach all of the Zombie bunnies. Let's see what no Gravity does. . .

3. In the PotatoAmmo prefab, turn off Use Gravity in the `Rigidbody` component.

4. Click Play, and test the potato gun.

The projectiles shoot straight out from the bazooka and congregate on the wall until they are destroyed (Figure 8-7). Unless you we shooting Nerf® balls, you would want them to be destroyed immediately on collision if you were not using gravity.

Figure 8-7. The projectiles without the use of gravity

5. Turn the Gravity back on in the prefab.

6. Stop Play mode.

About now you are probably itching to try out the new projectiles on the zombie bunnies. Let's activate them and see how it goes.

1. Locate the Zombie Spawn Manager and Zombie Zone object in the Garden 1 group, and activate them in the Inspector.

2. Click Play, and try your hand at shooting the pesky critters.

They bounce up a little when you hit them, giving some visual feedback for your efforts. This is due to the rigidbodies on both the zombie bunny and the projectile. You could get more bounce by decreasing the critter's Mass, but you will soon be replacing them with a "dead replacement," which will be a different object altogether. Let's work on the script that will remove the hit zombie bunnies from the scene first. The simplest solution will be to destroy them directly on collision. You will require a tag for the projectile so they won't be destroyed on colliding with the ground or each other.

3. At the top of the Inspector, click the Tag drop-down menu and select Add Tag.

4. In the blank Element 1 field, type **Ammo** (Figure 8-8).

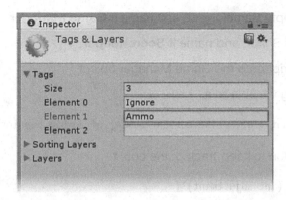

Figure 8-8. The new Ammo tag

5. Select the PotatoAmmo prefab in the Project view, and tag it as Ammo.

6. Create a new C# Script in the Game Scripts folder, and name it **ReceivedHit**.

7. Add the following OnCollisionEnter function:

```
void OnCollisionEnter (Collision collision) {
    if (collision.transform.tag == "Ammo") {
        // if it was hit by something tagged as a Ammo, process its destruction
        DestroyBun();
    }
}
```

8. Add the following function to destroy the object:

```
void DestroyBun () {
    Destroy(gameObject, 0.2f); // destroy it after a brief pause
}
```

In case you are wondering why you didn't just destroy it directly from the OnCollisionEnter function, it's because by separating it out, you can destroy it remotely. For example, you may decide that the potato should destroy anything within a particular radius, similar to a grenade. The DestroyBun function could be called from the projectile when it hits, once a sphere of influence is checked.

9. Save the script, and add it to the ZombieBunny prefab in the Project view.

10. Click Play, and shoot some critters.

If you are a pretty good shot, you may be able to get rid of all the originals before the next generation comes in. That will eventually signal a level or the game to be finished.

Now that you are able to remove the pests from the scene, you will want to update the current zombie bunny count, currentBunCount. If you remember, this variable is on the SpawnBunnies script on the Zombie Spawn Manager object. The only problem is that, at any given time, the entire garden may be deactivated. The answer, which will also be useful when you develop the GUI for the game, is to keep track of the count on an independent object.

1. Create a new Empty GameObject, and name it **Game Manager**.

2. Create a new C# Script, and name it **ScoreKeeper**.

3. Drag the new script onto the Game Manager object.

4. Add the following variable to it:

```
int currentBunCount = 0; // the current number of zombie bunnies
```

5. Add a little function to keep track of the count:

```
void UpdateCount (int adjustment) {

    currentBunCount += adjustment; // add or subtract the number passed in
    print ("new count: " + currentBunCount);
}
```

6. Save the script.

7. Open the SpawnBunnies script.

8. Add the following variable:

```
GameObject gameManager; // the master repository for game info
```

9. Find and assign it in the Start function, above the PopulateGardenBunnies line:

```
gameManager = GameObject.Find("Game Manager"); // identify and assign the Game Manager object
```

If you put the line below the StartCoroutine line, it may not get evaluated in time.

To update the count, you will use SendMessage to tell the UpdateCount function on the other script how many to add. Communication between scripts is a key concept in Unity, and there are many different ways to achieve it. SendMessage() will find the function on any of the gameObject's scripts, but it can pass only one argument.

10. In the PopulateGardenBunnies function, replace the currentBunCount += count line with the following:

```
// send the amount to update the total
gameManager.SendMessage("UpdateCount",count, SendMessageOptions.DontRequireReceiver);
```

The SendMessage function calls a function—in this case, UpdateCount—on *any* script on the contacted gameObject—in this case, the Game Manager. It has the option to send one argument—in this case, count. The last part, also optional, tells it not to report back to you via the console if a receiver can't be found. You've already added a print statement to the UpdateFunction, so you will know when it has been called. If you do not see results from a SendMessage, it is often a good idea to require it to report back to the console if it can't find a receiver. Simply remove the Dont.

11. Delete or comment out the print line that follows it.

12. Delete or comment out the int currentBunCount = 0 declaration.

13. Save the script.

14. Click Play, and watch the printouts as the zombie bunnies are added to the scene.

Now you can head back to the ReceivedHit script and have it report deceased zombie bunnies.

1. Open the ReceivedHit script.

2. Add the following variable:

```
public GameObject gameManager; // the master repository for game info
```

3. Find the Game Manager in the Start function:

```
gameManager = GameObject.Find("Game Manager"); // identify and assign the Game Manager object
```

4. In the DestroyBun function, add the following:

```
// send the amount to update the total
gameManager.SendMessage("UpdateCount",-1, SendMessageOptions.DontRequireReceiver);
```

5. Save the script.

6. Click Play, and test the new functionality.

This time the count goes down with each ravenous zombie bunny you destroy, inspiring you to shoot as many as possible.

7. Stop Play mode.

Particle Systems

Without special effects, your game is probably a bit boring. Sound effects are relatively easy to add and have a big impact on the enjoyment factor. Pyrotechnics can add even more excitement and incentive. In 3D games especially, these will usually involve particle systems. Particle systems are used for creating smoke, fire, dust, and many specialty effects requiring a large number of similar objects. While they *can* utilize 3D meshes, they most often are images on a quad (two triangles). The way the images are blended together at runtime lets you create a large variety of effects.

Legacy Particle System

While the legacy particle system is older than the newer Shuriken system, it continues to be useful for a couple of reasons. The first is that there are a great number of prefabs that can get you up and running [exploding] very quickly. The second reason is that they, unlike the newer Shuriken, have a parameter that will kill them when they have finished emitting.

Let's begin with a nice little explosion where the potato hits.

1. In the Project view, open the Standard Assets folder and inspect the contents of the Particles folder (Figure 8-9).

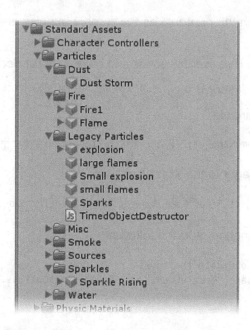

Figure 8-9. Particle system prefabs available from the ParticleSystem.unitypackage

These came in when you created the project with the ParticleSystem package. To see what they do and what they don't do, you will have to drag them into the Scene view.

2. Move the Gnomatic Garden Defender back to the Staging Area so your view won't be littered with zombie bunnies.

3. The Dust Storm prefab is rather subtle, so drag the Fire1 prefab into the Scene (Figure 8-10).

Figure 8-10. The Fire1 prefab in the scene

The results are rather spectacular. When a legacy particle system object is selected in the Hierarchy view, it is activated to give you a preview. Many particle system effects are a combination of multiple particle systems.

4. Delete Fire1 from the scene.

5. Drag Flame in but don't release the mouse button right away.

As you drag it in, you will see that Flame, besides the particles, includes a light.

6. Release the mouse button and zoom out (Figure 8-11).

Figure 8-11. *The Flame prefab with its smoke, fire and lighting*

Flame consists of 4 different objects: a light, a smoke particle system, and two flame configurations.

7.   Open Flame in the Hierarchy view to see its children.

8.   Click on each, and watch the viewport (Figure 8-12).

Figure 8-12. *The objects that make up the Flame prefab*

As you select each component, the others freeze in the viewport, allowing you to see only the one you have selected.

9. Delete Flame, and try out the other prefabs, deleting each when you are finished (Figure 8-13).

Figure 8-13. The Bubbles prefab

10. From the Legacy Particles folder, drag Explosion into the scene.

11. Deselect it, and click Play, watching it in both the Scene and Hierarchy views.

The explosion happens, drifts up, and disappears—both in the scene *and* in the Hierarchy view. Inspection will show that it has animation clips on both of the particle systems and a TimedDestructor script on the parent object. You be using the SmallExplosion prefab, modifying it to fit the need and then turning it off with a script.

1. Stop Play mode.

2. Delete the Explosion object in the Hierarchy.

3. Drag SmallExplosion into the scene, and rename it **SmallExplosion2**.

4. Inspect the components in the Inspector.

The Legacy parameters can be a bit cryptic. Because they are legacy, you won't be doing much with them other than tweaking them.

5. Near the bottom of the Ellipsoid Particle Emitter, turn on One Shot so you can see a single "shot" at a time.

6. Fill out its parameters as per Figure 8-14.

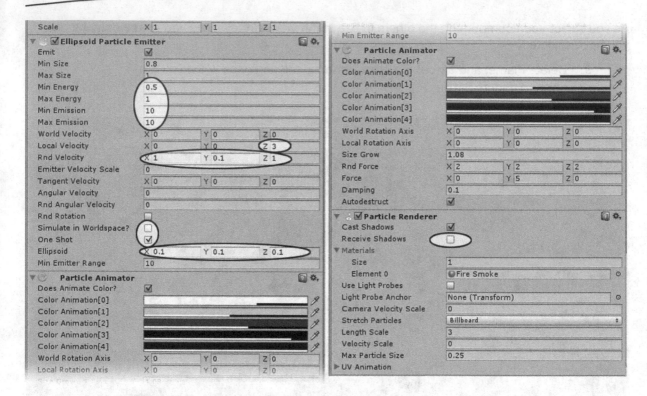

Figure 8-14. Settings for the legacy SmallExplosion2

Emission is the amount of particles. *Energy* is how long the individual particles live. (Try setting max to 6 to see the difference.) Velocity is the speed of the particles. *Ellipsoid* is the size of the emitter. The color array blends the color over the age of the particles. *Autodestruct* kills the particles when they have finished if One Shot is on. Shadows are not cast or received on billboard-type particles.

7. Click Play.

With One Shot turned on, the particle system destroys itself after it finishes.

8. Stop Play mode.

9. Create a new folder in the Prefabs folder, and name it **FX**.

10. Drag SmallExplosion2 into the new FX folder.

11. Delete the SmallExplosion2 object in the scene.

Next you will incorporate the explosion into the Projectile script.

1. Open the Projectile script.

2. Add a variable for the explosion:

```
public GameObject explosion; // the particle system associated with projectile
```

3. In the OnCollisionEnter function, above the //destroy the object line, add:

    ```
    Vector3 explosionPosition = transform.position; // the projectile's position at the hit
    Instantiate (explosion,explosionPosition,Quaternion.identity);
    ```

With an explosion of that magnitude, you would expect the potato to be obliterated at the same time.

4. Change the Destroy lines as follows:

    ```
    //destroy the object this script is on immediately
    Destroy(gameObject);
    ```

5. Save the script.

6. Assign the SmallExplosion2 to the PotatoAmmo prefab's Projectile component's Explosion parameter.

7. Click Play, and shoot the potato gun.

This time the zombie bunnies and the potato that hit them disappear to the accompaniment of a nice little explosion (Figure 8-15).

Figure 8-15. The new explosion when the PotatoAmmo hits

Dead Replacements

Now it would be nice if you could tell when you toasted a zombie bunny or when you missed. Let's begin with a "dead replacement." It will eventually need a healthy dose of black smoke to mark the event. If you think back to Chapter 6, you may remember setting up the ToastedZombie with a nice little animation.

The Toasted Zombie Parent will need to be instantiated from the ZombieBunny's ReceivedHit script.

1. Open the ReceivedHit script.

2. Add a variable for the dead replacement:

    ```
    public GameObject deadReplacement; // this will be the ToastedZombie
    ```

3. At the top of the DestroyBun function, add the following:

    ```
    if (deadReplacement) {
        // get the dead replacement object's parent
        GameObject deadParent = deadReplacement.transform.parent.gameObject;
        // instantiate the dead replacement's parent at this object's transform
        GameObject dead = (GameObject) Instantiate(deadParent, transform.position, transform.rotation);
        // trigger its default animation
        deadReplacement.GetComponent<Animator>().Play("Jump Shrink");
        // destroy the dead replacement's parent after a second
        Destroy(dead,1.4f);
    }
    ```

4. Now that you have a replacement, change the Destroy(GameObject,0.2f) line to

    ```
    Destroy(gameObject, 0.001f); // destroy it after a brief pause
    ```

5. Save the script.

6. Assign the ToastedZombie part of the Toasted Zombie Parent prefabto the ZombieBunny prefab's Dead Replacement parameter in the Received Hit component in the Project view.

7. Click Play, and test the new additions.

Now that the shoot/die sequence is together, you might want to shorten the pause before the animation starts. To change the animation clip, you must temporarily drag a prefab into the scene.

1. Drag the Toasted Zombie Parent into the Scene, and select the ToastedZombie child.

2. Open the Animation Window.

3. Select all of the keys, and drag them to the left so that they start at about **0:15**, 15 frames (Figure 8-16).

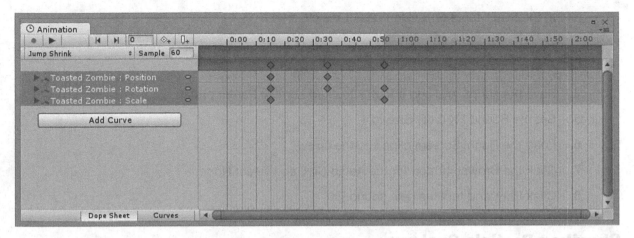

Figure 8-16. The ToastedZombie's animation keys shifted left to shorten the pause

4.   Drag the time indicator, and watch the object in the scene.

5.   Close the Animation view, and delete the ToastedZombie from the Scene.

6.   Back in the ReceivedHit script, change the Destroy(dead,1.4f) line to:

```
Destroy(dead,1.0f);
```

7.   Save the script.

You've probably noticed the BunnyScream audio clip in the Sound FX folder and are wondering when you will be using it. Until now, you've had nowhere to put it. If it was put on the zombie bunny or the potato, the object would be destroyed about the time you wanted the sound effect to play, so it would never be heard. With the dead replacement being instantiated about the same time, you now have a perfect container for the audio clip.

8.   Add an Audio Source component to the Toasted Zombie Parent prefab.

9.   Load the BunnyScream as its Audio Clip.

10. Do not turn off "Play on Awake."

11. Click Play and test.

The same sound effect played on every hit gets old fast. A little script to load a random sound from an array will improve things greatly. Audio.PlayOneShot is perfect for playing audio clips without the need to replace existing clips.

1.   Create a new C# Script, and name it **RandomSound**.

2.   Create a variable to hold the possible audio clips:

```
AudioClip SoundFX[]; // audio clips
```

3. In the Start function, assign one of the clips:

```
int num = Random.Range(0,soundFX.Length);// get a random number
audio.PlayOneShot(soundFX[num]);          // play that element
```

4. Save the script, and add it to the Toasted Zombie Parent prefab.

5. Set the Sound FX array Size to 4.

6. Load the BunnyScream clips into the array.

7. Click the Browse button for the Audio Clip, and select None.

8. Click Play, and test the new sound FX.

Shuriken Particle System

With a toasted dead replacement left in place of the original zombie bunny, a bit of black smoke to mark incendiary spot would be just the thing! This time you will be using the Shuriken Particle system to create the special effects. The Shuriken system is a lot more intuitive to use if you are already familiar with particle systems. It has a lot of parameters, complete with invasive tool tips; nonetheless, it can be intimidating. Fortunately, Shuriken is a lot more editor-friendly while setting up the system.

Smoke

The most basic of particle systems is smoke. Particles drift slowly upwards, fanning out, getting larger and fading out as they near the end of their lifetimes.

1. From GameObject, Create Other, choose Particle System.

2. Name it **Smoke**.

A rising funnel of cotton balls appears in the viewport (Figure 8-17).

Figure 8-17. *The default Shuriken particle system*

Rather than marching straight through the parameters, school-book style, let's approach them with a view to the result in mind. The most logical first step is to narrow the spread on the particles as they rise. In Shuriken, the spread is part of the Shape parameters.

The top half of the Particle System component is for the parameters that are always in play. The lower section has modules that are optional. Two, the Emission and the Shape, are turned on by default (Figure 8-18).

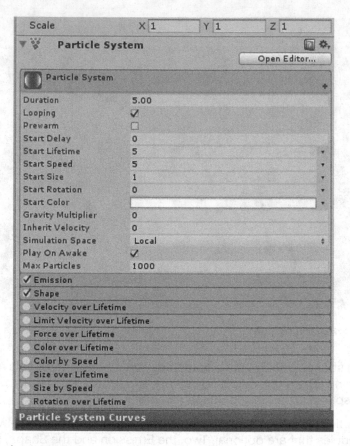

Figure 8-18. Shuriken in the Inspector

3.   Open the Shape section by clicking on the bar.

4.   Click on the drop-down list to see the Shape options, but leave it set to Cone (Figure 8-19).

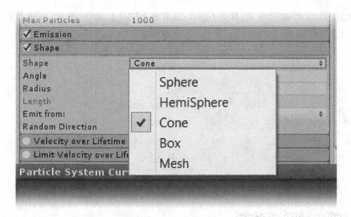

Figure 8-19. The Shape section, Shape options drop-down list

A cone with sizing handles appears in the Scene view (Figure 8-20).

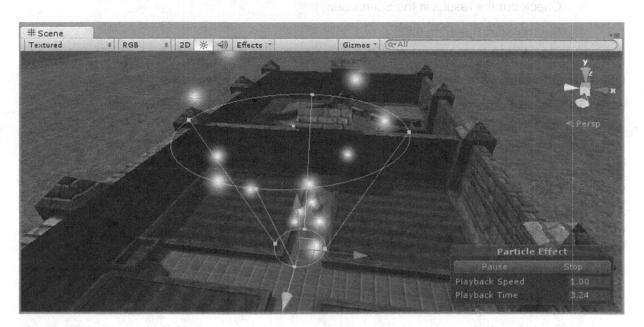

Figure 8-20. The Shape cone in the Scene view

    5.   Try adjusting the cone in the Scene view to see how it affects the emission.

The zombie bunnies are roughly box shaped, so it might make more sense to use a box emitter.

    6.   Change the Shape to Box, and set x, y, and z to **0.2** each.

There are several ways to affect the shape of the plume of smoke. By changing the lifetime, or how long each particle is on screen, the density will appear to taper off. Any parameter with a drop-down arrow has options appropriate to the parameter. For the Lifetime, you will choose random numbers between two constant numbers. The Start Lifetime is set in the top section.

1. Click the drop-down arrow at the right of the Start Lifetime to see the options (Figure 8-21).

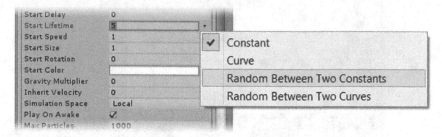

Figure 8-21. The drop-down options for Start Speed

2. Select Random Between Two Constants, and set the numbers to **1** and **5**.

3. Check out the results in the Scene view.

4. Set the Start Speed to **0.5**.

Slowing the Start Speed shortens the plume and makes it denser.

Let's look at the size next. Just as with the Start Lifetime, a bit of variation will improve things.

5. Click the drop-down arrow at the right of the Start Size, and select Random Between Two Constants.

6. Set the values to **0.75** and **1.2**.

Now as the particles reach the top of the plume and pop out of existence, you can see the new variation in size.

So far, you have seen random values. Let's have a look at the Gradient option for the Start Color. Most of the settings in the top section affect the particle system as a whole over its lifetime as will become clear when you specify a color gradient for the Start Color.

7. In the options for Start Color, select Gradient.

8. Click on the color bar to open the Gradient Editor (Figure 8-22).

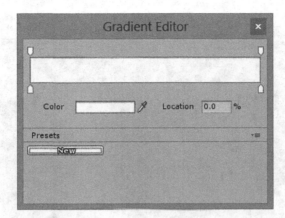

Figure 8-22. The Gradient Editor

The color bar in the Gradient Editor handles transparency on the top and color on the bottom.

   9.   Double-click the marker at the lower left of the color bar to open the color-picker dialog.

   10.   Select a color (Figure 8-23).

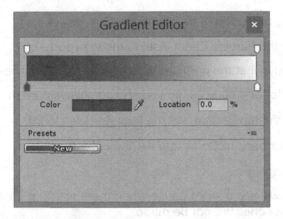

Figure 8-23. The color-picker dialog in the Gradient Editor

   11.   Check out the particle system in the Scene view.

The color loops through the gradient over its lifetime (the Duration parameter), using the default value of 5 seconds (Figure 8-24).

Figure 8-24. The gradient cycling over the particle system's Duration

12.   Uncheck Looping at the top of the component.

13.   Click Simulate in the Particle Effect inset in the viewport.

This time you can see exactly what the particle system looks like as a one-off.

Particle systems can use a lot of resources, so you should always pare them down.

1.   At the bottom of the top section, set the Max Particles to **20**.

2.   Set the Start Color back to Color, and set the color to white.

3.   Turn Looping on again.

With Looping back on, you will see a slight pause when there are 20 particles on screen. Until the current ones start to die, new ones will not be made.

4.   Increment the Max Particles by **5**, until they are once again continuous.
      A value of **30** should be sufficient.

To adjust the particles in respect their individual life spans, you will be using a few of the modules in the lower section. Let's start by revisiting the color. This time you will be adjusting the transparency to get a smoother start and finish.

1.   Rotate the Scene view so you can see a sunlit wall behind the particle system,
      or toggle off the scene lighting.

2.   Click to activate the Color over Lifetime module in the lower half of the
      Particle System component.

3.   Click on its title bar to open it.

4. Change the Color to Gradient from its option drop-down.

5. Click on the color bar to open the Gradient Editor.

The colors in the "Start Color" and "Color over Lifetime" will blend together, especially when they are not fully saturated, so the best way to control the outcome is to keep the Start Color to white and set the color fully from the "Color over Lifetime" section. The default shader for particle systems is also additive. That means when the particles overlap, the result will be brighter. To get a true reading for transparency, you will be setting the color to black before tweaking the transparency.

6. Click to activate the lower left Color marker, and change its color to black.

7. Click just below the gradient swatch, 70% of the way over, to create a new marker.

8. Set it to black.

9. Select the far right marker, and set it to gray.

10. On the top side of the color swatch, select the far left marker.

The Color picker swatch becomes an Alpha Slider.

11. Set the alpha value to **190**.

12. Click just above the gradient swatch at about 70% along, and create a new transparency marker.

13. Give it a value of **190** (Figure 8-25).

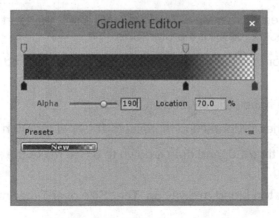

Figure 8-25. The "Color over Lifetime" settings in the Gradient Editor

14. Select the far right marker, and set the opacity to **0**.

The smoke is looking much better as the particles fade softly out (Figure 8-26). Next you will adjust the "Size over Lifetime" setting.

368 CHAPTER 8: Weaponry and Special Effects

Figure 8-26. The Smoke fading out nicely at the top

1. Click to activate the the "Size over Lifetime" module and then click on its title bar to open it.

By default, it is set to a Curve.

Click on the mini-curve to see a larger view. This curve will affect the Start Size of the particles, so 1.0 at the top left equates to 100% of the Start Size.

2. Position the cursor over the middle of the curve, right-click, and select Add Key.

3. A key with Bezier handles is created on the curve.

Time, at the bottom, is on the horizontal and represents 100% of the Start Lifetime of the particle.

4. Select the key at time 1.0, and drag it down to 0.5 to make the particle smaller at the end.

The plume of smoke is a bit too broad midway up. The "Size over Time" module is a good place to adjust it.

5. Drag the key you created down to about 75% (Figure 8-27).

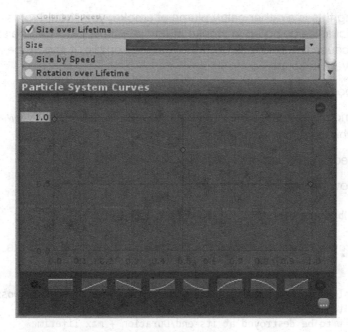

Figure 8-27. The "Size over Lifetime" curve at the bottom of the Inspector

6. Check out the results in the Scene view (Figure 8-28).

Figure 8-28. The finished smoke effect

In case you are thinking this is a rather paltry plume of smoke, you should remember the number of zombie bunnies that could be going up in smoke at any one time. Let's get the smoke added to the hit sequence next. Because the smoke is from the toasted zombie, it should be instantiated from the ZombieBunny's ReceivedHit script.

1. Uncheck Looping again.

2. Drag the Smoke object into the Prefabs' FX folder in the Project view, and delete it in the Hierarchy view.

3. Open the ReceivedHit script.

4. Add the following variable:

   ```
   public GameObject smokePlume; // smoke particle system
   ```

5. In the `DestroyBun` function, below the `Destroy(dead,1f)` line, add the following:

   ```
   GameObject plume = (GameObject) Instantiate(smokePlume, transform.position, smokePlume.transform.rotation);
   // trigger it to be destroyed at its end/Duration + max lifetime
   Destroy(plume,10f);
   ```

6. Save the script.

7. Select the ZombieBunny prefab in the Project view, and drag the Smoke prefab onto its Smoke Plume parameter.

8. Click Play, and test the new effect.

The smoke drifts up, enhancing the sequence (Figure 8-29).

Figure 8-29. The smoke added to the destroy sequence

Exploding Goo

A nice feature of the way Shuriken manages particle system manages the editing process is the ability to edit nested systems while seeing the parent and children in action at the same time. A nice splattering of green goo will give you an excuse to test that functionality.

1. Create a new Particle System object in the Scene view.

2. Name it **Splatter**.

3. Set the Duration to **2.5**.

4. Set the Start Speed to Random Between Two Constants, **2** and **6**.

5. Set the Start Size to Random Between Two Constants, **0.025** and **0.2**.

Goo splatters will have to fall back to the ground, but not too quickly. So this time you will be using the gravity Multiplier.

6. Set the Gravity Multiplier to **0.5**.

7. Turn on "Play on Awake" so the particles will start as soon as they are instantiated.

8. And set the Max Particles to **100**.

In Shuriken, the trick to making particles spray out all at once is found in the Emission rollout. Instead of using a constant rate, you will have the splatters come in *bursts*.

9.   Open the Emission module, and set the Rate to **0**.

10.   Click the + at the lower right of the rollout.

11.   Leave the Time at **0.00**, and set the Particles to **30**.

To make things more interesting, let's add another burst.

12.   Click the + again, and add 20 Particles at 0.25 Time (Figure 8-30).

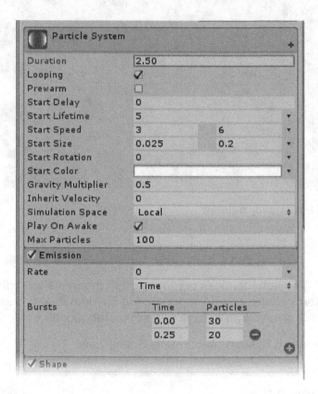

Figure 8-30. The burst-type emission

With the bursts activated, you can begin to fine tune the particle system.

1.   In the Shape module, set the Shape to Hemisphere and the Radius to **0.05**.

2.   Turn on the "Velocity over Lifetime" module and open it.

3.   Change it to Curve.

Because the Shuriken coordinate system uses Z as up, rather than Unity's Y as up, you will keep the Space set to Local and change only the Z curve. The velocity should slow down after the initial burst.

4.   Click on the X and Y thumbnail curves to hide their curves.

5.   In the curve editor, Particle System Curves, click on the key at 0 to activate the view.

6. Select the downward Fast/Slow preset at the bottom of the editor (Figure 8-31).

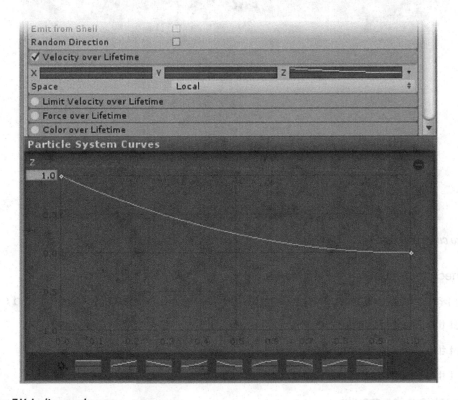

Figure 8-31. The Z Velocity speed curve

In the Scene view, there isn't much difference. Let's make it more apparent.

7. Move the far right key down to **-1**.

8. Select each key, and adjust the Bezier handles until the curve looks like Figure 8-32.

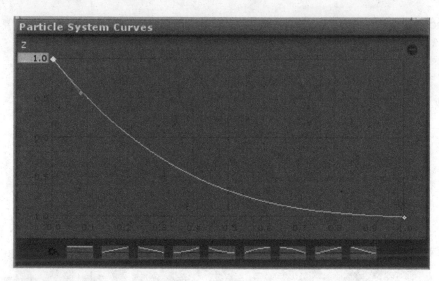

Figure 8-32. The curve adjusted

    9.   Check the effect in the Scene View.

This time the particles slow, then drop to earth. Now is a good time to reset the life and speed.

    10.   Set the Start Lifetime to **0.75**.

    11.   Set the Start Speed to **1.5** and **2**.

    12.   Set the Start Size to **0.01** and **0.08**.

    13.   Check out the results.

At this point, you will want to see the Splatter in combination with the Smoke.

    1.   Focus the view on Splatter.

    2.   Drag the Smoke prefab into the Hierarchy view, and use "Move the View" to align it with Splatter.

    3.   Drag Splatter, and drop it onto Smoke in the Hierarchy.

To see the combination properly, you will make use of the Simulate and Stop buttons for the Particle Effects. First, you will try out the Particle Effect Editor. It allows you to see the Particle System component for each object in the hierarchy. The one caveat is that the top parent must have a Particle System component.

    4.   Select the Smoke object.

    5.   In its Particle System component, click the Open Editor button at the top right of the component.

The editor opens. You may have to pull the divider to the right to see both objects' Particle System components (Figure 8-33).

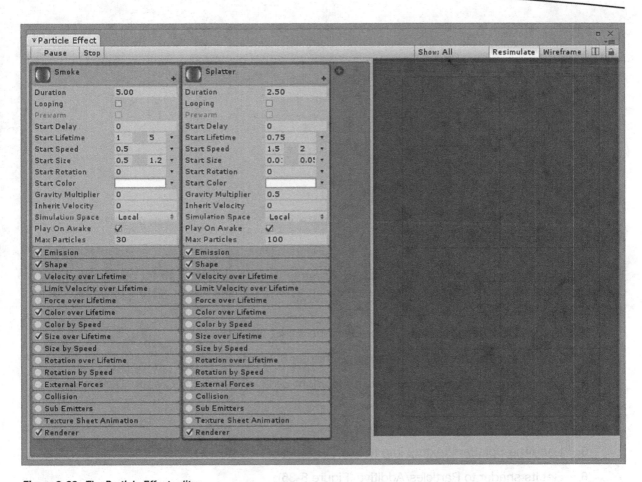

Figure 8-33. The Particle Effect editor

The Particle Effect editor has a Pause/Simulate button and a Stop button, but unlike the Particle Effect dialog in the Scene view, it doesn't have a duplicate Playback Speed adjustment.

6. Open the Splatter's "Color over Lifetime" module, and in the Gradient Editor, set the gradient color to green, tapering off to yellow-green, with the color fading off at the end (Figure 8-34).

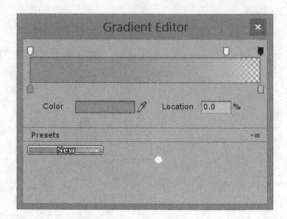

Figure 8-34. *The green goo color*

The effect is improving, but the default material, or rather its texture, isn't right for goo globs. For the right amount of variation, you can use a material with a texture sheet. Let's create a new material for the texture sheet.

1. In the Game Textures folder, right-click and select Import Asset.

2. Import the Splatters Texture from the Chapter 8 Assets folder.

3. In the Imported Assets, Materials folder, right-click, and from the Create sub-menu, select Material.

4. Name it **Splatters**.

5. Load the Splatters texture into it.

6. Set its shader to Particles/Additive (Figure 8-35).

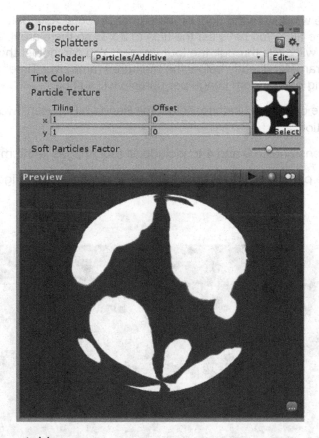

Figure 8-35. The new Splatters material

7. Select the Smoke object again.

8. In the Splatters particle effect, Renderer module, set the material to your new Splatters material.

9. If you observe the Splatters particles in the scene view right now, all four images on the texture will be on each particle.

To control which part of the texture is used on each particle, you will be using the Texture Sheet Animation module. This is also where you can set it to cycle through the images during the particle's lifetime, or, to just use a randomly chosen one for each particle.

1. Open and turn on the Texture Sheet Animation module.

2. Set the Tiles to X 2 and Y 2 to match the splat images on the texture sheet.

3. Leave Animation on Whole Sheet.

4. Slow the Playback Speed in the Scene view, and see if you can see the particle images change over time.

5. Click the "Frame over Time" curve.

The curve appears in the window to the right of the particle effects. As a default, "Frame over Time" is set to cycle through the tiles. You have set the tiles to 2 x 2, so there are 4 tiles total. Over the lifetime of the particle, it will cycle through the four images. You can adjust the number of cycles per lifetime in the Cycles parameter directly below the "Texture Frame over Time" parameter. For this particle system, just using one random image per particle will suffice.

6. For the "Frame over Time" setting, select the Random Between Two Constants option.

7. Set the two constants to **0** and **4** to include all four images in the mix.

8. Check out the particle effects in the Scene view at slow speed (Figure 8-36).

Figure 8-36. Smoke and splatters at the start of the Smoke's lifespan

9. Set the Playback Speed to **1** again, and uncheck the "Looping on the Splatters" effect.

10. Observe the effect in the Scene view.

11. Select the Smoke object, and clip Apply at the top of the Inspector to update the Smoke prefab to include the splatters.

12. Check the prefab in the Project view to assure yourself that it now includes the Splatter as a child, and then delete the Smoke in the Hierarchy view.

13. Click Play, and shoot some zombie bunnies.

The splatter gets lost in the rather excessive explosion. You may wish to increase the particle size, but you should definitely add a little delay.

1. Open the Smoke particle in the Project view.

2. Set the Splatter's Start Delay to **0.1**.

3. Click Play, and test the new settings.

Now the Splatters are not hidden by the explosion. With so much going on now, you may want to adjust the number and size of the particles in the Explosion particle system.

Trailing Particles

The last particle system you will look into is a means to make the slug leave a trail as he shoots through the garden. Unity has a Trail Renderer component, but it leaves particles standing up to face the camera. This time, the particles should remain where they were emitted, flat to the ground, until they fade out. The slug moves very fast, so you will slow him down while you block in the slime trail.

1. Drag the Slug prefab into the scene.

2. Open the Animator view, and select the default state, Slug Run.

3. In the Inspector, set the clip Speed to **0.1**.

4. Create a new Particle System, and name it **SlugSlime**.

5. Drag it onto the parent Slug in the Hierarchy view, and set its Rotations to **0**, **180, 0**.

6. Position it a short way in from the tail end of the slug and up off of the ground slightly.

7. In the Renderer module, set the Render Mode to Horizontal Billboard to keep the particles flat to the ground.

8. Set the Start Lifetime to **4**, the Start Speed to **0**, and the Start Size to **0.5**.

9. Set the Shape to Box.

10. Set its X and Y to **0** and its Z to **0.7**.

11. In "Color over Time," Set the Alpha to **145** at the first two markers and **0** at 100%.

12. Set the color to go from an electric blue to a strong green (Figure 8-37).

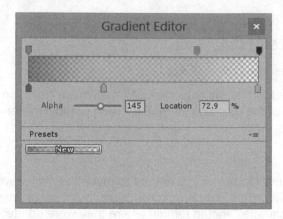

Figure 8-37. The Color over Time gradient for the slime

13.   In "Size over Lifetime," use the curve and move the end key down to 0 (Figure 8-38).

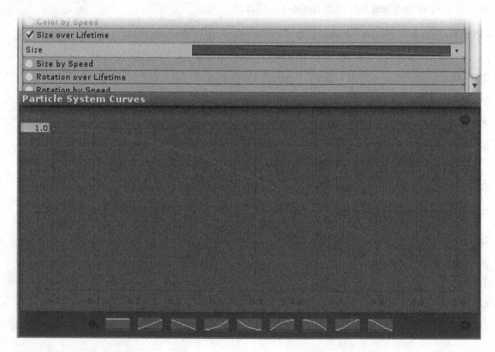

Figure 8-38. The "Size over Lifetime" curve

14.   Click Play.

You can see there is a major issue. The particles move along with the slug instead of being left behind. Fortunately, the solution is simple. By setting the Simulation Space to World, the particles no longer inherit the transforms of the parent emitter and stay in place until they fade out of existence.

1. Change Simulation Space to World.

2. Click Play, and watch the trail as it is left behind.

The trail is rather spotty but is behaving correctly. You will have to increase the number of particles to get a heavier trail.

3. Set the Emission Rate to **100**, and click Play (Figure 8-39).

Figure 8-39. The slug with its slime trail

Now there's one more thing to do. So far, you've been watching the slug move at 1/10th speed. Once the regular speed is reinstated, the trail will require some adjustment.

4. Select the slug.

5. In the Animator view, set the Slug Run's clip Speed back to **1**.

To compensate, you will shorten the particle life span and increase the emission rate.

6. Set the Start Lifetime to **0.75** and the Emission Rate to **300**.

7. Select the Slug, and click "Apply the Inspector" to update the prefab.

8. Check the prefab to make sure the slug was updated and then delete the slug in the scene.

Advanced Weaponry

As the saying goes, "*Close* only counts in horseshoes, hand grenades and nuclear weapons." As it stands, your player must make a direct hit to wipe out a zombie bunny. Given their tendency to cluster, it would help your player if the blast would work off of proximity rather than direct hits. In this section, you will alter the projectile code to do just that.

1. Open the Projectile script.

2. Comment out the first two lines in the OnCollisionEnter function.

In the earlier version, you simply used the hit point as the location to instantiate the explosion. In this version, you will also get and use the orientation of the object at the hit or contact point. It's not necessary for the giant fireball explosion, but if you wanted something more like sparks or shrapnel, they would have to be oriented at the *normal* to the surface that was just hit. A *normal* is a perpendicular to the face in the up or out direction. The normal to a piece of flat ground points upward. The normal to the garden wall will be perpendicular to the direction that the wall's surface is facing.

3. Change the OnCollisionEnter line to include an argument:

```
void OnCollisionEnter (Collision collision) {
```

4. Below the commented lines, add the following:

```
//get the contact point
ContactPoint contact = collision.contacts[0];
//get the normal of the contact point
Quaternion rotation = Quaternion.FromToRotation(Vector3.up, contact.normal);
// instantiate an explosion at that point, using its normal as the orientation
Instantiate (explosion, contact.point,rotation);
```

This time you will be using the argument passed in to the OnCollisionEnter function to obtain information about the collision.

5. In the Scripting Reference, do a search for the *Collision* type.

The Collision type's parameters include various useful parameters (Figure 8-40). When a collision event occurs, the following information is available:

Variables	
collider	The Collider we hit (Read Only).
contacts	The contact points generated by the physics engine.
gameObject	The GameObject whose collider we are colliding with. (Read Only).
relativeVelocity	The relative linear velocity of the two colliding objects (Read Only).
rigidbody	The Rigidbody we hit (Read Only). This is null if the object we hit is a collider with no rigidbody attached.
transform	The Transform of the object we hit (Read Only).

Figure 8-40. The parameters for the Collision type

6. Save the script.

7. Click Play, and test the explosion to make sure it continues to work as before.

To calculate the effects of the "blast," you will require a few new variables.

8. Add the following variables:

```
public float explosionTime = 1f; // how long the effect will last
public float explosionRadius = 0.5f; // the radius of the effect
public float explosionPower = 50f; // the force that will be applied to nearby objects
public int damage = 10; // the point amount of damage delivered
```

On the off chance you want to adjust the variable's values, you will have to do so by selecting the PotatoAmmo object in the Prefabs folder.

9. Beneath the `Instantiate` line, add the following:

```
// Find all nearby colliders and put them into an array
Collider[] hitColliders = Physics.OverlapSphere (transform.position,explosionRadius);
```

In this line, you are declaring a variable of an array of `Colliders` and filling it using the `Physics` function or method, `OverlapSphere()`. Every object with a collider that is intersected by the sphere will be added to the array. Armed with the objects within range that have a collider and using a foreach loop, you will apply a force if they have a `Rigidbody` component and send a message to destroy any with the appropriate receiver script.

10. Add the following code beneath the `Collider[]` line:

```
// Apply a force to all surrounding rigid bodies & destroy anything with a Terminator
function
foreach (Collider hit in hitColliders) {
    // Tell the rigidbody or any other script attached to it that the object was hit,
    // via the Terminator script
    hit.gameObject.SendMessage ("Terminator", damage, SendMessageOptions.
DontRequireReceiver);
    if (hit.rigidbody){ // if it has a rigidbody...
        hit.rigidbody.AddExplosionForce(explosionPower, transform.
position,explosionRadius);
    }
}
```

The last line sends a message [calls] any function by the name of "Terminator" on any of the object's scripts. In a more complicated version of the Explosion script, you could calculate a damage according to the distance from the explosion point. In this simple variation, you will send a hit damage amount just to see how it works. The function name to call is mandatory, but an argument and option message are optional. `DontRequireReceiver` prevents an error message if the object doesn't have a script with a `Terminator` function.

11. Save the script.

You are sending the message to destroy the hit objects directly from the Projectile script. Because you already abstracted the destroy sequence out of the ReceivedHits script's OnCollisionEnter function, this will be an easy task. Where before you called the DestroyBun function from the zombie bunny that was hit, now you will have an array of zombie bunnies that are within range of the projectile's contact point. You could call DestroyBun directly from the Projectile script, but by going through a more generic function, you can both filter out for damage points and allow other objects (such as cabbages) to be affected by the explosions also.

1. Open the ReceivedHits script.

2. Add the following variable:

    ```
    int damage = 0; // accumulated damage points
    ```

3. Add the following function:

    ```
    void Terminator (int newDamage) {
        damage += newDamage; // add more damage from
        print (damage);
        if (damage > 30) DestroyBun();
    }
    ```

With the Projectile script telling the nearby zombie bunnies they've been hit, you can comment out the OnCollisionEnter function in the ReceivedHits script.

4. Comment out the OnCollisionEnter function.

5. Save the script.

6. Click Play, and try to hit the zombie bunnies.

This time they take a couple of hits before they have enough damage to be destroyed. Having to shoot at each one twice is counterproductive. By altering the damage sent, you can set it to a 1-in-3 chance that the zombie bunny doesn't die and can receive the physics force.

7. Change the contents of the Terminator code to the following:

    ```
    if (damage > 10) DestroyBun (); // destroy only if there's enough damage
    ```

8. Comment out the print line.

9. Save the script.

10. Back in the Projectile script, change the SendMessage line to include a bit of randomness:

    ```
    hit.gameObject.SendMessage ("Terminator", damage + Random.Range(0,2), SendMessageOptions.DontRequireReceiver);
    ```

11. Save the script, click Play, and try again.

This time the zombies have a 1-in-3 chance of disappearing on the first hit or near hit, making it easier to clear the varmints out of the garden. With all of this fire power, you are probably thinking the plants should suffer as well. A simple little script with a `Terminator` function will do the trick.

1. Create a new C# Script in the Game Scripts folder, and name it **PlantRemover**.

2. Add the following variables:

```
public int hardiness = 1; // amount of damage required to destroy the plant
int damage = 0; // accumulated hit damage
```

3. Create the Terminator function:

```
void Terminator (int newDamage) {
    damage += newDamage; // add more damage from
    if (damage > hardiness) Destroy(gameObject);
}
```

4. Save the script, and add it to each of the plant prefabs, adjusting the Hardiness where necessary. (Cabbage, for example, might require 40 damage points to get rid of.)

5. Add a Sphere Collider, with Is Trigger checked, to each of the short plants and a Box Collider to the taller ones, adjusting as necessary.

6. Activate your Plant Zones, and test the new addition to your game play.

Post-Processing Effects

If you are using Unity Pro, there is one more effect you may want to try. Because the slug is electric in your little game, you might want a glow effect around him. Fake glows can be achieved for lights through the use of a billboard plane. There's even a parameter that creates the effect for you in the Light component. Other than the alpha sorting, it is fairly efficient. But a true glow is calculated after the frame has been drawn to the screen through the use of shaders. For this you will require Unity Pro's Image Effects.

1. If you are using Unity Pro, import the Image Effects (Pro Only) package.

An Image Effects folder is added in the Standard Assets folder. It consists of a few textures and a lot of shaders and scripts. Because it is a post-process effect, the component will be added to the main camera.

2. Drag the Slug prefab into the Staging area so it can be seen in the Game view (as rendered through the Main Camera).

3. Open the Main Camera Target's hierarchy, and select the Main Camera.

4. From the Component menu, Image Effects, Bloom and Glow, select Bloom (Optimized) (Figure 8-41).

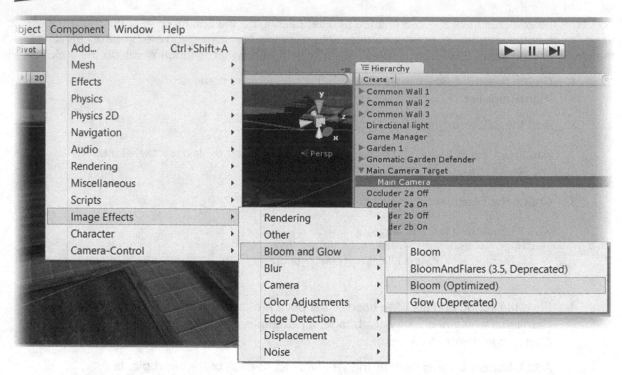

Figure 8-41. Bloom and Glow for Unity Pro

5.   Set the Intensity to **1.2** and the Blur Size to **1.85**.

The Game view has a nice soft, slightly saturated look (Figure 8-42, center).

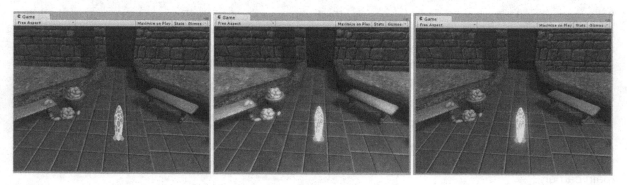

Figure 8-42. No Bloom, left, Bloom (Optimized), center, Bloom, right

6.   Disable the Fast Bloom component.

7.   Add the regular Bloom component.

8.   Set its Intensity to **11.2** and its Threshold to **0.83** (Figure 8-43).

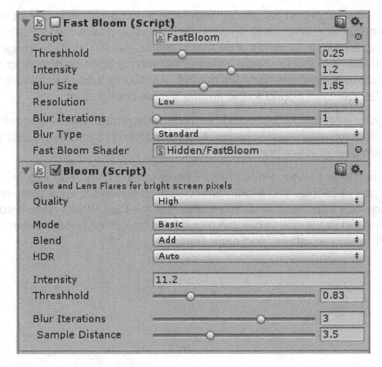

Figure 8-43. Setting for Fast Bloom and regular Bloom

Both blooms are affecting the brightest pixels in the rendered scene, but the regular Bloom is more selective.

9. Click Play, and see what the explosions and splatters look like with each of the Blooms.

10. Save the Scene, and save the project.

Feel free to use whichever bloom you prefer.

Summary

In this chapter, you got serious about keeping the zombie bunny threat to a manageable number. With a limitless supply of potatoes, you began by turning the gnome's bazooka into a potato gun. Rigidbodies, you found, could easily send the potatoes flying with the help of its velocity parameter. After a bit of experimentation, you restricted the player to a reasonable rate of fire through a small timer mechanism. By using Gravity and adjusting the Speed and mass of the projectiles, you were able to force the player to have to move the Gnomatic Garden Defender around the garden in order to reach all zombie bunny locations with his primitive weapon.

With the basics of pest control under way, you delved into the world of particle systems to improve the user experience and to provide better entertainment. Starting with a legacy explosion, you took full advantage of the opportunity for creating "dead replacements" as the zombie bunnies were dispatched.

You then moved on to the Shuriken particle system, where you began with a simple smoke effect to reinforce the crispy-critter scenario. Next, with the Splatter, you discovered the trick to explosion-type systems and had a chance to try out a texture sheet containing multiple images for your particles. Finally, you learned how to create a slime trail with particles by changing the Render Mode to Horizontal. The trick to leaving the particles behind, you found, was to use World for Simulation Space so the particles were not bound to the emitter's local coordinates.

Next, you revisited your weaponry scripts and converted the potato gun functionality from a single projectile type hit to a proximity based scheme. A quick addition to the plant prefabs made them prey to the potato gun's destructive purpose as well.

Finally, you had a quick look at Unity Pro's Image Effects where, if you had Pro, you experimented with two different types of Bloom. The Bloom effects, you discovered, are a post-process effect added after the scene has been rendered. You found that the Fast Bloom gave a soft washy look to your scene and increased saturation, while the regular Bloom component was easier to localize for a nice glow effect on the slug, splatters, and explosions.

Chapter 9

Incorporating Unity 2D

With Unity's major push into the mobile market and Adobe's announcement that Flash would not be supported for Mobile, Unity stepped in and beefed up its 2D capabilities with the addition of several very nice features and options. While your game is mainly 3D, you will be taking the opportunity in this chapter to cover some of the basics by incorporating a 2D warning system into the game as an added stressor for your player. Before jumping fully into the newer features, you will finish up the scoring system.

Finalizing the Game Play

Currently, you are tracking only the number of zombie bunnies in the garden. And because they are constantly being replenished, you are probably having a hard time eradicating them. The first thing to address is a means of rewarding the player as he scores more hits. It would be useful to have the current number displayed in the game.

Legacy GUI Text

Unity has a few different ways to put text on screen. You will begin with the oldest method, the GUI Text object. For nonprogrammers, it has the advantage of being a gameObject that can be seen and manipulated like any other. The newer UnityGUI, in contrast, is a solely script-based system. You will get a bit of practice with it as well, but as it tends to be too slow for most mobile applications, you won't spend much time on it.

Let's see about getting the score on screen first. Putting text on screen is fairly easy, but in the code, the numbers will have to be converted to characters. Because 2D objects do not show in the Scene view, this is a good time to switch to the Default layout.

1. If you aren't already using it, switch to the Default layout and click the "Game view" tab.

2. Delete the Slug from the scene, and disable the Plant Zone objects for now.

3. From the GameObject menu, Create Other, select GUI Text.

4. The text "Gui Text" turns up in the center of the Game View.

5. Name it **Bunny Count**.

6. Turn on "Maximize on Play" at the top right of the Game view.

7. Click Play.

The text remains the same size even when the game window changed size. As a default, the text object stays in pixel size.

8. Stop Play mode, and check out the object's Position transforms.

It uses X/Y screen space. Z can be used to order GUI objects in z space (back into the viewport) when ambiguity exists. The position value is in unit values; 1 equals 100% of the screen width and height.

9. Set its X Position value to **0.85**.

The text shifts to the right, showing that 0 is on the left and 1 is on the right for the X Position.

10. Set its Y Position value to **0.95**.

The text shifts to the top, showing that 0 is on the bottom and 1 is on the top for the Y position.

11. Set the Font Size to **30**.

12. Change its Color to a nice orange.

The most logical place to put the controlling code is on the Scorekeeper script.

1. Open the Scorekeeper script.

2. Add the following variable:

```
public GameObject bunnyCounter; // GUI Text object
```

3. Inside the UpdateCount function, below the print line, add the following:

```
bunnyCounter.guiText.text = "test";
```

4. Comment out the print line.

5. Save the script.

6. Select the Game Manager, and drag the Bunny Count object onto its Bunny Count parameter.

Let's try a quick test.

7. Change the bunnyCounter.guiText.text line to:

```
bunnyCounter.guiText.text = currentBunCount; // change the gui text's text
```

8. Save the script.

9. Check the console.

The error message says it can't convert an `'int'` [integer] to a `'string'`. So you will have to convert or *cast* the `currentBunCount` to a string before sending it off to the GUI Text object.

10. Change the line to:

```
bunnyCounter.guiText.text = currentBunCount.ToString(); // change the gui text's text
```

11. Save the script, and click Play.

With the zombie bunny count clearly visible, the player is motivated to reduce the count as quickly as possible. While doable, it is a bit challenging.

If you think back to the firing mechanism, you may remember that you had to constrain the rate of "reload" so the player couldn't fire a steady stream of potatoes into the scene. It would be nice, though, to reward the player's marksmanship by increasing the firing rate with, say, every 10 zombie bunnies that are eradicated. Because the population grows in hops and bounds, you will have to keep a total for the removed count as well as the current total.

1. In the ScoreKeeper script, add the following variables:

```
int killCount = 0; // player hits
int hitsRequired = 10; // hits required for reward
```

2. In the UpdateCount function, below the GuiText line, add the following:

```
// manage player rewards
if(adjustment == -1){ // if it is a removal...
  killCount ++; // increment the count

}
```

For the reward, you will use a little modulus math. The % operator returns the remainder from a division operation. You will be dividing by the `hitsRequired` number, 10. When the remainder is 0, providing the `killCount` is greater than 0, you will know the player has destroyed another 10 zombie bunnies.

3. Below the killCount line, add the following:

```
int remainder = killCount % hitsRequired; // do the calculation
print("remainder = " + remainder + ", " + killCount + " dead");
if (remainder == 0 && killCount >0){
   print("reward time!");
}
```

4. Save the script.

5. Click Play, and watch the console as you destroy the zombie bunnies.

With the mechanism in place, you can add the reward. The reward will be a rate increase in the firing code, but the number will have a ceiling, or floor in this case.

1. Open the PotatoLauncher script.

The `loadRate` variable is the value you will be changing, so the `ScoreKeeper` script would require access to both the PotatoLauncher script and the `loadRate` variable. In C#, you would have to make the variable `public`. That would expose it to the Inspector. You have another option. You can designate it as `internal`. This keeps it from being exposed to the Inspector, yet allows it to be accessed by other scripts.

2. Change the `float loadRate` line to:

```
internal float loadRate = 0.5f; // how often a new projectile can be fired
```

3. Save the script.

4. Back in the ScoreKeeper script, add the following variable:

```
public PotatoLauncher launcher; // the PotatoLauncher script
```

5. Inside the `UpdateCounter` function, change the print statement contents, "reward time!", as follows to test the communication:

```
print("current rate: " + launcher.loadRate);
```

6. Save the script.

The PotatoLauncher script resides deep in the Gnomatic Garden Defender's hierarchy, on the Fire Point object.

1. Locate the Fire Point object, and drag it onto the Game Manager's Score Keeper's Launcher parameter.

2. Click Play, and watch the console as you shoot the zombie bunnies. When you reach 10 hits, you will see the `loadRate` value printed in the console.

If this was a simple matter of changing the value, as with a Boolean type, you could change it directly. But this one not only requires a bit of math, it also has to be clamped so it cannot be decremented indefinitely. This is a good time to use `SendMessage`.

3. Add the following line above the `print("current rate:" +` line:

```
launcher.SendMessage("RewardTime", SendMessageOptions.DontRequireReceiver);
```

4. Comment out the two `print` lines.

5. Save the script.

In the PotatoLauncher script, you will do all the necessary calculations. Let's put a cap of nothing shorter than 0.1 seconds for the reload time.

6. In the PotatoLauncher script, create the `RewardTime` function:

```
void RewardTime () {
    if( loadRate > 0.1f) loadRate -= 0.1f; // decrease the loadRate by 0.1
}
```

7. Save the script.

8. Click Play, and test the new reward system.

At some point, you may notice that things have gotten out of hand (Figure 9-1). The loadRate has dropped below 0.1, the potatoes seem to be hitting each other on the way out, and the zombie bunny count is off, with more reported kills than there were zombie bunnies.

Figure 9-1. Excessive explosions and an erroneous zombie bunny count

So what is wrong? The most likely culprit is frame rate. In this scenario, where you can have multiple hits very close together, the calculations may not always get a chance to finish. With the zombie bunnies, because there is a delay after the hit before they are destroyed, they could be "hit" more than once. For that, you can introduce a flag to track the first hit.

9. In the ReceivedHit script, add the following:

    ```
    bool alreadyDead = false; // flag to prevent duplicate 'deaths'
    ```

10. At the top of the DestroyBun function, add the following:

    ```
    if (alreadyDead) return; // bypass the rest of the function
    alreadyDead = true; // set the flag
    ```

Here's what is happening: The alreadyDead flag is false the first time through, so the if clause is not activated. The flag, because this is the first time through, is now set to true and the rest of the code is carried out. Now, if a second strike happens before the zombie bunny is removed from the scene, the if clause catches it and tells it to *return*, or exit the function immediately.

11. Save the script and test.

The current zombie bunny count is now better behaved, but the loadRate continues to be an issue. Let's use a similar tactic on the code that sends the message to implement the reward. You've already got the code that checks the reload value. Once the minimum value has been reached, there is no reason to carry out the rewards code. Because you are dealing with floats, it is safer to test for less than 0.2 than == 0.1 in the conditional.

1. In the ScoreKeeper script, just above the // manage player rewards section, add the following:

   ```
   if(launcher.loadRate < 0.2f) return; // no rewards available
   ```

2. Comment out the print line in the // manage player rewards section.

3. Save the script, and test again.

This time, the potato launcher's reload rate stops short of a serious cooking oil fire.

With the task of eradicating the zombie bunnies becoming attainable, it's time to give the poor player another break. Because it can sometimes be difficult to locate the last zombie bunny standing, you are going to at least stop the zombie bunny procreation when there is only one left. For the sake of argument, you can consider zombie bunny procreation and birth to be instantaneous, so if there is only one left, the player will not be plagued by more of the ravenous creatures.

If you think back to when you were populating the garden, you may remember creating and using a canReproduce variable that is checked before PopulateGardenBunnies() can be called after the first time. This is how you will stop them once the target number of 1 has been reached.

1. Open the ScoreKeeper script.

2. Add the following variable to identify the SpawnBunnies script:

   ```
   public SpawnBunnies spawner; // the SpawnBunnies script
   ```

3. Above the if(launcher.loadRate < 0.2f) line, add the following:

   ```
   if (currentBunCount == 1) { // stop the population explosion!
       spawner.canReproduce = false;
   }
   ```

4. Save the script.

An error appears in the console (Figure 9-2).

```
Assets/Game Scripts/ScoreKeeper.cs(30,33): error CS0122: 'SpawnBunnies.canReproduce' is inaccessible due to its protection level
```

Figure 9-2. Protection-level error for the canReproduce variable

As with the loadRate variable, the canReproduce variable must also be made available to other scripts, but not to the Inspector through the use of internal.

5. Open the SpawnBunnies script.

6. Change the canReproduce line as follows:

```
internal bool canReproduce = true; // flag to control reproduction of zombie bunnies
```

7. Save the script.

The SpawnBunnies script lives on the Zombie Spawn Manager object.

8. Drag the Zombie Spawn Manager object onto the ScoreKeeper's new Spawner parameter.

9. Click Play, and test the new means of zombie bunny birth control.

You may have noticed that if the timer was already running, you got one more batch of zombie bunnies before they stopped reproducing. The flag is used before the timer is reset. You can easily add a return clause to the PopulateGardenBunnies() function.

10. In the SpawnBunnies script, at the top of the PopulateGardenBunnies function, add the following:

```
if (!canReproduce) return; // cancel the latest population explosion
```

11. Save the script.

12. Click Play, and test the result.

Finally, the garden is free of the zombie bunny pests (Figure 9-3).

Figure 9-3. Invaders eradicated!

At this point, `currentBunCount = 0`, the garden is secure, so the game should either end or open up a new level. You won't deal with levels until Chapter 10, but you can block in the code for whatever eventuality you will end up providing for.

13. In the ScoreKeeper script, add the following above the
    `if (currentBunCount == 1)` section:

```
if (currentBunCount == 0) { // garden secure
    GardenSecure();
    return;
}
```

14. And then add the `GardenSecure()` function:

```
void GardenSecure(){
    // if game over

    // if more gardens

    // if more levels

}
```

There are obviously lots of things you can do here, so at this point, it makes sense to block in the options with no code.

There's one last detail of game play that you will add before getting into the 2D section of this chapter. Now that the zombie bunnies can be fully eradicated, some of the pressure has been taken off of the player. To make the player work a little harder, you will introduce the concept of battery life for the Gnomatic Garden Defender's power source.

In effect, this is just another sort of timer. The battery life will drop throughout the game. If the player gets rid of all of the zombie bunnies before the battery runs out, the game is won. If the battery runs out first, the player has lost. Let's start the countdown once the Gnomatic Garden Defender has entered the garden. You will create a GUI Texture to hold the countdown.

1. Duplicate the Bunny Count GUI Texture object, and name it **Battery Life**.

2. Set its X Position value to **0.05**.

3. Create a new C# Script in the Game Scripts folder, and name it **BatteryHealth**.

4. Add the following variables just beneath the class declaration:

```
public float batteryFull = 70.0f; // battery life in seconds
float batteryRemaining; // remaining battery life in seconds
int percentRemaining; // converted to percent
bool trackingBattery = true; // timer not started
GUIText guiTxt; // the GUI Text component
```

5. In the Start function, identify the GUI Texture component and set the starting battery value:

```
batteryRemaining = batteryFull; // full charge
guiTxt = GetComponent<GUIText>(); // the GUI Text object
guiTxt.text = "100%"; // full charge- assigned
```

6. In the Update function, add the timer:

```
if(trackingBattery) {
    if (batteryRemaining > 0){
        batteryRemaining -= Time.deltaTime; // second countdown
        percentRemaining = (int)((batteryRemaining / batteryFull) * 100); // round off for
          percent
        guiTxt.text = percentRemaining.ToString() + "%";
    }
}
```

This timer counts downward. The variable, batteryRemaining, is the updated time left. Subtracting Time.deltaTime subtracts a second at a time, but the time is divided over a second's worth of frames. The current value is sent to the GUI Text component. Because batteryRemaining is a float, it is converted or cast to an integer, using (int), before it is converted to a string to update the text value in the component.

7. Save the script.

8. Put it on the Battery Life object.

9. Click Play, and watch it count down.

When the battery runs out, the Gnomatic Garden Defender must be disabled. It should neither be able to move nor shoot. Let's disable the weapon first. Now you can switch the flag on from the BatteryHealth script.

1. Open the BatteryHealth script.

2. Below the if (batteryRemaining > 0) clause, add an else:

```
else {
    GameOver(); // it has run out
    trackingBattery = false; // turn off    battery timer
}
```

3. And create the GameOver function:

```
void  GameOver(){
    // deactive the potato gun firing
    GameObject.Find("Fire Point").SetActive(false);
}
```

4. Save the script.

5. Click Play, and try to fire potatoes after the battery has run out.

To disable the Gnomatic Garden Defender's navigation, you will have to prevent movement and the two mouse looks. With the weapon, you could deactivate the object because there was no Mesh Renderer on it. With the Gnomatic Garden Defender, you will be disabling the CharacterMotor and MouseLook scripts.

6.   Inside the GameOver function, add the following:

```
// disable navigation
GameObject.Find("Gnomatic Garden Defender").GetComponent<CharacterMotor>().enabled =
false;
// disable turning
GameObject.Find("Gnomatic Garden Defender").GetComponent<MouseLook>().enabled = false;
//disable weapon aiming
GameObject.Find("Arm Group").GetComponent<MouseLook>().enabled = false;
```

7.   Save the script.

8.   Click Play and test.

The character no longer responds, but the zombie bunnies keep falling.

Unity 2D

While the text countdown gives the player the information about the remaining battery life, it is rather boring. More typically, you will see progress bars for things like health and other parameters that work on percent of a whole. HUDs, or *heads up displays*, provide a means of keeping the player informed without having to suspend game play to access a separate menu or stats page.

With the addition of several new features, Unity has made the authoring of HUDs and fully 2D games much easier. The dedicated 2D physics engine and sprite tools are well implemented and easy to use. For your 3D game, you will be adding a few sprite-based embellishments to entertain and distract your player.

Basics

This game is obviously 3D in nature, but it will definitely benefit from some 2D elements. You will be using textures for those, but their preparation is quite a bit different than textures used on the 3D objects.

2D Mode

There are a few things you can do to make 2D authoring more efficient. If your game is going to be fully 2D, you can select the option when you create a new project (Figure 9-4).

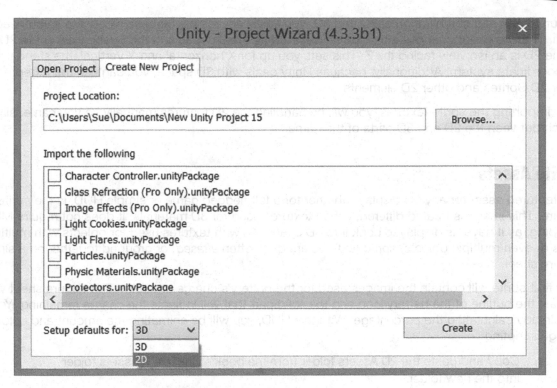

Figure 9-4. *The 2D mode option in the Project Wizard*

To change the mode after you have already started your game, you can access the Project Settings.

1. From the Edit menu, select Project Settings, Editor.

2. Under Default Behavior Mode, locate 2D mode, but do not change it (Figure 9-5).

Figure 9-5. *The 2D mode option in the Editor Settings*

If your project is a combination of 2D and 3D, you easily access the features when and if you need them. The two major changes are textures imported as Sprite types and the Scene view set to 2D. Scene 2D is an iso view facing the Z. This sets you up for X horizontal and Y vertical, the standard 2D coordinate system. Additionally, because Unity deals with 3D space, you can use the Z depth to order 2D Sprites and other 2D elements.

After importing the sprite textures, you will be handling the 2D features manually so you can easily switch between the 2D and 3D parts of the game.

Sprite Assets

The featured asset for any 2D display, whether for a full-fledged game or simple HUD, is the sprite texture. This image is treated differently than textures used for 3D materials. It does not require MIP mapping, as it never is displayed back into 3D space. As with textures used for objects with multiple parts or even multiple objects, sprite textures are quite often *altased*, or grouped together on a single texture sheet.

Your first sprite will contain the images used for the battery's charge or health. The texture sheet will contain the outline of the battery icon and the solid part that will indicate the charge remaining. You are already calculating the percentage. With this HUD, you will be animating the amount and color though scripting.

1. Copy and paste the 2D Assets folder from the book's Chapter 9 Assets folder into the new folder.

2. In the 2 x 3 Layout, switch to the Two Columns Layout to see the thumbnails of the new additions.

The folder contains four texture sheet-type images. Imported in 3D mode, they will appear as shown in Figure 9-6, where it has not been assumed that the alpha channel is used for transparency.

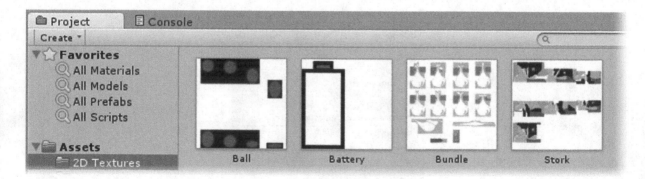

Figure 9-6. The new textures for the game's 2D assets imported in 3D mode

3. Select the Battery texture in the Inspector.

4. Check out its diffuse and alpha components (Figure 9-7, left and center).

Figure 9-7. The "Texture" Texture Type (left), its alpha channel (center), and the "Sprite" Texture Type (right)

5.   Change its Texture Type to Sprite (Figure 9-8).

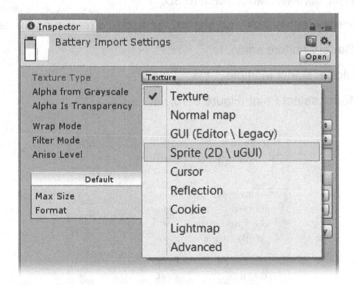

Figure 9-8. The Sprite Texture Type

6.   With Sprite chosen as the texture type, transparency is assumed and several of the other import options have changed.

For four textures, setting each to Sprite takes very little time, but if you had lots of textures to convert, it would be well worth switching to 2D Mode.

7.   From Project Settings, Editor, change the Default Behavior Mode to 2D.

8.   Delete the 2D Assets folder and then import it once more.

This time the textures come in set as Sprite Texture Type where the alpha channel is being used for transparency (Figure 9-9).

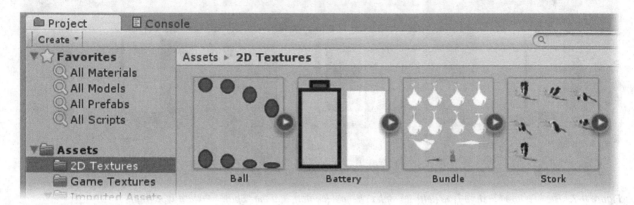

Figure 9-9. The Sprite Texture Type

9. Set the Default Behavior Mode back to 3D.

Because the setting affects textures only on import, the textures remain as Sprite Texture Types.

1. Select the Battery texture again.

2. For Sprite Mode, select Multiple.

3. For Filter Mode, select Point (Figure 9-10).

Figure 9-10. The Sprite texture settings

Point filtering preserves hard edges in the source texture, keeping the sprite sharp and clean.

This texture sheet contains two battery images, so you will use the Sprite Editor to separate them for use.

4. Click the Sprite Editor button.

5. The sprite texture appears in the editor.

6. Click the Slice button at the upper left, and read the note about obtaining more accurate slicing results (Figure 9-11).

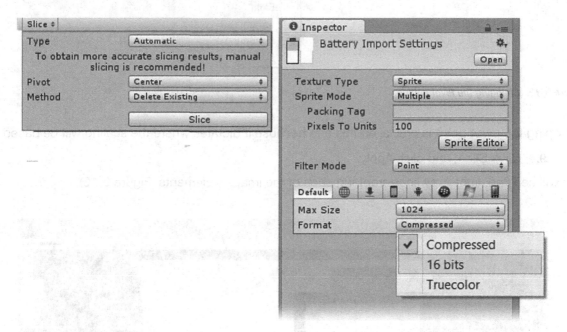

Figure 9-11. The compression warning

Because automatic slicing of compressed textures can give less-than-perfect results, you can change the Format to try Automatic slicing. Most 2D sprites have a limited color palette, so 16 bit should be sufficient.

7. Select "16 bits," and click Apply.

Back in the Sprite Editor, the message regarding compressed textures has disappeared.

8. Click the Pivot drop-down, and select Bottom (Figure 9-12).

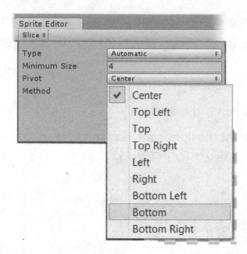

Figure 9-12. Changing the Pivot setting

Changing the pivot point is crucial on this one because it dictates where the scaling will be based.

9.   Click Slice, and click Apply.

You will see fine, light-gray lines cropping each of the image's elements (Figure 9-13).

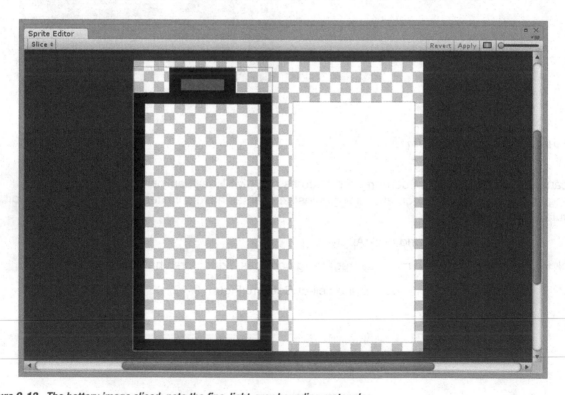

Figure 9-13. The battery image sliced; note the fine, light-gray bounding rectangles

10.   Close the Sprite Editor.

In the Project view, the Battery asset now has a drop-down/fly-out where you will find the two newly generated sprites (Figure 9-14).

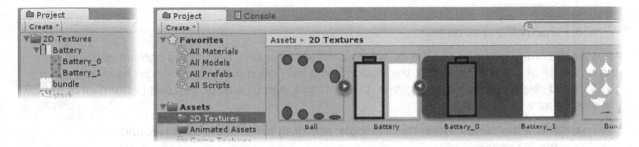

Figure 9-14. The new sprites in the One Column Layout and the Two Column Layout

Unlike the GUI Text object, sprites will show up in the Scene view. To work with the 2D sprites, however, you must first switch to the 2D display. If you had turned on 2D mode through the editor or at project creation, it would already be in 2D mode. For a combination project, you will be more likely to switch back and forth.

1.   Change the scene view to 2D, and toggle off scene lights (Figure 9-15).

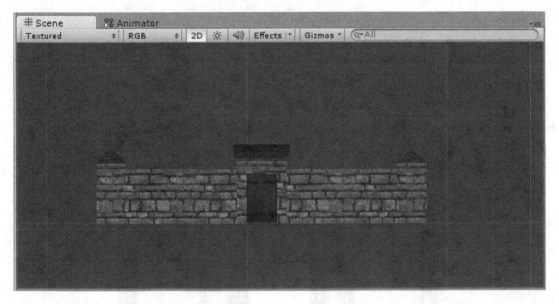

Figure 9-15. The 2D Scene view with lights toggled off

The first thing you will notice is that the Scene Gizmo is gone. You are prevented from inadvertently rotating the view out of whack. A little investigation will show that you are looking at an ortho Back view of the 3D scene.

2. Drag each of the battery sprites from the Project view into the upper left of the Scene view.

3. Focus the view on them.

At close proximity, you can see the selected sprite will have blue dots at the corners and a blue ring at the pivot point (in this case, the Bottom). You will notice that you no longer have a transform gizmo in 2D display. With the new gizmo, the rectangle with blue dots, you can perform all of the 2D transforms as well as constraints.

4. Place the cursor inside the rectangle, and drag to move the sprite around in the 2D space.

You can constrain the movement to the closest direction by holding the Shift key down while dragging.

5. To scale, place the cursor over a side or corner and click and drag.

6. To rotate, move the cursor just outside of the gizmo until the icon changes to indicate rotation (similar to Photoshop rotation).

Note that the scale changes in the Inspector and that it is a uniform scale.

7. Move the white sprite over the outline sprite.

To control the layering of this simple combination, you can use the Z depth.

8. Select Battery_0, the energy bar, and adjust the Z Position from the Inspector until it is behind the outline sprite.

9. In the Inspector, drag its Y Scale up and down for a preview of how you will match it to the remaining battery life percent.

Because you set the Pivot of the sprites to Bottom, you will be able to set the scale correctly.

10. In the sprite's Sprite Renderer component, change the Color to a nice green (Figure 9-16).

Figure 9-16. The energy bar on top of the outline (left), behind the outline (center), and scaled and colored (right)

You will eventually be setting the color according to the percent remaining.

11. Set the Y Scale back to **1** and the Color back to white.

Cameras and Layers

By now, you have probably noticed that, unlike the GUI Text objects, the sprites are not showing in the Game view. To have a 3D scene overlaid by 2D sprites, you will be using a second camera. This will allow you to keep the sprites together and scaled to the scene regardless of what the Main Camera is looking at.

1. Create a new camera, and name it **Camera GUI**.

2. Remove its Audio Listener component.

The Game view now shows the view from the new camera, but as yet, no battery. The mystery can be quickly solved with a quick trip back to the 3D scene.

3. Toggle the scene back to 3D, and switch to a Perspective Top view.

You can now see where the sprite exists in the 3D world and that the camera must be moved back for the battery to come into view (Figure 9-17).

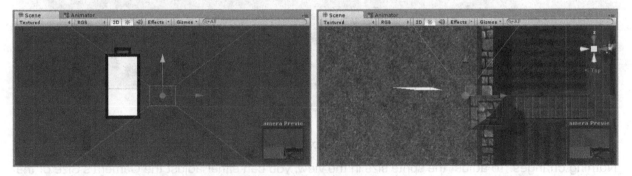

Figure 9-17. The camera and sprites in 2D space (left) and in 3D space (right)

4. Move the camera back until the Battery appears in the Game view (Figure 9-18).

Figure 9-18. The battery sprites visible in the Game view

Now you can easily see another problem. Perspective may be good for 3D scenes, but 2D should be flat or orthographic.

5.   In the Inspector, set the Camera component's Projection to Orthographic.

The view in the Game window is properly flat, but the battery is now very small (Figure 9-19).

Figure 9-19. The Camera GUI view properly orthographic

6.   Try moving the camera in closer to the battery sprites in the Scene view.

Nothing changes. To adjust the sprite size in the view, you can either adjust the Camera's Size or the sprite's X and Y Scale.

7.   Try adjusting the Size and location of the Orthographic Projection in the Camera component until the battery is displayed large and behind the Battery Life Gui Text object in the upper left (Figure 9-20).

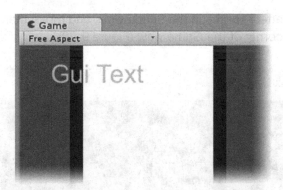

Figure 9-20. The camera's Orthographic Size reduced to increase the battery size in its view

If you have been wondering why the GUI Text objects are always visible in the Game view, it is because Camera components come with a GUI Layer that renders them.

8. Disable the GUILayer component for Camera GUI to turn off the Battery Life and Bunny Count Gui Text objects.

Next you will be turning off some of the rendering in the Camera GUI so you can see both the Main Camera and the Camera GUI's sprites.

9. Under Clear Flags, select Depth only (Figure 9-21).

Figure 9-21. Depth only on the Camera GUI, allowing the Main Camera's view to show through

With Main Camera's 3D scene visible once again, the GUI Text objects are back. They will draw on any camera with an enabled GUILayer component.

10. Set the Camera GUI's Size to **4**.

11. Set the Scene view to 2D again.

12. Select the two battery sprites in the Scene view, and move them so they are in the upper left corner of the Game view (Figure 9-22).

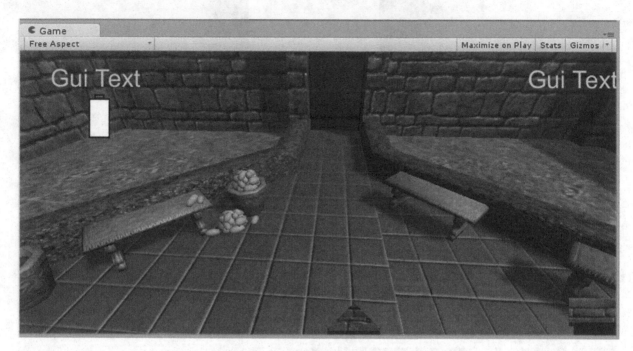

Figure 9-22. The sprites in position

Layers

At some point, you may have noticed that part of the garden from the Camera GUI is also showing in the foreground of the Game view. Unity has a robust layering system to control what objects can be rendered by each camera. Similar to tags, layers serve as a filtering mechanism. To prevent Camera GUI from rendering the garden-related objects, you will create a layer just for the sprites.

1. In the top left of the Unity editor, click Layers and select Edit Layers (Figure 9-23).

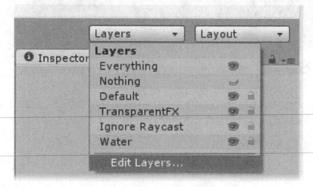

Figure 9-23. Edit Layers

2. In User Layer 8, type in **Sprite**.

3. Select Camera GUI, and set its Culling Mask to Nothing, and then to Sprite.

Everything from Camera GUI disappears.

4. Select Battery Life, Bunny Count, Battery_0, and Battery_1, and assign them each to the new Sprite layer at the top of the Inspector (Figure 9-24).

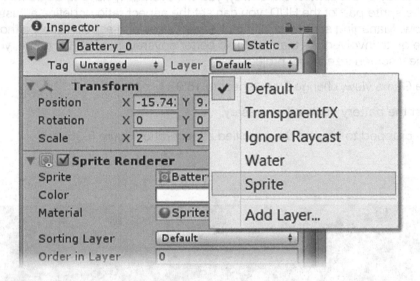

Figure 9-24. Assigning the Sprite layer

5. Enable the Camera GUI's GUILayer component to see the GUI Text objects again.

Let's take a few minutes to see how sprites behave with different aspect ratios.

1. With the Game View set to Free Aspect, try adjusting the size and aspect ratio of the window in the editor (Figure 9-25).

Figure 9-25. Sprite location problems with different aspect ratios

The sprites are clearly affected by the screen ratio, but the GUI Text position, using a percent of the screen size, is not. If you were to enable the GUI Layer in the Camera GUI object, you would find that the text is rendered in the exact same place for both cameras.

The first rule for using sprites is that you will have to manage your screen size. You can restrict the player to predefined sizes, or you can adjust the Orthographic Projection Size to the screen's size and script the camera's position to adjust accordingly. With the latter, you will probably lose the "pixel perfect" display of the sprites. Either way, you will eventually have to do some scripting. For setting up the sprite part of the HUD, you can set the aspect ratio or define a custom size in the Game window. Managing sprites for different screen sizes and aspect ratios, although certainly possible, can be quite involved. As that is a topic better covered in a fully 2D game, you will be limiting the game's screen size in this project.

2.   In the Game view, change Free Aspect to 16:9.

3.   Adjust the battery sprites if necessary.

The view is now cropped to present the specified aspect ratio (Figure 9-26).

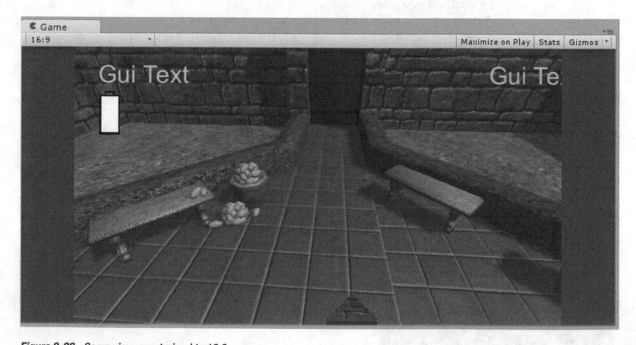

Figure 9-26.   Game view constrained to 16:9

Depending on where the Main Camera is pointing, it may be possible for it to see the sprites because they do exist in World space. So once you create a layer and a camera specifically for the layer, you will want to tell other cameras—in this case Main Camera—not to render the sprites.

4.   Select the Main Camera, and from its Culling Mask drop-down menu, uncheck Sprite.

Now each camera renders the appropriate objects.

Orthographic Size

If you are a 2D purist, you already know that the sprites will be "pixel perfect" only at certain screen resolutions. If the screen size varies from the optimal size, the sprites will be drawn to fit the size and may not scale cleanly. In a fully 2D game, this can be an important issue, especially if the 2D assets are small. For HUD elements, it is probably not as crucial, but it's worth covering.

The orthographic size denotes how many [2D] world units are contained in the top *half* of the camera projection. For example, with an orthographic size of 5, the vertical extents of the viewport will contain 10 units of world space. The horizontal size is dictated by the aspect ratio.

1.   Select the Battery asset in the Project view.

2.   In the Inspector, locate the "Pixels to Units" value.

It tells you that 100 pixels equal 1 unit. With an orthographic Size of 5, you could stack ten 100-pixel-high sprites vertically in the viewport and they would be displayed at their native size. As long as the sprites or the orthographic size are increased in multiples of 2, the sprites should retain a clean appearance. It is essential to make sure that all of your sprites are the same scale or at least in multiples of 2 so they can be sized in the game using the orthographic size. For a more in-depth discussion on this topic, check out http://www.third-helix.com/2012/02/making-2d-games-with-unity/ by Josh Sutphin. His article was written before Unity revamped its 2D features, but it remains a valuable source of 2D information.

The remainder of the sprites created for this game are meant to be used with the default 5 orthographic size, so let's get that locked in and adjust the battery size accordingly.

3.   Select the Camera GUI, and set the Size to **5**.

While you are scripting the energy bar's animation, it will be useful to have it display larger.

4.   Select both battery sprites in the Hierarchy view, and set their X and Y Scale to **2**.

5.   Move the battery sprites to the top left. Don't worry about the text.

6.   Set Battery_1's Color to a fully saturated green.

At this point, you should make an executive decision about where the text should be rendered. With the Camera GUI rendering the text, the text is rendered on top of the sprites. If you wanted it behind the sprites, you would have to turn on the Main Camera's GUILayer and remove the text from the Sprite layer.Let's continue with the battery setup.

1.   Select the Battery Life object.

2.   Set its X Position transform to **0.02** and its Y Position transform to **0.71**.

3.   Set its Text parameter to "**00%**" and its Font Size to **24.**

4.   Move the battery sprites above it.

With the battery in place, you can go ahead and script the functionality.

5.   Open the BatteryHealth script.

6. Add the following variables:

    ```
    public GameObject energyBar; //the battery's energy bar sprite
    float baseScale; // the energy bar's base y scale
    ```

7. In the Start function, get and store the energy bar's base scale:

    ```
    baseScale = energyBar.transform.localScale.y; // get the base scale
    ```

The progress bar will be updated at the same time as the text value, so you will call a little function from inside the Update function.

8. Inside the Update function, beneath the percentRemaining = (int)... line, add the following:

    ```
    UpdateBattery(); // update the sprite graphic
    ```

9. Block in the function that does the work:

    ```
    // animate the battery's energy bar sprite to match percent remaining
    void UpdateBattery () {

    }
    ```

10. Inside the function, add:

    ```
    // adjust battery's energy bar sprite
    Vector3 adjustedScale = energyBar.transform.localScale; //store the sprite's scale in a
    temp var
    adjustedScale.y = baseScale * (batteryRemaining / batteryFull); // calculate the actual
    y scale
    energyBar.transform.localScale = adjustedScale; // apply the new value
    ```

11. Save the script.

12. Select the Battery Life object.

13. Drag Battery_1 into the Energy Bar parameter of its Battery Health component.

14. Click Play, and watch the bar drop in response to the percent of charge remaining (Figure 9-27).

Figure 9-27. The battery sprite's animating with the percent

The bar works nicely, changing with each drop in percent.

You are probably thinking it would be better if the color changed as the charge dropped lower and lower. When scripting color values, Unity has a few presets from the Color class. Color.green, for instance, will produce the fully saturated green used in the battery. Custom colors must be set with a Color struct. The catch is that unlike the familiar [to some of us, at least] (256,256,256) format, you must use the unit values, Color(1.0f,1.0f,1.0f). As this is essentially a percent, it works out quite well for changing the color in response to the percent of charge remaining.

For this added functionality, let's consider the green color good until 50%. At that point, it should morph to yellow until 25% (remaining). And from there, down to red at 0%. Before tackling the math, it is helpful to find out what the RGB numbers are for each of the target colors. You can do this in any color picker that gives you an RGB read out. Saturated green is (0,255,0), or Color(0,1f,0). Remember, most array values start at 0 rather than 1, so 256 becomes 255. Yellow is (255,255,0), or Color(1f,1f,0). Red is (255,0,0). So the logic will be from 50% down to 25%, the R value will increase by 0.4 each percent. At 25%, the G value will decrease by 0.4 each percent. Each color change works over 1/4 of the 100%, so each percent adds 4 x 1% to the affected color.

1. Below the scaling code in the UpdateBattery function add:

```
// if less than 50% and greater than 25%, adjust color- raise red to get yellow
if(percentRemaining <= 50 && percentRemaining > 25) {
    float adj = (50- percentRemaining) * 0.04f; // adjusted for current percent
    energyBar.GetComponent<SpriteRenderer>().color = new Color(0f + adj,1f,0f);
}
```

Because you are setting the color absolutely, you must calculate using the offset of the percentage where the change is taking place (50- percentRemaining). If this is confusing, just try working out the numbers manually to assure yourself that the value is changing properly.

2. Add the code to bring the color to red:

```
// if less than or equal to 25%, adjust color drop green to get red
if(percentRemaining <= 25 ) {
    float adj = (25 - percentRemaining) * 0.04f;
    energyBar.GetComponent<SpriteRenderer>().color = new Color(1f,1f - adj,0f);
}
```

In either case, there is only one of the RGB values changing, so the other is set to 1 or 100%. Blue is never used and remains at 0.

3. Save the script.

4. Click Play, and watch the color change as the battery's charge gets lower and lower.

To reward your player for eradicating the threat, you will freeze the battery drain when the zombie bunnies are no longer able to reproduce. In the BatteryHealth script, the trackingBattery variable controls the battery energy drain, so you will be changing its state from the ScoreKeeper script.

1. Open the ScoreKeeper script.

2. At the top of the // stop the population explosion! conditional, add:

```
// stop the battery drain - the threat is almost neutralized
GameObject.Find ("Battery Life").GetComponent<BatteryHealth>().trackingBattery = false;
```

3. Temporarily set its condition to 10 zombie bunnies remaining while testing:

```
if (currentBunCount == 10) { // stop the population explosion!
```

4. Save the script.

An error in the console reports that the variable is not accessible due to its protection level. Once again you will have to add internal to gain access.

5. In the Battery Health script, change the variable declaration to:

```
internal bool trackingBattery = true;
```

The internal allows you to access it from other scripts without exposing it to the Inspector as would using public. Functions will have to be marked as public if they are being called directly from other scripts, as you will discover later in the project.

6. Save the script.

7. Click Play, and shoot all but the currently set limit of zombie bunnies.

The battery stops dropping, allowing the player to eradicate the remaining pests at his leisure.

Animated Sprites

With the battery, you used multiple sprites derived from a single texture sheet as individuals. Another use is to convert multiple images on the sheet into a single animated sprite. To warn your player about an impending zombie bunny population explosion, you will fly an animated stork across the top of the screen. Eventually, it will drop its bundle of zombie bunnies, signaling the onslaught of new zombie bunnies dropping into the 3D scene.

The stork, minus its lower beak, will be an animated sprite. The lower beak, bundle and payload (baby zombie bunnies), will be separate sprites that will be mostly animated with physics.

1. In the Project view, select the Stork asset from the 2D Assets folder.

2. Change its Sprite Mode to Multiple.

3. Change its compression to 16 bit, and click Apply.

4. Open it in the Sprite Editor.

5. Open the Slice dialog and, using the default Type, Automatic, and Minimum Size, 4, click Slice.

The stork, sliced with the default settings, is shown in Figure 9-28.

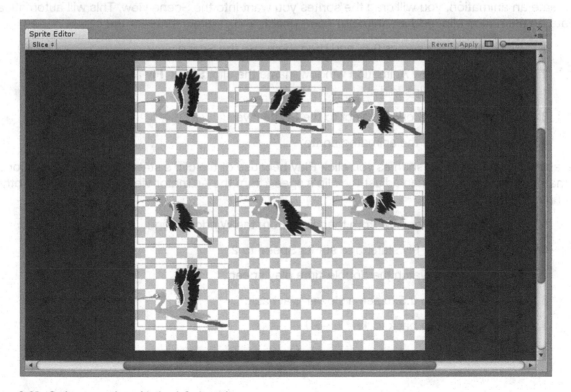

Figure 9-28. Sprite generation with the default settings

Note the wasted space on the texture sheet. To conserve memory, you can atlas different sprites together on the same sheet, as you will see in the Bundle asset, or, if you have Unity Pro, you can make use of its Sprite Packer option from the Edit menu, Project Settings, Editor section. The Sprite Packer will internally pack your sprites for optimal memory usage. The sprite's Packing Tag parameter determines which sprites can be grouped together for more efficient use of space/memory. Only similar texture sheets should be atlased (e.g., those that use different compression or alpha channels).

6. Click Apply, and close the Sprite Editor.

7. In the Project view, click to expand the Stork asset.

8. Just as with the Battery, it now shows the newly generated sprites (Figure 9-29).

Figure 9-29. Stork sprites in the Single Column Layout and the Two Column Layout

To create an animation, you will drag the sprites you want into the Scene view. This will automatically create an animation clip, add an Animator component, and create a state for the clip.

1. Select the Stork sprites 0-6, and drag them into the Scene view.

2. At the Create New Animation window, name the clip, **Stork_Fly** and put it in the Animation Clips folder.

3. Assign the new Stork_0 object to the Sprite layer.

4. Click Play to see the animated sprite.

The animation happens as soon as you click Play because of the clip's state that was created for the Animator component. You can adjust the clip's speed from the Animator view, just as with any other Mecanim-driven animation.

5. Open the Animator view from the tab or from the Window menu.

6. Select the Stork_Fly state, and set its Speed to **2**.

7. Click Play, and watch the double-time play speed.

8. Set the Speed to **0.5** to see a slower playback.

9. Set the Speed to back to **1**.

The Stork bobs up and down because the center of each of the auto-sliced sprites is at a different height. That may not be an issue or may even be a serendipitous surprise with some animations. You will be trying something different with the stork. Anyone who has ever held a live chicken in their hands knows that you can move the body and the chicken's head attempts to retain its initial location. With this animation, you will attempt the same effect but for a more mundane reason. The stork's head must remain still while the wings move the body up and down so the parented sprites will always be registered properly. One way to insure that is to slice the sprites with the grid option. Providing the registration point is exactly the same for each sprite, the animation will play as designed. To better illustrate this, let's try a classic bouncing ball.

10. Select the Ball asset from the 2D Assets folder.

11. Change its Sprite Mode to Multiple, set its Format to 16 bits, and click Apply.

12. Open the Sprite Editor.

13. Click Slice.

The various ball poses are cropped close as expected (Figure 9-30).

Figure 9-30. The cropped balls in the sprite sheet

14. Click Apply, and then drag the ball's sprites into the Scene view.

15. Name the animation **Ball Test**, and put it in the Animation Clips folder.

16. Click Play, and watch it in the Scene view.

As expected, there isn't much movement, though it squashes nicely.

1. Select the Ball asset in the Project view again.

2. In the Sprite Editor, change the Type to Grid, set the Pixel Size to 128 x 256, and set the Pivot to Bottom (Figure 9-31).

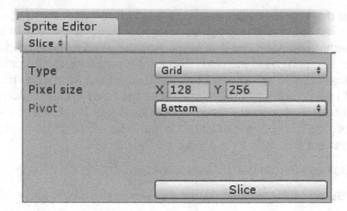

Figure 9-31. Grid settings for the Ball

3.   Click Slice.

This time the divisions follow the specified grid (Figure 9-32).

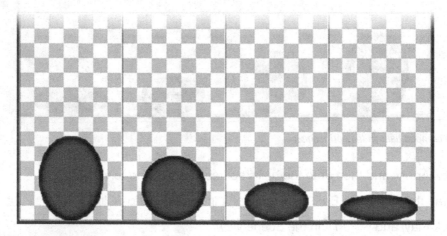

Figure 9-32. Grid divisions for the ball

4.   Click Apply, and close the dialog.

5.   Click Play, and watch the results in the Scene view.

This time the ball drops and is squashed correctly. The animation, however, is only the dropping part of the bounce cycle. Rather than create the rest of the cycle with what are essentially duplicates, you can clone the keys in the Dope Sheet.

1.   Select the Ball_0 in the Scene view, and open the Animation view (Ctrl + 6).

2.   Click the arrow to the left of the Ball_0 : Sprite line to see the thumbnails in the Dope Sheet.

3. Turn on Record (by clicking the red button on the left), and drag the time indicator to the second-to-the-last key (Figure 9-33).

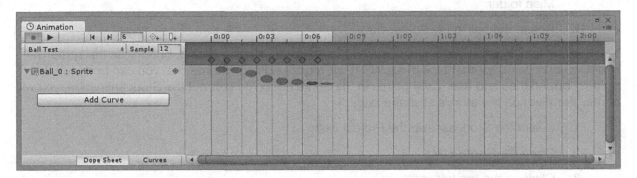

Figure 9-33. The Ball sprites in the Dope Sheet

4. Select the key.

5. Copy the key with Ctrl + C (copy).

6. Move the time indicator to the next position after the last key and press Ctrl + V (paste).

The copied key/sprite is added to the animation clip, but there is an easier way to add sprite keys. You can drag them directly into the Animation editor from the Project view. You may wish to use the Two Panel Layout for this operation to see the clip thumbnails.

7. Drag the sprites from the Inspector into the Ball Test animation clip until all, including the first sprite, are mirrored (Figure 9-34).

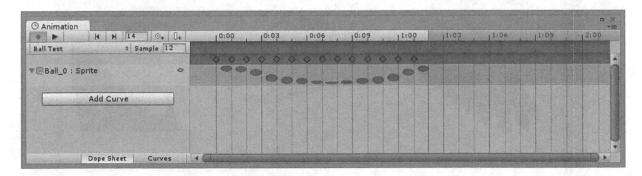

Figure 9-34. The duplicated keys and the sprites they represent

8. Click Play in the Animation view, and watch the ball bounce.

The timing is much nicer. The Animation editor allows you to adjust the timing of the individual keys. The default time for each sprite is 0.1 second. If you wish to slow down or speed up the clip, you can do so by adjusting the Speed in the clip's state in the Animator view.

9. Close the Animation editor.

10. Select the Ball_0 object in the Hierarchy view, and drag it into the Prefabs'
    Misc folder.

11. Delete the ball in the Scene view.

You may be thinking that you should use Grid for the Stork's sprite slicing, but unless the sprite sheet was prepared for that type of slicing, it will require editing. It turns out, you can both edit the sprites' boundaries and their pivot points in the Sprite Editor. To sort out the Stork animation, you will center the pivot on the stork's eyeball's pupil.

1. Select the Stork asset in the Project view.

2. Open the Sprite Editor.

3. Click on the top left sprite.

The now-familiar 2D transform gizmo appears.

4. Use the middle mouse roller or upper left scroll bar to zoom in close enough
    to see the eye's pupil.

5. Click and drag the pivot to the pupil (Figure 9-35).

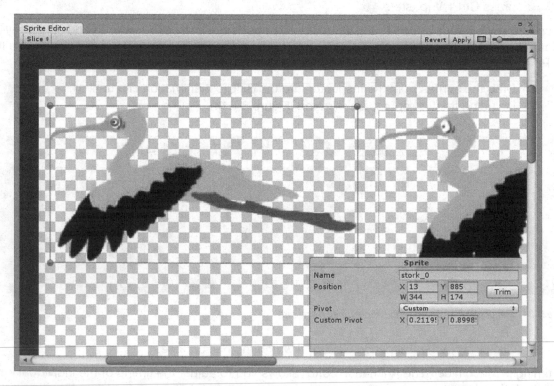

Figure 9-35. The custom pivot located at the stork's eye

6. Repeat for the rest of the sprites.

7. Close the editor, and click Play to see the difference.

The stork doesn't have a lower beak or a payload yet, but you can get him moving across the scene in the meantime. Because he's just doing a simple fly-by with no obstacles to navigate, using physics would be overkill. A simple transform animation will do the job. In order to retain control of the animations of the various parts of the stork and his payload, you will put him on a parent object.

8. Create a new C# Script, and name it **FlyBy**.

9. Create a variable for speed:

```
public float speed = -5f; // send the 2d sprite left
```

10. In its Update function, add:

```
transform.Translate ( speed * Time.deltaTime, 0, 0);
```

Because of the Camera GUI's orientation, world x, y, z space is also screen x, y, z space, so the minus x value will send the object from right to left.

11. Save the script.

12. Focus in on the Stork_0 in the Scene view.

13. Create an Empty GameObject, and name it **Stork Group**.

14. Assign it to the Sprite layer.

15. Add the FlyBy script to Stork Group.

16. Add the Stork_0 object to Stork Group.

17. Position the Stork Group to the right side of the Game view, just out of view.

18. Click Play, and watch the stork flap his way across the screen.

The stork will make several trips across the screen throughout the game, so you will want to save the starting location, as well as deactivate him when he's reached the other side. The location is calculated in world space, and the screen bounds or viewing frustum are relative to the Camera GUI.

You are probably wondering why you aren't going to Destroy and Instantiate the stork as you have with other characters that come and go. If you plan on developing games for mobile at some point, you will discover that the Destroy/Instantiate method is rather costly. Typically in mobile, objects that make several appearances are deactivated and reactivated. It tends to require more work on your part, but it is a worthwhile method of controlling temporary objects to try out.

The first thing to do is to see what happens when the object is deactivated and then reactivated.

19. Select the Stork Group.

20. Click Play, and then deactivate it from the top of the Inspector when it is about half way across the screen.

21. Now reactivate it.

It carries on just where it left off. This means location is retained during deactivation, so you will have to specify its starting location each time he starts the fly-by.

22.   Add the following variables:

```
Vector3 startLocation; // starting spot
Vector3 endLocation;   // out of view
```

There is no rotation involved, so you need only save the three position values in a Vector3 struct. When the object is reactivated, you will have to set it back to the start position. By setting up a function to handle the task, you can call it from both the Start function and any other object.

1.   Holding the shift key down to constrain to a horizontal transform, drag the Stork Group to the left of the screen until it is no longer showing in the game view.

2.   Make note of the X position, and calculate a safe total distance of change.

A distance value of -25 should be more than enough.

3.   Add the offset variable:

```
float offSetX = -25f; // distance to the other side
```

The stork will have to be deactivated at the start, so you will set up the values in the Awake function instead of the Start function. Awake is evaluated before the Start function and is used to locate and identify objects that will be deactivated in the Start function.

4.   Above the Start function, create an Awake function:

```
void Awake () {
    startLocation = transform.position; // store the starting location
    endLocation = new Vector3(startLocation.x + offSetX , startLocation.y,
       startLocation.z);
}
```

You can initiate the action from the Start function so the player will get a preview of what happens when the garden is overrun with zombie bunnies.

5.   In the Start function, add:

```
Initialize(); // set location
```

6.   Next, create the Initialize function:

```
void Initialize () {
    // reset the start position
    Vector3 tempLocation = transform.position; // make a variable to hold the value
    tempLocation = startLocation;                // change the value
    transform.position = tempLocation;           // assign the new value
}
```

7. In the Update function, above the Translate line, add the "stop" condition:

```
if (transform.localPosition.x < endLocation.x) gameObject.SetActive (false);
// deactivate
```

8. Save the script.

9. Click Play, and watch the stork in the Hierarchy view to make sure it is deactivated after it goes out of view in the Game window.

The stork fly-by will be initiated in the Zombie Spawn Manager's SpawnBunnies script.

1. Open the SpawnBunnies script.

2. Add the following variable to access the stork:

```
public GameObject stork; // the Stork Group
```

3. In the StartReproducing function, just above the audio.Play() line, add:

```
stork.SetActive (true); // reactivate the stork
stork.SendMessage ("Initialize", SendMessageOptions.DontRequireReceiver); // initialize
    the stork
```

4. Save the script.

5. Assign the Stork Group to the Zombie Spawn Manager's Stork parameter.

6. Click Play, and watch the stork fly by with each new zombie bunny addition.

With the stork now making a fly-by, you will want to move the Clacking sound effect to the stork and set it to looping.

7. Add an Audio Source component to the Stork Group.

8. Load the Clacking clip, turn "Play on Awake" on and set the clip to Loop.

9. Disable or remove the Audio Source component from the Zombie Spawn manager.

10. In the SpawnBunnies script, change the audio.Play() line to:

```
stork.audio.Play(); // play the sound effect that signals the repro populating
```

11. Save the script, and click Play to test the sound effect.

The clacking sound effect now matches up with the stork's fly-bys.

Next up is the stork's payload: a bundle of Zombie bunnies. You will do the usual sprite slicing, but this time, you will be using Mecanim and key-frame animation to cue the action. Unlike a "canned" animation, by animating the various parts individually, you will be able to cue the bunny-drop sequence at any (random) time.

1. Select the Bundle asset in the 2D Assets folder.

2. Set the Compression to 16 bit.

3. Set it to Multiple, and open the Sprite Editor.

The Bundle asset contains images for 3 carried bundles, 3 falling bundles, 3 hit bundles, a lower beak, and a baby zombie bunny (Figure 9-36).

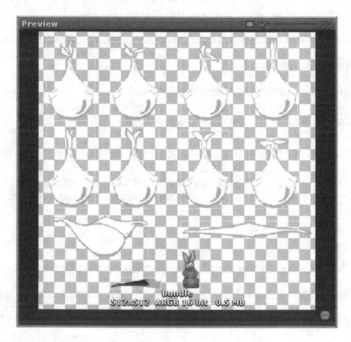

Figure 9-36. *The atlased Bundle sprite sheet*

1. Do an Automatic slice with the Pivot at Bottom.

2. Zoom into the lower beak, and click to edit the sprite.

3. Set its pivot as per Figure 9-37.

Figure 9-37. *The lower beak's custom pivot location*

4. Click Apply, and close the editor.

5. In the Inspector, click through the new Bundle sprites until you find the beak, or select it directly if you are using the Two Columns Layout.

6. Drag it into the Scene view, and position it at the stork.

7. Rename it **Lower Beak**, and assign it to the Sprite layer.

8. Adjust its Z depth (Position) to move it behind the Stork_0 object (Figure 9-38).

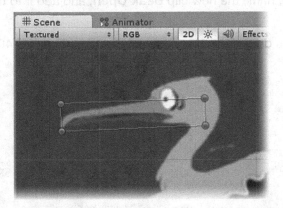

Figure 9-38. The lower beak in position

The higher numbers are drawn first, so the beak should be a positive number higher than the stork's 0 value.

1. Position the cursor just off the gizmo until you can see it change to the rotate icon.

2. Rotate the beak to an open position to make sure the location and Pivot location are correct for this pose (Figure 9-39).

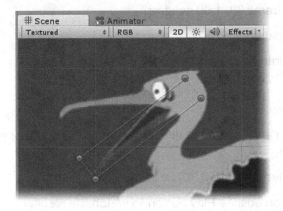

Figure 9-39. The beak in its open pose

3. Make any correction necessary, and then rotate the beak back to an almost closed position.

4. In the Hierarchy view, drag the sprite onto the Stork Group.

5. Click Play, and watch the stork and beak fly by.

Next you will create a one-shot animation for the beak.

1. Select the Lower Beak, and open the Animation editor.

2. Click Add Curve, name the new clip **Beak Open**, and add it to the Animation Clips folder.

3. In the Transforms drop-down menu, select Rotation (Figure 9-40).

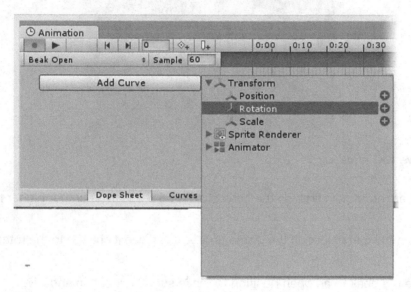

Figure 9-40. Adding a Rotation track

A key is set at frame 0 and frame 60, 1:00 second.

4. Move the time indicator to 0:10.

5. Rotate the beak into its open orientation in the Scene view.

A new key is added.

6. Select the new key.

7. Copy the key (ctrl + C), move the time indicator to 0:20, and paste to make a duplicate.

8. Move the key at time 1:00 to 0:30.

9. Click the Animation editor's Play button to watch the result.

The beak opens farther than it should have because of the default smooth tangents Unity uses when there are more than two keys. To fix the problem, you will adjust the two "open" key's tangents.

1. At the bottom of the Animation editor, switch to Curves and select the Rotation track.

You can now see why the beak opens farther than you set it to open (Figure 9-41).

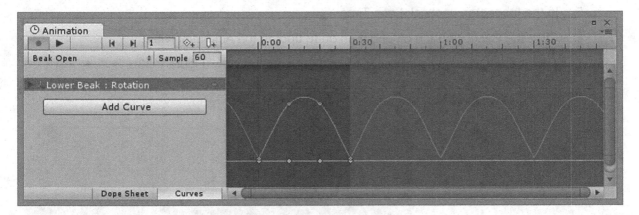

Figure 9-41. *The smooth tangents on the Beak Open curve*

2. Select the key at time 0:10, and right-click on it.

3. From the right-click menu, select Right Tangent, Constant (Figure 9-42).

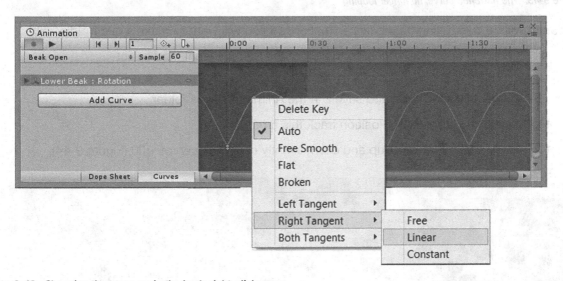

Figure 9-42. *Changing the tangency in the key's right-click menu*

The curve flattens out between the two "open" keys.

Now that you've seen what it looks like, you can also change the tangent types in the Dope Sheet if you can do without the visual feedback.

This will be a one-off animation, so you will have to turn off the default loop setting for the clip.

4. Select the clip in the Animation Clips folder in the Project view.

5. In the Inspector, uncheck Loop Time.

6. Click the Record button off and then on to update the Animation view.

7. The ghosted curves no longer show in the Animation view (Figure 9-43).

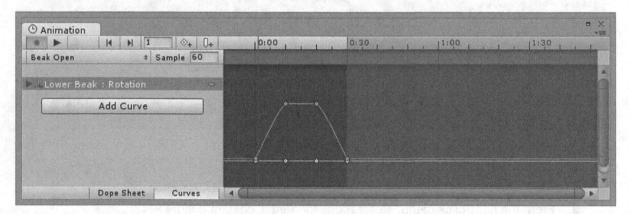

Figure 9-43. *The flattened curve, no longer looping*

Mecanim will be controlling the beak's animation, so you will want to make a quick "idle" clip.

8. Click the open arrows just to the left of the Sample label, and select [Create New Clip].

9. Name it **Beak Clack**, and save it in the Animation Clips folder.

10. Select the Transform, Position track this time.

11. Move the Lower Beak up and down slightly over the span of 1:00 (Figure 9-44).

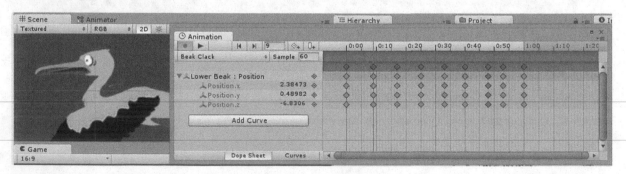

Figure 9-44. *The clacking animation showing the beak at its down position*

You can copy and paste the keys if you wish, but the key generated at 1:00 will ensure a proper loop cycle. The stork should look as if he's muttering to himself.

12. Close the Animation view.

The Animator setup will be fairly simple. The two clips you made for the beak have automatically been added. To trigger the Beak open, you will be creating a Trigger parameter.

1. With the Lower Beak selected, open the Animator view.

2. Right-click over the Beak Clack state, and choose "Set as Default."

3. In the Parameters area, at the lower left, click the plus sign and create a new Trigger type parameter.

4. Name it **Cue the Beak**.

Trigger type parameters are Booleans that are automatically set back to `false` after they have been triggered, which saves you lots of scripting.

5. Create a transition from Beak Clack to Beak Open.

6. Set its Condition to "Cue the Beak."

7. Create a transition from Beak Open to Beak Clack.

8. Leave its Condition set to Exit Time.

9. Click Play, and watch the stork as he mutters to himself while making his way across the screen.

10. With the beak selected, click to turn on the "Cue the Beak" parameter halfway across.

The beak opens once, closes, and then resumes its clacking behavior.

11. Exit Play mode and uncheck the "Cue the Beak" parameter.

When you change a parameter during runtime, it does not revert to its prior state when you exit Play mode.

To cue the beak open, you will return to the SpawnBunnies script where you cue the stork. The Animator component must be identified, but the triggering is a single line of code.

1. Open the SpawnBunnies script.

2. Add the following variable:

```
public Animator beak; // the lower beak's animator component
```

3. In the `StartReproducing` function, change the `3f` in the second `yield return new` to a random number between 1 and 2:

```
yield return new WaitForSeconds(Random.Range (1f,2f)); // finish the adjusted time
```

4. Below that `yield return` new line, add:

    ```
    beak.SetBool("Cue the Beak", true); // trigger the beak drop
    ```

5. Save the script, and select the Zombie Spawn Manager object.

6. Drag the Lower Beak object onto its Beak parameter.

7. Click Play, and watch the action when the stork makes his drop runs.

8. Stop Play mode.

Next up is the bundle. It will require multiple clips.

1. Select the first three sprites in the Bundle asset in the Project view.

2. Drag them into the Scene view.

3. Name the new animation clip **Bundle Carry**, and save it in the Animation Clips folder.

4. In the Animation Editor, drag another Bundle_1 sprite to the end to make a better looping animation.

5. Rename the object Bundle, and position it at the beak.

6. Adjust the Z position until the bundle is in back of the stork but in front of the Lower Beak (Figure 9-45).

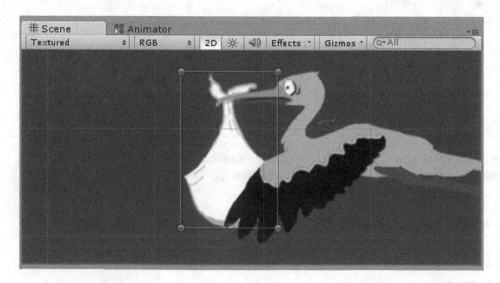

Figure 9-45. The Bundle in position

7. Add the Bundle object to the Sprite layer, and then drag it into the Stork Group.

8. Click Play, and watch the assets fly by.

Depending on where in the Z depth you placed the battery elements and the stork elements, you may discover that the stork goes in front of the battery, while the bundle and Lower Beak go behind it (Figure 9-46). To fix the problem, you could move the battery farther back in the scene with its Z position, or you could adjust its Order in Layer.

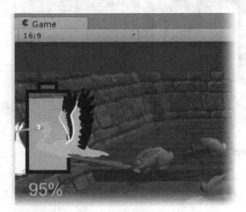

Figure 9-46. The Bundle and Lower Beak behind the Battery sprite

In a fully 2D game, you would want to make use of Unity's Sorting Layers. Using these layers, which are similar to camera Layers and accessed from the same place, you can create layers for things like background and foreground sprites so you won't have to adjust the Z depth for every sprite on an individual basis. The Sorting Layer is assigned to sprites in the Sprite Renderer component. The lower element numbers are drawn first, so you would create a background layer first, a character layer next, and then a foreground layer.

In this game, there are very few sprites and they are currently all on the same layer, the Default layer. Let's use the "Order in Layer" parameter to move the two battery sprites back behind the stork sprites.

9.   Select the Battery_0 sprite, and give it an "Order in Layer" value of **-1**.

That immediately puts it behind Battery_1, the energy bar.

10.   Set Battery_1's "Order in Layer" value to **-2**.

The energy bar is back behind the outline.

11.   Click Play, and watch as the stork flies over the battery.

The Stork and bundle are now both in front of the battery sprites during the fly-by (Figure 9-47).

Figure 9-47. The stork, bundle, and lower beak in front of the battery sprites

The bundle requires two more animation clips: a fall sequence and a hit/open sequence. They will be added to Bundle.

1. Select Bundle, and open the Animation editor.

2. From the drop-down menu showing Bundle Carry, select [Create New Clip].

3. Name it **Bundle Fall**, and save it in the Animation Clip folder.

4. Drag the Bundle_3 asset from the Project view into the Animation editor.

A Sprite Renderer, Sprite track is created with Bundle_3 at frame 0.

5. Zoom the Animation window to show up to about 0:20.

6. Drag Bundle_4 into the editor at time 0:05.

7. Drag Bundle_5 into the editor at time 0:10.

8. Drag Bundle_4 into the editor again at time 0:15.

9. Click Play, and watch the falling animation clip play.

10. Create another new clip named **Bundle Open**.

11. Drag the last 4 Bundle sprites (6, 7, 8, 9) into it about 0:1 apart from each other.

12. Zoom out in the Animation editor by using the middle mouse roller, and pan until you can see time 4:00.

13. Drag one more fully open bundle sprite into the Animation editor, and position it at time 4:00.

14. Select the Bundle Open clip in the Project view, and uncheck Loop Time.

15. Cloes the Animation view.

16. Select Bundle, open the Animator tab, and view the three clip/states.

Because the three clips will be triggered by outside events, you will not have to add transitions or create Trigger type parameters to change the states in the animator controller, Bundle_0. You will be setting the active state directly from your code. The bundle-dropping event will involve several steps, so you will create a little function to make it easier to manage.

1. In the SpawnBunnies script, add the variable to identify the Bundle's Animator component:

```
public Animator bundle; // the bundle's animator component
```

2. Under the beak.SetBool line, add:

```
DropBundle();
```

The bundle will require a collider and a rigidbody. And, when the bundle is triggered to fall, you will have to remove it from the parent Stork Group and activate the physics.

3. Block in the DropBundle function:

```
void DropBundle () {
    bundle.Play("Bundle Fall");      // start the fall animation
    bundle.transform.parent = null; // remove the bundle from the Stork Group
}
```

4. Save the script, and drag the Bundle onto the Zombie Spawn Manager's new Bundle parameter.

5. Click Play.

Now when the beak opens, the bundle is left behind.

Unity's 2D physics engine works a lot like the 3D version, but it uses the 2D versions of the familiar colliders and rigidbody.

1. Select the Bundle object in the Hierarchy view.

2. In the Animator component, uncheck Apply Root Motion.

3. From Components, Physics 2D, add a Box Collider 2D component to it.

4. Also from Physics 2D, add a Rigidbody 2D component to it.

5. Turn on Is Kinematic to prevent it from dropping immediately.

Is Kinematic prevents the object from responding to any physics actions. You may have noticed that the Rigidbody components have no enable/disable parameter. Is Kinematic is used for that purpose.

6. Click Play.

7. When the bundle is left behind, uncheck Is Kinematic to see it fall.

8. Stop Play Mode.

9. Back in the SpawnBunnies script's `DropBundle` function, add:

```
bundle.rigidbody2D.isKinematic = false; // turn on the physics
```

10. Save the script, and click Play.

The bundle drops nicely but leaves the scene. To stop it, you can create a Box Collider 2D at the bottom of the Camera GUI's view.

1. From Create Other, create a new Sprite and name it **2D Ground**.

2. Add it to the Sprite layer.

3. Add a Box Collider 2D, and remove or disable the Sprite Renderer component.

4. Set the collider's Size to **50**, X, and **1**, Y.

5. Move it somewhere below the battery and stork.

For final positioning, you will have to get the Camera GUI's viewing frustum showing in the Scene view.

6. Select the Camera GUI, and from the GameObject menu, choose "Align View to Selected."

7. Move the 2D Ground so that the top of its box collider is barely above the bottom of the Scene view.

8. Click Play, and watch as the bundle drops and hits the ground.

9. Stop Play mode, and adjust the 2D Ground object's position further if necessary to put the bundle at the bottom of the Game view when it hits.

The next step is to register the collision and use it to trigger the Bundle Open clip. The collision detection is easy, but you will also have to get the bundle back to its starting position and re-parented in time for the next bunny drop. If you re-parent it to the Stork Group, which should already be deactivated, it will inherit the deactivation. You can reuse a lot of the FlyBy's code.

1. Create a new C# Script in the Game Scripts folder, and name it **BundleManager**.

2. Add the following variables:

```
public GameObject stork;  // the Stork Group object
Vector3 startLocation;     // the bundle's original location
public Animator animator; // the bundle's animator component
```

3. In an Awake function, store the start position:

```
void Awake () {
    startLocation = transform.localPosition; // store the starting location
}
```

4. In the Start function, call a function to set the bundle to its starting state:

    ```
    Initialize(); // set location
    ```

5. Create the Initialize function:

    ```
    void Initialize () {
        // set the animation state back to Bundle Carry clip/state
        animator.Play ("Bundle Carry");
    }
    ```

Using animator.Play, you set the Bundle Carry state/clip to the currently active state in the Animator. Note that animator.Play, unlike audio.Play, requires the *name* of the clip, so the name is in quotation marks. As you have seen before, this also provides you with a means to put an object directly into a new state without it going through a transition that is meaningless for sprites.

To detect the collision, you will use the 2D version of OnCollisionEnter. From that function, you will tell the bundle to go directly into the Open clip/state. Then you will call a coroutine to wait for 2 seconds and re-parent the object to the Stork Group. The trick here is that by re-parenting the bundle after the stork has left the scene and been deactivated, the bundle will inherit that deactivation without its own being changed. When the Stork Group is activated for the next pass, the Bundle will automatically be activated again because its own Active parameter was never turned off.

6. Add the collision detector:

    ```
    void OnCollisionEnter2D () {
        animator.Play ("Bundle Open"); // trigger the open clip
        StartCoroutine(Deactivator()); // start the coroutine
    }
    ```

7. And add the Deactivator function:

    ```
    IEnumerator Deactivator () {
        yield return new WaitForSeconds(3.5f); // wait 3.5 seconds
        // turn off the physics
        rigidbody2D.isKinematic = true;
        // add the bundle back into the Stork group' transform
        transform.parent = stork.transform;
        // reset the start position
        Vector3 tempLocation = transform.position;
        tempLocation = startLocation;
        transform.localPosition = tempLocation;
    }
    ```

8. Save the script, and add it to the Bundle object.

9. In the Inspector, drag the Stork Group in as the Stork and the Bundle in for the [Bundle's] Animator.

You could have assigned the animator in the Start function, but this is a quick way to get the job done with a one-off assignment.

    10.   Click Play, and watch the action.

The reactivation causes the default animation clip to be reset. Each time the bundle is activated, the Bundle Carry clip will be playing.

Watching the sequence play out, you are probably thinking it would be nice if the 3D zombie bunnies didn't appear in the garden until the delivery was made (e.g., the bundle hits the ground). To do so, you can take the call to repopulate and move it to the BundleManager script's OnCollisionEnter2D function.

    1.   In the SpawnBunnies script, in the StartReproducing function, below the DropBundle() line, comment out the PopulateGardenBunnies line.

    2.   Save the script.

    3.   Open the BundleManager script.

    4.   Add the following variables:

```
public int litterSize = 8; // Maximum litter size on spawning
public GameObject zSpawnManager; // where the SpawnBunnies script is
```

    5.   At the bottom of the OnCollisionEnter2D function, add:

```
zSpawnManager.SendMessage("PopulateGardenBunnies", litterSize,
SendMessageOptions.RequireReceiver);
```

The litterSize is the argument that must be passed to the PopulateGardenBunnies function to tell it the base number of zombie bunnies to make.

    6.   Save the script.

    7.   Assign the Zombie Spawn Manager to the Bundle's ZSpawn Manager parameter in the Bundle Manager component, and click Play.

Now the zombie bunnies hold off popping into the scene until the bundle hits the ground.

The only thing missing from the sequence is a bunch of zombie bunnies bouncing out from the opened bundle. . .

    1.   Stop Play mode, and drag the last Bundle sprite, the baby zombie bunny, into the Scene view, near the center top of the Game view.

    2.   Rename it **Baby ZB**.

    3.   Assign it to the Sprite layer.

Just as with the bundle, the Baby ZB will have a Rigidbody component so it can make use of physics on landing. Additionally, you will be adding a Physic Material to its collider.

4. From Physics 2D, add a Circle Collider 2D and a Rigidbody 2D component to it.

5. From the Create submenu, create a new Physics 2D Material in the 2D Assets folder.

6. Name it **Bouncy 2D**.

7. Set its Bounciness to **1** and its Friction to **0.3**.

8. Add it to the Baby ZB's Circle Collider's Material parameter.

9. Click Play, and watch it drop and bounce.

If you arrange it so it will hit the bundle, the bundle will get knocked out of place. So it follows that if it is with the bundle when Is Kinematic is turned off, the bundle will suffer. Just as with regular physics, you can exclude physics interactions by layer. Right now, all of the 3D objects are in the Sprite layer. If you create a layer for the baby zombie bunnies and have the sprite layer ignore it, the ground will no longer stop them. So you will have to make a layer for both.

1. Click on the Layer drop-down menu, and select Edit Layer.

2. Set Layer 9 to **Buns** and Layer 10 to **Ground**.

3. Assign the Baby ZB to the Buns layer and the 2DGound to the Ground layer.

The Baby ZB will no longer be drawn by the Camera GUI, so you will have to add the new Buns layer. The ground isn't rendered anyway, so it is good to go.

4. Select the Camera GUI and, under Culling Mask, add the Buns layer.

The code to manage the ignore functionality is from the Physics2D class and is global, so it really doesn't matter where it resides. The most logical object is the Game Manager, but currently it has only the ScoreKeeper script. It is typical to create a script for general game-related code, so let's go ahead and do that now.

5. Create a new C# Script in the Game Scripts folder, and name it **GameMisc**.

6. Add the following to the Start function:

```
// prevent baby zombie bunnies from colliding with bundle
Physics2D.IgnoreLayerCollision(8,9,true);
```

The arguments 8 and 9 are the layers involved. The collisions between objects belonging to the two layers will be ignored if the third argument is set to true. The Boolean argument allows you to turn the ignore on and off at will.

7. Save the script, and add it to the Game Manager object.

8. Click Play, and watch the action.

This time the bouncing baby zombie bunny is not able to affect the bundle.

With that little issue taken care of, you can orchestrate the drop and release of the Baby ZB from the bundle.

1. Select the Baby ZB.

2. Set its Rigidbody to Is Kinematic, and drag it onto the Stork Group object in the Hierarchy view.

You may be wondering why you aren't adding the Baby ZB to the Bundle rather than the Stork Group. When a parented object is unparented, its local transforms, the offset from its parent, are converted to world coordinates. Re-parenting it using the original transforms will work for a child but break down for a grandchild. As long as the Baby ZBs objects are re-parented to the Stork for the reset, you can parent them to the bundle afterwards for the drop.

3. Adjust the Baby ZB's Z position until it is behind the bundle, and give it a bit of rotation (Figure 9-48).

Figure 9-48. The baby zombie bunny nestled in the bundle

When the bundle hits, the baby zombie bunny should bounce out. You will be turning off its Is Kinematic property and letting physics do the rest. The only problem is that it will pop back up to where it was when the bundle was dropped. Just as you did with the bundle, you will have to unparent the Baby ZB *before* turning the physics on. It will also eventually have to return to its original position just like the Stork and bundle, so you will be creating a similar script to the BundleManager. Feel free to copy and paste code to speed things up.

4. Create a new C# Script in the Game Scripts folder, and name it **BabyZBHandler**.

5. Add the following variables:

```
Vector3 startLocation; // the object's original location
float zRotation; // the object's original z rotation
GameObject bundle; // the bundle
GameObject stork; // the stork
```

6. Set the location, and find the gameObjects in an Awake function:

```
void Awake () {
    startLocation = transform.localPosition; // store the starting location
    zRotation = transform.localEulerAngles.z;
    stork = GameObject.Find("Stork Group"); // locate the parent object
    bundle = GameObject.Find("Bundle"); // locate the parent object
}
```

The Baby ZB is put into the Stork Group in the Hierarchy view, but once the game starts, you will transfer it to the Bundle. This way it will be able to retain its starting location through all of the re-parenting.

7. Add the following to the Start function:

```
transform.parent = bundle.transform; // move the baby zb into the bundle group
```

You will be calling a little function from the Bundle when it hits the ground to set the Baby ZBs in motion.

8. Add the following function:

```
public void Escape() {
    // unparent the object
    transform.parent = null;
    //turn on the physics!
    rigidbody2D.isKinematic = false;
    // add some spin
    rigidbody2D.AddTorque(-50f.50f); // on the z, the only option for 2D torque
    // bounce the bun up with a random x force and random y force
    rigidbody2D.AddForce(new Vector2(Random.Range(-100f,100f),Random.Range(-200f,700f)));
    // start the coroutine that will manage the reset
    StartCoroutine(Deactivator());
}
```

In this function, you unparent the Baby ZB just before turning the physics back on. Then you add some torque to send it spinning. In Physics 2D, you can only spin a sprite relative to the screen, on its z axis. Next you send it off with some force within a small range of its x and y directions. Finally, you call the coroutine that will take care of resetting the Baby ZB at the end of its routine.

The Deactivator function is a bit different than the one on the bundle in that it also manages the results of the physics forces and torques.

9. Create the Deactivator function:

```
IEnumerator Deactivator () {
    yield return new WaitForSeconds(Random.Range (4f,5f)); // wait 4 to 5 seconds

    // turn off the physics
    rigidbody2D.isKinematic = true;
    rigidbody2D.velocity = Vector2.zero; // clear the velocity
    rigidbody2D.angularVelocity = 0; // clear the spin velocity
```

```
                    // add the bundle back into the Stork Group's transform
                    transform.parent = stork.transform;

                    // reset the start position
                    transform.localPosition = startLocation;

                    // reset the rotation
                    Vector3 tempRot = transform.localEulerAngles;
                    tempRot.z = zRotation;
                    transform.localEulerAngles = tempRot;

                    transform.parent = bundle.transform; // move the baby zb into the bundle group
          }
```

In the `Deactivator`, you allow 4-5 seconds for the Baby ZBs to bounce around before they wink out of existence. They are then returned to their initial locations and re-parented to the Stork Group, where they inherit its deactivation. After resetting their orientations, the physics are turned off, and then any residual velocity is cleared. Having made sure they are safely in the Stork group and their position is correct, you move them into the bundle group for the next pass.

10.   Save the script.

11.   Drag the script onto the Baby ZB.

12.   Drag the Baby ZB into the Prefabs' Characters folder to create a prefab for it.

13.   Drag 3 or 4 more Baby ZBs into the scene, and arrage them in the bundle.

To set all of the Baby ZBs in motion, you will call their `Escape` function in the Bundle's `OnCollisionEnter` function. You could use BroadcastMessage to contact all of the Baby ZBs that will reside on the Bundle parent, but it tends to be rather slow, as it must check each component looking for the function you want to trigger. To manage the Baby ZBs here, you will put them into an array at the start of the game and iterate through them to call their `Escape` functions.

1.   Open the BundleManager script, and add the following variable for the array:

```
GameObject[] buns2D; // array to hold the baby buns sprites
```

2.   In the Awake function, collect the Baby ZBs'as follows:

```
buns2D = GameObject.FindGameObjectsWithTag ("Buns2D");
```

With `FindGameObjectsWithTag`, the scene will be searched for all objects with the specified tag. The collected objects are put into an array of type GameObject. The Baby ZBs will require the tag.

3.   Click the Tag drop-down menu on the Baby ZB, and Add Tag.

4.   In the next open Tags slot, add **Buns2D**.

5.   Select the Baby ZB again, and assign the Buns2D tag to it.

6. At the top of the BundleManager script's `OnCollisionEnter2D` function, add:

```
foreach(GameObject bun2D in buns2D) {
    bun2D.GetComponent<BabyZBHandler>().Escape();
}
```

This `foreach` loop iterates through the array of gameObjects and calls the `Escape` function on the object's `BabyZBHandler` script.

7. Save the script, and click Play.

After the initial fly-by, the Baby ZBs bounce chaotically around the 2D screen with each drop (Figure 9-49).

Figure 9-49. The bouncing baby zombie sprites

Now when you play through, shooting at the 3D zombie bunnies, you should note that you will have a fly-through and drop of the 2D elements even after the 2D zombie bunny count has reached the "can't reproduce" state you set in the ScoreKeeper script. You left it at 10 for ease of checking the functionality. Let's get the stork fly-through respecting the condition as well.

1. Open the SpawnBunnies script.

In the PopulateGardenBunnies function, you return immediately if canReproduce is false. You can't use return inside the coroutine, so if the first yield return new WaitForSeconds is running when the limit is reached, the stork will be cued. You can, however, wrap the code that follows the yield statement in a conditional to achieve the same result.

2. Inside the IEnumerator StartReproducing, below the first yield return new WaitForSeconds, add:

    ```
    if (canReproduce) { // check the status before continuing after the pause
    ```

3. At the bottom of the IEnumerator StartReproducing, below the if (canReproduce) StartCoroutine(StartReproducing(10f)) line, add the closing curly bracket and indent the contents.

To be safe, you should prevent the bundle from dropping if the limit is reached while the stork has the bundle in its beak.

4. Add another if (canReproduce) { line after the second yield line, yield return new WaitForSeconds(Random.Range (1f,2f)).

5. The if (canReproduce) in front of the StartCoroutine(StartReproducing (reproRate)) line is now redundant and can be removed.

6. Add the closing curly bracket after it.

The last conditional (minus earlier code that was commented out) should look as follows:

```
yield return new WaitForSeconds(Random.Range (1f,2f)); // finish the adjusted time
if (canReproduce) {
    beak.SetBool("Cue the Beak", true);
    DropBundle();
    StartCoroutine(StartReproducing(reproRate));
}
```

7. Save the script.

8. From Garden 1, activate the Plant Zone[s] and click Play.

9. Shoot down to 11 zombie bunnies remaining, and wait for the stork to fly by before shooting the next one.

The stork, fully loaded, continues on without dropping his bundle (Figure 9-50).

Figure 9-50. The stork's aborted mission as the limit is reached while in flight

    10.   Save the scene, and save the project.

In the next chapter, you will create a simple end for the game to cover both the successful eradication of the zombie bunny menace and the tragic overrunning of the garden should the Gnomatic Garden Defender run out of battery life before finishing the job.

Summary

In this chapter, you began by finalizing the game play. Starting with Unity's older 2D system, you used the GUI Text objects to display the bunny count and battery life values for your player. You discovered that, as a default, they retain their pixel size independent of screen size, but retain their screen location in relationship to the screen's aspect ratio. That they could not be viewed in the Scene view was logical when you found their rendering was controlled by the camera's GUILayer component.

With the Battery HUD, you got your first look at Unity's 2D sprite system. You learned the basics of creating sprites from texture sheets, from slicing the sprites to selecting their pivot points. You found a quick way to import textures for use as Sprites with the Default Behavior Mode accessed in the Editor section of the Player Settings. You discovered you could also set the texture Type manually as well as change the Scene view to 2D display while working on your 2D elements.

The sprite object also introduced you to the concept of camera Layers where you discovered both 2D and 3D objects could be assigned and included in or excluded from a particular camera. 2D objects, you found, are better suited to a camera with an orthographic projection. With multiple camera layers to produce the final view, you learned that Clear Flags gave you a further means of controlling what each camera renders.

Once in the Scene view, you found that the 2D objects had a new transform gizmo in the guise of a rectangle with blue dots at the corners. You were able to perform the various transforms by watching the cursor icons and dragging from different spots on the gizmo. While setting up a means to animate the scale of the battery sprite's progress bar, you had a chance to animate its color using its RGB values with Unity's Color struct.

With the addition of the "delivery" stork sprite, you got some practice with customizing pivot points and learned how easy it was to let Unity generate an animated sprite from a sprite sheet. Getting deeper into the topic, you were able to customize the sprite animation as well as use traditional key-frame animation to move, rotate, or scale them. With the addition of the beak and bundle to your stork, you made use of Sorting Layers to dictate the draw order between the various sprites occupying the same camera layer.

To top off your 2D experience, you had a go at combining Unity's 2D physics system with the traditional sprite and key-frame animation. You were able to make use of the 2D counterparts of already familiar physics components, including Rigidbody2d. As you managed the 2D baby zombie bunnies, you found it necessary to use the very powerful `Physics2D.IgnoreLayerCollision` to allow or prevent interaction with the various other 2D objects. With the addition of a Physics2D Material, you completed the chaos introduced by the hapless delivery stork.

As a takeaway from this chapter, you had a look at the concept of orthographic cameras and "pixel perfect" sprite displays. You learned that there are pros and cons to using 2D elements and most importantly, that there are several issues involved with authoring for different screen sizes and aspect ratios.

Finally, while much of the chapter dealt with art assets, you also refined many of your existing scripts to control and improve the user's experience. A couple of notable discoveries were modulus math, which uses the remainder of a division operation to calculate rewards for your player, and the requirement to expose variables to other scripts but not the Inspector with the use of `internal` rather than `public`.

Chapter 10

Menus and Levels

In the previous chapter, you implemented a means to end the game, the current level, or maybe just the current garden. With most of the game play in place, you will be delving into the concept of using levels for menus as you begin wrapping up the game. In the book, your game will have only one garden level, but the menus you will add can also be considered levels. With the addition of the menus and the elements required to navigate between them, you will be using the second of Unity's GUI offerings, Unity GUI.

Unity GUI is a solely scripted feature, but it has the benefit of a CSS-type implementation that makes it easy to create visual continuity throughout the game's GUI (graphical user interface). But because Unity GUI is very slow on mobile devices, Unity is in the midst of developing a third GUI system that promises to make layout, sizing, and speed top priorities. As no hints of a release date have been made at the time of this writing, you will be using Unity GUI for the remainder of the project. When the new GUI becomes available, be sure to check the book's page on the Apress website for an introduction to the new system using this chapter's GUI assets.

Ending the Game

Currently, when the player has run out of battery life, the game is over. Conversely, if the player has destroyed all of the invading zombie bunnies, the game, level, or individual garden has been secured. In the first scenario, as well as the out-of-battery scenario, the player should be offered the option to "Play Again" or "Quit." With both scenarios, it will also be nice to have a message telling the player whether the garden has been lost to the invading hordes or secured.

For the end-of-game GUI, you will simply add the text and buttons to the existing scene.

Unity GUI

In the previous chapter, you used GUI Texture objects to add text to your HUD. This time you will be using the script-based Unity GUI. Besides the scripting API that creates the functionality, the Unity GUI has several preset templates that are associated with elements such as buttons, boxes, sliders, and labels.

Although you can put code for the GUI elements on multiple scripts, the best practice is generally to keep it all in one place. This way, you can control the layering order by using the order in the script rather than explicitly adding code to do so. Let's begin by creating a large message to let the player know the game is over. For testing, once again, you will want to be able to end the game quickly. You will begin with a winning game scenario.

You should already have the value 10 set to stop bunny drops, but this will be a good time to make it even easier to reach the goal while setting up the end-game scenarios. The biggest drawback to setting public variables is remembering that once they are exposed their values take precedence.

1. Open the GardenLevel1 scene.

2. Open the ScoreKeeper script, and create a new variable:

    ```
    public int stopPopX = 1; // variable for stopping extra zombie bunny drops
    ```

3. Change the `// stop the population explosion!` line to

    ```
    if (currentBunCount <= stopPopX) { // stop the population explosion!
    ```

4. Save the script.

5. Select the GameManager object, and set its Scorekeeper's Stop Pop X to **20**.

The most logical place to add the Unity GUI is to the Game Manager object. To keep it easy to find, you can create a script expressly for the in-game GUI elements.

6. Create a new C# Script, and name it **EndGameGUI**.

You will create several scripts for the GUI and menus, so now is a good time to create a new folder to keep them separate from the rest of the game scripts.

7. Create a New Folder in the Project view, and name it **Menu Scripts**.

8. Drag the new EndGameGUI script into it.

9. Open the script, and add the following variable:

    ```
    string finishedMessage= "Garden Secure"; // message for finished garden
    ```

10. Add the following function:

    ```
    void OnGUI () {

        GUI.Label(new Rect(0,0,1000,100), finishedMessage);

    }
    ```

The Unity GUI script is handled in an `OnGUI` function that is called every frame. With Unity GUI, you will be able to see the GUI elements only during run-time and only in the Game view. The "controls," buttons, labels, scroll bars, etc., are defined by starting with a rect, which is a rectangular position and size.

1. Save the script, and drag it onto the Game Manager object in the Hierarchy view.

2. Click Play.

The text appears at the top left corner of the Game view (Figure 10-1).

Figure 10-1. The Unity GUI Label element at runtime

The text is drawn on screen at the upper left of the viewport, telling you that 0,0 is the top left corner of the screen. The text starts at the far left of the rectangle you specified to start at 0 x, 0 y, with a width of 1000 and a height of 100. Let's see what happens with a full-screen view.

3. Toggle on "Maximize on Play," and click Play again.

The text remains the same size as before and is now dwarfed by the battery sprites (Figure 10-2).

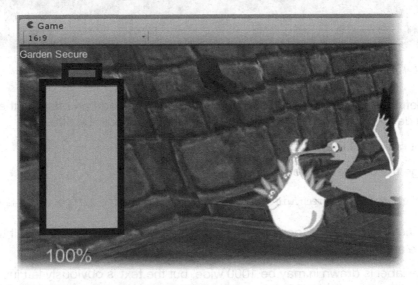

Figure 10-2. The Unity GUI Label element in the maximized Game window at runtime

The first issue to tackle is the positioning. In the previous chapter, the decision was made to lock the player into a single screen aspect ratio. While this would allow you to safely hard-code in the label's location, a better solution is to access the screen size directly. This method also makes it easier to test without using "Maximize on Play."

4. Change the GUI.Label line to

    ```
    GUI.Label(new Rect(Screen.width / 2, Screen.height / 2,1000,100), finishedMessage);
    ```

5. Save the script, and click Play again.

This time, the label is rendered near the center of the screen (Figure 10-3).

Figure 10-3. The Label at half screen width and height

The text, being left justified, reminds you that you will also have to add an offset to the label's location. Having defined the rectangle as 1000 wide, the offset should be 500.

6. Do not get out of Play mode.

7. Change the GUI.Label line to

    ```
    GUI.Label(new Rect(Screen.width / 2 - 500, Screen.height / 2,1000,100), finishedMessage);
    ```

8. Save the script, change focus by clicking in the Game view, and wait for it to update and show the recent change.

The rectangle the label is drawn in may be 1000 wide, but the text is obviously left justified inside it. Fortunately, you will be able to change this.

To affect the label layout, you will have to access the template used for that Label control or element. The templates are part of a GUI Skin asset. To change it or even inspect it, you will have to create a new one.

9. Turn off Play mode, and turn off "Maximize on Play."

10. From the Project view's right-click menu, Create, create a new GUI Skin in the Menu Scripts folder.

11. Name the new skin **Garden GUISkin**.

12. Select the skin, and examine it in the Inspector.

The GUI Skin contains templates for the various elements or controls, a place to define custom templates or styles, and a small Settings section (Figure 10-4).

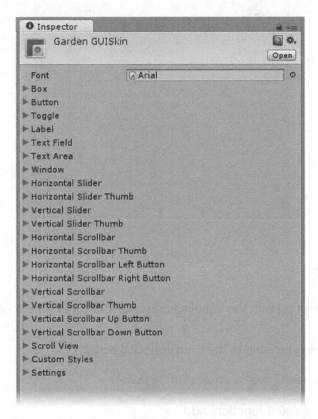

Figure 10-4. The templates available in the new GUI Style asset

At the top is the default font, Ariel. Ariel is a system font that comes with both Windows and Mac operating systems. System fonts have the advantage of being able to be dynamically sized during runtime. That means a texture sheet will not have to be generated for each and every size of the font you wish to use. You will have a chance to experiment with fonts later in the chapter. For now, let's look at the Label template to see what can be done with it.

1. Open the Label template by clicking the expand arrow next to its name (Figure 10-5).

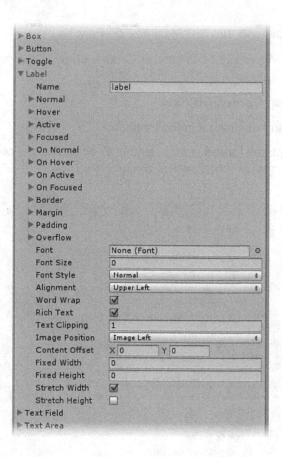

Figure 10-5. The Label template

Before you start experimenting with the Label's parameters, you will have to tell the script to use the new GUI Skin asset.

2. Add the following variable to the EndGameGUI script:

```
public GUISkin newSkin; // custom skin to use
```

3. At the top of the OnGUI function, add

```
GUI.skin = newSkin;
```

4. Save the script, and assign the Garden GUISkin to the New Skin parameter in the Game Manager's EndGameGUI component.

5. Click Play so you will be able to see the changes as you experiment with the Label template.

The GUI Skin is one of the few parameters that will not throw an error when missing. If you forget to assign one, the default skin will be used. It is also one of the objects that can be permanently changed during Play mode.

6. Select the Garden GUISkin from the Project view, and set the Label template's Alignment (it's about 3/4 of the way down the parameters) to Middle Center.

7. Set the Font Style to Bold and Italic.

8. Increase the Label's Font Size until the text takes up a large part of the screen (Figure 10-6).

Figure 10-6. The adjusted Label text

The vertical position of the text is too low, especially because you will be placing the two option buttons below it. You could use the Content Offset parameters to make the adjustment, but in this case, it will be better to add the adjustment to the script.

1. Change the GUI.Label line to

    ```
    GUI.Label(new Rect(Screen.width / 2 - 500, Screen.height / 2 - 200,1000,100),
    finishedMessage);
    ```

2. Save the script.

A 200-pixel offset is too much for the small Game view, but it should be good with "Maximize on Play" and a font more in keeping with the full-size window.

3. Set the Font Size to **180**.

4. Stop Play mode.

5. Turn on "Maximize on Play," and click Play.

The text all but disappears because it has wrapped to fit inside the 1000 x 100 rectangle set for the Label control (Figure 10-7). Let's turn off Wrap mode first, and then reset the rectangle and offset sizes.

Figure 10-7. *The non-wrapped text clipped in its rectangle, but showing again*

6. Stop Play mode, uncheck Word Wrap, and click Play.

The words appear again but are cropped on all sides. For super-size text, where you may have to make several adjustments, you might consider using variables to help with the offsets. In this case, this is the last adjustment you will make, so you will change the code to fit the Size.

7. Change the GUI.Label line to

```
GUI.Label(new Rect(Screen.width / 2 - 800, Screen.height / 2 - 250,1600,200),
finishedMessage);
```

8. Save the script.

The 1600 width size is obviously more than you require for a 1280 x 720 screen. You could just as easily use the following:

```
Screen.width / 2 - 700, Screen.height / 2 - 250,1400,200
```

or:

```
Screen.width / 2 - 640, Screen.height / 2 - 250,1280,200
```

With the text being centered, as long as it isn't cropped at the edges, it doesn't really matter for this game.

This time, there is no doubt about the outcome (Figure 10-8).

Figure 10-8. The repaired, super-sized label text

It would be nicer if the font color was something other than white. Let's change it to a nice yellow. Most of the regular template parameters are associated with the type of functionality associated with the type of control it is. Because a label has almost no interactive functionality, most of the parameters—such as Hover, Active, Focused, etc.—are never used. Normal, the top behavior, is where the very basics are set. In the Label's case, there is no background set as a default, but that is where you can set the color of the text for all of the Label controls that use the Garden GUI Skin.

9. Stop Play mode.

10. Expand the Label's Normal parameter, and change the Text Color to yellow, RGB,**255,255,0**.

Let's add the two buttons before hooking the new GUI up to actual scene events.

11.   In the OnGUI function, below the Label line, add

```
// Play Again
if (GUI.Button( new Rect (Screen.width / 2 - 325, Screen.height / 2,300,60),
"Play Again")) {
   // call function here
}

// Quit
if (GUI.Button( new Rect (Screen.width / 2 + 25, Screen.height / 2,300,60), "Quit")) {
   // call function here
}
```

GUI Button controls are always waiting for a pick event, so they are wrapped in a conditional. Usually, you will call a function if the pick event is detected. Once again, the pixel size and offset are specified in the Rect. This time, because the text will always be the same, the strings are added directly to the code.

12.   Save the script.

13.   Click Play, and check out the changes in the game view. (Be sure to pick in the window to change focus.)

The buttons are a nice size and well placed, but their visual appearance, though clean and elegant, is not bold enough to stand out (Figure 10-9). The font size will require some adjustment, but this time you will assign a texture to both the Normal and Hover parameters.

Figure 10-9. *The newly added Button controls*

1. Bring the GUI Assets folder from the Chapter 10 Assets folder into the Project view.

In Settings, the Editor was left on 2D as the Default Behavior Mode, so the textures come in set up as sprites.

2. Among other assets, it contains a few blue and orange circular button images and some carrots (Figure 10-10).

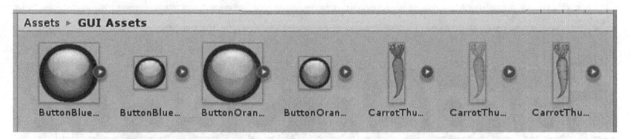

Figure 10-10. The blue and orange button images and some carrots

3. Select the button and carrot textures in the GUI Assets folder, set their Texture Type to GUI (Editor/Legacy), and click Apply.

4. Select the Garden GUI Skin, and open the Button template.

5. Expand the Normal and Hover parameters.

6. Assign the ButtonBlueGlass to the Normal Background (Figure 10-11).

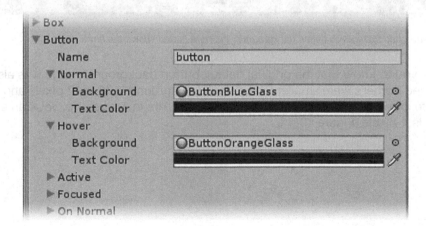

Figure 10-11. The textures assigned to the Button template's Normal and Hover sections, and Text Color set to Black

7.   Assign the ButtonOrangeGlass to the Hover Background (Figure 10-11).

8.   Set Both Text Colors to black (Figure 10-11).

9.   Toggle off "Maximize on Play."

10.   Click Play, and look at the result.

The round button textures are oddly stretched (Figure 10-12).

Figure 10-12.   The stretched textures as button backgrounds; the right button shows the hover color

It might surprise you to know that the original default button background image was also square, though its rounded corners were smaller. The default background is 12 x 12 pixels and is a layer in a composite texture used internally for the default GUI Skin. In a close-up, you can see that its rounded corner is 4 pixels (Figure 10-13).

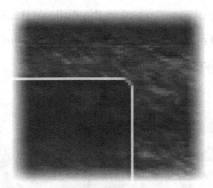

Figure 10-13. The rounded corner of the default background texture

So how is it that the original texture was not stretched? The Border parameter is set to 4 and 4 for the Left and Right. This is commonly called "slice 9," as it divides an image into 9 sections where the corners are retained and the center sections are stretched. The imported button textures are both 64 x 64, so the Border should be half that size.

1. Set the Border Left and Right values to **32** each.

The buttons round out correctly while allowing the button to stretch to the rectangles' dimensions (Figure 10-14).

Figure 10-14. The button textures with the correct Border offset; the right button shows the hover color

2. Try clicking the button.

The Active state also requires the new orange texture for its background, but you can leave the Text Color as white.

3. Assign the ButtonOrangeGlass texture to the Active's Background.

4. Set the Font Size to **30** and the Font Style to Bold and Italic.

The updated font is shown in Figure 10-15.

Figure 10-15. The updated font; the right button shows the Active state (being pressed)

The proper font can make or break the look and feel of your game. There are many fonts that are free to use, but few that can be freely redistributed. One of the fonts you will use for this game is Comic Sans. Feel free to use a font of your choice if you have something you prefer.

5. From Windows, locate Comic Sans Ms in the Windows, Fonts folder. On a Mac, OS 10.5, Location: /Library/Fonts.

6. Copy and then paste, or drag it into the GUI Assets folder, and look at it in the Inspector.

Because it is a system font, you will not see anything for its material or texture sheet. Those are created internally.

7. Select the Garden GUI Skin and, at the top, assign Comic as the Font.

8. Adjust the Font size for the Button and Label templates if necessary.

The newly assigned font with "Maximize on Play" (Figure 10-16).

Figure 10-16. The Comic Sans font

With the GUI in place, it's time to add the code for the buttons. Both calls are very simple.

1.   Open the EndGameGUI script.

2.   In the Play Again button's conditional, add

```
Application.LoadLevel("GardenLevel1");
```

3.   In the Quit button's conditional, add

```
Application.Quit();
```

4.   Save the script.

While the code is simple for both, there are a few caveats. `Application.Quit()` won't stop the application when you are running it through the editor. To see if it works, you will have to do a build. `Application.LoadLevel` also requires the level to have been added to the build before it can be found. You can call a level either by name or by its build index number.

5.   Save the scene, and save the project.

6.   From the File menu, open Build Settings.

7.   Click the Add Current button to add GardenLevel1 to the build.

8. Make sure PC, Mac & Linux Standalone is chosen for the Platform setting and the appropriate Target Platform is selected (Figure 10-17).

Figure 10-17. The Build Settings dialog ready to build for Windows

9. Click Build and Run.

10. Name it **GardenTest**, and save it somewhere outside of the project folder.

The Configuration dialog appears.

1. At the configuration dialog, select 1280 x 720, Fantastic, Windowed and then click Play.

2. Go into the garden, shoot a few zombie bunnies and then select Play Again.

The game starts all over.

3. Next, select Quit.

The game closes in a well-behaved manner.

4. Close the Build Settings window.

It would be nice if the game would stop Play mode with the quit button when you are working in Unity. It turns out you can add "editor" code to customize the Unity editing environment. While that is generally beyond the scope of this book, having Play mode stop is too valuable to pass up.

5. In the EndGameGUI script, change `Application.Quit` to the following:

```
#if UNITY_EDITOR
    UnityEditor.EditorApplication.isPlaying = false;
#else
    Application.Quit();
#endif
```

6. Save the script.

7. Turn off "Maximize on Play," and click Play. Then click the Quit button in the scene.

Play mode ends.

Now, of course, you will want to have the appropriate message appear when the game has ended. Because the end message exists only as code, you will begin by creating a flag to suppress it until it is triggered.

Add the following variable to the EndGameGUI script:

```
bool showEndGUI = false; // flag to hide/show end message and options
```

8. In the onGUI function, beneath the GUI.skin line, add

```
if (showEndGUI) {
```

9. Add the closing curly bracket after the Quit conditional, and then indent the contents for better readability:

```
} // close end message conditional
```

Next you will create a little function that will turn on the flag and update the message according to who calls it.

1. Add the following function:

```
public void TriggerMessage (string results) {

    finishedMessage = results; // set the correct message
    showEndGUI = true; // turn on the message
}
```

2. Save the script, and click Play to make sure the GUI no longer shows.

3. Stop Play mode.

4. Open the ScoreKeeper script.

5. Add the following variable:

```
public EndGameGUI endGameGUI; // the script that handles the GUI
```

You've already created a GardenSecure function in the event of the Player reaching a 0 zombie bunny count. From that function, you will directly call the EndGameGUI script's TriggerMessage function, passing in the appropriate text message.

6. In the GardenSecure() function, under // if game over, add the following:

```
endGameGUI.TriggerMessage("Garden Secure");
```

7. Save the script.

8. Select the Game Manager object in the Hierarchy view, and drag it onto its In Game GUI parameter in the Score Keeper component.

9. Click Play, and test the "0 zombie bunnies left" ending.

The end GUI pops up on cue.

The other ending is triggered when the battery life runs out before the zombie bunny hordes have been eradicated.

1. Stop Play mode.

2. In the Battery Life object, set the Battery Full to **10** for a quick battery drain.

3. Open the BatteryHealth script.

4. Add the following variable:

```
public EndGameGUI endGameGUI; // the script that handles the GUI
```

5. In the GameOver function, add

```
// end of game options
endGameGUI.TriggerMessage("Garden Overrun");
```

6. Save the script.

7. Select the Battery Life object in the Hierarchy view, and drag the Game Manager object onto its End Game GUI parameter in the Battery Health component.

8. Select the Game Manager, and set the Score Keeper's Stop Pop X parameter to **10** to make sure the battery will drain.

9. Click Play, and let the battery run out.

The "Garden Overrun" message appears when the battery life reaches 0.

You are probably thinking that the text color for the failure message would look better if it was a less cheery color. It turns out, you can override the text color fairly easily. For that, you will require a flag to tell it when it should override.

1. Add the following variable to the EndGameGUI script:

```
bool overrideColor = false; // flag for message colors
```

In the TriggerMessage function, above the showEndGUI line, you *could* add

```
if(finishedMessage == "Garden Overrun") overrideColor = true;
else overrideColor = false;
```

Instead, because the variable is a Boolean, you can evaluate the same expression and assign its result directly to a variable. Take a minute to work this one out in your head if it is confusing.

2. In the TriggerMessage function, above the showEndGUI line, add

```
overrideColor = (finishedMessage == "Garden Overrun");
```

3. In the OnGUI function, at the top of the if (showEndGUI) clause, add

```
if (overrideColor) GUI.color = new Color(0.8f,0,0); // a dark red
```

4. Underneath the GUI.Label line, add

```
GUI.color = Color.white; // return it to white, a pre-defined color
```

Several colors are predefined in the Color class, such as black, white, red, blue, and a few others. A custom Color, if you remember, uses unit values rather than the more familiar 256 value for each color channel.

5. Save the script

6. Click Play, and wait for the battery to run out.

This time, the text color is suitably gloomy.

7. Select the Game Manager, and set the Score Keeper's Stop Pop X parameter to **1**.

8. Select the Battery Life, and set the Battery Full parameter back to **70**.

9. Save the scene.

Starting the Game

If working on the start of the game at the end of the project seems more than a bit backwards to you, consider the following issues. Game play is the most important part of the game. Until you have a game at least partially fleshed out, there's no point in spending a lot of time on a start menu. The game play, theme, or artistic style could change dramatically as ideas are tested and refined. The game itself may even be abandoned for any number of reasons.

Having reached the point where the game runs well, it's time to get it off to a conventional start by creating a Start screen as a portal for your player to enter the game. Besides having "Play Game" and "Quit" options, you may want to allow the player to see some navigation instructions, credits, and maybe even some game-play strategies. In games that require skills, you may even opt to allow players to change the difficulty level.

As there are a few game-play issues remaining, you will tackle the most basic parts of the Start screen first.

Start Screen

Because the game theme itself is along the lines of a train wreck, the Start screen will reflect the monumental task awaiting the player. Besides giving a preview of the major elements, it will also present a plausible back-story to help engage the player.

The premise is simple. Our player, charged with protecting the (costly) vegetable garden from hordes of ravaging zombie bunnies, has found instructions for modifying a common garden gnome statuette into a potato gun-wielding Gnomatic Garden Defender. When the scene opens, the dubious-looking construct stands ready to exterminate the voracious invaders.

Let's begin with the new level or scene that will be the Start screen.

1. From the File menu, create a New Scene.

2. Save it as **MenuBase**, and put it in the Scenes folder.

The Main Camera should automatically be set to Orthographic projection because the Default Behavior Mode remains set to 2D.

3. Set its Size to **3.75**.

4. Check to make sure its z position is **-10**.

5. If you are not already in it, switch to the 2 x 3 Layout or tear off one of the views so you can see both the Scene and Game views at the same time.

This scene will be a combination of 2D and 3D objects that will blend together better without pixel-perfect sizing. The texture sheet for the main elements is already 1024 x 1024, so in this case, rather than quadrupling the size and putting them on a 2048 x 2048 sheet, you are compromising by setting the camera to a smaller orthographic size.

6. In the Scene view, toggle the view to 2D and pan the view until the camera is centered.

7. Create a Quad object, and name it **Stone Wall**.

8. Set its x, y, and z Positions to **0,0,1**.

To cover the 16:9 aspect ratio, you will have to scale the quad to be wider than it is high.

9. Set its Scale to **18, 11, 1**.

The quad should now easily cover the Game view screen, leaving no blue background showing.

10. In its Mesh Renderer component, set the Stone Wall's Material Element 0 to StoneTextureColored by clicking the browse button to the right of the field and locating the material.

Even though the Quad is a simple plane in a 2D projection, the material uses a normal map to give the illusion of texture, so you can set up the lighting for the effect you prefer.

11. Add a Directional light to the scene, and rotate it until the light hits the wall from the upper left.

Directional lights are location independent, so you can place them anywhere in the scene.

12. Using the Global coordinate system, move the light up in the Scene view until it is clear of the wall.

13. Turn on "Maximize on Play," and click Play.

The stone texture is a bit large for a full-sized screen. You can adjust the tiling or repeats for the texture, but in order to preserve the correct tiling on the regular garden walls, you will have to create a duplicate material for the menu backdrops.

1. Stop Play mode.

2. Double-click on the material in the Element 0 slot to locate it in the Project view.

3. Use CTRL+D to duplicate it from there.

4. Change the Base and Normalmap Tilings to **2** (Figure 10-18).

Figure 10-18. The duplicate material, with texture maps tiled

5. Name the clone **StoneTextureMenus**.

6. Drag the new material onto the Quad in the viewport.

7. Save the scene, and then choose Save Scene As and name it **StartMenu**.

This will provide you with a quick way to create the submenus later in the chapter.

Besides the wall that provides continuity from the menus to the 3D levels, you will also add a rustic "wood" fence so you can have extra information pop up from behind it. This object will also require a tiling texture, so you can create another simple Quad object for it.

1. Create another Quad in the scene, and name it **Wood Fence**.

2. Center it on the Stone Wall, and then set its Z Position to **0** so it is out "in front" of the Stone Wall.

3. Set its X Scale to **15.4** and the Y Scale to **5.1**.

4. From the GUI Assets folder, select WoodFence and change its Texture Type to Texture and click Apply.

5. Drag the WoodFence texture onto the Wood Fence quad.

A material is generated for the texture with the Diffuse shader.

6. Select the quad, and set its WoodFence material's x Tiling to **2**.

7. Position the fence so that the bottom of it is just below the viewing frustum of the Game view (Figure 10-19).

Figure 10-19. The Stone Wall and Wood Fence in the Game view

If you are wondering why a 0 z depth is closer than the Stone Wall's 1 depth, remember that you are in 2D view where you are looking forward from the Back view.

The remaining objects for your menu, aside from the buttons, will be sprites.

1. From the GUI Assets folder, select the StartScreen image and change it to Sprite Mode, Multiple.

2. In the Sprite Editor, click and drag directly in the image to manually define each sprite.

3. Click to edit each one to refine its size, and position them as per Figure 10-20.

Figure 10-20. The StartScreen texture sheet, sliced manually

4. Click Apply, and close the Sprite Editor.

Next you will be adding the new sprites to the menu scene.

1. Drag the sprites from the Project view into the Scene view.

2. Set the Z Position for the gnome, plants, and title block to **-0.5** so they all appear in front of the quads.

3. Name them **Plants**, **Gnome**, and **Title Block**.

The Gnome belongs in the left lower corner, the plants in the right lower corner, and the title block at the top, center position.

The two information panels will slide up from behind the fence.

4. Name the two information panels **Weaponry** and **Navigation** to match their titles.

5. Set their Z Positions to **0.7** and their Z Rotations to **270**.

6. Hold the Shift key down while adjusting the Y position to constrain to vertical movement on the Weaponry panel.

The panel's corners should just peek over the fence (Figure 10-21). When you are happy with the location, center the Title Block.

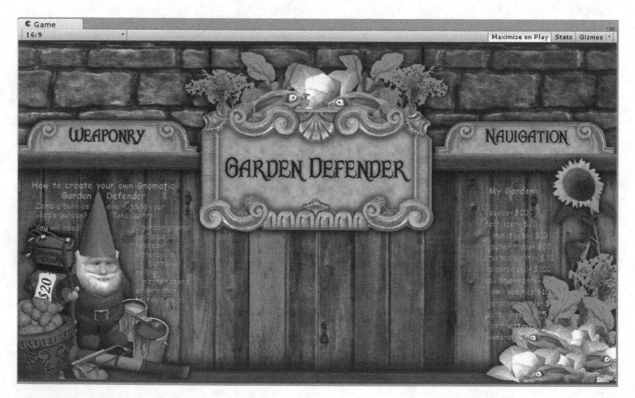

Figure 10-21. The sprites in position

7. Toggle off the 2D display, and orbit the viewport to see the manual layering of the sprites and quads (Figure 10-22).

Figure 10-22. The sprites and quad objects layered in 3D space

8. Return to the 2D display in the Scene view.

9. Resize the Game view to assure yourself that the sprites and quads objects play well together regardless of window size.

10. Save the scene.

Next, you will handle the information panel slide-outs with animation clips and Mecanim. Each will require a simple pop-up animation. For the pop-down animation, you will simply create another state that uses a negative speed of the same clip.

1. Select the Weaponry sprite in the Hierarchy view.

2. Open the Animation editor from the Window menu or by using Ctrl+6.

3. Click Add Curve, and create a new animation clip named **Weaponry Up** in the GUI Assets folder.

4. Select the Transform drop-down menu, and choose Position by clicking the plus sign to its right (Figure 10-23).

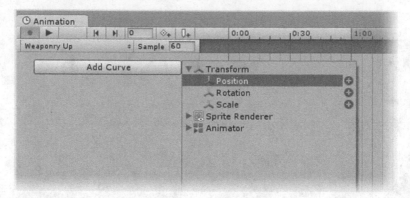

Figure 10-23. Adding the Position Transform track

5. Move the right keys to **0:20**, frame **20**.

The time indicator moves to frame 20, and the Record button is now on.

6. In the Scene view, select the Move tool, place the cursor inside the 2D transform gizmo, and hold the Shift key down to constrain movement to vertical when you (carefully) pull up or down.

7. Move the Weaponry panel up in the scene view until it is high enough to see the text information and just below the top of the viewing frustum in the Game view (Figure 10-24).

Figure 10-24. The Weaponry sprite in its "up" position

8. Slide the time indicator back and forth to make sure the panel animates correctly.

With only two keys, the curve will be linear. For nonlinear animations, you will want a classic ease-in/ease-out curve.

9. Select all of the keys and, from the right-click menu, select Flat.

Flat, in this case, refers to the tangency handles being horizontal or "flat." Feel free to switch from the Dope Sheet to the Curves view, select the keys, and press F to frame them and check out the curve (Figure 10-25).

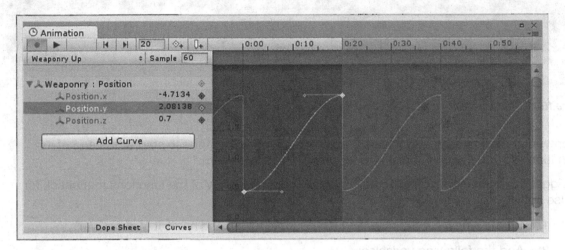

Figure 10-25. The looping ease-in/ease-out curve

10.   Close the Animation panel.

The next step is to turn off the Loop wrap type. Aside from preventing the animation from looping, this will also "hold" the object in its final position as long as it remains in that state. When you turn on the Weapon Up state, the panel will go up and stay there until it is told to go to a different state.

11.   Select the Weaponry Up clip in the GUI Assets folder, and uncheck its Loop Time in the Inspector.

When you created the clip, an Animator component was automatically created.

1.   Select the Weaponry object in the Hierarchy view.

2.   Double-click on its Animator component's Controller parameter to open the Animator view.

3.   Clone the Weaponry Up state by right-clicking and choosing Copy, and then right-click and choose Paste.

4.   Rename it **Weaponry Down**, and set its Speed to **-1**.

5.   Right-click over it in the view, and select Set as Default (Figure 10-26).

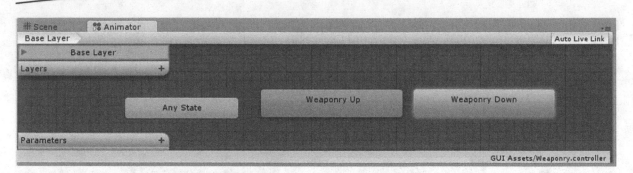

Figure 10-26. The animation states in the Animator view

To prevent it from playing automatically on start up, you will script it to start at the end of its animation clip, where it immediately goes into a "holding pattern."

To trigger the animation, you will create a small script and a few of the functions that check for mouse activity.

1. Create a new C# Script in the Menu Scripts folder, and name it **MouseOver**.

2. Add the following variables:

```
Animator animator; // the component
public string clip1;
public string clip2;
```

3. Identify the Animator component in the Start function:

```
animator = GetComponent <Animator>();
```

4. Also in the Start function, below the line that finds and assigns the animator, tell the clip2 to start playing at the end, 1 or 100%, of its animation:

```
animator.Play (clip2,0,1f); // start the state in layer 0 at the end of its animation
```

5. Add the following three functions:

```
void OnMouseDown () {
    print("ouch!");
}

void OnMouseEnter () {
    animator.Play (clip1);
}

void OnMouseExit () {
    animator.Play (clip2);
}
```

6. Save the script.

7. Add it to the Weaponry object.

8. In the Mouse Over component, type in the Animation state names for Clip 1 and Clip 2, being careful to type them exactly as they were named in the Animator (Figure 10-27).

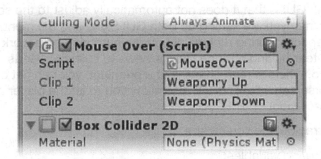

Figure 10-27. The state names in the Mouse Over component

If you click Play now and try to mouseover or click the Weaponry tab, nothing will happen. That is because 2D and 3D objects *must* have a collider in order to catch mouse events. It doesn't matter if they are set to Is Trigger or not.

9. From the Components menu, Physics 2D, add a Box Collider2D to the Weaponry sprite.

10. Click Play, and test.

Nothing happens yet because the two 3D objects have colliders that are blocking the mouse events from reaching the panel even though there is space between the sprites and quads. The fence *should* block the mouse events where it covers the panel, but the wall should *not* interfere at all.

1. Select the Stone Wall, and disable its Mesh Collider component.

2. Click Play, and test the mouseovers and picks.

This time, the panel goes up and down with mouse enter and mouse exit events and prints the "ouch!" message out to the console when picked.

3. Comment out the print line, and save the script.

4. Set up the Navigation panel to match the Weaponry panel, naming the animation clip **Navigation Up** and the animation states **Navigation Up** and **Navigation Down**.

Next up are the buttons that will take your player into or out of the game. For those, you will once again be using the Unity GUI.

1. Create a new C# script in the Menu Scripts folder and name it **StartMenuGUI**.

2. Create an Empty GameObject in the scene, and name it **GUI Holder**.

3. Add the script to the new object.

One downside of the UnityGUI is that it does not automatically adjust to the screen size unless you add the math to do so. When you are setting up both GUI Skins and the menu GUI, it is important to have access to the Inspector during runtime. If you are authoring on a work station with multiple monitors, you can easily tear off and arrange Unity's views to suit your needs. If you are mobile and authoring on a laptop, where screen space is at a premium, you can get creative by adjusting the layout in response to screen size. This will also allow you to let the player adjust the size of the window (but not the aspect ratio).

The first step is to keep track of the screen size.

4. Create the following variables:

```
public GUISkin newSkin; // custom skin to use
int screenW; // screen width
int screenH; // screen height
```

5. Create the OnGUI function, and define the variables it will require:

```
void OnGUI () {
    GUI.skin = newSkin;

    //manage layout
    print (Screen.height);
    screenW = Screen.width;
    screenH = Screen.height;
    int yOffset = 30; //default offset
    if (screenH < 800) yOffset = screenH / 50; // adjusted offset

}
```

6. Save the script.

7. With "Maximize on Play" on, click Play and adjust the Unity editor window size (toggle out of maximize for the Unity editor if necessary), while watching the printout in the console when you release the mouse button.

The console reports the window height each time you pause after resizing the Unity editor.

To make the buttons easier to position as a whole, you will be putting the buttons into a GUI Group. This will allow you to shift the parent group to get the spacing right without having to adjust each button individually.

8. Comment out the print line.

9. Add the following to the OnGUI function, below the // manage layout section:

```
// Constrain all drawing to be within a 500x500 pixel area centered on the screen.
GUI.BeginGroup (new Rect (screenW / 2 - 250 , screenH - screenH/2 - 150, 500, 500));

    // add controls here

// must match all BeginGroup calls with an EndGroup
GUI.EndGroup ();
```

The group placement for the X is straightforward; it centers the group using half the screen width. The vertical positioning is a bit trickier. It references from the bottom of the screen, gets the halfway value, and then adds an extra offset.

Rather than hard-coding the sizes and locations of the buttons, you will set up variables for those values.

10. Add the button code below the // add controls here line:

```
int ySize = 64; // button width
int xSize = 400; // button height
int y = 150 + yOffset * 3; // adjust the starting vertical location
according to screen size
int x = 250-xSize/2; // the horizontal location

// Play Game
if (GUI.Button( new Rect (x,y,xSize,ySize), "Play Game")) {
    // start game
    Application.LoadLevel("GardenLevel1");
}
y += ySize + yOffset;
// Settings
if (GUI.Button( new Rect (x,y,xSize,ySize), "Main Menu")) {
    // go to settings menu
    Application.LoadLevel("MainMenu");
}

y += ySize + yOffset;
// Quit
if (GUI.Button( new Rect (x,y,xSize,ySize), "Quit")) {
    // quit application
    #if UNITY_EDITOR
    UnityEditor.EditorApplication.isPlaying = false;
    #else
    Application.Quit();
    #endif
}
```

11. Save the script.

Note how the button code is set in relation to the group's location. By using level names instead of index numbers, you will have less to change as you add more menus. The downside is that you will get an error if the level you try to load has not yet been added to the build.

1.   Drag the Garden GUISkin onto the GUI Holder's New Skin parameter.

2.   Click Play, and adjust the size of the editor window.

The button locations adjust themselves to stay relatively correct (Figure 10-28).

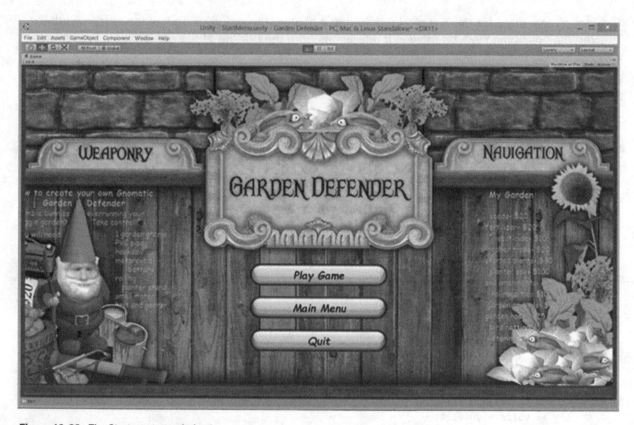

Figure 10-28. The Start menu maximized

3.   Stop Play mode, and uncheck "Maximize on Play."

4.   Click Play, and adjust the Game view size.

The buttons adjust their position, allowing you access to the Inspector during runtime with limited screen space (Figure 10-29).

Figure 10-29. The Unity GUI buttons in the Start menu

The math involved here is nothing fancy. Obviously you could code button sizes to be affected by the screen size, but for testing during the authoring process, this will get the job done. Feel free to improve the logic and equations that control the button placement. Also, if you decide not to allow the player to resize the game window during run time, you could move the screen height and width assignments into the Start function to conserve resources.

Adding the New Level to the Build

With the visual aspects of the start screen sorted out, you can add the new level to the build.

1. Stop Play mode, and save the StartMenu scene.

2. Open Build Settings from the Files menu.

3. Click the Add Current button.

The Start menu is added to the build, but its index number is 1. For it to be the first scene shown, it will have to be index 0.

4. Click on the GardenLevel1 scene, and drag it below the StartMenu scene.

The StartMenu is now index 0.

5. Click Build and Run, and overwrite GardenTest.

6. Play the game, and make sure the GardenLevel1 (now index 1) loads from the Play Game button.

There's one thing you may have noticed that is inconsistent with a shooter-type game. The cursor is visible throughout the game. You can suppress it during regular game play and bring it back whenever the GUI controls are active. This code can be on any script, but it will be easy to find and turn back on from the OnGUI functions.

1. In the StartMenuGUI script, below the `// Start Game` line, add

    ```
    Screen.showCursor = false; // hide the cursor
    ```

2. Save the script.

3. Click Play, and test.

You probably won't see the expected results unless you are using "Maximize on Play" or make a new build, but it should be turned back on when the game is won or lost.

4. In the EndGameGUI script, `TriggerMessage` function, add the following above the `showEndGUI` line:

    ```
    Screen.showCursor = true; // show the cursor
    ```

5. Save the script.

6. Turn on "Maximize on Play," and test.

The cursor disappears and reappears on cue.

7. Save the scene.

Refining the Starting Game Play

When you were originally setting up the garden level, the Gnomatic Garden Defender was in the staging area. This gives the player time to practice navigation and weaponry before beginning the challenge. Currently, however, both the zombie bunnies and the battery countdown begin at scene start-up.

The best scenario would be for the original zombie bunny drop to happen at start-up but have nothing else triggered until the Gnomatic Garden Defender has entered the garden for the first time. On the off chance the player leaves the garden and then returns, the triggering should happen only once.

1. Open the GardenLevel1 scene.

2. Move the Gnomatic Garden Defender back into the staging area if you haven't already.

Let's begin by preventing the battery drain at the start. You may remember it already has a tracking variable that you left in the on position while testing.

3. Open the BatteryHealth script.

4. Set the `trackingBattery` variable to `false`:

    ```
    internal bool trackingBattery = false; // timer not started
    ```

5. Save the script.

It would also make sense to hide the HUD until the garden is entered. For the GUI Text, you will disable the GUILayer component on the GUI Camera. The battery sprites are gameObjects, so the simplest solution to control them will be to put them into a group and activate and deactivate the group. The problem with this is that deactivated objects cannot be "found." In most cases, you identify and store the object in an Awake function before it has been deactivated so the script can turn it back on later in the game. If it doesn't exist in the current level or scene, you can turn off the renderer component. In this case, there are only two objects, so you could easily turn them off individually. If you had several objects, you would want a way to iterate through them and do the required processing in a more generic and flexible manner. To keep the code reusable, you can make a simple script that can be called from several different places.

6. Create a new Empty gameObject, and name it **Garden HUD**.

7. Drag, Battery_0, and Battery_1 into it in the Hierarchy view.

8. Create a new C# Script in the Game Scripts folder, and name it **ChildVisibility**.

9. Add the array variable that will hold the children of the object the script is on:

    ```
    public Component[] spriteRenderers;
    ```

10. Also add a variable to hold the Camera GUI's GUILayer:

    ```
    public GUILayer hudText; // the Camera GUI's GUILayer component
    ```

11. Create the function that does the work:

    ```
    public void SpriteToggle(bool newState) {
        spriteRenderers = GetComponentsInChildren<SpriteRenderer>();
        foreach (SpriteRenderer sprite in spriteRenderers) {
            sprite.enabled = newState;
        }
        hudText.enabled = newState;
    }
    ```

In this function, you are creating an array of all of the object's children with a Sprite Renderer component, and then iterating through it and turning it on or off depending on the state passed in to it.

12. In the Start function, find the GUILayer and turn off the sprites and text:

    ```
    hudText = GameObject.Find("Camera GUI").GetComponent<GUILayer>();
    SpriteToggle (false); // turn off at start
    ```

13. Save the script, and add it to the Garden HUD object.

Next you will block the automatic start-up zombie bunny drops.

1. Open the SpawnBunnies script.

2. Move the four StartCoroutine lines from the bottom of the Start function to its own function:

```
public void StartCountdown () {

    int tempLitterSize = litterSize * 3; // increased for first drop only
    PopulateGardenBunnies (tempLitterSize);  // create new zombie bunny
    prefabs in the scene
    float tempRate = reproRate * 2; // allow extra time before the first drop
    StartCoroutine(StartReproducing(tempRate)); // start the first timer- pass in
reproRate seconds
}
```

3. Save the script.

4. Turn off "Maximize on Play," and turn off the 2D toggle in the Scene view.

5. Click Play, and wait to see what happens.

The staging area is quiet and peaceful, and the garden remains zombie-bunny free.

The decision now is when to trigger the rest of the action. If you waited until the Gnomatic Garden Defender is fully in the garden, having triggered the door open, he could stand outside happily watching the garden being overrun—a clear dereliction of duty. A better scenario is to consider "game on" as soon as the gates open. You have the SensorDoor script that opens the doors, but it has no idea what it is opening them onto. You obviously wouldn't want the game to start if he goes through the wrong door.

The OcclusionManager script, on the other hand, tracks the areas that the Gnomatic Garden Defender is about to enter, but it does so before the gate is open. Theoretically, the player could trigger "game on" without ever seeing the garden. So a good solution would be to add some intelligence to the SensorDoor script.

Remembering that the script can be put on any door, you will want to create a flag that marks it as a "game on" activator. When it is triggered, you will be turning on the Garden HUD, setting the trackingBattery flag to true, and triggering the StartReproducing coroutine, so you will want to create variables to make contact with them.

To activate the various elements, you will use a Boolean variable. False says it can't activate the "game-on" functionality, and true says it can. Because activation for a particular garden is a one-time deal, as soon as it is triggered, the state switches to false, or can't activate.

6. Open the SensorDoors script.

7. Add the following variables:

```
// variable that can trigger 'game on'
public bool canActivateGame = false;

//objects that must be informed of the 'game on' state
public GameObject gardenHud; // where the battery sprites are & text controlled
public SpawnBunnies bunnySpawner; // the SpawnBunnies script
public BatteryHealth batteryLife; // the script for the battery charge
  (on Battery Life object)
```

8. Save the script.

9. Select the GardenGates object from Common Wall 2, and set its Can Activate Game parameter to `true`.

10. Leave any doors that do not lead into a garden as `false`.

11. In the `OnTriggerEnter` function, inside the `...` `tag == "Player"` conditional, add the following:

```
if (canActivateGame) SetGameOn(); // get the game underway
```

The logic to this system is that you must start the game from a non-garden area. Once the game is underway, the Gnomatic Garden Defender should not be able to enter other garden zones until the current one is finished.

1. And then create the `SetGameOn()` function that does the work:

```
void SetGameOn () {
    // turn off the flag
    canActivateGame = false;
    // activate the Garden HUD sprites
    gardenHud.GetComponent<ChildVisibility>().SpriteToggle(true);
    // send a message to start the additional bunny drops
    bunnySpawner.StartCountdown();
    // set battery drain on
    batteryLife.trackingBattery = true;
}
```

2. Save the script.

3. Select the GardenGates object from Common Wall 2.

4. Drag the appropriate objects into the three new parameters (Figure 10-30).

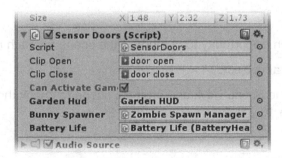

Figure 10-30. The new parameters loaded in the Sensor Doors component

The other two GardenGates objects do not open onto gardens, so you can leave the parameters empty.

5. Click Play, and drive the Gnomatic Garden Defender into the garden.

The Battery and HUD text appear, and the stork continues to make his deliveries.

6. Stop Play mode.

7. Save the scene.

8. Open the StartMenu scene, and play through to the end.

At the end, when you select Play Again, the game bypasses the start menu and loads the GardenLevel1 scene.

Options and Player Settings

When the game restarts at the GardenLevel1 scene, the player no longer has access to the StartMenu scene. By creating a new scene for the main menu and settings menu, the player will be able to access either from inside the game. The settings menu will be accessible from the main menu.

The Main Menu

Let's begin by refining the MenuBase scene that you stared earlier in the chapter. It provides continuity between the various individual menus, yet allows for some quick differentiation. By combining 2D with a 3D background, you will be able to incorporate a few of the 3D elements into the scene as well.

1. Open the MenuBase scene.

2. Toggle the Scene view to 2D.

3. Double-click the Main Camera to see it in the Scene view

4. Set its Size to **5**.

A little terrain will give you an opportunity to customize the scene for each menu.

5. Create a new Terrain object.

6. Toggle 2D off in the Scene view, and orbit the scene to check the position of the terrain (Figure 10-31).

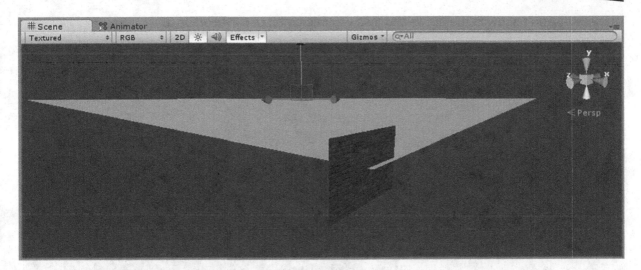

Figure 10-31. The Terrain with respect to the Quad

7.   In the Terrain's Settings section, set its Terrain Length and Width to **20** and its Height to **2**.

8.   Set the Terrain's Y Position to about **-5.3**, and move it to center it on the Quad in the x and z (Figure 10-32).

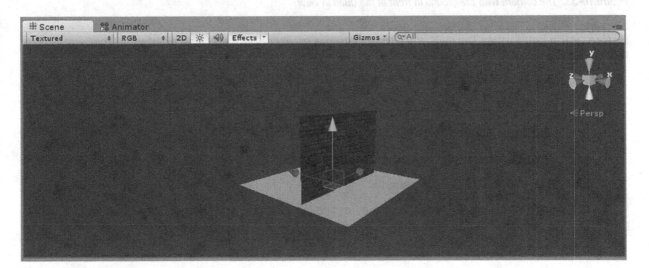

Figure 10-32. The mini-terrain in position

9.   In the Paint Textures section, add the dirt texture of your choice.

The terrain won't show in the 2D view unless you paint a bit of elevation on it.

    10.   Paint a couple of mounds with the Raise/Lower Terrain tool.

    11.   Select the camera, and move it backwards (away from the camera icon)on the z until its clipping plane covers the ground in front of the Quad (Figure 10-33).

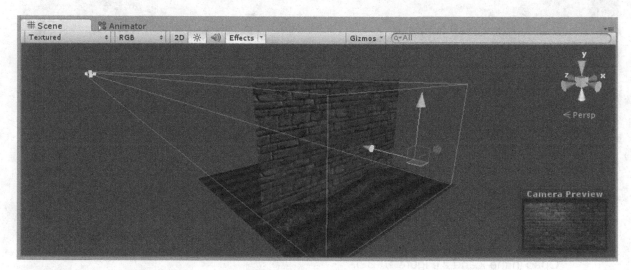

Figure 10-33. The camera with the ground in front of the Quad in view

Before going any further, you will want to update the newly enhanced base scene and make a few duplicates.

    1.   Save the scene.

    2.   Duplicate it in the Scenes folder, and name it **MainMenu**.

    3.   Duplicate it again, and name it **SettingsMenu**.

    4.   Duplicate it again, and name it **Credits**.

    5.   Open the new MainMenu scene.

    6.   Drag a prefab or two into the scene, and adjust their size and location by watching the Game view. Keep the center area clear for the menu (Figure 10-34).

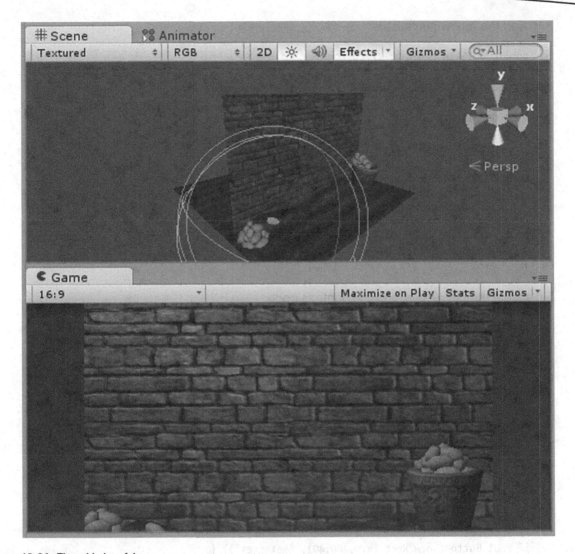

Figure 10-34. The added prefabs

7. Save the scene.

For the menu itself, you will use the same setup as with the start menu's buttons. They will be places in a GUI Group. This time, because there are more buttons, you will be using a couple of variables to make layout much easier.

1. Create a new Empty GameObject, and name it **Main Menu**.

2. Create a new C# Script in the Menu Scripts folder, and name it **MainMenuGUI**.

3. Add the following variable:

    ```
    public GUISkin newSkin; // custom skin to use
    ```

4. Block in the OnGUI function:

    ```
    void OnGUI () {

        GUI.skin = newSkin;

        // Constrain all drawing to be within a 600x600 pixel area
        GUI.BeginGroup (new Rect (Screen.width / 2 - 300, Screen.height /
        2 - 350, 600, 600));

        // must match all BeginGroup calls with an EndGroup
        GUI.EndGroup ();
    }
    ```

5. Inside the GUI.Group, add the controls code:

    ```
    // Draw a box in the new coordinate space defined by the BeginGroup.
    GUI.Box (new Rect (0,0,600,600),"Main Menu");

    int y = 60; // base Y position
    int x = 60; // base x inset
    int yOffset = 60; // y offset

    // Play Game
    if (GUI.Button( new Rect (x,y,200,40), "Play / Resume")) {
        // start game
        Screen.showCursor = false; // hide the cursor
        Application.LoadLevel("GardenLevel1");
    }
    y+= yOffset;
    // Settings
    if (GUI.Button( new Rect (x,y,200,40), "Settings")) {
        // go to settings menu
        Application.LoadLevel("SettingsMenu");
    }
    y+= yOffset;
    // Quit
    if (GUI.Button( new Rect (x,y,200,40), "Credits")) {
        // got to credits
        Application.LoadLevel(3);
    }
    y+= yOffset;
    // Quit
    if (GUI.Button( new Rect (x,y,200,40), "Quit")) {
        // quit application
        Application.Quit();
    }
    ```

The x and y values will make layout much easier as you create the skin templates for the controls. Because the final skin will change the layout drastically, there is no reason to calculate more realistic values for the x and y variables at this point.

As you get each menu/level finished, you will be adding it to the build.

6.   Save the script, and add it to the Main Menu object.

7.   Click Play to see the results (Figure 10-35).

Figure 10-35. The Main Menu with default skin

8.   Arrange the Game view in the editor so that the GUI box control (the large box) is fully visible and the Project and Inspector views are easily accessible.

9.   Stop Play mode.

The components are there, but they will benefit greatly from a custom GUI Skin.

1.   Duplicate the Garden GUISkin, and name it **SubMenu GUISkin**.

2.   Assign it to the Main Menu's New Skin parameter.

3.   Click Play, and check out the results.

The Label is the super-sized set for the end-game GUI, but it is not used in this menu. Other than the font, which will have to be changed, you will have to do a bit more customizing to whip the Garden GUISkin into shape for use in the main menu. Before making any other decisions, you should nail down a background image.

4. Select the SubMenu GUISkin, and expand the Box template.

5. In the Normal section, assign the SubMenu Background texture as the Background Image.

For the Box's font, you have two options. The font used in this project for the Box title is *rm_ginger*, a *ttf* font (true type font) created by Ray Meadows. Ray has graciously allowed it to be distributed with the rest of the book's assets. The font is a pure ASCII 128 font suitable for only the English language, and it does not handle European umlauts. He has since refined it considerably and released a more professional version as "RM Victoriana" on the MyFonts website at `http://www.myfonts.com/fonts/ray-meadows/rm-victoriana/`, where it can be purchased for a very reasonable $19. It is worth noting that while there are a great many free-to-use assets available on Unity's Asset Store and elsewhere on the Web, when you calculate the number of man-hours you will have in creating even a simple game, the cost of purchasing unique assets can be a wise investment. If you require fonts for non-English languages, be sure they can handle the extra ascii characters before making the design decision to include them in your game.

When using fonts other than Ariel (a system font for both Windows and Mac), you will have to include the font in the project just as any other asset. If a font is capable of being dynamically created on the OS, you can use a single copy of it. If not, you will have to create a copy of the font and specify the font size for each size usage. This is because a texture sheet is made internally for each sized font. For more information on using fonts in Unity, check out the documentation under Reference at `http://docs.unity3d.com/Documentation/Components/class-Font.html`.

You can find rm_ginger in the GUI Assets folder. Be sure to check out the Material and texture sheet generated by Unity when the font was imported.

6. Turn off "Maximize on Play," and turn on Play mode to see your changes while you enter them.

7. Set the Box template's Font to rm-ginger.regular.

8. Set the Text Color to Black and its Font Size to **85**.

9. Set the Content Offset Y to about 180 to drop it below the background's border.

10. Set the Font Style to Bold.

The font doesn't have a true bold version, so it crowds together, giving it a nice fabricated wrought iron appearance.

Next, the buttons could stand to be scaled down for the smaller submenus.

Expand the Button template.

1. Put the ButtonBlueGlassSm in the Normal's Background slot and the ButtonOrangeGlassSm in the Hover and Active slots.

2. Set the Border Left and Right values to **16**.

3. Set the Font Size to **24**.

With a clear view of the final controls in the Game view, you can now tweak the x and y offset variables in the code.

4. In the MainMenuGUI script, set the x and y values as follows:

```
int y = 265; // base Y position
int x = 200; // base x inset
```

5. Save the script.

6. All four buttons line up correctly (Figure 10-36).

Figure 10-36. *The Main Menu, with the Play/Resume button showing Hover behavior*

7. Stop Play mode.

8. Save the scene.

9. Add the new menu to the Build Settings, and move it into the level 1 position, putting the GardenLevel1 into the number 2 slot.

10. Click Build, and overwrite.

11. Close the Build Settings.

To view the Main Menu, once the player has left the StartMenu, you will have to give the player a way to access it from in the game. Depending on the platform, that could be via keyboard, mouse pick, or screen touch. In this game, the cursor is suppressed while the player is controlling the Gnomatic Garden Defender in the garden, so the most logical option is a keyboard key. The code is not object specific, so it should be put on the object that will exist in only the garden level(s).

1. Open the GardenLevel1 scene.

The Game Manager object has a GameMisc script that should be the perfect place for your code. The F1 key is quite often used to bring up help menus, so that would be a good choice. A search for "keycodes" in the Scripting Reference will give you a complete list to choose from.

2. Open the GameMisc script.

3. In the Update function, add

```
if (Input.GetKeyDown(KeyCode.F1)) {
    Screen.showCursor = true; // show the cursor
    Application.LoadLevel(1); // load the Main Menu
}
```

4. Save the script, and test by pressing the F1 key while in the garden level.

The menu comes up, but there isn't much you can do until the other menus are finished.

5. Save the scene.

The Settings Menu

The options offered to the player are minimal for this little game. The "difficulty" will be adjustable and the audio volume for the ambient sounds will also be adjustable. Both will use Horizontal Sliders from the Unity GUI. You can repurpose a lot of the MainMenu to speed things up.

1. Open the blocked-in SettingsMenu scene.

2. Focus in on the Main Camera.

3. Add a new Empty GameObject, and name it **Settings Menu.**

4. From the Menu Scripts folder, duplicate the MainMenuGUI script and name it **SettingsGUI**.

5. Open the script, and change the class declaration to match the new name:

```
public class SettingsGUI : MonoBehaviour {
```

6. Add the following variables:

```
float diffSliderValue = 5.0f; // difficulty slider
float ambSliderValue = 1.0f; // ambient volume slider
```

7. In the OnGUI function, clear the contents of the GUI Group as follows:

```
void OnGUI () {

    GUI.skin = newSkin;

    // Constrain all drawing to be within a 600 x 600 pixel area centered
    on the screen.
    GUI.BeginGroup (new Rect (Screen.width / 2 - 300, Screen.height /
    2 - 350, 600, 600));

    // must match all BeginGroup calls with an EndGroup
    GUI.EndGroup ();
}
```

This code is pretty standard. You are once again creating a group and visualizing its size and location with a Box. You will also be using variables again to make tweaking the control element's layout easier to refine.

8. Add the controls inside the GUI Group:

```
// Draw a box in the new coordinate space defined by the BeginGroup.
GUI.Box (new Rect (0,0,600,600),"Settings");

int y = 240; // base Y position
int x = 200; // base x inset
int yOffset = 60; // y offset

// difficulty slider
GUI.Label(new Rect (x - 50, y, 300, 60), "Difficulty");
y+= yOffset;
diffSliderValue = GUI.HorizontalSlider (new Rect (x, y, 200, 60),
diffSliderValue, 10.0f, 0f);
y+= yOffset;
// ambient volume slider
GUI.Label(new Rect (x - 50, y, 300, 60), "Ambient Sound Volume");
y+= yOffset;
ambSliderValue = GUI.HorizontalSlider (new Rect (x, y, 200, 60),
ambSliderValue, 0.0f, 1.0f);

if (GUI.Button( new Rect (156200,y + 40,200,40), "Main Menu")) {
    // Back to Main Menu

    Application.LoadLevel("MainMenu"1);
}
```

For the controls, you are using GUI.Label and GUI.HorizontalSlider. Note how the slider values set themselves recursively. The slider ranges are set in the controls, but the default values are read from the variable declarations.

1.   Save the script.

2.   Drag it onto the Settings Menu object.

3.   Drag the SubMenu GUISkin onto its New Skin parameter.

4.   Click Play, and check out the menu.

The Label is in dire need of adjustment.

5.   Expand the Label template.

6.   Set its Normal Text Color to black.

7.   Set its Font to None, its Font Size to **22,** and its Font Style to Bold.

8.   Set its Alignment to Middle Center.

The label text is back under control.

Here comes the fun part. The sliders are looking okay, but you can have a bit of fun with the indicators.

1.   Expand the Horizontal Slider Thumb template.

2.   For its Normal background image, select CarrotThumb.

3.   For its Hover background image, select CarrotThumb_Hover.

4.   For its Active background image, select CarrotThumb_Active.

5.   Set the Fixed Width to **25** and the Fixed Height to **50**.

6.   Under Overflow, set the Top to **10**.

With the skin elements locked down, you can experiment with the sliders to see how the different images are used during interaction.

7.   Just above the `// ambient volume slider` line, subtract 25 from the offset to improve the spacing:

```
y+= yOffset - 25;
```

8.   Stop Play mode.

9.   Add a few prefab objects if you wish.

The Settings menu is ready for interaction (Figure 10-37).

Figure 10-37. The Settings menu

10. Be sure to check the placement of the extra scene objects with "Maximize on Play" turned on.

11. Save the Scene.

Next, you will be adding some of the functionality controlled by the sliders. The difficulty will be updated according to its value when you are in the regular garden levels. You will have to provide a sound for the player to adjust in this level. Let's begin by checking up on the values of the two sliders.

1. Add the following line at the bottom of the OnGUI function:

```
print (diffSliderValue + "   " + ambSliderValue);
```

2. Save the script.

3. Adjust the sliders, and watch the new values being reported in the console.

The sliders stay within their respective ranges and are updated dynamically. To test the ambient sound volume, you must have an audio clip to sample.

1. Stop Play mode.

2. Add an Audio Source component to the Settings Menu object.

3. Assign the Birds audio clip as its clip.

4. Set it to Loop.

As this scene is essentially a 2D still shot, there is no reason to use a 3D sound. Instead of turning the Volume Rolloff to Linear, this time you will change the audio clip.

5. From the Sound FX folder, duplicate the Birds clip and name it **Birds2D**.

6. Uncheck 3D Sound, and click Apply.

7. Assign Birds2D as the Audio Source component's Audio Clip.

With Unity GUI, you can track when the user makes changes in the GUI. This cuts down on the resources so that the values in the menu are updated only when the player actively changes any of them.

8. Add the following code below the `GUI.EndGroup()` line:

```
if (GUI.changed) {
    audio.volume = ambSliderValue; // adjust the audio clip's volume
}
```

9. Comment out the `print` statement.

10. Save the script.

11. Click Play, and adjust the volume with the slider.

The volume changes with the slider. In the Inspector, the component's Volume slider will update only if you deselect and then reselect the Settings Menu.

12. Stop Play Mode, and save the scene.

13. Add the scene to the Build Settings, moving it above the GardenLevel1 scene.

14. Click Build and select Overwrite when the dialog appears.

15. Close Build Settings.

You will be creating the code to make use of the settings near the end of the chapter.

Credits

The Credits scene is very simple. Once again you can repurpose most of the code. Here you will learn a simple technique for overriding a GUI Skin on a one-to-one basis.

1. Open the blocked-in Credits scene.

2. Focus in on the Main Camera.

3. Add a new Empty GameObject, and name it **Credits.**

4. From the Game Scripts folder, duplicate the MainMenuGUI script and name it **CreditsGUI**.

5. Open the script, and change the class declaration to match the new name:

```
public class CreditsGUI : MonoBehaviour {
```

6. Change the Box control's text to "Credits."

7. Replace the rest of the current contents of the GUI Group with

```
int y = 240; // base Y position
int x = 150; // base x inset
int yOffset = 60; // y offset

// title
GUI.Label(new Rect (x, y, 300, 60), "Game Design");
y+= yOffset;

// person
GUI.Label(new Rect (x, y, 300, 60), "your name here");
y+= yOffset;

// date
GUI.Label(new Rect (100, 370, 400, 40), "XXIV");
y+= yOffset;

// Main Menu
if (GUI.Button( new Rect (200,420,200,40), "Main Menu")) {
    // Back to Main Menu
    Application.LoadLevel("MainMenu");
}
```

8. Save the script, and add it to the Credits object.

9. Assign the Sub-Menu GUISkin as its New Skin.

10. Click Play.

Besides being centered, the two label lines are on top of each other in the center. Ideally, you would like one label to be right justified and one to be left justified. The last label, the date, is fine as is. It turns out, you can both create your own templates, or GUI Styles, and you can use them to selectively override those in the current GUISkin.

1. Select the Sub-Menu GUISkin, and expand the Custom Styles section and the Element 0 style.

2. Set the Name to **left_label**.

3. Change its Font Size to **20.**

Its Alignment is already Upper Left.

4. Increase the Custom Styles array Size to **2.**

The left_label style is cloned to create the next element.

5. Change its Name to **right_label** and its Alignment to Upper Right.

6. In the CreditsGUI script, change the // title label as follows:

```
GUI.Label(new Rect (x, y, 300, 60), "Game Design","left_label");
```

7. In the CreditsGUI script, change the person label as follows:

```
GUI.Label(new Rect (x, y, 300, 60), "your name here", "right_label");
```

8. Move the y+= yOffset line from below the Game Design label line to above it:

```
y+= yOffset;
// title
GUI.Label(new Rect (x, y, 300, 60), "Game Design","left_label");
```

9. Save the script, and click Play to see the results.

10. Stop Play mode.

11. Add some prefabs if you wish (Figure 10-38).

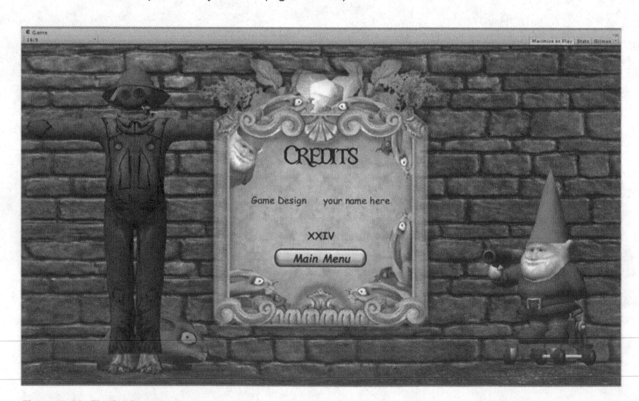

Figure 10-38. The Credits screen

> **Tip** If you wish to add any characters, you should drag the assets rather than the prefabs into the scene to avoid any animation or controller script issues.

12. Save the scene.

13. Add it to the Build Settings, and move it up above the GardenLevel1.

14. The Build levels should now look as shown in Figure 10-39.

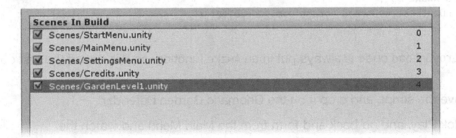

Figure 10-39. The final level order in the Build Settings

15. Click Build and select Overwrite when the dialog appears.

Because you are using names rather than index numbers to load the levels through your scripting, the order (other than the starting level, index 0) isn't important.

Retaining Data

With all of the new menus loaded and the game built, you should be able to test navigation between them and some of their functionality.

1. Load the StartMenu.

2. Click Play, and the test menus to see how they handle.

The most obvious issue is that the garden scene restarts every time you select Play Game from the Main menu. In this simple game, you won't be saving games, so you don't need to offer a "load previous game" option. You will, however, have to save some of the data from the garden level when the player is visiting the menu layers.

DontDestroyOnLoad

If it was simply a matter of retaining the character's transform and a score, things would be fairly simple. Unfortunately, all of those pesky, instantiated zombie bunnies have to be accounted for. Rather than just passing on a few choice bits of data, you will carry the pertinent gameObjects through whenever you change levels, setting them as active or inactive according to level. This is where moving the garden level to the end of the level list works nicely.

The most important thing to understand about DontDestroyOnLoad is that it will happily add duplicate gameObjects every time a scene is restarted. In this game, if for instance, you told the Gnomatic Garden Defender to DontDestroyOnLoad every time you went out to the Main menu and came back, a new Gnomatic Garden Defender would be created. Let's try a quick test.

1. Open the GardenLevel1 scene.

2. Create a new C# Script in the Game Scripts folder, and name it **LevelManager**.

3. Add the following code to it:

```
void Awake () {
    DontDestroyOnLoad (transform.gameObject);
}
```

The DontDestroyOnLoad code is always put in an Awake function, so it is one of the first commands to be read.

4. Save the script, and drop it on the Gnomatic Garden Defender.

5. Click Play, and go back and forth from the Main Menu and watch the Hierarchy view (Figure 10-40).

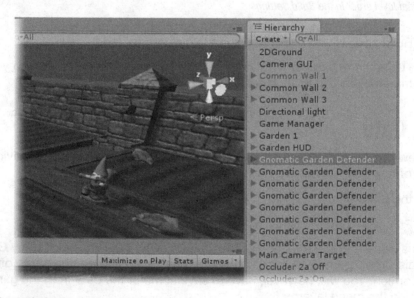

Figure 10-40. *The Gnomatic Garden Defender duplicate problem*

6. Stop Play mode, and remove the Level Manager component from the Gnomatic Garden Defender.

Let's get a bit more serious about managing the levels. Along with LoadLevel(), the Application class has some other useful static variables, such as loadedLevel and loadedLevelName. With these, you can track what level your game is currently running. Armed with that information, you can control which of your persistent objects are active. Let's add a bit more code to the LevelManager script.

1. Add the following variable:

    ```
    int currentLevel; // the currently active level
    ```

2. Add the following to the Start function:

    ```
    print("Starting " + Application.loadedLevelName);
    currentLevel = Application.loadedLevel; // its index number
    ```

In the Start function, you initialize the currentLevel variable to the currently loaded level.

3. Add the following to the Update function:

    ```
    if (Application.loadedLevel != currentLevel) {
        currentLevel = Application.loadedLevel;
        print("new level =  " + Application.loadedLevel + ",  " +
        Application.loadedLevelName);
    }
    ```

In this conditional, you are checking to see if the current level is no longer the same as the value of the variable holding the last-known current level. If not, the new number is assigned as the current level.

4. Save the script, and save the scene.

5. Open the StartScene.

6. Create a new Empty gameObject, and name it **Level Manager**.

7. Add the LevelManager script to it.

8. Click Play, and go between the various levels, watching the console level report as you go (Figure 10-41).

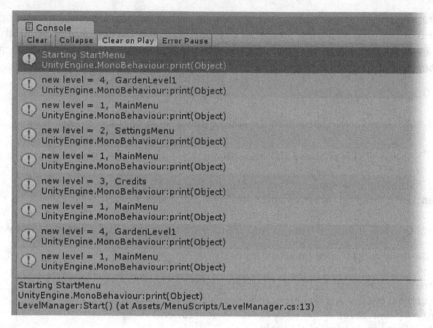

Figure 10-41. *Level hopping*

9. Comment out the `print` statements in the `Start` function and the `Update` function, and save the script.

10. Save the StartMenu scene.

The most crucial task now is to determine what has to be retained while the player is accessing the main menu. The number one question is whether or not the game has begun. If the Gnomatic Garden Defender remains in the staging area, you could either do a clean restart or just save the location and orientation of the Gnomatic Garden Defender.

The stork fly-bys uncover a different problem. Once a coroutine is invoked, it can't be canceled and then restarted at a particular point in its duration. The `StartReproducing` function, however, does have several yields controlling the drop sequence. If the drop hasn't started yet, you can trigger the fly-by again. If it has, you can simply trigger the 3D zombie-bunny drop in the scene when the game resumes without worrying about the 2D warning system—e.g., the fly-by.

Let's begin with the simpler tasks. The Gnomatic Garden Defender's transform must be stored right before the level change to the Main Menu, but only if the current level is a garden level. The SensorDoor script is in charge of starting the actual game play.

To manage the data exchange, you will be tracking the currently loaded level and the state of the game itself. You will be creating a new variable named `gameState`. State 0 will mean you have not yet entered a garden level. You can only be in a menu at this point. State 1 means you have entered a garden level, but the game is not yet underway. You are in, or have been in, the staging area or have gone into one of the menus via the main menu. State 2 means the game has started. At this point, you could be anywhere other than the start menu.

1. Open the SensorDoors script.

2. Add the following variable:

```
LevelManager levelManager; // the script that holds the data between levels
```

3. Find it in the Start function, and assign it if found:

```
if(GameObject.Find("Level Manager")) {
    levelManager = GameObject.Find("Level Manager").GetComponent<LevelManager>();
}
```

Because the Level Manager exists only in the StartMenu scene in edit mode, you can't drag and drop it in the GardenLevel1 scene. It can be found only *after* the level has started. And it can be assigned only if it has been found.

If the SensorDoor script has been started—e.g., you are in a garden level—you will find out what state the game is currently in and, if it is currently set as state 0, you will update it to state 1.

4. In the Start function, below the levelManager = line, add the following:

```
if(levelManager.gameState < 1) levelManager.gameState = 1; // in staging area
```

If the player has triggered the door and the game is not already in play, the game is now in play, so you will report the new gameState, 2, to the Level Manager.

5. In the SetGameOn function, add

```
// game is running, inform the LevelManager
if(levelManager) levelManager.gameState = 2;
```

6. Save the script.

The LevelManager script is where the gameState value will be kept.

7. In the LevelManager script, add the following variable:

```
public int gameState = 0; // 0, new game, 1, staging area, 2, in garden
```

8. Save the script.

9. Open the StartScene, and select the Level Manager object.

10. Click Play, and go into the game.

11. Resize the Inspector panel to force the update so you can see the new game state, 1.

12. Drive into the garden, and force another update to see the new state value, 2.

13. Stop Play mode, and save the scene.

Managing the Gnomatic Garden Defender

The Gnomatic Garden Defender has two values that must be stored: its position (a Vector3 construct), and its y rotation (a simple float). The Level Manager will require the original transform at the start, but it will also want the Gnomatic Garden Defender's updated position right before the level changes from a garden level to a menu level. The code to go from GardenLevel1 to the MainMenu level is in the GameMisc script, so that will be a good place to handle the data.

1. Open the GardenLevel1 scene.

2. Open the GameMisc script, and add the following variables:

    ```
    LevelManager levelManager; // the script that holds the data between levels
    public Transform gnomeTransform; // the gnome's transform
    ```

3. In the Start function, add the following:

    ```
    if(GameObject.Find("Level Manager")) {
        levelManager = GameObject.Find("Level Manager").GetComponent<LevelManager>();
        // if this is a new game, send the initial data
        if(levelManager.gameState == 0) LevelPrep ();
    }
    ```

As before, the Level Manager can be found only after the level has loaded, which is a drawback of using DontDestroyOnLoad. By checking first to see if it has been found, you can avoid errors when testing the level directly. The call to the LevelPrep function is where data will be gathered and sent to the LevelManager script.

4. Create the LevelPrep function:

    ```
    void LevelPrep () {
        if(levelManager) {
            // send the gnome's transform off to be saved if the levelManager has
            been found
            Transform temptrans = gnomeTransform;
            levelManager.gnomePos = temptrans.position;
            levelManager.gnomeYRot = temptrans.localEulerAngles.y;
        }
    }
    ```

5. Do not save the script yet.

If you are a chess player and are good at thinking things through, you may have spotted a bit of a conflict between the code you added to the GameMisc script and the SensorDoors script. The first time the player enters GardenLevel1, the gameState will be 0. If the GameMisc script is executed first, LevelPrep() will be called. If the SensorDoors script is executed first, the state will have been changed to 1 before the GameMisc script is executed and the LevelPrep() function will not be called. To make sure the GameMisc is executed first, you will specify the execution order between the two scripts.

1. Select a script in the Project view.

2. Near the top of the Inspector, click the Execution Order button.

3. Click the plus sign to Add Script, and select LevelManager.

4. Click the plus sign again, and add GameMisc.

5. Click the plus again, and add SensorDoors.

6. Click Apply.

With the execution order locked down, you can return to the GameMisc script. The data has been sent off to the LevelManager at the start of the garden level, so next you will make sure it is sent to update the LevelManager before the garden level is exited.

1. In the Update function, call the LevelPrep function *before* loading the new menu level:

```
if (Input.GetKeyDown(KeyCode.F1)) {
    Screen.showCursor = true; // show the cursor
    LevelPrep (); // do data collection before going to the new level
    Application.LoadLevel("Main Menu"); // load the Main Menu
}
```

The little bit of data you are storing now should be no problem, but when there is a lot of data to be processed and to store, you will want to play it safe and add a little pause before loading the MainMenu scene.

2. In the Update function, replace the Application.LoadLevel line with

```
StartCoroutine(LoadTheLevel());
```

3. Create the coroutine that now starts the new level:

```
IEnumerator LoadTheLevel() {
    // makes sure all the storage tasks have been completed
    yield return new WaitForSeconds(0.1f);
    Application.LoadLevel("MainMenu"); // load the Main Menu
}
```

4. Save the script.

Before you can assign the Gnomatic Garden Defender, you will have to add the two new variables to the LevelManager script.

1. In the LevelManager script, add the gnome's variables:

```
public Vector3 gnomePos; // the gnome's position
public float gnomeYRot; // the gnome's Y rotation
```

2. Save the script.

3. In the GardenLevel1 scene, assign the Gnomatic Garden Defender to the new parameter in the Game Manager's Game Misc component.

4. Save the scene.

Next, you will create the script that uses the stored data to put the Gnomatic Garden Defender into its previous position when the player returns to the game.

1. Create a new C# script in the Game Scripts folder, and name it **SetTransform**.

2. Add the following function:

```
public void UpdateTransform (Vector3 newPos, float newYRot) {
    // set the new position
    Vector3 tempPos = new Vector3(transform.position.x,
transform.position.y,transform.position.z);
    tempPos = newPos;
    transform.position = tempPos;
    // set the new y rotation
    Vector3 tempRot = new Vector3(transform.localEulerAngles.x,
transform.localEulerAngles.y,transform.localEulerAngles.z);
    tempRot.y = newYRot;
    transform.localEulerAngles = tempRot;
}
```

3. Save the script.

4. Add it to the Gnomatic Garden Defender's prefab in the Project view.

5. While you are there, rename the prefab **Gnomatic Garden Defender** to match the updated name in the Hierarchy view.

Finally, in the LevelManager script, you will tell the gnome's data to be updated.

6. In the LevelManager's Update function, below the print statement, add

```
ManageLevels (); // do stuff according to the level just entered
```

7. Create the ManageLevels function:

```
void ManageLevels () {
   if (currentLevel > 3) { // you are in a garden level
       // reposition & re-orient gnome
       GameObject.Find("Gnomatic Garden Defender").GetComponent<SetTransform>()
.UpdateTransform(gnomePos,gnomeYRot);

       if (gameState == 1) return; // still in staging area, just repopulate a new game
   }
}
```

8. Save the script, and save the scene.

You have now reached the "point of no return" in your game, or more accurately, the "point of must return." Because the Level Manager is *only* present in the StartMenu scene and is carried forward with each loaded level, you must always play from the StartMenu scene to check the "scene hopping" functionality.

1. Open the StartMenu scene.

2. Click Play, and test the gnome's repositioning by accessing the main menu from inside the garden and then returning to the game.

All works reasonably well when you leave the *active* game for the MainMenu and then return to the game. The Gnomatic Garden Defender is put into its former location and orientation. Conspicuously missing, however, are the zombie bunnies and the HUD.

Let's tackle The HUD next. There are only two pieces of data that must be saved: the zombie-bunny count and the battery life remaining. Both must be saved in their current value just before the level change.

1. In the LevelManager script, add the new storage variables:

    ```
    internal int bunCount = 0; // number of buns in garden
    internal float batteryRemaining; // time in seconds
    ```

2. Save the script.

3. In the GameMisc script, add the following variables:

    ```
    // needed for level hopping
    public ScoreKeeper scoreKeeper; // where the current bun count is kept
    (on the Game Manager)
    public BatteryHealth batteryHealth; // where the battery charge is tracked
    (on the Battery Life)
    ```

4. In the LevelPrep function, inside the if(LevelManager) clause, add the following to inform the LevelManager of the current values:

    ```
    // send the current zombie bunnie count
    levelManager.bunCount = scoreKeeper.currentBunCount;
    // send the battery info
    levelManager.batteryRemaining = batteryHealth.batteryRemaining;
    ```

5. Save the script.

The console reports the two variables are inaccessible due to their protection level. The GameMisc script, acting as a "middle man" doesn't have access to the variables on either end unless they are made public or internal. You set the LevelManager's new variables as internal, but you will have to locate and change the other two on their respective scripts.

6. In the ScoreKeeper script, set the CurrentBunCount variable to internal.

7. In the BatteryHealth script, set the batteryRemaining variable to internal.

8. Save both scripts

The console is once again clear and happy.

1. In the GardenLevel1 scene, select the Game Manager.

2. In its Game Misc component, load the Game Manager into its Score Keeper parameter and the Battery Life object into its Battery Health parameter (Figure 10-42).

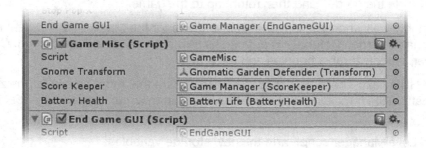

Figure 10-42. The Game Misc component on the Game Manager object

With the data flying back and forth between the scripts, the next task will be to have the Level Manager process it. The GameObject.Find function can be slow, so any scripts that will be contacted regarding more than one piece of information or function call can have a temporary local variable to hold them. This uses less memory than making the variable global to the whole script and cuts down on access time, making it a compromise between speed and memory use.

1. In the LevelManager script's ManageLevels function, below the if (gameState == 1) line, add

```
// game state must be 2, the game is on
// use the LevelManager's stored values to update and turn on HUD stuff
GameObject.Find("Game Manager").GetComponent<ScoreKeeper>().currentBunCount = bunCount;
// update the zombie bunny count in the HUD
GameObject.Find("Bunny Count").GetComponent<GUIText>().text = bunCount.ToString ();

// manage the battery HUD
BatteryHealth batteryHealth = GameObject.Find("Battery Life").GetComponent<BatteryHealth>();
batteryHealth.batteryRemaining = batteryRemaining;
batteryHealth.trackingBattery = true;    // restart the drain
// turn on battery sprites again
GameObject.Find("Garden HUD").GetComponent<ChildVisibility>().SpriteToggle(true);
GameObject.Find("Camera GUI").GetComponent<GUILayer>().enabled= true; // activate GUI Text
```

2. Save the script, and save the scene.

3. Click Play from the StartMenu scene.

4. Once in the garden, shoot until about 10 zombie bunnies remain, and then access the Main Menu by pressing F1.

5. Experiment with the submenus and then press Resume Game.

The count and the battery life have been retained, but the zombie bunnies would have originally been generated the first time the Gnomatic Garden Defender hit the occluder object and triggered the code from the DoorSensors script.

If you call the same code from the LevelManager, the stored number, bunCount, will be randomized and therefore changed. Rather than add yet another variable to use as a flag, you can play with numbers to have the bunCount do double duty as a value *and* a flag.

1. Open the LevelManager script.

2. In the ManageLevels function, just under the GameObject.Find("Bunny Count") line, add

    ```
    // repopulate the zombie bunnies and related functionality
    SpawnBunnies spawnBunnies = GameObject.Find("Zombie Spawn Manager")
    .GetComponent<SpawnBunnies>();
    // repopulate the zombie bunnies, adding 100 as a flag not to randomize
    spawnBunnies.PopulateGardenBunnies(bunCount + 100); /// repopulate
    // restart the drop timer
    spawnBunnies.RestartCountdown();
    ```

3. Save the script.

The SpawnBunnies script will require the corresponding changes.

4. In the SpawnBunnies script, change the protection level on the PopulateGardenBunnies function:

    ```
    public void PopulateGardenBunnies (int count) {
    ```

5. Wrap the count = Random.Range and gameManager.SendMessage lines in a conditional to handle the "100" flag:

    ```
    if (count < 100) { // check for the resuming game flag
        count = Random.Range(count*3/4,count +1); // randomize the count number
        // send the amount to update the total
        gameManager.SendMessage("UpdateCount",count,
        SendMessageOptions.DontRequireReceiver);
    }
    else count -= 100; // strip off the extra 100, the resume to level flag
    ```

6. Add the RestartCountdown function:

    ```
    public void RestartCountdown  () {
        StartCoroutine(StartReproducing(reproRate));
    }
    ```

7. Save the script.

8. Play through from the StartMenu scene.

The correct number of zombie bunnies are dropped.

If you were lucky (or skilled) enough to shoot down to 1 zombie bunny before you went out to the menu, you will have discovered that the canReproduce variable and the battery-tracking flag were reset to their default values, allowing more zombie-bunny drops after you re-entered the game. Rather than add two more variables for the LevelManager to track (and all of the associated code), you will call a little function in to update those values.

1. In the Level Manager script, ManageLevels function, below the
   GameObject.Find("Camera GUI") line, add

   ```
   GameObject.Find("Game Manager").GetComponent<ScoreKeeper>().StopTheMaddness(bunCount);
   ```

2. Save the script.

3. In the ScoreKeeper script, add the new function:

   ```
   public void StopTheMaddness (int bunCount) {
      if(bunCount <= stopPopX) {
          // stop the battery drain and refresh GUI
          BatteryHealth batteryHealth = GameObject.Find ("Battery Life")
   .GetComponent<BatteryHealth>();
          batteryHealth.trackingBattery = false;
          batteryHealth.UpdateBattery();
          // stop bun drop
          spawner.canReproduce = false;
      }
   }
   ```

4. Save the Script.

To correctly update the battery GUI, you will have to do a little rearranging of the UpdateBattery function. When it is called from the Update function, the math has already been calculated. You will be moving the calculations down to the UpdateBattery function so it will be fully self contained.

5. In the BatteryHealth script, set the UpdateBattery function to public.

6. In the Update function, move the two lines above the UpdateBattery() line to the top of the UpdateBattery function.

7. In the Update function, move the line below the UpdateBattery() line to the bottom of the UpdateBattery function.

8. Save the script.

9. Open the GardenLevel1 scene, and change the GameManager's Stop Pop X value to **15** so you can quickly test the new code.

10. Save the scene, and return to the StartMenu.

11. Play and then access the MainMenu once you have shot enough zombie bunnies to halt the battery and bunny drops.

The battery remains stopped at its previous charge, and the stork will no longer bring more zombie bunnies to destroy your garden.

Player Settings

There are a few remaining issues that could be improved, but now that you can go back and forth from the game and menus, you can see about implementing the player options. To begin, you will send the updated values to the LevelManager before returning to the main menu.

1. Open the SettingsGUI script.

2. Add the following variable:

```
LevelManager levelManager; // the script that holds the data between levels
```

3. Add the usual code to identify the LevelManager in the Start function:

```
if(GameObject.Find("Level Manager")) {
    levelManager = GameObject.Find("Level Manager").GetComponent<LevelManager>();
}
```

4. In the OnGUI function, inside the if (GUI.changed) clause, add

```
// Send updated values back to LevelManager
if (levelManager) {
    levelManager.ambientVolume = ambSliderValue;
    levelManager.difficulty = (int)(diffSliderValue);
}
```

Once again, you may wish to run the game directly from the garden level during testing, so you are checking for the existence of the LevelManager before sending it the updated information. This will prevent communication errors when there is no LevelManager present, but any functionality related to the Level Manager will not be accessible.

The sliders use float values, but the difficulty functionality will be easier to manage as a rounded-off integer, so the float is *cast* or converted to an integer where it becomes a number from 0 to 10. Because the number will be used mainly to adjust timing, a high number will give the player longer to get things done and a lower number will cause things to happen more frequently, so the difficulty will range from 10 down to 0.

5. Save the script.

Next, you will add the variables that will store the ambient sound volume and the game difficulty.

6. In the LevelManager script, add the following variables:

```
internal float ambientVolume = 0.8f; // volume for all ambient sounds/music
internal int difficulty = 5; // affects battery life
```

7. Save the script, click Play from the StartMenu level, and go to the Settings menu.

8.   Select the Level Manager in the Hierarchy view, and adjust the sliders in the viewport.

9.   Resize the views to force an update so you can see the changed values in the Inspector.

10. Stop Play mode.

The implementations of the two settings are a bit different. Ambient volume should carry through to all, menu and garden levels alike.

Adjusting the Ambient Sound Volume

Because a game could easily have its audio categorized as ambient, voice, and special effects, you will create a tag to identify the audio source components that must be adjusted. Each time the game enters a new level, the components are located, put into an array, and then processed with the new value.

1.   Open the SettingsMenu scene.

2.   Create a new tag, and name it **Ambient**.

3.   Select the Settings Menu in the Hierarchy view.

It is the object that contains the Audio source for the ambient sounds.

4.   Set its tag to the new Ambient tag.

5.   Save the scene.

With the new tag in place, you can add the scripting that will make use of it.

6.   In the LevelManager script, at the top of the ManageLevels function, add

```
ProcessAudio(); // adjust the ambient volume no matter what the level is
```

7.   Create the ProcessAudio() function:

```
void ProcessAudio() {
    GameObject[] ambientTags =  GameObject.FindGameObjectsWithTag("Ambient");
    foreach (GameObject ambientTag in ambientTags) {
        ambientTag.audio.volume = ambientVolume;
    }
}
```

In this function, you are finding all gameObjects in the current level with the "Ambient" tag and putting them into an array, and then iterating through the array and changing the volume setting on each. You aren't performing a check to make sure the object has an Audio Source component first, so it is up to you to check for one when you change the object's tag. A more likely scenario is that you will forget to change the tag on an object.

1.   Save the script.

Although the only ambient sound you have at the moment is the test sound in the SettingsMenu scene, it should be able to retain its setting from previous adjustments. For that, you will have to use the value set by the Level Manager as the slider's starting value.

2. In the SettingsGUI script's `Start` function, under the `levelManager` assignment, add

```
ambSliderValue = levelManager.ambientVolume; // set the volume to the stored value
diffSliderValue = levelManager.difficulty;   // set the difficulty to the stored value
```

The Audio Source component was already updated from the LevelManager script, so you should be ready to test.

3. Save the script, and save the scene.

4. Click Play from the StartMenu, and test the Settings menu by adjusting the ambient sound, returning to the main menu and then going back to the settings menu.

The volume setting and volume of the test Audio Component are retained between menus. The Difficulty value is also retained.

As a final test, you can add some ambient sound effects to the garden scene. Unlike you did with the visual elements of your scene, you will want to keep the audio separate from the rest of the garden groups so it will always be active and able to be adjusted. Sound clips in Unity are 3D by default. That means they automatically adjust their volume internally depending on how far away the main camera (the camera with the Listener component) is from the object holding the Audio Source.

1. Open the GardenLevel1 scene, and focus in on the Gnomatic Garden Defender.

2. Create a new Empty GameObject, and name it **Sound FX Birds**.

3. Move it to the center of the staging area, about 1 meter off of the ground.

4. Add an Audio Source component to it.

5. Load Birds as its Audio Clip, and check Loop.

6. Assign the Ambient tag to it.

The falloff is spherical, but the character doesn't go into the corners, so you can adjust the falloff curve so that the sound will stay pretty much "inside" the walled area. If you wanted full control, you could add a box collider and have the Audio Source turn off and on using an `OnTriggerEnter` and `OnTriggerExit`. Let's rely on the falloff to do all of the work this time. The enclosures are about 10 x 10 meters, so you can begin by setting the range.

1. Set the Max Distance to **9** (Figure 10-43).

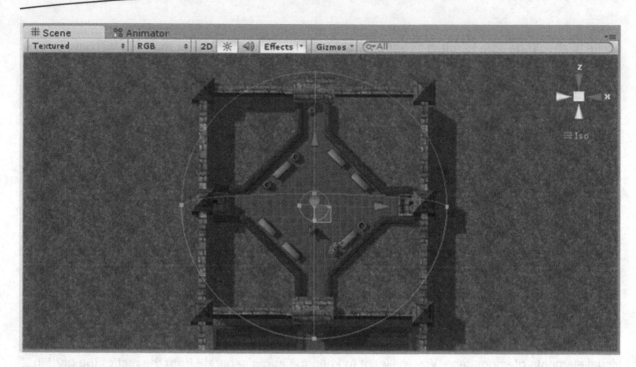

Figure 10-43. The Max Distance gizmo showing the spherical range

2. Set the Volume Rolloff to Custom Rolloff.

The Curve changes to a classic ease-in/ease-out curve (Figure 10-44, left).

3. Position the cursor midway along the curve, right-click over it, and select Add Key to create a new key.

4. Move it up and over to the right to keep the volume loud until the edge of the falloff.

5. Add another key, and adjust the locations and handles as per Figure 10-44, right.

6. Click on the first and last keys so you can adjust their handles to make the curve tangent to them (Figure 10-44, right).

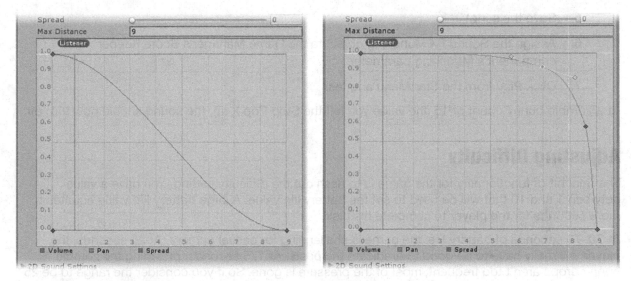

Figure 10-44. The default Custom Rolloff (left), and the adjusted curve (right)

7. In the 2 x 3 layout, click Play and drive the Gnomatic Garden Defender into the garden, watching the location of the Listener in the falloff curve (the vertical red line), as the character (camera) moves away from the Audio source.

8. Stop Play mode.

You are probably thinking the garden is too quiet now. Ideally, it would be nice to have each zombie bunny come with its own randomly chosen munching sound effect. That way, when it was exterminated, its sound would go with it. To move the project along, you will just reuse the object you just made and use a single clip. The only difference is that this one should be turned off when the zombie bunny count drops to 1.

1. Duplicate Sound FX Birds, name it **Sound FX Munching**, and move it to the center of the garden enclosure.

2. Load Munching in as its Audio Clip.

3. Open the ScoreKeeper script, and add the following variable:

    ```
    public AudioSource munching; // the sound effect component for the overrun garden
    ```

4. Inside the UpdateCount function, at the top of the if (currentBunCount == 0) clause, add

    ```
    if (munching) munching.enabled = false; // turn off the munching sound
    ```

5. Save the script.

6. Assign the Sound FX Munching object to the Game Manager's Score Keeper component's Munching parameter.

7. Click Play from the StartMenu and test.

At a zombie bunny count of 15 (the value you left the Stop Pop X at), the sound should now turn off.

Adjusting Difficulty

The final bit of functionality for the game is to flesh out the difficulty setting. You have a value between 1 and 10 that will be used to set the battery life value. A large battery life value equates to more seconds for the player to complete his task.

At 70–75 seconds of battery life, the game is challenging for casual gamers. At 25 seconds, the player will really have to be good to eradicate the pests. At 175 seconds, providing the zombie bunny drops aren't too frequent, most of the pressure is gone. So if you consider the range to be 25 to 175, that gives you a range of 150, which puts the default difficulty at about 50%, or 75 seconds.

Up to this point, where the battery time was fixed, it made sense to track the batteryRemaining, or seconds remaining. Now, however, the battery time, batteryFull, will be calculated using fixed amounts and the Difficulty value, so the battery remaining will require recalculation every time the player changes the Difficulty setting. Now it makes more sense to track the percent, as it will remain the same regardless of the total time and time remaining.

Let's begin by substituting percentRemaining for batteryRemaining in a few places.

1. Open the GameMisc script.

2. In the LevelPrep function, change the levelManager.batteryRemaining line to

   ```
   levelManager.percentRemaining = batteryHealth.percentRemaining;
   ```

3. Save the script.

4. In the BatteryHealth script, set the percentRemaining variable to internal:

   ```
   internal int percentRemaining = 100; // remaining battery life in percent
   ```

5. Create the new function to calculate the battery charge:

   ```
   public void UpdateBatteryLife (float newBatteryFull, int newPercentRemaining) {
       percentRemaining = newPercentRemaining;
       batteryFull = newBatteryFull;
       batteryRemaining = (batteryFull * percentRemaining * .01f);

   }
   ```

6. Save the script.

7. In the LevelManager script, change the `batteryRemaining` variable to

   ```
   internal int percentRemaining; // % of battery remaining
   ```

8. In the `ManageLevels` function, move the `Find("Battery Life")` line to just below the `GameObject.Find("Gnomatic Garden Defender")` line

9. Below that, add the following:

   ```
   // update full battery value, use inverse, add offset
   float newBattery = (150f * difficulty * .1f) + 25f;
   batteryHealth.UpdateBatteryLife(newBattery,percentRemaining);
   ```

The player can change the battery life before the game has started running, so the code identifying the Battery Health component is moved earlier in the function so it is useful in both places where the component is accessed. The equation that calculates the new battery life value uses the base amount, 150, times the difficulty, multiplies it to get the percent, and then adds the 25-second offset.

The `batteryRemaining` value will now be recalculated in the function, so you must comment out or remove the original line.

1. Under the `// manage battery HUD` line, comment out or remove the `batteryRemaining` line:

   ```
   // batteryHealth.batteryRemaining = batteryRemaining;
   ```

2. Save the script, and save the scene.

3. Click Play from the Start menu, and then increase the difficulty to the full amount.

4. Enter the garden, and watch the battery charge drop quickly.

5. Press the F1 key to access the Main menu, select the Settings menu, and set the Difficulty to the lowest setting.

6. Get back into the game.

The battery life remaining should be the same, but the rate at which it drops should now be much slower.

7. Play again from the start, and set the Difficulty to the easiest setting.

8. Go into the garden, and wait for the first zombie-bunny drop.

The time, completing the task may take longer, but the zombie bunnies multiply just as quickly as they did before. There's several things you could do to make the game easier. You could decrease the number of zombie bunnies that can appear, increase the time between drops, or increase the time before the first drop. The most noticeable option would be to use the `difficulty` value to adjust the time between drops.

1. At the bottom of the SpawnBunnies script's `StartReproducing` function, change the `StartCoroutine(StartReproducing(reproRate))` line to the following:

    ```
    if (levelManager) StartCoroutine(StartReproducing(reproRate +
    levelManager.difficulty));
    else StartCoroutine(StartReproducing(reproRate));
    ```

Once again, you are checking for the LevelManager before accessing it. The `else` clause allows you to test the level directly without going through the Start menu. You will, of course, have to find and assign the LevelManager before you can test the code.

2. Add the variable:

    ```
    LevelManager levelManager; // the script that holds the data between levels
    ```

3. Find it in the Start function:

    ```
    if(GameObject.Find("Level Manager")) {
        levelManager = GameObject.Find("Level Manager").GetComponent<LevelManager>();
    }
    ```

4. Save the script, and test from the StartMenu scene.

The zombie-bunny drops may be a bit too fast yet for the "easy" setting because of the randomization of the time between drops. This is another place where you can use the difficulty value to affect game play.

5. At the top of the `StartReproducing` function, change the `float adjustedTime = Random.Range` line to the following:

    ```
    // wait for this much time before going on
    float adjustedTime;
    if (levelManager) adjustedTime = Random.Range(minTime, minTime +
    levelManager.difficulty);
    else adjustedTime = Random.Range(minTime, minTime + 5f);
    ```

6. Save the script, and play through from the StartMenu level.

The zombie-bunny drops are better behaved for the different difficulty settings.

The last little task is to re-instate is the occlusion culling. Any object with the HideAtStart script will require its state to be saved and handled by the LevelManager any time the player is entering or leaving the garden level. The LevelManager only has to store a Boolean value.

7. Open the GardenLevel1 scene.

8. In the GameMisc script, add the following variable:

    ```
    public GameObject[] hideShows; // the objects that are affected by occlusion culling
    ```

9. In the `LevelPrep` function, inside the `if(levelManager)` conditional, add

```
// send the hide/show areas' current active states off to be stored
for (int x = 0 ; x < hideShows.Length ; x++) {
    levelManager. areaVisibility [x] = hideShows[x].activeSelf;
}
```

10. And create the function the LevelManager will call to set the objects' active state:

```
public void LoadVis () {
    // retrieve the hide/show areas' current states and apply them
    for (int x = 0 ; x < hideShows.Length ; x++) {
        hideShows[x].SetActive(levelManager. areaVisibility [x]);
    }
}
```

11. Save the script.

The rest of the code is added to the LevelManager script.

1. In the LevelManager script, add the following variable:

```
public bool[] areaVisibility; // active state of the garden areas
```

2. In the `ManageLevels` function, directly below the `if (currentLevel > 3)` line, add the following:

```
// set the occlusion areas' visibility
GameObject.Find("Game Manager").GetComponent<GameMisc>().LoadVis();
```

3. Save the script.

With the code in place in both scripts, you can fill in the new parameters.

1. In the Game Manager's Game Misc component, set the Size of the new array to **5** and load each of the objects affected by the occlusion culling system into it (Figure 10-45).

Figure 10-45. The areas affected by occlusion culling added to the Hide Show array

2. Enable the HideAtStart components on the objects you added to the Game Misc component's Hide Shows array.

3. Save the scene, and open the StartMenu scene.

4. In the Inspector, set the Level Manager's new Area Visibility's array Size to 5;

5. Save the scene and click Play, watching the areas' visibility in the Scene view as you go between levels and menus.

There are obviously lots of refinements that could make the game better for game play, visual effect, and stability, but as most real-life projects have a time or budget limitation, now would be a good place to stop and consider the current version of the game as "finished."

Final Build

With the game in a relatively "finished" state, it's time to revisit the Player settings and then do an almost-final build. There are a lot of settings that can be adjusted, but most are better left as advanced topics.

1. From the Assets menu, Project Settings, select Player.

2. At the top of the Inspector, set Company name to **Gnomatic Solutions**.

3. The Product name should already be Garden Defender.

4. For Default Icon, click Select and locate the GnomeIcon image.

5. In the "Resolution and Presentation" section, open the Supported Aspect Ratio section and uncheck all but 16:9.

6. In the Splash Image section, select ConfigBanner for the Config Dialog Banner.

The image used for the splash/config banner should be 432 x 163. It can be smaller, but not larger. If you do not have Unity Pro, you can manually replace the default image for the Windows exe by locating it in the game's _data folder. Its name is ScreenSelector.bmp.

Before saving the project, you will have to return to the garden level and set the Stop Pop X value back down to 1.

1. Open the GardenLevel1 scene.

2. In the Game Manager, Score Keeper component, set the Stop Pop X parameter back to **1**.

3. Save the scene, and save the Project.

4. From Files, select Build Settings.

5. Click Build And Run.

6. Find a suitable location for the last build, and name it **TheGardenDefender**.

7. Select Windowed at the Config Dialogue splash screen, select your favorite screen size and quality, and click Play (Figure 10-46).

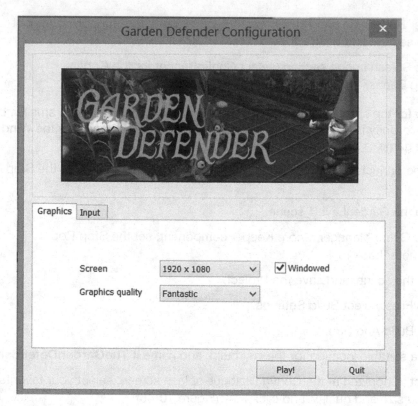

Figure 10-46. The Configuration dialog screen

With the aspect ratio restricted, you may notice that the game cannot be maximized. Also note that the name on the title bar of the window is Garden Defender, the Product name. All in all, however, you now have a quite respectable mini-game. There are, of course, any number of refinements and improvements that could be made. A few choice features will be added in Chapter 11, the "bonus" chapter.

Summary

In this chapter, you delved into the basics of the UnityGUI system for putting 2D text and control elements on screen. You began by putting a rather large text message across the 3D scene to mark the end of the game and added a couple of buttons to allow the player to quit or play again. Application.Quit, you discovered, doesn't work in the editor or in a browser without some special editor code. You also learned that the solely scripted UnityGUI doesn't adjust to the screen size unless scripted to do so.

With the help of GUI Skins, you were able to set up a template for font and control elements that added continuity to your GUI. In doing so, you learned that you could create your own template "Styles" that you could use to override those that were automatically assigned to your control elements. The template styles, you found, contained parameters that were not necessarily used for every GUI control.

When dealing with the Label element, you discovered that you could override the font on an individual level. If it was a dynamic font (where it was handled by the OS), you could even change its size. Other parameters of note dealt with its wrap type, offsets, and other useful options. With the addition of button elements , you discovered how you could define a border size that allowed the interior of the image to be stretched while preserving the outer corners.

Next you created several scenes or levels that functioned solely as menus. You got a chance to combine 2D, both sprite and UnityGUI, and 3D elements to create a start screen that provided a bit of back-story for the game, along with instructions for navigation and weaponry. Making use of Mecanim for some tab-type animation, you discovered that to register mouse events, an object, whether 2D or 3D, requires a collider.

With a handful of levels to navigate between, you then set up the logic and scripting that allowed the player to access the menus or levels during game play. The mainstay of level hopping, `DontDestroyOnLoad`, you found, either required scripting to prevent duplicate objects or had to be carried through into each level on its own. With the levels on their way to behaving themselves, you added them to the build, getting some practice with re-arranging their order, and you were consequently able to move back and forth between scenes during runtime.

Returning to your Settings menu, you added a couple of very simple player settings through the use of sliders. You allowed the player to adjust the volume on any audio components that were tagged as "Ambient," and you allowed the player to set the difficulty of the game. You did this through adjusting the life of the battery and the frequency of the zombie-bunny drops. Throughout the process, you handily dealt with little issues that cropped up.

Finally, you returned to the Player Settings, where you made some executive decisions on the Player's options, added a new game icon and configuration dialog image, and did a final build. After being able to play through the final game and, hopefully, giving yourself a pat on the back for a job well done, you have probably already come up with a list of improvements, refinements, and extra functionality.

Bonus Features

With your game in a "finished" state, you may occasionally have the opportunity to add a few of those missing details that got cut due to time or budget. In this chapter, you will revisit Mecanim to give your Gnomatic Garden Defender another weapon to fight the zombie-bunny hordes, bring the electric slug in as a power-up, and introduce a means of locating that last pesky zombie bunny required to win the game. You will begin with the feature that will most help the player to finish the game.

Creating a Zombie-Bunny Locator

While testing the game during its various stages of completion, you have undoubtedly discovered that the last one or two zombie bunnies can be difficult to find. You probably checked the Hierarchy view for the clones to make sure the count remaining was correct. And after a few more sweeps of the garden, you may even have resorted to checking the Scene view from a top projection to locate the miscreants. About that time, it probably occurred to you how nice it would be to allow the player to have a bird's eye view of the garden as well.

Fortunately, creating that type of functionality is fairly straightforward. A new camera and some more layer control will help you on your way.

Spy Map

With Unity Pro, you can render a camera view to texture, enabling you to create security cameras that play on in-game monitors. A simple HUD-type display, however, requires only a camera and a new layer.

1. From Edit, Project Settings, Editor, set the Default Behavior Mode back to 3D.

2. Open the GardenLevel1 scene.

3. In the Scene view, toggle off 2D and arrange a top iso view to get a good view of the garden.

4. Create a new camera, and name it **Camera Spy View**.

5. Remove its Audio Listener component.

6. From the GameObject menu, use Align With View.

7. Set the Projection to Orthographic and the Size to about **7.7** so the walls are clipped about halfway on the top and bottom (Figure 11-1)

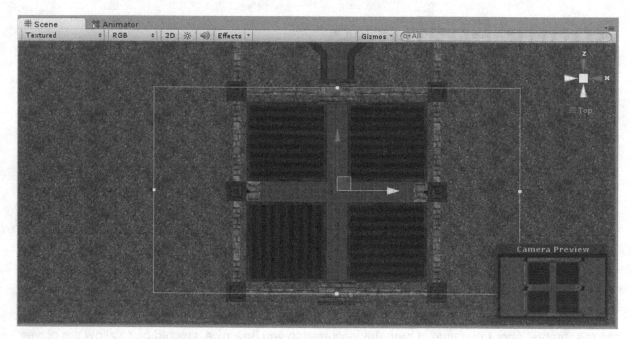

Figure 11-1. The Camera Spy View clipping the walls at top and bottom

To fit the camera on screen over the regular view, you will have to adjust a few more of its parameters.

8. Set the Clear Flags to Solid Color, and set the Background color to black.

To make things easier to see, you will adjust the camera's far clipping plane. The most common place for the zombie bunnies to hide is between the walls and raised beds. By clipping the camera bounds to not include the ground, the natural camouflage of the zombie bunnies is no longer in play.

1. Set its Y position to **40**.

2. Set the Far Clipping Plane to **50**, and then slowly decrease it until the ground and bottom of the tower basins are no longer rendered, about 39.75 (Figure 11-2).

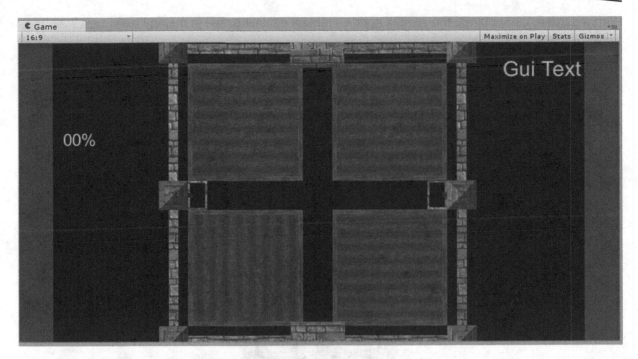

Figure 11-2. The Camera's Far Clipping Plane adjusted

To fit the camera's view on screen in a less obtrusive manner, you will be adjusting its Viewport Rect. The location and size values are all given as a percent of screen, where 1 is 100% of the screen. Let's locate the spy view in the lower right of the screen.

3. Set the W to **0.28** and the H to **0.5**.

4. Set the X position to **0.7** and the Y to **0.03**.

5. Turn off the GUILayer component.

The Main Camera's Depth is -1, but the Camera GUI's depth is the default 0. To keep the 2D zombie bunnies from bouncing across it, you can set the Camera Spy View's Depth to a higher number so it will be drawn last.

6. Set the Camera Spy View's Depth to **1**.

7. Disable the GardenLevel1's HideAtStart component.

8. Click Play, and test.

9. Exit Play mode.

If you were to allow the player to change the aspect ratio of the game window, you would have to calculate the W value when the window changed. In this case, because you have specified the aspect ratio, you will not have to script any adjustments.

With a garden full of plants, the zombie bunnies remain difficult to see in the spy view.

1. Exit Play mode, create a new Layer, and name it **Hide from Spy**.

2. Select the Camera Spy View, and uncheck Hide From Spy in its Culling Mask list.

3. In the Prefabs, Plants folder, assign the "Hide from Spy" layer to each of the plant prefabs.

4. Click Play.

The zombie bunnies are much easier to spot (Figure 11-3).

Figure 11-3. The plants are no longer rendered by the Camera Spy View

Unfortunately, it is possible for sneaky little critters to be missed by the spy cam's clipping plane if they are on the terrain ground and on their side. Rather than trying to fine-tune the clipping plane, it might be more fun to try a different approach. You will repurpose the slug's particle system and tailor it to show in the spy map.

1. Exit Play mode.

2. Drag the Slug prefab into the scene, and drag the SlugSlime out of it.

3. Agree to losing the prefab, and then delete the Slug.

4. Rename the SlugSlime to **ZB Spot**.

5. Drag it into the middle of the garden so you will eventually be able to see it in the spy map.

6. In the Inspector, set its Start Size to **3** and its Gravity Multiplier to **-5** (so it moves up into the clipping plane).

7. Set the Max Particles to **1**, open the Shape rollout, and set its Box Z to **0.1**.

The particle should now be pulsing happily in the middle of the spy view (Figure 11-4).

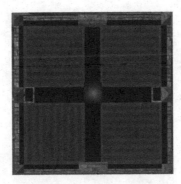

Figure 11-4. The repurposed particle system in the spy map

8. Drag a zombie-bunny prefab Into the Scene view, and position it at the new particle system (Figure 11-5).

Figure 11-5. The zombie-bunny prefab at the ZB Spot

9. Drag the ZB Spot onto the ZombieBunny in the Hierarchy view.

10. Select the ZombieBunny and at the top of the Inspector, and click Apply to update the prefab.

11. Delete the prefab from the scene.

12. Click Play, and drive the Gnomatic Garden Defender into the garden.

The zombie bunnies fill the spy map looking like little glow bugs (Figure 11-6).

Figure 11-6. The zombie bunnies clearly visible in the spy map

The problem is, of course, that the glow planes can be seen rising up in the regular view. Once again, you can create a layer to control which objects are rendered.

1. Exit Play mode.

2. Create a new layer, and name it **Spy View Only**.

3. In the Project view, assign the new layer to the ZombieBunny prefab's ZB Spot object.

4. In the Main Camera's Culling mask, uncheck Spy View Only.

5. Click Play, and test.

This time the particle systems appear only in the spy map.

If you have played down to one zombie bunny a few times, you are probably thinking it would be nice if it was easier to see which direction the Gnomatic Garden Defender is pointing. You've already got a layer set up, so it will be easy to add an arrow to the top of the Gnomatic Garden Defender that renders only in the spy map. And what could be more appropriate than a nice red cone shape?

1. Focus the Scene view on the Gnomatic Garden Defender.

2. From the Chapter 11 Assets folder, import the Gnome Arrow asset into the Imported Assets folder in the Hierarchy view.

3. Under Rig, set its Animation Type to None and click Apply.

4. Drag the new asset into the Hierarchy view, and use "Move to view" to center it on the Gnomatic Garden Defender.

5. Rotate the arrow to align it in the proper direction (Figure 11-7).

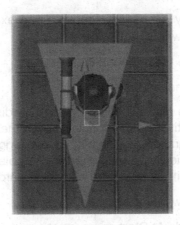

Figure 11-7. The gnome's arrow

6. Raise the arrow's Y Position until it clears the gnome's hat.

7. Uncheck Cast Shaddows and Receive Shadows.

8. Assign it to the Spy View Only Layer.

9. Add the arrow to the Gnomatic Garden Defender object in the Hierarchy view.

10. Click Play, and test.

Now there is no doubt about the direction the Gnomatic Garden Defender is facing (Figure 11-8).

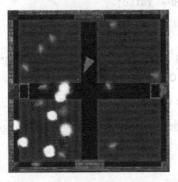

Figure 11-8. The Gnomatic Garden Defender at work as seen from the spy map

In this game, because it is being developed for desktop deployment, you may not have seen a drop in frame rate with the addition of the Camera Spy View. It is always worth considering ways to optimize your game, even when not entirely necessary.

1. In the Prefabs folder, assign the Gnomatic Garden Defender object, the ZombieBunny's ZombieBunny child, and the Toasted Zombie to the Hide From Spy layer. Agree to adding it to the children when prompted.

2. Update the Gnomatic Garden Defender prefab using Apply on the one in the Hierarchy view to add the arrow to the prefab.

3. Assign the Hide From Spy layer to the Smoke, Small explosion2, and PotatoAmmo prefabs as well.

4. Save the scene, and save the project.

5. Open the StartMenu Scene, and play through.

The newly added spy map helps the player reach his goal of eradicating the zombie horde, but it probably shouldn't be visible the entire game, especially when the garden is hidden. You could set it (the Camera component) to hide and show with a keyboard toggle, just as you did with the main menu. Or you could have it automatically appear when the zombie bunny count dropped to, say, 5. By putting it in the Garden 1 group, it will be visible only if the garden area is visible.

1. Drag the Camera Spy View into the Garden 1 group.

2. Enable the Garden 1's Hide At Start component again.

3. Open the ScoreKeeper script.

4. Add the following variable:

```
public Camera cameraSpyView; // the spy map camera
```

5. In the UpdateCount function, below the if (currentBunCount == 0) conditional, add

```
// show spy map
if (currentBunCount <= 5) cameraSpyView.enabled = true;
else cameraSpyView.enabled = false;
```

6. Save the script.

7. Back in the GardenLevel1 scene, assign the Camera spy View in the Game Manager's Score Keeper component.

If the garden has been secured, you can hide the spy map.

8. In the GardenSecure function, below the TriggerMessage line, add

```
cameraSpyView.enabled = false;
```

9. Save the script.

10. Disable the Camera Spy View's Camera component, and save the scene.

11. Return to the StartMenu scene, and play through.

The spy map functionality adds to the game with a nominal amount of effort. There are, of course, lots of options as to how it could have been handled. One variation could allow the player to toggle the map on and off, but increase the battery drain while it is being displayed.

Adding a Power-Up

You were probably wondering if the electric slug would ever make an appearance showing off his neon slime. In this section, you will use what will be a rare occurrence to give the player a chance to replenish his battery life in the heat of the battle.

1. Open the GardenLevel1 scene, and drag the Slug prefab into the Staging Area in the Scene view.

2. Arrange it so that it faces the doorway to the garden, approximately a meter or so in front of the door.

3. Click Play to make sure it heads into the garden (Figure 11-9).

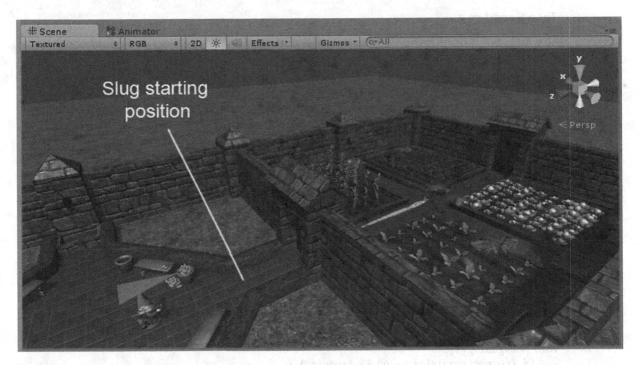

Figure 11-9. The slug streaking through the garden

4. Stop Play mode.

You could easily update the prefab to store the new transform and save yourself some scripting. On the other hand, if you had more than one garden or level, it would be better to be able to instantiate it at a given location.

5. Focus the Scene view to the slug.

6. Create a new empty gameObject, and name it **Slug Start**.

7. Copy the Slug's Transform component and Paste Component Values to the Slug Start object's Transform component.

You've seen what the slug does, so now it's time to define its behavior. As usual, there are several different things you could do. If it passed through on a regular basis, its speed might be inversely proportionate to the amount of battery left. The more desperate the player, the faster the slug. Another option would be to have it appear only when the battery dropped below a certain threshold. Before deciding, you should do a test or two. Let's begin by using 1/10th of the percent of battery life for speed, 10%.

1.   Open the slug's Animation Controller, Slug Controller.

2.   Set the Slug Run clip/state to **10**.

3.   Switch to the Scene view, and click Play.

The slug streaks by, leaving only its slime trail. A setting of 1/25th might be more realistic.

4.   Try a Speed of **4**.

It's also pretty fast, but it does have a pause near the middle of the garden, so you *could* consider that the top speed.

5.   Set the Speed back to **1**.

With either option, the action will be based on the battery's percent remaining, so it might be a good idea to plan on instantiating the slug from the BatteryHealth script.

6.   Open the BatteryHealth script, and add the following variables:

```
public GameObject slug;      // the slug prefab
public Transform slugDrop; // this could be updated to the current zone
bool running;                // flag for active slug
```

7.   In the Update function, inside the if (batteryRemaining clause, at the bottom, add the following:

```
ManageSlug(); // check to see if the slug should make a run
```

8.   Create the new function:

```
void ManageSlug(){
    if (percentRemaining == 90 && !running) {
        Instantiate (slug,slugDrop.localPosition, slugDrop.localRotation);
        running = true;
    }
}
```

9.   Save the script.

10.   For the Battery Life object, assign the Slug prefab from the Project view to the Slug parameter and the Slug Start object to the Slug Drop parameter.

In case the slug escapes the garden before being hit, you will have to set it to be destroyed when its run is finished. If it is hit, its Slug Hit state/clip will be triggered.

1. Select the Slug in the Hierarchy view, and open the Animation view (Ctrl+6) to inspect its read-only Slug Run clip.

2. Zoom out on the tracks until you have about 7 seconds showing, and then turn on the record button and scrub the time indicator.

Watching the Scene view while scrubbing the time indicator, you can see that 6 seconds will give the slug plenty of time to get through the garden.

3. Close the Animation editor.

4. Create a new C# script in the Game Scripts folder, and name it **SlugManager**.

5. Add the following variables:

```
BatteryHealth batteryHealth; // the script
public float life = 6f;      // time to go through the garden
```

6. In the Start function, "find" the BatteryLife script and start the timer with a coroutine:

```
// Use this for initialization
void Start () {
    batteryHealth = GameObject.Find("Battery Life").GetComponent<BatteryHealth>();
    StartCoroutine (TimedDestroy()); // start timer for auto destroy
}
```

7. Add the coroutine:

```
IEnumerator TimedDestroy () {
    yield return new WaitForSeconds(life);
    DestroySlug();
}
```

The destroy gets called separately because it will also be changing the running flag in the BatteryHealth script in case you want more than one run, and it will also get called if the slug is hit.

8. Create the DestroySlug function:

```
void DestroySlug () {
    batteryHealth.running = false;
    Destroy(gameObject);
}
```

9. Save the script.

The console reports that the running variable is not accessible due to its protection level. You will have to make a small change.

10.   In the BatteryHealth script, change the bool running line to

```
internal bool running; // flag for active slug
```

11.   Save the script.

12.   Drag the SlugManager script onto the Slug prefab in the Project view.

13.   Click Play, and watch the Scene view to make sure the slug is destroyed after it has left the garden (Figure 11-10).

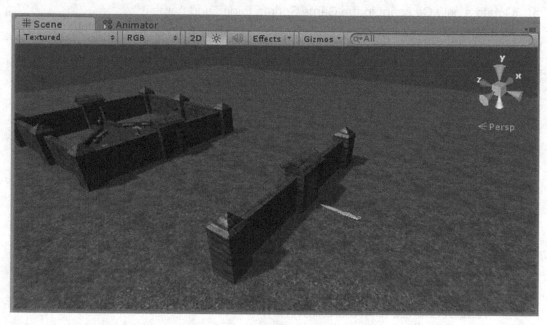

Figure 11-10. The slug clear of the garden, just before it is destroyed

14.   Select the Slug in the Hierarchy view, and in the Inspector, click Apply to update the Slug prefab. Then delete it from the Hierarchy view.

15.   Click Play, and drive the Gnomatic Garden Defender into the garden.

The slug zips through the scene when the battery has reached 90%.

Before refining the slug triggering mechanism, you will want to set it up for a hit by the potato gun. When hit, it will go into its Slug Hit clip/state before it is deleted, so you will use another coroutine.

1.   Add the following to the SlugManager script:

```
void OnCollisionEnter (Collision collision) {
    if (collision.transform.tag == "Ammo") {
        StartCoroutine (HitDestroy()); // if it was tagged as Ammo,
process its destruction
    }
}
```

If you check the PotatoAmmo prefab, you will see that it is tagged as Ammo.

2. Add the coroutine:

```
IEnumerator HitDestroy () {
    GetComponent<Animator>().Play("Slug Hit");
    audio.Play(); // play death fx
    yield return new WaitForSeconds(1);
    // reset battery
    DestroySlug();
}
```

3. Save the script.

4. Add an Audio Source component to the Slug prefab in the Project view, and assign the SlugZap audio clip to it.

5. Uncheck Play On Awake.

6. Click Play, drive the Gnomatic Garden Defender into the garden, and try to shoot the slug as it goes through.

The slug jumps into the air when hit, accompanied by a nice high-voltage crackle.

Once the slug is hit, you will want to refresh the charge on the battery.

7. In the SlugManager, under the //reset battery line, add the following:

```
batteryHealth.batteryRemaining = batteryHealth.batteryFull;
```

8. Save the script.

9. Click Play, and test.

The battery is recharged.

To set it to full each time is probably too easy, especially as you will be setting the slug to run through when the charge is a lot lower.

1. Change the line to

```
batteryHealth.batteryRemaining = batteryHealth.batteryFull / 2; // half charge
```

2. Save the script.

3. In the BatteryHealth script, add a new variable:

```
int slugTime; // battery % to cue the slug
```

4. In the Start function, add

```
slugTime = Random.Range(30,10);
```

5.   Add the same line in the ManageSlug function under the running = true line.

6.   Change the 90 in the SlugManager conditional to slugTime:

```
if (percentRemaining == slugTime && !running) {
```

7.   Save the script, and save the scene.

8.   Play through from the StartMenu scene, and test.

The player is now given a reprieve when the zombie bunnies have gotten out of hand.

Feel free to experiment with the functionality. You may decide that the battery should be reset only once, so you can comment out the line that resets the battery in the SlugManager script. Or you may want to experiment with multiple runs and variable speeds. To adjust the speed of the Slug clips, you would set animator.speed for the slug's animator component.

Upgrading the Armaments

In this final section, you will be revisiting Mecanim for a look at custom masking. You may remember that one of the animation clips opens the gnome's hat to expose what looks to be a laser beam device. Once the ability to do so is added to the game, you will be adding the beam through the very useful physics raycast functionality.

Mecanim Masks and Layers

Masks let you isolate parts of the character and control them with different animation clips. To activate a layer, you generally create a Parameter (which is essentially a variable), in the state engine and call it from a script. Let's start by defining a mask.

1.   Open the GardenLevel1 scene.

2.   In the Animated Assets folder's Animator Controllers folder, right-click, and from Create, select Avatar Mask.

3.   Name it **Hat Node Mask**.

4.   In the Inspector, click on Humanoid.

A humanoid body template appears. With humanoids, the bone systems are similar so that masks can be used on any humanoid character. The gnome character doesn't even have bones, so you will make a custom mask from its skeleton.

5.   Close the Humanoid section, and open Transform.

6.   Load the GardenGnomeAvatar in the "Use Skeleton from" field, and then click the Import Skeleton button.

The GardenGnome's hierarchy appears in the panel.

7.   Click the Gnome Motion Root check box to clear the selections, and then click the Hat Node to define the masked parts (Figure 11-11).

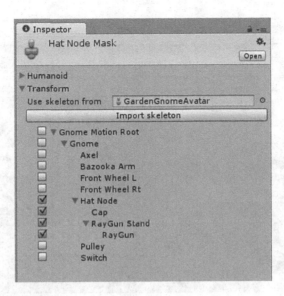

Figure 11-11. Creating the Hat Node Mask

8. Next, double-click the Gnome Controller in the Project view to open the Animator component.

9. In the upper left corner, click the plus sign to the right of Layers to create a new Layer.

10. Name it **Laser**, and select the Hat Node Mask as its Mask (Figure 11-12).

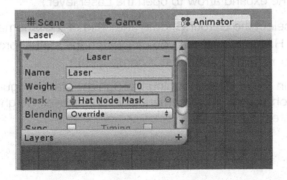

Figure 11-12. The new Laser layer

When you created the new layer, the view changed to it instead of the Base layer. Now you can load the three hat-related states into the layer.

1. Expand the GardenGnome asset in the Project view so you can see the animation clips that you set up in Chapter 6.

2. Drag the Gnome arming, Gnome armed, and Gnome disarming clips into the view to create their states.

3. Create transitions between them (Figure 11-13).

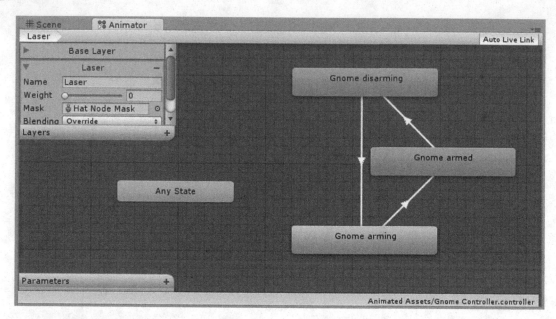

Figure 11-13. The Laser layer states

The default transitions, if you remember, are set to Exit Time. As soon as the clip is nearly finished, the transition to the next state is triggered.

4. Switch to the 2 x 3 Layout, or tear off the Animator view so you can see it and the Game view at the same time. (You may have to open the Animator view again and click the expand arrow to open the Laser layer.)

5. Click Play, and select the GardenGnome (the child of the Gnomatic Garden Defender) in the Hierarchy view so you can watch the states' progress bars. (The GardenGnome holds the Animator component.)

The progress can be seen in the Animator looping through the states (Figure 11-14), but to see the layer in action in the viewport you will have to manually set the layer Weight to 1 to fully override the Base layer's current states.

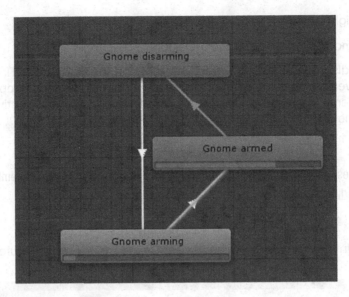

Figure 11-14. The Laser layer's states at runtime

6. In the Laser layer, set the Weight to **1**.

Now the Hat Node mask overrides the Base layer states for its objects only (the Hat Node and its children), and the armed animations play through. Because the Gnome Armed clip is so short, it is almost always being blended with another state during the transition. It will require something more than the Exit Time in some of the transitions, but for now, you can use Mute to see the animations better.

1. Select the transition from Gnome armed to Gnome disarming, and mute it (upper left in the Inspector (Figure 11-15).

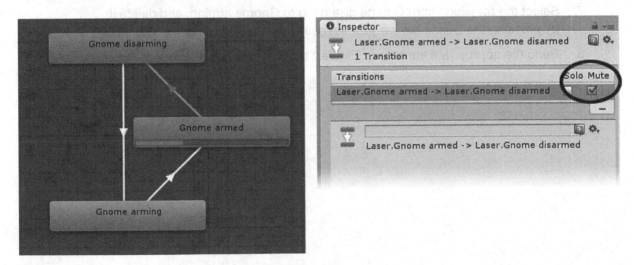

Figure 11-15. Muting a transition—the red arrow indicates the muted transition

2. Set the Weight back to 1 in the Laser layer.

3. Stop Play mode, and un-mute the transition.

Muting the armed-to-disarming transition effectively turns off the default Exit Time condition so that the armed state is never left after it is entered. There are a couple of things happening here that require some adjustment. To begin with, the whole sequence should not be activated until you are ready for it. To implement that functionality, you will be adding an Empty state.

> **Tip**   Making changes to the Transitions will set the layer Weight back to 0. Always remember to check the value after making adjustments.

4. Right-click in the Animator view, and select Create State, Empty (Figure 11-16).

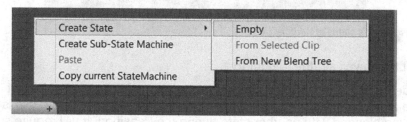

Figure 11-16. Creating an empty state

5. Right-click on it and select Set As Default.

6. In the Inspector, name the new state **Closed**.

7. Select the transition from Gnome disarming to Gnome arming, and delete it by pressing the Delete key on your keyboard.

8. Redo the appropriate transitions (Figure 11-17).

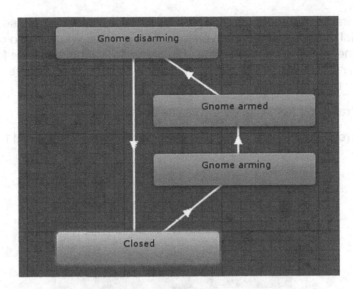

Figure 11-17. The Laser layer states, re-wired for the new empty layer, Closed

To control the entry and exit from the armed state, you will create a Parameter. A Parameter is just a variable that will be used for communication between scripts and the Mecanim state engine.

1. In the lower left corner of the Animator view, click the plus sign to create a new parameter and select Bool (Figure 11-18).

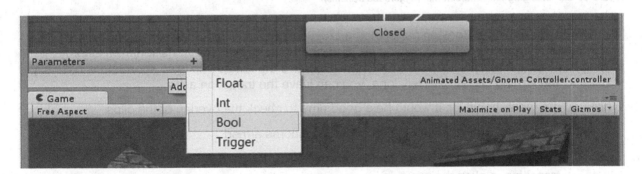

Figure 11-18. Creating a new Parameter

2. Name it **Armed** (Figure 11-19).

Figure 11-19. The new Boolean Parameter

You will access the parameter through scripting via its name, in string format, so the name is not restricted to the normal variable naming conventions. Many times, you will also need to create a matching variable in the script. A good practice is to name the variable and the Mecanim parameter accordingly, e.g., myVariable and "My Variable." With a new parameter in place, you can refine the conditions for some of the transitions.

3.   Select the transition from Closed to Gnome arming.

4.   Click the arrows at the right of Exit Time, and select Armed (Figure 11-20).

Figure 11-20. Changing the condition that triggers the transition

The default value for the Boolean parameter is true, so you are all set on this one. The empty Closed state has no animations to blend, so you are also good to go there. The transition from Gnome arming to Gnome armed is set to use Exit Time. Because the armed clip is so short and is basically static and the arming clip is relatively long, you can leave the transition as is.

While you are there, however, it would be a good time to check the overlap of the clips.

5.   Select the Transition for Gnome arming to Gnome armed.

6.   Scrub the time indicator in the Preview window to assure yourself that the transition is okay the way it is.

7.   Next, select the transition from Gnome armed to Gnome disarming.

8.   Set the Condition for this one to Armed and false (Figure 11-21).

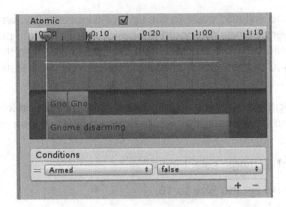

Figure 11-21. The condition for the Gnome armed-to-Gnome disarming transition

9. Click Play in the preview to see the transition.

The Gnome disarming-to-Closed transition is already set to trigger on Exit Time, so it requires no extra attention.

With the new conditions set, you can test the functionality manually through the Animator view.

1. Click Play, and set the Laser layer's Weight to **1**.

The progress bar loops happily in the Closed state.

2. Set the Armed parameter to on or true.

The hat opens and the laser is raised. The progress now loops through the armed state. Because of the mask, the rest of the gnome is animated using the Base layer states.

3. Click the Base Layer bar in the upper left of the Animator to view its progress.

4. Click the Laser layer to return to it, and uncheck the Armed parameter.

5. Watch as the progress heads up to the Gnome disarming state and then down to the Closed state once the clip has finished.

6. Stop Play mode.

You are probably thinking it would be pretty handy to be able to control the arming/disarming sequence with a key press. You are also probably wondering how all of this ties together with the scripting, so now is a good time to create a script to make use of Mecanim's functionality.

7. In the Game Scripts folder, create a new C# script and name it **LaserController**.

8. Open it, and add the following variables beneath the class declaration:

```
Animator animator; // var to hold the animator component
```

9. In the Start function, add the following to assign the Animator component:

```
animator = GetComponent <Animator>(); // assign the object's animator component
```

To check for player input, you will add code to the Update function. This way, the engine is checking for input from the Player every frame. You could check for a specific key press as you did to open the main menu, but that could become ambiguous if the player mapped the same key to any of the functionality already assigned in the Input Manager. Instead, you will create two custom virtual Input keys.

While it would be nice to toggle the armed state off and on with a single key, the code to prevent immediate retriggering of the opposite state gets tedious so you will keep things simple with a two key system.

1. From Edit, Project Settings, select Input.

2. Open the Axes, and set the Size to **16**.

3. Rename the duplicate Jump to **Arm**.

4. Set the Descriptive name to "Press to arm laser."

This will appear in the Player Preferences dialogue that will appear at the start of the game.

5. Set the Positive button to 1, the 1 key on the keyboard (Figure 11-22). If you prefer the 1 key from the keypad, use [1].

6. Set the Axes the Size to **17**, and repeat the process to create a `Disarm` input that uses the 2 key (Figure 11-22).

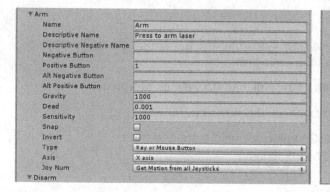 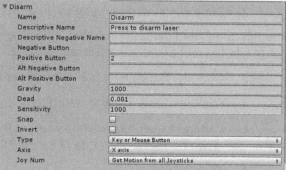

Figure 11-22. The new virtual inputs

7. Back in the LaserController script, add the following to the Update function:

```
if (animator) { // check for its existance first
    if(Input.GetButtonUp("Arm")) OpenHat ();
    if(Input.GetButtonUp("Disarm")) CloseHat ();
} // end if animator
```

8. Create the two functions that change the clips:

```
public void OpenHat () {
    animator.SetBool("Armed", true);
}

public void CloseHat () {
    animator.SetBool("Armed", false);
}
```

The first line checks for the existence of the Animator component. The next two lines wait for an on key up event from the virtual keys you created earlier. If a key press is detected and *finished*, the function is called that tells the Animator to toggle the parameter on that triggers the Gnome arming animation. The arming state goes directly into the Gnome armed state when it has finished. If you wanted to trigger a weapon firing, you would use GetButtonDown or GetKeyDown where the message is sent at the *start* of the action rather than the end. The animator parameter changes are sent from their own functions so that they can be triggered by events other than key presses, which is also why the little functions are marked as `public`.

9. Save the script.

10. Drag it onto the GardenGnome object (where the Animator component resides).

11. Make sure the Weight of the Laser layer is set to **1**.

12. Click Play, and press the 1 key to trigger the arming sequence.

13. Press the 2 key to disarm and close the hat.

14. Update the Gnomatic Garden Defender prefab.

As a fail-safe for the Weight value resetting to 0 after an adjustment, you can add it to the script to avoid having to remember to set it to 1 every time you make adjustments to the transitions.

A search of the Unity community will tell you that the Weight assignment is also lost if the Animator component is deactivated and reactivated. The community also suggests that using `OnEnable` rather than `Start` is the best place to put the code. `OnEnable` is evaluated before `Start`, so you will have to identify the animator there as well. The bug may have been fixed by now, but it certainly won't hurt to use `OnEnable` just in case.

1. Create the `OnEnable` function as follows:

```
void OnEnable () {
    if (animator.layerCount >=2) { // if there is more than one layer...
        // set the Laser layer's weight to 1, (base layer is index 0, so Laser is 1)
        animator.SetLayerWeight(1, 1f); // layer index, weight
    }
}
```

2. Move the `animator=` line from the `Start` function to the top of the `OnEnable` function.

3. Save the script.

4. Set the Weight to **0**, click Play, and test to make sure everything still works.

The weight goes to 1 as soon as you click Play.

Creating a Laser Beam

With the "mechanical" bit in place, it's time to create a laser beam graphic. For this, you will be using a Line Renderer component. The beam length will be controlled with scripting.

1. Hold the Alt key, and select the GardenGnome to expand it in the Hierarchy view.

2. Deactivate the Cap and the Gnome Arrow.

3. In the Scene view, focus in on the Raygun and create a new Empty GameObject.

4. Name it **Laser Point**.

5. Position it at the front of the RayGun mesh, and in Local coordinates, make sure its Z points forward (Figure 11-23).

Figure 11-23. The new Laser Point object in place

6. Drag and drop it onto the RayGun object in the Hierarchy view.

7. From Component, Effects, add a Line Renderer component to the Laser Point object.

8. Uncheck Use World Space.

The magenta-colored line (a simple quad by default) appears at the Laser Point (Figure 11-24).

Figure 11-24. *The Line Renderer Component (seen in Textured Wire display)*

9. Under the Parameters section, set the Line Renderer's Start Width and End Width to **0.05** (Figure 11-25).

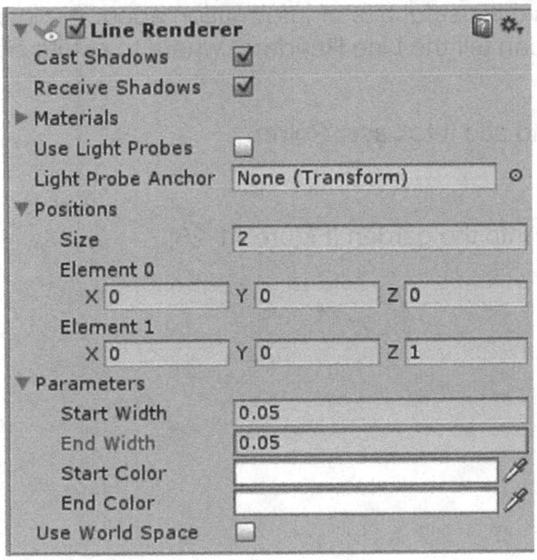

Figure 11-25. *The adjusted Line Renderer width*

The length is specified with the Size elements. Element 0 is at a 0 offset from the parent, Laser Point. Element 2 will also be at an offset, but it will be set by scripting.

Creating the Beam

To control the laser beam, you will be using Physics.Raycast.

1. Do a quick search for physics.raycast in the Scripting Reference.

The (overload) version you will be using begins with a location, uses a direction, and then checks for an intersection with anything with a collider within the specified range.

2. Create a new C# Script in the Game Scripts folder, and name it **LaserBeam**.

3. Open the new script, and add the following variable:

```
int range = 30; // the distance to check within
```

4. Inside the Update function, add

```
// Did we hit anything?
RaycastHit hit; // holds some of the object properties that are detected with the raycast
if (Physics.Raycast (transform.position, transform.forward, out hit, range)) {
    Vector3 pos = new Vector3(0, 0,hit.distance);     // create the new end value
    //update end position
    GetComponent<LineRenderer>().SetPosition (1,pos); // also on the Laser Point
}
```

Take a minute to read the comments.

5. Look up RaycastHit in the Scripting Reference.

You can see that it stores several useful bits of information about the intersection. The first one you will need is *distance* so you can tell the Line Renderer where to set its element 1 x, y, and z location in a Vector3 format.

6. Save the script, and add it to Laser Point.

7. Click Play.

The laser "beam" shoots out into the garden (Figure 11-26).

Figure 11-26. The laser beam projected into the garden

8. Turn the Gnomatic Garden Defender around.

9. Try raising and lowering the laser with the 1 and 2 keys.

The beam goes up and down with the device, but the device itself does not *rotate* up and down like the gnome's arm. Just as with the Arm Group, the RayGun will require a MouseLook component.

1. Exit Play mode, and select the Arm Group.

2. Right-click over its Mouse Look component label, and select Copy Component.

3. Select the RayGun, right-click over any of its component labels, and select "Paste Component as New."

4. Click Play, raise the device, and test the mobility.

This time, the beam is fully mobile within the ranges already set in the original MouseLook. The only problem is that the beam can intersect the base of the cap (Figure 11-27).

Figure 11-27. The laser beam intersecting the hat base

5. In the RayGun's Mouse Look component, Decrease the Minimum Y until the beam no longer intersects the cap base, somewhere around **-35**.

6. Stop Play mode, and make the change permanent.

Now would be a good time to address another little detail. Currently, the top of the cap is deactivated. The problem is, of course, that the beam comes through even if it were closed. Obviously, you will want to turn it off and on to coincide with the Gnome armed state. It should only be *on* during the Gnome armed state.

There are a lot of ways you could implement this functionality, but for this task you will be accessing the Animator component's state information.

1. Open the LaserController script.

The script resides on the GardenGnome object where the Animator component is located. It will require access to the Laser Point.

2. Add the following variable:

```
public GameObject laserPoint;
```

3. In the Update function, below the two if (Input lines, add the following:

```
//check for hat state
if(animator.GetCurrentAnimatorStateInfo(1).IsName("Laser.Gnome armed") ) BeamOn();
else BeamOff();
```

Using the GetCurrentAnimatorStateInfo for layer 1 (layer 0 is the base layer), you check to see if the active state is named "Laser.Gnome armed." If it is, you call the little function that activates the Laser Point with its Line Renderer component. If not, you call the function that deactivates it.

4. Add the BeamOn and BeamOff functions:

```
void BeamOn () {
    laserPoint.SetActive(true);
}

void BeamOff () {
    laserPoint.SetActive(false);
}
```

You will also want to make sure the beam is off on startup.

5. Add the following to the Start function:

```
BeamOff();
```

6. Save the script.

7. Select the GardenGnome.

8. Assign the Laser Point object as the Laser Point parameter.

9. Activate the Cap object.

10. Click Play, and try activating and deactivating the laser with the 1 and 2 keys.

The laser behaves correctly.

The beam, however, is not very convincing as a sharp-edged, magenta-colored strip. An animated texture, or more precisely, animated mapping (the offsetting of the UV mapping coordinates), will improve its appearance greatly. Let's begin by creating a material for the Line Renderer.

1. Stop Play mode.

2. From the Chapter 11 Assets folder, Import the SoftEdges texture into the Game Textures folder.

At the beginning of the chapter, you changed the Default Behavior Mode from 2D back to 3D. On the off chance you missed this step, you should double-check the texture's import settings.

3. Make sure it imported as a Texture for its Texture Type.

4. Check out its alpha channel in the Inspector (Figure 11-28).

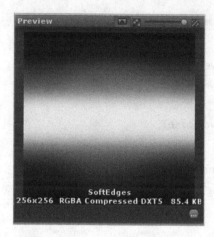

Figure 11-28. The alpha channel of the SoftEdges texture

The texture has a slight flare in the center of the alpha channel.

5. In the Animated Assets, Materials folder, right-click in the Project view and select Create, Material.

6. Name it **Laser Beam**, and assign the Particles, Additive (Soft) shader to it.

7. Assign the SoftEdges texture to it.

8. Assign the new material to the Laser Point object by dragging and dropping it directly onto the object.

9. Select the Laser Point object, and set the shader's Tiling x field to **20**.

The length of the beam will vary as the laser moves around the scene. With a bit of math, you could dynamically adjust the tiling according to length in the LaserBeam script.

The Additive (Soft) shader, as you probably noticed, has no color field. To color your laser beam, you will return to the Line Renderer.

1. In the Line Renderer component's Parameters section, set the Start and End Colors to a classic red color.

2. Click Play, and check out the improvements (Figure 11-29).

Figure 11-29. The improved laser beam

With the addition of the material, the laser beam may be a bit thin.

    3.   Stop Play mode.

    4.   Set the Start Width and End Width to **0.1**.

You may also have noticed that the beam gets darker near the shadowed side of the wall. Shadow calculations are usually expensive, so it's a good practice to turn them off whenever an object warrants it.

    5.   Uncheck Cast Shadows and Receive Shadows.

Creating the UV Animator Script

For the pulsing effect, you will be animating the shader's X Offset. A UV animator script comes in handy for lots of things, so as long as you are adding code to animate the regular texture, you will include the means to animate a bump as well. Since you may not want to use both all the time, you will make them both optional.

Texture offsets work on a 0 to 1 basis, where 1 is a full loop. You can adjust the offset in the shader to see the effect before you begin.

    1.   Select the Laser Point and zoom in on the line renderer in the Scene view (Figure 11-30).

Figure 11-30. Experimenting with the x Offset value

2. In the Laser Beam material, try adjusting the x Offset by **.2** or **.5** to see the texture shift.

3. Create a new C# Script in the Game Scripts folder.

4. Name it **UVAnimator**.

5. Open it in the script editor.

6. Add the following variables:

```
public int materialIndex  = 0;        // in case the object has more than one material
public Material theMaterial;          // the object's material[s]

public bool animateUV = true;         // flag for option to scroll texture
public float scrollSpeedU1 = 0.0f;    // variables to scroll texture
public float scrollSpeedV1 = 0.0f;

public  bool animateBump = false;     // flag for option to scroll bump texture
public  float scrollSpeedU2 = 0.0f;   // variables to scroll bump texture
public  float scrollSpeedV2 = 0.0f;
```

In the Start function, you will assign the material so it will be available throughout the rest of the game.

7. Add the following to the Start function:

```
theMaterial = renderer.materials[materialIndex];
```

To animate the Offset for the main texture and bump maps, you can use `Time.deltaTime` and the speed to control the Offset.

8. Change the `Update` function to a `FixedUpdate` function.

9. Add the following in the `FixedUpdate` function for the main texture:

```
// texture offset variables
float offsetU1 = Time.time * -scrollSpeedU1;
float offsetV1 = Time.time * -scrollSpeedV1;
// animate the UVs
if (animateUV) { // if the flag to animate the texture is true...
    Vector2 offset1 = new Vector3(offsetU1,offsetV1);
    theMaterial.SetTextureOffset ("_MainTex",offset1);
}
```

You have no need for animating a bump texture on the laser, but animating a materials bump texture can produce some very interesting water-type effects.

10. Add the following to change the bump texture offset value:

```
// bump texture offset variables
if (animateBump) {
    float offsetU2 = Time.time * -scrollSpeedU2;
    float offsetV2 = Time.time * -scrollSpeedV2;
    if (animateUV) { // if the flag to animate the texture is true...
        Vector2 offset2 = new Vector3(offsetU2,offsetV2);
        renderer.materials[materialIndex].SetTextureOffset ("_BumpMap",offset2);
    }
}
```

You can access the material through the renderer component with `renderer.material` if there is only one material, or `renderer.materials[`_index number_`]` if there might be more than one. Setting the index number to 0 will use the first material unless otherwise specified.

The trickiest part about this script is discovering what the _internal name_ of the shader parameter is in the script, so you can feed it into the `SetTextureOffset` method. Unlike regular variables/parameters, those used in shaders do not necessarily coincide. A good place to begin your search for internal shader parameter names is the UnityAnswers post, `http://answers.unity3d.com/questions/501797/can-i-get-the-a-list-of-the-properties-in-a-shader.html`, where robertbu has generated a list of internal names for several of the Unity shaders. If you are feeling adventurous, you may want to download the Unity default shader package from `http://unity3d.com/unity/download/archive`. It contains the source code for each of the built-in shaders and takes the guess work out of identifying the correct parameter names. Once you track down the shader you are looking for, spotting the names is easy.

11. Save the script.

12. Add the UVAnimator script to the Laser Point object.

13. Set the Scroll Speed U1 to **5**.

14. Click Play, and check out the subtle pulsing effect.

You may have noticed at some angles, the beam texture is blurred so much that it goes all the way to the edges of the line renderer, spoiling the effect of the beam (Figure 11-31). This is due to anisotrophic filtering. Aniso filtering (for short) is what blurs the texture when you are seeing it at a shallow angle. It helps prevent the shimmering artifacting sometimes seen on ground textures at a short distance from the player or character. You can increase the Aniso levels for the texture to fix the problem, but doing so can be expensive resource-wise, so use it carefully.

Figure 11-31. Anisotropic filtering adversely affecting the laser beam

15. Select the SoftEdges texture in the Project view.

16. Set its Aniso Level to **4**, and click Apply.

The beam is looking much nicer, but it would look even better if it produced a bit of light where it hit an object. You will be using the hit position for its location.

1. Stop Play mode.

2. Create a new Point Light, and name it **Laser Light**.

3. Set its Range to **0.8**, its Color to match the laser beam, and its Intensity to **2**.

4. In the LaserBeam script, add the following variable:

```
public Light hitLight; // the light for the end of the laser
```

5. Inside the Physics.Raycast conditional, add

```
hitLight.transform.position = hit.point; // move the light to the hit point
```

One issue to think about is that as soon as you turn off the laser, the active light will stay where it was last positioned. But by parenting it to the Laser Point object, it will be activated and deactivated the same time as the laser beam. Because it is a child of the Laser Point, the code calculating the offset from the hit point has to use local position to actually place the light.

6. Save the script.

7. Assign the Laser Light object to the Hit Light parameter on the Laser Point's Laser Beam component.

8. Drag the Laser Light onto the Laser Point object in the Hierarchy view.

9. Click Play, activate the laser, and test by running the laser over the various scene objects.

The laser and light do well on most surfaces, but occasionally, the light cannot be seen. The issue may be that the light is too close. On a flat surface, the light is on the same plane and its rays have nothing to hit. If you want to refine the light's performance, you can make a second variable for the hit distance minus a small offset and use that to position the light.

1. In the LaserBeam script, replace the `hitLight.transform.localPosition` line with the following:

```
Vector3 lightPos = new Vector3(0, 0,hit.distance-0.2f);
// calculate and offset from the hit pt
hitLight.transform.localPosition = lightPos;
// move the light to the hit point
```

2. Save the script, and test.

You have probably noticed that the light never shines on the gate. If you watch the beam in the top view as you point it at the gate, you will see that it stops short. Thinking back, you may realize that there are colliders on the Occluder that trigger various events. This time, the solution is fairly simple. There is already an Ignore Raycast layer that works internally and requires no extra scripting!

1. Stop Play mode.

2. In the Project view, assign the Ignore Raycast layer to the Occluder prefab.

3. Check the objects in the Hierarchy view to make sure they now have the layer assigned to them.

4. Click Play, and test the laser on the gate.

This time. the beam goes all the way to the door and the light spot appears. Because the GardenDoor material uses a simple Diffuse shader, the light spot is more subdued.

5. Stop Play mode.

There are also several objects in the garden area that will block the laser from making contact with the zombie bunnies. The Zombie Zone and the Plant Zones all have colliders that will intercept the hits. Basically, any object that is not rendered but has a collider must be examined and possibly excluded from raycast detection.

6. Assign the Ignore Raycast layer to the Zombie Zone and each Plant Zone.

An additional special effect often used with lasers is sparks to let the player know when he has hit something worthy. You will be using a Sparks prefab that has already been prepared for you. It is a variation on the particle system that you created for a zombie-bunny hit. Feel free to check it out in the Inspector.

1. In the LaserBeam script, add the following variable:

    ```
    public GameObject hitParticles; // the sparks prefab
    ```

2. In the Raycast conditional, above the //update end position line, add

    ```
    if (hitParticles) { // if particles were assigned, instantiate them at the hit point
        GameObject temp = (GameObject) Instantiate(hitParticles, hit.point,Quaternion
    .FromToRotation(Vector3.up, hit.normal));
        Destroy(temp, 0.3f);
    }
    ```

If hitParticles have been assigned, they are instantiated at the hit point, but they are *oriented* to the face normal of hit surface so they spray back towards the player. Then the prefabs are allowed to live for 0.3 seconds before being destroyed. This solution is also commonly used to simulate bullets hits where there is no actual mesh for the bullets. A "normal," if you remember, is a perpendicular to the face on the side it is drawn.

3. Save the script.

4. Import the Sparks.unitypackage from the Chapter 11 Assets folder, and move it from the Prefabs root folder into the FX folder.

5. Assign the new prefab to the Laser Point's Hit Particles parameter.

The particle system uses a Standard Assets material, but it does not recognize it as the same one already existing in the scene. You can easily remedy the problem.

6. Select the Sparks prefab, and open the Particle System component's Renderer rollout.

7. Assign the Spark material to its Material parameter.

8. Click Play, and test.

The sparks complete the visual aspect of the laser beam nicely. The next task is to actually destroy zombie bunnies with it. With the potato gun, you used a proximity scheme to calculate hits. With the laser always on, you will consider only direct hits. For that functionality, you will make use of tags.

1. Create a new tag named **Invader**.

2. Assign it to the ZombieBunny prefab.

Electric slugs are oddly immune to lasers, so you can leave the Slug prefab as is.

3. Open the LaserBeam script.

4. Below the hitLight.transform line, add

    ```
    if(hit.collider.tag == "Invader") {
        hit.collider.SendMessage ("DestroyBun",SendMessageOptions.DontRequireReceiver);
    }
    ```

5. Save the script.

6. Click Play, enter the garden, and try lasering the zombie bunnies (Figure 11-32).

Figure 11-32. Lasering the zombie bunnies

Here you are directly calling the DestroyBun function in the ReceivedHits script, so you are bypassing the explosion from the potato ammo and the green globs. Also, because the laser is set to destroy only objects with the Invader tag, it will not destroy plants. This will afford the zombie bunnies hiding in the corn patch a bit of protection.

A little sound effect, say of a sizzling sound, would be a nice touch. The sound should come from the hit point, but the zombie bunny already has a death scream assigned to its Audio Source. The Laser Light will be close enough to do the job, and the LaserBeam script already has access to it.

7. Select the Laser Light object.

8. Add an Audio Source component.

9. Assign the Zap audio clip to it, and uncheck "Play on Awake."

10. Back in the LaserBeam script, add the following beneath the SendMessage line:

```
hitLight.audio.Play(); // cue the fx
```

11. Save the script.

12. Activate the Gnome Arrow again.

13. Click Play, and test.

The laser is much more efficient than the potato gun. In fact, it's hardly sporting, not to mention it makes the game too easy to win. It might be fun to automatically activate it around the same time the slug is sent zipping through the garden, a sort of "Hail Mary," or last-ditch attempt, to help the player get control of the situation. The aim is quite a bit off from the potato gun, so the player will have to make a quick choice on how best to deal with the remaining zombie bunnies.

Before adding that last refinement, you will want to make sure the laser is turned off when the battery runs out. Also, in keeping with the concept of the battery powering the Gnomatic Garden Defender, you should change the state of the GardenGnome so that it no longer plays the idle animation when the battery is dead. You can take care of all three tasks in the BatteryHealth script.

1. Select the GardenGnome, and open its Gnome Controller.

2. In the Animator view, right-click somewhere and select Create State, Empty.

3. Name it **Dead Battery**.

4. Open the BatteryHealth script.

5. At the bottom of the GameOver function, add

```
// turn off gnome animations
Animator gnome = GameObject.Find("GardenGnome").GetComponent<Animator>();
gnome.Play("Dead Battery"); // turn off the gnome animation
gnome.SetBool("Armed", false); // close the hat
gnome.SendMessage("BeamOff", SendMessageOptions.DontRequireReceiver);
// deactivate the laser stuff
```

6. Save the script.

7. Click Play, and test by losing the game.

Now when the game is lost, the Gnomatic Garden Defender and its related functionality is turned off.

The final task is to decide when the player will have access to the laser weapon. An easy solution is to piggy-back onto the slug activation in the BatteryHealth script. By activating the laser shortly before the slug, the player can be tricked into missing the slug power-up.

8. At the top of the BatteryHealth script's ManageSlug function, add the following:

```
if (percentRemaining == slugTime + 10) {
    GameObject.Find("GardenGnome").SendMessage("OpenHat",SendMessageOptions
.DontRequireReceiver);
}
```

9. Save the script.

And finally, to prevent the player from activating the laser prematurely, you will add a flag in the laser controller.

1. In the LaserController script, add the following variable:

    ```
    internal bool activated; // flag to allow laser
    ```

2. In the Update function, change the if(animator) line to

    ```
    if (animator && activated) { // check for its existance and activation flag first
    ```

You can turn the flag on when the hat is opened by an outside source.

3. In the OpenHat function, add

    ```
    activated = true;
    ```

4. Save the script.

5. Click Play, and make sure the hat cannot be opened by the player but opens when the battery charge gets low.

6. Save the scene, and open the StartMenu scene.

7. Play through the game from start to finish.

8. When you are satisfied with the ensuing chaos, make a final build!

As always, one can continue to think of ways to improve the game, and there are undoubtedly bugs that will be discovered as the game is tested by a larger number of people, but this last chapter's additions will be as far as the book goes. Be sure to follow the book's thread on the Unity forum (search the book's title in the Learning forum) for discussion, errata, tweaks for version changes, and just to say hi.

Summary

In this final chapter, you had the opportunity to add a bit of extra functionality to the game. An overhead map, the appearance of the electric slug as a power-up, and a hat-based laser gun provided the player with some extra options for accomplishing his goal.

The overhead map, a HUD feature, showing the location of the last few zombie bunnies was implemented with another camera layer. With the help of the Viewport Rect parameters, you learned how to inset one camera's view into another's without making use of the Pro-only render-to-texture feature. Making good use of the camera's Culling Mask, you were able to pick and choose what was shown on the simplified view.

In creating an opportunity for a power-up that extended the life of the battery, you were able bring the electric slug into the game for a cameo appearance. After experimenting with its speed, you settled on activating it when the battery reached a critical level.

In the final section, you revisited Mecanim and learned how to create a mask that would allow part of the character's body to animate independently of the rest. Creating a new layer in the Gnome Controller, you were finally able to make use of the hat animation that exposed a secret laser gun.

To implement the laser, you were introduced to the Line Renderer component. Through scripting, you were able to control its length with Physics.Raycast. In that code, you were able to check for intersections with colliders and position both a small point light and the sparks prefab at the hit points. To make the laser more interesting, you created a useful little script that helped you gain access to shader parameters in order to animate the textures UVs or mapping offset. Finally, you discovered the Ignore Raycast layer that allowed you to selectively ignore the raycast intersection with certain colliders without adding a single bit of code.

Appendix A

Rigging with Mixamo

Mixamo is a software tool that allows you to quickly rig your own character. In addition, you can also create a new character from one of the preset Mixamo characters and add preset Mixamo animations to your characters. As of this writing, you are allowed two free rigs for your own prebuilt characters for your personal use. Mixamo characters and Mixamo animations must be purchased. Mixamo is at www.mixamo.com.

Before Starting Mixamo

To have Mixamo rig your character, there are a few things you will have to do to prepare it.

1. Use your favorite digital content creation software to create your character.
2. Make sure your character is in the standard T-pose (Figure A-1).

Figure A-1. *The classic T-pose*

3. Export your character using the .FBX format.

4. If you will be adding Mixamo animations, make sure that "enable media" is checked when exporting so that the animations can be imported back into your software after rigging.

Important   If, at any time, you get a message to upgrade to Get All Access (Figure A-2), do NOT click on the button until you finished downloading your two free rigs. Otherwise, it will assume you want to pay for unlimited access to Mixamo for a full year (which costs $1499/year at the time of this writing). Once you click this button, you will lose your two free rigs and the program assumes you will be paying from this point forward.

Figure A-2. Do not click this button!

Rigging a Character with Mixamo

The scarecrow from Chapter 6 was rigged with Mixamo and will serve as an example to take you through the rigging procedure. To begin the process, you will have to create an account at Mixamo.

1. Create an account at Mixamo.

As of this writing, regardless of which type of account you choose (personal project or student project), you get two free rigs as a trial.

2. Select "Rig" from the menu (Figure A-3).

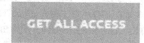

Figure A-3. The Mixamo toolbar

3. From the next screen, click "Upload file."

On a PC, the Windows Explorer window will pop up.

4. Navigate to your character file's location, and select it.

The orientation window comes up.

5. 5.Click "Yes" if you see your character.

You should see your character in the correct position (Figure A-4, left).

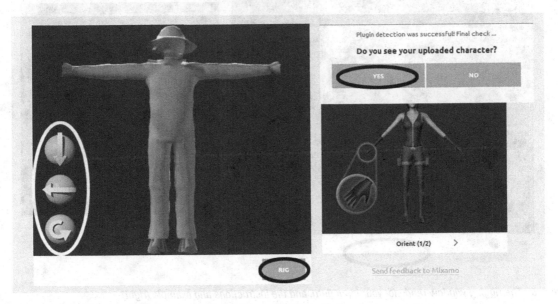

Figure A-4. The orientation window, with the rotation buttons on the lower left

5. Use the buttons on the lower left side to rotate your character into position if necessary.

6. Once the character is in the correct T-pose position and facing forward, click the "Rig" button at the lower right of the window.

If you cannot see your character, verify that your Unity web player works, click "No," and repeat the steps starting at step 2.

If all went well, you should now see the rigging window (Figure A-5).

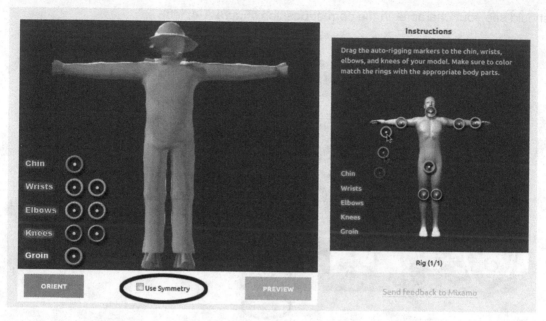

Figure A-5. The rigging window ready for your input (left), and the instructions and example (right)

1. If your character was created with symmetry, check "Use Symmetry" (Figure A-5, left).

To rig, you will drag each marker to the appropriate target area as shown in the example (Figure A-5, right).

2. Drag the chin marker into place first (Figure A-6).

The area is zoomed for more accurate placement (Figure A-6, left, upper right).

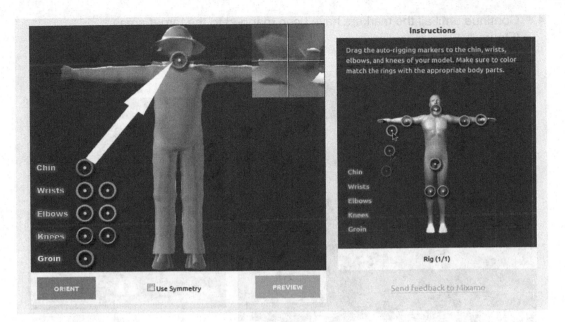

Figure A-6. Setting the markers

3. Next drag the wrist marker to the target area (Figure A-7). If "Use Symmetry" is checked, it will place the other marker for you.

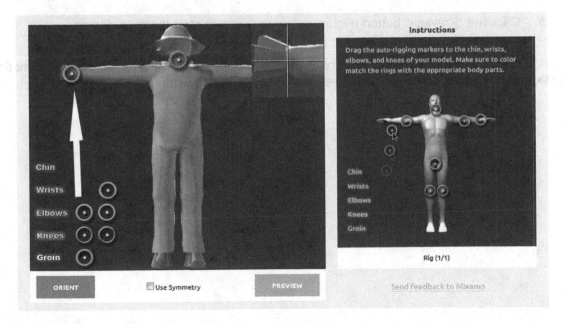

Figure A-7. Setting the wrist markers

4. Continue until all the markers have been mapped to the target areas (Figure A-8).

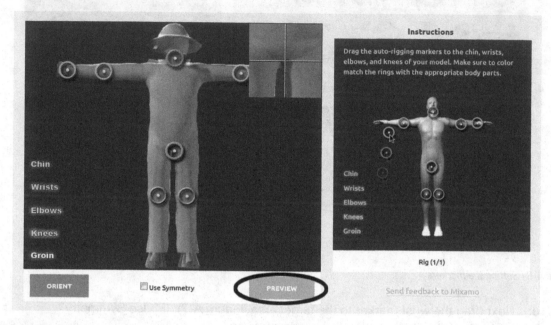

Figure A-8. The markers in position

5. Click the "Preview" button (Figure A-8, lower right) to start the auto-rigging process.

Once rigging is completed, you can click on the video buttons (Figure A-9) to see the idle animation that Mixamo has put on the character to see how well the rigging works.

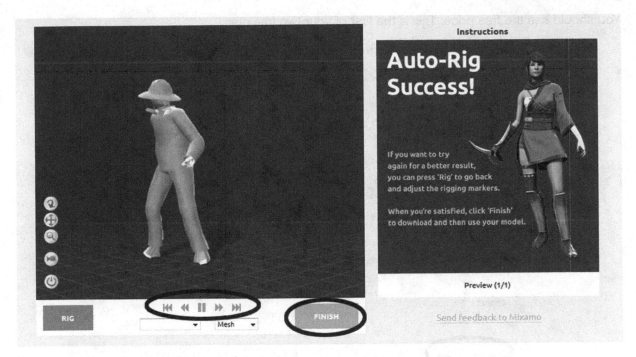

Figure A-9. The video buttons and successful auto-rigging

6. Click "Finish" to accept the rig (Figure A-9, lower right).

7. Click the "Download" button to download the rig (Figure A-10).

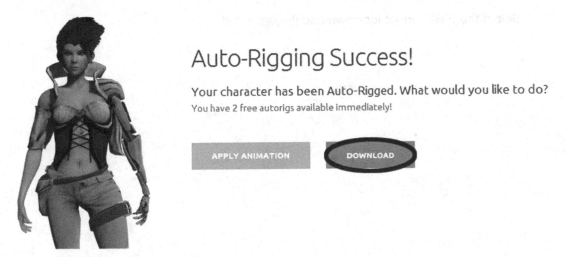

Figure A-10. Auto-rigging was successful; selecting Download

You should see the free price. This is the first of your two free rigs.

8.   Select "Checkout" (Figure A-11).

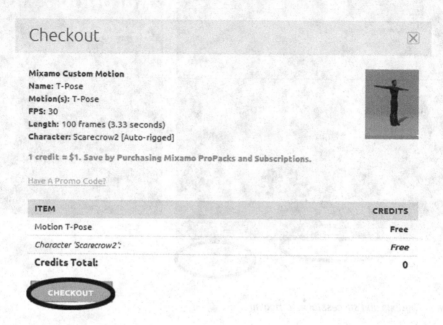

And finally, you will select the export format.

9.   Select the .FBX format for download (Figure A-12).

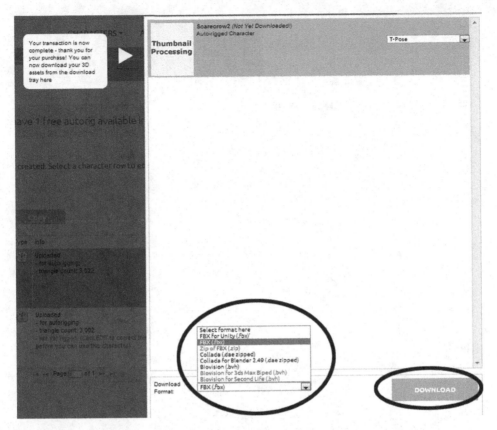

Figure A-12. Choosing .FBX for the export format for your rigged character and selecting Download

10. Click the "Download" button (Figure A-12, right).

11. Save the file.

You've completed the Mixamo rigging process.

Note that the character is rigged and *ready* for animations, but it does not yet contain any. At this point, you can bring it back into your digital content creation software to create your own animations, or bring it directly into Unity and use many of the animations available for Mecanim from the Unity asset store.

> **Tip**   If later on you find that you need to go back to your character and adjust the rig, Mixamo will allow you to go back to your two free rigs and re-rig, based on your account (as of this writing). So don't forget your username and password!

Index

Get the eBook for only $10!

Now you can take the weightless companion with you anywhere, anytime. Your purchase of this book entitles you to 3 electronic versions for only $10.

This Apress title will prove so indispensible that you'll want to carry it with you everywhere, which is why we are offering the eBook in 3 formats for only $10 if you have already purchased the print book.

Convenient and fully searchable, the PDF version enables you to easily find and copy code—or perform examples by quickly toggling between instructions and applications. The MOBI format is ideal for your Kindle, while the ePUB can be utilized on a variety of mobile devices.

Go to www.apress.com/promo/tendollars to purchase your companion eBook.